Protecting the Best Men

Protecting the Best Men

An Interpretive History of the
Law of Libel
by Norman L. Rosenberg

The University of North Carolina Press

Chapel Hill and London

© 1986 by The University of North Carolina Press

Manufactured in the United States of America

Library of Congress Cataloging in Publication Data

Rosenberg, Norman L., 1942–

  Protecting the best men.

  (Studies in legal history)

  Bibliography: p.

  Includes index.

  1. Libel and slander—United States—History.

I. Title.   II. Series.

KF1266.R67   1985   346.7303'4   85-1174

ISBN 0-8078-1665-5   347.30634

For all of the members of the Rosenberg,

Schwimmer, Ginsburg, and Anderson families—

and especially for my father, the memory

of my mother, and Emily.

Contents

Acknowledgments

As friends and acquaintances have learned by now, I am among the most tardy and delinquent of correspondents. Thus, I will seize this opportunity to thank, in one quick stroke, all of you who took the time to talk with me about ideas that ultimately influenced the general shape of this book. Certain people deserve special mention: Jack Sosin, David Trask, David Burner, Robert Marcus, Jackson T. Main, Richard Archer, Garry Wills, Thomas Daniels and my colleagues in the history department at Macalester College (especially the late Ernest Sandeen and James Stewart, who deserves extra commendation for reading through an early version of this study). I'd like to express greatest thanks to John Pratt, who first suggested the subject of libel law. Harlan Abrahms and Joseph Gorrell provided important encouragement at key points.

In the case of one special colleague, words such as helpful and influential are simply inadequate. As Emily knows, "my" book pales in comparison to the discussions, debates, and fights we have had over the past twenty years about the meaning of life and American history.

Grants from NEH, the Jerome Foundation, the Bush Foundation, and Macalester College helped to support portions of this study. Much of the discussion of Thomas Cooley appeared, in slightly different form, in the *University of Puget Sound Law Review*, and permission to incorporate this material is gratefully acknowledged. In the final stages, Macalester Library's Peggy Feldick proved indispensable in helping to locate elusive secondary materials. My editors at North Carolina—Lewis Bateman, G. Edward White, Gwen Duffey, and Nancy Margolis (a skilled and compassionate copyeditor)—have been both patient and supportive. Macalester College students have always been willing to listen and help with ideas; Kris Hoover, Tim Hodgdon and Juliette Ramirez provided the special text-processing skills that I lacked, and Amy Zhe offered critical help on bibliographical matters.

Finally, this book about speech and communication has gained more than can ever be calculated from the support of my family. I do not, quite honestly, remember learning anything about libel from Sarah, Molly, Ruth, and Joe, but they did teach me a great deal about the "politics of communication." Similarly, all of my family—the Rosenbergs, Ginsburgs, Schwimmers, and Andersons—showed me how *real* communication, about both "large" and "small" politics, should proceed. My uncles, the late Herman Ginsburg and Hymen Rosenberg, patiently gave the best education in law, and my brother Ron has continued my legal training. It is to my family—especially to my parents and to Emily—that I dedicate this book.

Protecting the Best Men

Introduction | Toward an Understanding
of Defamation Law

Protecting the Best Men began its own history more than a few years ago.[1] The complexity, if not the sheer irrationality, of libel doctrines presents numerous problems for the lawyer who has to "try" a case; it can throw up many more for the historian "trying" an article or a book. Even William Prosser, a legal-writer who could generally create at least the illusion of doctrinal order out of a mass of chaotic precedents, admitted the impossibility of ordering defamation law. "A great deal of the law of defamation . . . makes no sense," he confessed.[2]

Most people know something about the law of libel. Although trials for libel seldom attract as much attention as cases involving murder or sex, legal conflicts over reputation (which can, sometimes, include questions of sex and violence) often receive extensive publicity. In fact, law professor Leon Green once complained that "the highly publicized libel action today is a sort of show piece to attract attention to the court house and dress an ordinary personal injury action in 'Million Dollar Old Lace' for the advertisement of the lawyers and of the party plaintiff."[3] Although some libel suits do become "legal circuses," action inside the center ring has also required careful attention to numerous rules and doctrines, many of ancient origin.

Defamatory statements or publications—oral defamation is called slander and written or printed called libel—are ones that, according to an often-cited definition, "tend to expose one to public hatred, shame, obloquy, contumely, odium, contempt, ridicule, aversion, ostracism, degradation, or disgrace, or to induce an evil opinion of one in the minds of right-thinking persons, and to deprive one of their confidence and friendly intercourse in society."[4] Although the common-sense view may be that defamatory statements are false ones, at common law (a term, some critics have contended, that is the antonym of common sense) falsity has not been the "essense of the action."[5] This has been particularly true in *criminal* prosecutions for libel.

The common law crime of libel can claim a long and broad—if, in the view of libertarians, disreputable—ancestry. It bears some relationship to "constructive treason," an offense that could be stretched to apply to any comment critical of the state or of governmental officials. Legal genealogists also can trace it back to the Middle Ages when the political implications of defamation led the king's courts to intervene in verbal tussles between men of great wealth

3

and power. Because disputes over the reputations of great magnates of the realm often resulted in violence rather than in recourse to local or church courts, creation of new criminal penalties seemed one means of halting such breaches of the king's peace. In addition, attacks upon the good names of England's "best men" raised ominous dangers in a feudal order held together not by an absolutist state but primarily by personal bonds of honor and loyalty. In such a society, when one lord of the realm falsely impugned the honor of another, he also attacked the whole basis of feudal society. Such considerations prompted enactment of *De Scandalis Magnatum* in 1275. Reenacted in 1378 and again in 1388 (in the wake of the Peasants' Revolt), this act made it a crime to slander the leading men of England. In the words of the 1378 measure, slanderous falsehoods threatened "great peril and mischief . . . to all the realm, and quick subversion and destruction of the said realm."[6]

Criminal penalties against defamation changed their character with the transition from a feudal to a nascent capitalist order, with the rise of a powerful national state, and with the introduction of the printing press into England during the Tudor era. Fearing the revolutionary potential of critical political publications and of heretical religious tracts, the Tudors invoked their royal prerogative over the new print medium. Under Henry VIII and Elizabeth I, a complicated system of prior restraints—involving appointment of official government printers, grants of special privileges and monopolies, and royal licensors—loomed over the presses. In addition, the prerogative Court of Star Chamber dealt with the crime of "seditious libel," an offense akin to constructive treason and the old *scandalum magnatum*.[7]

Between 1606, when Sir Edmund Coke prosecuted the landmark Star Chamber case of *De Libellis Famosis*,[8] and 1641, when the Long Parliament abolished the infamous body, the judges of Star Chamber refined the basic principles of criminal libel. Under the Stuarts, Star Chamber moved with special energy against "seditious libel," any political statement that had the "bad tendency" of lowering the public's estimation of the government, its laws, or its officers. Thus, in contrast to *scandalum magnatum*, which distinguished between accurate and false attacks, the new Star Chamber law proscribed all criticism of the state and its officials. In practice, seditious libel was a vague offense, and royal judges could construe almost any comment on public affairs to be illegal. The essence of the crime of libel was the fact of publication; the writer's intent and accuracy were irrelevant. So-called libels on the government or on public officials, even if true, tended to lower public respect for authority. Star Chamber also applied criminal penalties to libels on purely private individuals on the theory that unless the law offered a means of official redress, such defamation would inevitably lead to violent retaliation. Here, too, truth was not a legal consideration. When it came to criminal prosecutions, even against nonpolitical libels, the judges of Star Chamber argued that accuracy was no guarantee against breaches of the king's peace by people who had been defamed. Thus in Star Chamber libel prosecutions, once a defamatory statement was shown to have been communicated, the only important legal question was whether or not the defendant, in point of fact, was the person who had disseminated the offensive material. Royal officers, lesser public officials, and private litigants all found that they possessed considerable legal advantages in Star Chamber libel prosecutions, and actions for seditious libel, as well as for ordinary criminal libel, became frequent.[9]

After abolition of Star Chamber in 1641, during the English Revolution, common law courts assumed jurisdiction over criminal libel prosecutions. After some controversy, the courts retained the basic outlines of Star Chamber's libel doctrines. In common law prosecutions for libel, judges ruled on the "law of the case"—whether publication was libelous—and juries decided the "facts of the case"—whether defendants had really published the libels.[10]

As every late twentieth-century One-L or cub reporter is supposed to know, however, the greatest dangers in libel have for many years been not from fines or jail terms but from civil suits for monetary damages. Once, English local and church courts, rather than common law tribunals, heard civil defamation cases. But during the first half of the sixteenth century, common law courts began to accept jurisdiction in at least some types of defamation cases. The rise of commercial-capitalist relationships, for example, placed increased importance on the reputations of leading merchants, and seventeenth-century common law courts began to grant money damages for slanderous attacks upon the good names of England's commercial elite.[11] Because Star Chamber effectively controlled printed libels, common law courts dealt almost exclusively with slander. Although truth ultimately became an issue in most civil suits, common law defamation cases did not, at the outset of the trial anyway, turn on the falsity of the statement.[12] If the offending words fell within the bounds of defamation law, a defendant could begin an action.[13] And in strict legal theory, courts did not focus on any actual personal injury to the plaintiff—such as emotional damage from the libel—but on the injury to the litigant's reputation, on any injury that might affect relationships with other people.[14]

Long before the rise of modern mass communication media, then, the law of civil defamation involved the process of true public "communication." Defamatory statements, for example, were not actionable unless "communicated" to a third party.[15] Persons who insulted their neighbors in a one-to-one showdown in colonial America could get themselves, as we shall see, into legal difficulties; but, under strict common law theory, a suit for defamation required that a third party must have heard the critical statements.[16] Similarly, libelous statements contained in a letter from one person to another were not actionable because they were not "communicated" to a third party.

Although defendants in common law defamation suits were not in as bad a position as the targets of criminal libel prosecutions, they still had difficulties.[17] Once it was established that the words or statements had been defamatory and had been directed at the plaintiff, defendants were required to offer some type of "justification" in their defense. Defendants found themselves, in effect, trying to prove their "innocence." The usual defense to civil libel was proof of truth. But although there was a popular eighteenth-century maxim that "truth could be no libel," common law jurists rejected such a view as incompatible with the basic theory of libel law. The truth could be "libelous," most common law lawyers insisted, even in civil suits; but if defendants established the truth of their libelous statements, the law could offer no legal redress because any type of recompense would give plaintiffs something to which they had no right—an unblemished reputation. Therefore, in civil libel cases, though not in criminal actions, proof of truth eventually became an "absolute justification."[18]

Other circumstances that could legally "justify" defamation in a civil suit came to be called "privileged occasions." The law allowed defendants, for instance, an "absolute privilege" for defamatory statements made in the course of judicial proceedings.[19] The common law also recognized a number of "qualified privileges." Masters, for example, possessed a qualified privilege to comment critically—and in some cases even incorrectly—on the performance of servants. The victims of such defamation could not sue successfully unless it could be established that the defamatory false statements had been made "maliciously." In cases involving qualified privilege, trials turned on the proper legal definition of "malice" and upon whether or not the actions of defendants had, in fact, been "malicious."[20] Much of this study involves the ways in which legal writers and courts have applied the theory of qualified privilege to political libel cases.

The "New" Legal Histories

The last decade has brought not only an explosion in the number of books and articles published in legal and constitutional history, but also an expansion in the types of legal issues studied and in the methodologies employed. Recently, a number of excellent historiographical essays have examined "the new legal history," and there seems no need to offer another such examination here.[21] But it does seem necessary to indicate how *Protecting the Best Men* fits into the existing literature.

Addressing general issues related to the study of law and the history of law, John T. Noonan, Jr., has followed the familiar technique of law professors: answering one question with another. The question, "What is law?" Professor

Noonan correctly observed, cannot be answered "without asking another— 'Why do you want to know?' The definition of law depends on the purpose of the definer."[22] The same questions, I believe, apply to the problem of writing the history of libel law.

Traditionally, the people defining and writing the history of American law, particularly those who have focused on the work of common law courts, came from the law schools. Around the end of the nineteenth century, lawyer-historians began to direct their scholarly attention in the same general direction as their professional interest—toward the decisions, rules, and doctrines generated by common law courts. This traditional type of legal history—what Daniel Boorstin has called "legal genealogy"—amounted to a search for the ancient ancestors of modern legal doctrines.[23] The emphasis in traditional legal histories was upon the steady evolution of some legal rule, or group of rules, within the minds of judges and legal scholars, not upon the interaction between the law and the larger society. Although few, if any, traditional historians would have claimed that the law bore no imprint of the surrounding society, or that the Anglo-American legal system was completely autonomous, these traditionalists felt quite comfortable in generally ignoring the external dimension of the American legal system in favor of detailed examinations of its internal character, especially the evolution of doctrine. As a result, the history of American law remained a field unto itself; rather than seeking links with other areas of historical research, the vast majority of lawyer-historians dealt with matters "*distinctly legal*."[24] The connection between this "conservative" tradition in legal history and the needs of the legal profession was clear, and quite natural. Legal history provided support for the view that an autonomous legal system, one dominated by independent and specially trained legal minds, produced a neutral and organic body of legal rules.[25]

This has now changed. With historians from the law schools often leading the way, scholars have begun to develop a variety of new approaches, including what Robert Gordon has called an "external" history of American law—a body of scholarship that seeks to examine the complex interaction between legal institutions and the broader society. In one sense, then, *Protecting the Best Men* seeks to interpret the tangled history of what many scholars now call "the law of public libel"—what I still prefer to call "the law of political libel"[26]—by examining forces that are not distinctly legal, especially changes in political practices, in ideas of social and political order, and in the nature of American journalism. Other nonlegal themes—such as the changing nature of the profession of journalism and of other news-producing institutions—also have a place in this history. But, as Professor Gordon has observed, one cannot get too far from the "internal" legal system without abandoning the field of legal history altogether. More important, some of the most exciting new work in legal history has involved fresh looks, often utilizing new modes of critical analysis, at legal doctrines; doctrinal studies, their practitioners have shown, not only help to illuminate changes and contradictions in legal consciousness, but also throw valuable light on broader historical processes. Thus, I have still dealt with things distinctly legal, especially the formulation, in different historical periods, of the major rules and doctrines used in political libel cases. And I have sought to examine the interaction between the internal and external realms, to suggest how social influences have helped to shape libel law and how defamation itself can relate to broader themes in the history of the United States.[27]

Protecting the Best Men weaves through a somewhat eclectic variety of primary and secondary sources. No one type of source material or one single historiographical approach, I became increasingly convinced, could help to illuminate the many dimensions of the law of libel. This book does offer, I think, a good deal of new material, especially on the late eighteenth and nineteenth centuries. But it also seeks to reexamine and refocus earlier studies about libel law during the colonial period and during the twentieth century. The desire to sketch a broad picture has led to this general history rather than to one that concentrates upon a particular jurisdiction where the resources are especially rich (say, New York or Pennsylvania) or upon a particular time period such as the late nineteenth century.[28] At various points in the on-again-off-again history of this study, I reluctantly concluded that certain lines of research could not be represented fully. For example, the issue of governmental officials' tremendous power to affect the reputations of individuals and groups—a question raised most pointedly during the cold-war era—deserves more attention than it has received here. Similarly, I have only been able to note, without expanding upon the point, that the politics of reputation remains an important part of American life, even though ordinary citizens have no expectation that their reputational disputes—in contrast to those of the "best" men and women—will ever be acknowledged by the public court systems.

Rather than trying to cover every facet of defamation, then, I have tried to give this study one recurrent focus. Disputes involving the world of "large" politics—questions related to the power of citizens to criticize the character and conduct of those people (for most of American history, men) in the forefront of political life—and the relationship between libel law and the major media institutions form the core of analysis. What must necessarily be sacrificed in a study of this shape can, I trust, be balanced by the overall coherence and by the comparative dimension that this book attempts to provide. Perhaps this broad interpretive study will provide the framework for more specialized work on particular jurisdictions and more limited time periods.

This study was completed against the background of growing debate over the social-political value of "rights talk," in general, and First-Amendment discourse, in particular. Although all the tangled issues have yet to be joined, critics have succeeded in raising troubling questions about the "First Freedom." To what extent, David Kairys asks, has the "ideology of free speech" served to provide misleading images that actually conceal the real limits on communication, especially in the so-called private sectors of American life? Whatever the supposed content of First-Amendment doctrines, ask other commentators, is it realistic to expect that the costly and complex process of judicial review can offer significant protection to unpopular speakers and writers? And might the reduction of complicated social-political relationships, such as policies toward the poor and homeless, to questions of whether or not welfare-rights protestors are legitimately exercising their First-Amendment rights actually serve to deflect attention from the fundamental moral-political issues at stake?[29]

Although I have resisted the temptation to use this history of defamation law to comment at length on these and some of the other new First-Amendment issues, readers should be aware that *Protecting the Best Men* seeks to break from the more traditional modes of legal history. It does not, for example, purport to find any "original understanding" about the meaning of the First Amendment, and it rejects the conventional liberal view that the history of First-Amendment adjudication is the story of steadily expanding liberties, a theme still dominant when I began work on the issue of libel law.

I would like to avoid the suggestion of reductionism; but if forced to label this work, I would prefer to call it "anti-Whiggish," rather than "neo-revisionist" or "neo-Marxist." In most areas of history, of course, an anti-Whiggish stance has been conventional for some time. But in the history of American law and in the history of American journalism certain Whiggish tendencies have persisted. (In both fields, for example, the word "development," used to imply some type of orderly and natural long-term "evolution," pervades the literature.)

In contrast to most Whiggish historians of American journalism, however, I do not see the modern mass media, despite its obvious virtues, as the "natural development" of older libertarian ideals and principles.[30] As a historian familiar with recent work in American political and social history, I find it extremely difficult, for instance, to reduce the history of defamation law to a story of how the law of libel has steadily "become the law of free communication" and to conclude that by the late nineteenth century, "the law of libel had assumed its current character and during the last fifty years has reached its mature doctrinal status."[31]

The writing of First-Amendment history contains numerous pitfalls. On the one hand, the meaning of words such as "freedom" or "libertarian," which recur throughout this book, must be grounded in a historical setting.[32] Historians of free expression must constantly ask themselves questions such as "freedom for and from whom?" and "more libertarian than what?" Christopher

Hill, for example, has properly rebuked revisionist historians for sneering at John Milton's *Areopagitica* because the poet-theorist's essay on free expression refused to extend toleration to Roman Catholics. Critiques of Milton's libertarian reputation, Hill argues, cannot ignore the historical context of his writings, especially the pervasive anti-Catholicism of seventeenth-century English Protestantism and Milton's own association with radicals whose ideas and political activities (in Hill's phrase) turned the traditional English world "upside down." As Hill suggests, "Milton knew very well what he was doing, and it is evidence of the complete change in the politico-religious atmosphere since his day that this [Milton's conviction that Catholics represented a foreign-controlled conspiracy against English liberties] still has to be explained."[33]

On the other hand, histories can do more than recreate the historical context of previous disputes. It is possible, without violating the historian's obligation to seek "truth," to use the study of the past as a means of offering critical perspectives on contemporary issues. Here, however, historians of civil liberties need to take great care. First, there is the problem already noted: the danger of adopting an ahistorical approach. Thus, scholars must not employ their view of how past issues *should have been* conceptualized or decided simply to unmask the "intolerance" or to praise the "tolerance" of an earlier age. Second, those who use history as a means of social criticism need to be honest about their own perspectives.

My own approach to free speech issues, as I have indicated in an earlier article, rejects the liberal marketplace model of Louis D. Brandeis, Oliver Holmes, Jr., and many other interpreters of First-Amendment issues.[34] The footnotes and list of secondary works make evident my debt to recent critical scholarship, especially to the work of Claus Mueller, Todd Gitlin, Herbert Schiller, Mark Tushnet, and Alvin Gouldner. I have particularly benefited from Gouldner's thoughtful examination of European critical theory. Gouldner rightfully stresses a crucial point: although the news-producing system in the United States contains contradictions grounded in the capitalist economic system, it also lacks some of the corruptions evident in state-dominated socialist societies.[35] Those concerned with greater freedom of expression must work, both intellectually and politically, to create the vision and the reality of societies that transcend the limitations of corporate capitalism and state-dominated socialism. When we can do that, we will have moved closer to an "ideal speech situation."

This study derives its title, *Protecting the Best Men*, from what I consider to be one of the central themes in the history of defamation law. The old law of seditious libel asserted that any criticism of the government or leading state officers, whether true or false, carried a "bad tendency" and could be made the subject of criminal prosecution. Over time, as this book explains, indictments for general criticism of the government came to be conducted under standards more generous to political critics and later fell into general disrepute. Eventually, astute public officials recognized that public criminal trials for the speaking or writing of words alone created more trouble than they were worth. As the history of the post–World War II period has shown, for example, political critics can be neutralized and discredited without resort to potentially divisive political trials. A vast national security bureaucracy and a full-scale national surveillance state have all but replaced formal prosecutions for sedition as the means for dealing with political dissent.[36] But well before the rise of surveillance institutions, during the first years of the nineteenth century, in fact, public officials and leading political figures had generally come to substitute civil libel suits for criminal prosecutions.

From the early nineteenth century on, those who dealt with these political libel suits invariably insisted that even in a polity grounded on the principle of popular sovereignty, indiscriminate political defamation should not be allowed to wound the reputations of important public figures. The old saw that "sticks and stones may break my bones but words can never hurt me"—a saying that I remember from earliest childhood—expressed a broad popular attitude, but it was never accepted as a formal part of the law of political defamation. As soon as nineteenth-century courts began to hear libel suits involving political figures, creators of legal doctrine insisted that despite guarantees for freedom of political expression, the good names of the "best men" could not be left totally unguarded. Some type of protection for their right of reputation was required; otherwise, framers of political libel rules argued, the process of political communication would become corrupted and the general population might be denied the public services of the "best men"— the most virtuous, wise, and talented members of the community.

Meanwhile, as this study argues, the realities of libel litigation came to mean that only a select few—important politicians or other powerful public figures—could reasonably hope to mobilize the resources needed to mount a credible defamation suit against an increasingly well-fortified journalistic establishment. Indeed, the prominent libel battles of the mid-1980s—*General Ariel Sharon* versus *Time, Inc.*, *William Tavoulareas* versus *Washington Post Co.*, and *General William Westmoreland* versus *CBS*—assumed the character of trench warfare involving elite members of the modern corporate-military order. If, as some observers insist, late twentieth-century politics revolves around a new kind of "feudalism," might not many modern libel trials be seen as contemporary versions of baronial conflict among the self-styled best men?[37]

Chapter One | The Politics of Reputation in Seventeenth-Century America

Free Expression in Colonial America: The Scholarly Debate

For much of the twentieth century, an essentially Whiggish vision of an ever-expanding empire of liberty has inspired American histories of free expression. Following historical trails blazed by patriotic writers of the nineteenth century, many scholars have located the origins of free expression in the colonial and Revolutionary eras, when "Apostles of Freedom," such as Roger Williams and John Peter Zenger, conquered the forces of suppression. This expansionist interpretation has become enshrined in constitutional histories and in American constitutional law. In this view, the Founding Fathers had written their broad interpretation of freedom of speech and press into the First Amendment to the United States Constitution. Zechariah Chafee, Jr. and Oliver Wendell Holmes, Jr., for example, both concluded that the First Amendment's free-speech and free-press clauses abolished the English common law of seditious libel and guaranteed Americans wide latitude to criticize the actions of government and the conduct of public officials. The task of succeeding generations, libertarians of the 1940s and 1950s believed, was to build upon this heritage and further expand the frontiers of First-Amendment liberties.[1]

Skeptics always existed, of course, but the antiexpansionist view remained undeveloped until publication of Leonard Levy's *Legacy of Suppression* in 1960. Citing legal statement after legal statement and piling example of suppression upon example of suppression, Levy built an imposing case for several "revisionist" propositions. He argued that until 1798, when partisan conflict broke out over passage of the nation's first Sedition Act, American theories of free expression were "quite narrow," narrower even than contemporary English ideas about freedom of speech and press; that suppression of political speech, especially by legislatures, continued throughout the colonial era; and that not even the framers of the First Amendment intended to overturn the Blackstonian view of seditious libel.

According to Levy, most colonials accepted the views of eighteenth-century English jurists on the law of seditious libel. In both England and America, Orthodox Whigs upheld the importance of "free" expression, but they also drew a clear distinction between "liberty" of speech and press and "licentious-ness." Looking back upon a century of revolution and several decades of political instability, England's eighteenth-century political and legal elites desired restraint and order in political affairs—and in political discussions. Although the king's ministers preferred to manage the nation's constantly expanding political press by more subtle means—especially by subsidizing court "scribblers" or buying off talented opposition publicists—libel prosecutions under strict doctrines, first developed in the Court of Star Chamber, continued throughout most of the century. In 1704, for example, Sir John Holt warned, while presiding over a libel prosecution, that the government could not tolerate *any* criticism—even if justified by the facts—of its policies or its officials. "If people should not be called to account for possessing the people with an ill opinion of the government," he charged a jury, "no government can subsist." The obvious tendency of any criticism, he believed, was to diminish popular respect for authority. According to a standard treatise, *Hawkins' Pleas of Crown*, it was "far from being a justification of a libel, that the Contents thereof are true, or that the Person upon whom it is made has a bad Reputation. . . ."[2]

This view of criminal libel became enshrined after mid-century in several opinions by Lord Mansfield and in the celebrated *Commentaries* of Sir William Blackstone. In a civil defamation action, Sir William wrote, "the truth of the accusation may be pleaded in bar of the suit." But in a criminal prosecution for libel, "the tendency which all libels have to create animosities, and to disturb the public peace is the whole that the law considers." This orthodox construction of libel law, focusing upon the "bad tendency" of the publication, did not violate "the liberty of the press, properly understood. . . ." Freedom of the press, Blackstone acknowledged, "is indeed essential to the nature of a free state; but this consists in laying no previous restraints upon publications, not in freedom from censure for criminal matter when published." Employing the common law's penchant for arguing by analogy, Blackstone drew the following parallel: just as a man "may be allowed to keep poisons in his closet, but not publicly to vend them as cordials," so people possess the liberty to think what they might in private so long as they do not try publicly to disseminate "bad sentiments, destructive of the ends of society." For if officials were to tolerate licentious political unrest, Blackstone believed, the foundations for both popular liberty and civil order would collapse. Thus, "it will be found that to censure the licentiousness is to maintain the liberty of the press."[3]

Although opponents of England's ruling aristocracy rejected the Star Chamber-Holt-Blackstonian position, it took considerable time for articulate dissenters to attack the law of seditious libel. Only after the abolition of England's system of prior restraints in 1694 did libertarians focus upon England's libel laws. And even then, critics accepted the basic theories of seditious libel: that political authorities could prosecute all political statements that criticized the existing order and that government could be harmed by words alone. Rather than meeting seditious libel head-on, libertarians in England and America pressed for narrower definitions for libelous publications and liberalization of the rules under which government prosecuted its critics. Thus, eighteenth-century opposition lawyers urged courts to adopt the "Zengerian" principles, to permit truth as a defense, and to allow jurors to determine "the law of the case" and not simply the fact of publication. But judges consistently rejected the Zengerian position. Levy concluded that the orthodox view, immortalized in Blackstone's popular *Commentaries*, dominated English and American writings on free expression.

Levy carefully specified the limits of his revisionist thesis. Admitting that anti-Blackstonian ideas, especially the Zengerian principles, were undoubt-edly "in the air," he narrowed his legalistic focus to "the precise meaning of freedom of speech and press in legal ideas." In the hard ground of legal doctrine, unlike the "thin air" of popular opinion, Levy argued, Blackstonian rather than Zengerian principles flourished. He also adopted a strict, lawyer-like approach to colonial sources: "believe nothing unless proved beyond a reasonable doubt by the evidence." And anticipating a major point of critics, Levy conceded that the common law of seditious libel did not prevent "wide-spread discussion of affairs of state by the common people."[4]

In the best tradition of free speech, *Legacy of Suppression* provoked impas-sioned dissent. Some critics searched through colonial newspapers and tracts, claiming to discover statements that refuted Levy's assertion that early liber-tarian theories had remained narrow. Others attempted to demonstrate what Levy had already conceded; pointing to numerous pamphlets, broadsides, and newspaper pieces, they argued that the "law on the books" was not nearly as restrictive as the "living law." In practice, they insisted, the law of criminal libel was woven from gossamer threads. A third group of critics avoided Levy's preoccupation with legal controls altogether and examined a wide range of nonlegal restraints, especially the economic ones that most colonial printers constantly confronted.[5]

Over a twenty-five year period, Levy himself slowly backed away from some of his initial contentions, and in 1985 he issued a revised, expanded version of his now classic work. Entitling it *Emergence of a Free Press*, Levy announced that "I am revising myself." First, he unequivocally stated that if "a legacy of suppression had existed at all, the realms of law and theory had perpetuated it, not the realm of practice." More important, he now rejected as too sweeping his earlier conclusion that there had been no change in ideas about freedom of speech and press during the colonial period. Although he still insisted that there was no substantial body of libertarian thought that rejected "the core idea of seditious libel, that the government may be criminally assaulted by mere words," he nevertheless concluded that the "relationship between the press and the electoral process had become so close that popular government and political parties depended upon the existence of a free press." Finally, and most important, Levy continued to cling—correctly, I believe—to his "principal thesis" that the "core idea" of seditious libel remained in place.[6]

The towering influence of Levy's work still makes it difficult to write about political communication before 1800 without first acknowledging the contribution of *Legacy of Suppression* to the store of legal knowledge and the process of historical debate. But with the publication of *Emergence of a Free Press*, it seems appropriate to move beyond old frameworks and debates, to look at the dynamics of political expression during the colonial era from new perspectives, and to place analysis of the issue of political libel in a framework that includes the broad sweep of America's legal and cultural history.

The Dynamics of Political Expression in Seventeenth-Century America

A brief comparison between seventeenth-century America and our own times can help to illuminate the dynamics of political expression in the early colonial era. Today, courts almost never adjudicate civil suits for slander or hear criminal prosecutions for either slander or libel. The vast majority of defamation cases now involve civil libel suits against the mass media or other large business corporations. These lawsuits, which comprise only a small fraction of the total judicial business, require application of exceedingly complex, seemingly inconsistent legal doctrines. During most of the twentieth century, attorneys who represent plaintiffs have generally found themselves outgunned, especially by the more experienced and better-financed libel specialists who have represented the press. In addition, as students of modern tort law have observed, the sheer complexity of mid–twentieth-century defamation law has discouraged most ordinary citizens from filing libel suits. Plaintiffs, once they decide to sue, almost always press for sizable damages; suits designed merely to vindicate one's good name cost too much in both time and money. During the 1960s successful litigants started to collect increasingly high awards, sometimes reaching seven figures. Recognizing that such large judgments might inhibit discussion of controversial public issues, the Supreme Court began in 1964 to rule that state defamation laws must meet new, stringent First-Amendment standards. As a result of decisions such as *New York Times* v. *Sullivan* (1964) and *Rosenbloom* v. *Metromedia* (1971), critics of the media claimed that the courts had all but eliminated defamation law.

Although after the mid-1970s the Supreme Court announced new constitutional standards, somewhat more favorable to libel plaintiffs, it still rejected the dominant pre-*Sullivan* view that the libelers had to account for all defamatory falsehoods.[7]

Seventeenth-century defamation suits took place in a quite different legal culture. During the earliest years of English settlement, the various colonial legal systems generally encouraged private citizens to initiate civil defamation suits aimed at recovering monetary damages or eliciting public apologies. In contrast to most modern defamation cases, where plaintiffs sue large corporate publishers in front of juries of twelve strangers, seventeenth-century lawsuits pitted ordinary citizens against one another. In most early American defamation trials, jurors knew the litigants and, very likely, something about relations between the two parties. (Defamation suits oftentimes accompanied, or closely followed, other types of disputes.) People almost always handled their own cases, and courts applied flexible rules that in many ways resembled the practices of local and church tribunals of medieval England more than the complicated doctrines and procedures of modern defamation law.

Few seventeenth-century plaintiffs could expect a sudden financial windfall from a defamation suit. Although plaintiffs won more often than they lost, juries usually awarded court costs and relatively small damages. A judgment of even as much as several pounds was unusual. But a monetary award was not the only remedy available to successful plaintiffs. Following the practice of local and church courts in England, colonial tribunals also required many defendants to acknowledge in open court or some other public forum that they had wrongly defamed the plaintiff. News of such retractions traveled quickly in small villages, and plaintiffs could hope to have their reputations effectively vindicated.

In such civil defamation cases, then, seventeenth-century courts placed little emphasis on determining winners and losers according to a monetary calculation. Instead, their primary aim was to restore, if possible, the *status quo ante libellis*—to minimize feelings of hostility and "to make a balance" between the parties.[8]

Courts also invoked criminal penalties to reestablish "a balance" between individuals and to control "licentious" expression. Proclaiming that "a good name is better than precious ointment" and that slanders were "worserer than dead flies to corrupt and alter the savour thereof," a Rhode Island law of 1647 proscribed both defamatory comments and false reports.

Several years later, in 1652, the Rhode Island legislature again denounced "some ill-effected and rude persons" who were vilifying other people. Besides harming particular individuals, the assembly argued, defamatory statements tended "much to the disparidgement, not only of the government here established, but also reflect upon the State and Commonweale of England, our honorable protectors." The laws of Pennsylvania also condemned people who defamed either private citizens or public officials as "Enemies to the Peace and Concord of the Province" and provided for criminal and civil remedies. The Connecticut Code of 1650 included all of these justifications for punishing slanderers. Denouncing witting lies as sins against God, as "pernicious to the public weale," and as "injurious to particular persons," the code established criminal penalties that increased after each offense.[9]

Cases involving libel and slander—the legal categories most familiar to modern jurists—were not the only criminal restraints upon expression in seventeenth-century America. Colonial officials possessed a number of other criminal actions that could be used against speakers and writers. Pennsylvania's statute books, for example, contained a sedition act, a "Law Against the Spreaders of False News" about either "magistrates or private persons," and a "Law Against Scolding," which authorized justices of the peace to punish "any persons [who] shall be Clamorous, Scolding & Railing with their tongues. . . ." Persons convicted under the Scolding Law were to "stand one whole hour in the most publick place where such offense was committed, with a Gag in their mouth, or pay five shillings."[10]

Officials and citizens insisted upon enforcement of these laws. Douglas Greenberg's careful study based upon a sample of criminal prosecutions in New York between 1691 and 1776, for example, provides some quantitative perspective. Six percent of all criminal accusations sampled involved "contempt of authority"—a highly plastic legal category that could reach a tavern keeper who said that King William was "nothing but a nose of wax" and a thirteen-year-old boy who appended a personal epithet to a posted proclamation. The same study suggested that jurors, as well as thin-skinned public officials, took such accusations seriously. The rate of conviction for contempt of authority ran above the average for all crimes in New York. And though the incidence of most other crimes varied according to geographic location, prosecutions for contempt of authority occurred fairly evenly throughout the province. Similarly, Kai Erikson's study of "wayward Puritans" revealed prosecutions for contempt of authority to have been a major item of business in Essex County, Massachusetts, during the late seventeenth century.[11]

Such prosecutions reflected a general policy: to provide extensive legal controls over expression that seemed to threaten the reputation of government or social harmony. Thus, judicial and legal records from various parts of seventeenth-century America reveal prosecutions for a variety of different offenses including making "lascivious speeches" about a woman; uttering "reproachful words"; spreading "false news"; telling "pernicious" or "damaging" lies; and, most important, speaking "abusively" or "contemptuously" about governmental officials.[12]

At least in Massachusetts, authorities used legal penalties against people from all social and economic groups, not just against unpopular or isolated dissenters. In 1645, for instance, eighty-one citizens from the town of Hingham formally petitioned the Massachusetts General Court, protesting certain actions by Deputy Governor John Winthrop. The legal struggle over the limits of Winthrop's authority revealed significant factional opposition to the deputy governor and his supporters, but Winthrop ultimately prevailed. As a result, all of the petitioners, who included some of Hingham's leading residents, were fined for supporting the remonstrance. Charges against Winthrop, it was held, constituted "false and scandalous" challenges to political authority.[13]

In all of these kinds of criminal actions, penalties could be quite severe. In 1631 the Court of Assistants of Massachusetts Bay ordered one Philip Ratliffe to be whipped, to have his ears cut, and to be banished for "mallitious and scandalous speeches" against the government and the church of Salem. Such severe penalties were not limited to Puritan New England. Several years earlier, for instance, an unfortunate Virginian fared even worse than poor Ratliffe. The General Court sentenced Richard Barnes, who had been convicted of making "detracting speeches" against one of the colony's leading citizens, to forfeit all his weapons, to have his tongue bored through with an awl, to run a gauntlet of forty men and be "butted," to be "footed" out of Jamestown, to be banished forever from the town, and to post a £200 good behavior bond if he remained in the colony.[14]

The manner and type of punishment varied according to the seriousness of the statement and the demeanor of the defendant. In 1672, for example, the Suffolk County Court initially sentenced John Veering, convicted of calling a minister "a black hypocritical rogue," to suffer a severe whipping and to stand "in the open market place in Boston, exalted upon a Stolle for an houres time . . ." with a paper fastened to his breast, which proclaimed that he was "A Prophane and Wicked Slanderer & Impious Reviler of a Minister of the Gosple. . . ." But when Veering humbly apologized, the court reduced his sentence to the payment of a small fine and the posting of three good behavior bonds.[15]

Judged by modern constitutional standards, use of good behavior bonds to control future statements raised the issue of an illegal prior restraint. In the seventeenth century, however, courts commonly assessed good behavior, or peace, bonds against people considered likely to cause trouble with their tongues. Bonds could even be used before there had been any formal determination of criminal guilt or innocence. Courts required persons "bound to good behavior" to secure one or more acquaintances who would pledge some of their own assets as well. The Suffolk County Court, for example, required John Veering to post a twenty pound bond and two friends to post bonds of ten pounds apiece. All three men would be liable for the value of these recognizances if the court later found that Veering had violated his pledge of good behavior. According to *Dalton's Country Justice*, a commonly used seventeenth-century handbook for justices of the peace, a bond could be declared forfeited without any actual breach of the peace. By "using wordes or threatenings, tending or inciting to the breach of the peace," people opened themselves to forfeiture. In societies without regular police or prisons, good behavior bonds offered inexpensive and apparently fairly effective deterrents to recidivism in minor disputes, and courts often employed them in seventeenth-century cases.[16]

Thus, colonial officials sought to settle most disputes over reputation as quickly and as economically as possible. As the struggling English outposts became more stable and secure, criminal penalties tended to become less harsh. In some cases, courts applied no formal sanctions at all; they merely admonished citizens to speak more carefully in the future or bound them to good behavior. In contrast to the drastic action against Richard Barnes in 1624, for example, the Governor's Council allowed several "seditious" Virginians to escape unpunished in 1699 after they confessed their crimes, begged forgiveness, and promised to behave themselves. In criminal cases, courts sometimes encouraged contrition by giving defendants a simple choice: pay an outrageously large fine or make a humbling apology. Most took the latter option. Courts used similar techniques in civil cases. They could, for instance, propose retractions in court or more public types of apologies as substitutes for payment of sizable money damages.[17] In agrarian societies where money was scarce and individual fortunes small, few people could afford to do anything but apologize. Similarly, people bound to their own good behavior or the good behavior of their neighbors possessed a considerable economic stake in not having these recognizances forfeited.

Therefore, the first generation of white colonials believed that all types of expression could unsettle their struggling communities. Even private defamation did more than damage individual reputation, the primary interest protected by modern libel and slander law. Like other types of expression—such as false reports, abusive speeches, and contemptuous language toward authorities—private slanders were considered serious enough to warrant the invocation of formal legal sanctions. According to one survey of early colonial court records, cases of defamation or slander "amounted to 17 per cent of the criminal business of all courts."[18]

The Politics—Large and Small—of Reputation

Despite abundant evidence of the use of legal restraints, historians must do more than locate the early colonial era near the restrictionist end of some libertarian-restrictionist continuum or chide colonials for possessing unenlightened ideas about freedom of expression. No analysis should isolate legal ideas and practices from the nature of early American society and politics. Why did the earliest colonial settlers place so much importance upon the control of "loose" talk? Why did they devote so much of their time and legal resources to the protection of personal and governmental reputation?

Older histories of libel law provide few answers, particularly for questions involving private defamation suits. The vast majority of lawyers, judges, and common law scholars have snorted at most private defamation suits. To these busy people, the ordinary libel or slander case merely uncovered some petty dispute between the quarrelsome and litigious. Reflecting upon the development of defamation law, for example, an English common law scholar once complained about the prevalence of slander suits in medieval courts. He considered the sensitivity of English villagers "very curious." Even worse, local tribunals did not try to distinguish types of insults according to common law principles. "Everything that might by even fastidiously minded persons be regarded as militating against personal honor was cognizable."[19]

Similarly, most American lawyer-historians have shown scant sympathy toward private defamation suits and little interest in seeking social explanations for their frequency during the early colonial era. In general, historians have been most concerned about the legal issues raised by "political" libel cases, ones involving public leaders. "Private" defamation suits between anonymous citizens have seemed far too removed from the world of public affairs and from great constitutional issues. But recent studies on the nature of legal process, on conflicts over reputation in small European villages, and on early American society all help to explain not only the prevalence of criminal restraints in seventeenth-century America but also the relationship between frequent private defamation suits and the larger system of political communication in premodern societies.

Evidence of extensive legal restrictions upon expression does not mean that seventeenth-century courts ruthlessly stamped out public dissent and effectively controlled private discord. From all that historians now know about political and social unrest in colonial America, it seems evident that these restraints reflected conflict as much as they suppressed it. In some cases, defamation actions signified the existence of other types of conflict. The injunction to report suspected cases of sexual misconduct, for example, sometimes triggered actions for defamation. Similarly, persons who feared that they might be charged with witchcraft sometimes filed defamation suits in hopes of bringing their accusers' evidence into the open before the charges gained credibility.[20] Moreover, the system of controls over expression, tight as it might have been by twentieth-century standards, never could have reached every person who technically violated prohibitions mandated by statute books, local court traditions, or village customs. Whether or not colonials actually enforced criminal sanctions or instituted civil suits depended upon a variety of circumstances.

Formal conflict in the courtroom, studies of the legal process have shown, may be viewed as a game, one whose rules can both repel and attract players.[21] The game and player perspective explains in part the prevalence of legal restraints on expression during the early seventeenth century. Before deciding to enter formal legal combat, colonials could have chosen a number of alternative courses. Mediation and conciliation of disputes over reputation by some third party offered an obvious and less drastic alternative to litigation. Many seventeenth-century communities, particularly in New England, actively encouraged mediation of private disputes. In Massachusetts Bay, unlike in England, members of the established church could take disputes, including defamation cases, to separate ecclesiastical courts.[22] Alternatively, villagers could adopt the apparently quite common remedy of "self-help," matching their own vocal resources against that of their detractors and hoping that this trial by battle of tongues would not provoke authorities to seek formal legal restraints against one or both parties. Finally, either private citizens or public officials could adopt the easiest course of all: simply to "lump it." For one reason or another, citizens and officials could decide to take no legal action whatsoever.[23] In a situation involving "contemptuous" words, for example, political leaders might have decided that rigid enforcement of the law would have inflamed rather than healed wounds in the body politic.[24] Yet, despite such considerations and despite the availability of alternatives to litigation and adjudication, the fact remains that the early colonial era was a time when employment of both criminal sanctions and civil controls upon expression occurred with considerably more frequency than in any other period of American history. Why?

Put quite simply, the earliest colonial "legal system"—using the term legal system in the special sense suggested by legal historian Lawrence Friedman—encouraged the use of formal institutions to resolve disputes over reputation.[25] First, the very structure of the early American legal machinery contributed to the relatively heavy defamation caseload. In contrast to the modern American judicial structure, colonial courts were readily accessible; they were not located in an imposing building "somewhere downtown." In addition, these bodies were not dealing in some "mysterious science" known only to those people trained in the common law. In cases involving expression, most of the legal rules were fairly simple; court procedures were flexible; and the catalog of potential remedies was long. The legal system, then, erected few institutional, procedural, or doctrinal barriers to the speedy resolution of controversies over reputation.

Finally, and perhaps most important, the "legal culture"—those values and attitudes that help determine "when and why and where people turn to government, or turn away"—favored use of formal restraints over expression.[26] In deciding whether or not to participate in the seventeenth-century legal game, potential litigant-players in the category of defamation law could be encouraged by the fact that the likelihood of a decision in favor of restriction was great. Free speech in the colonial era did not include the liberty to speak licentiously, particularly about political affairs. Unlike nineteenth-century liberals, for example, colonials did not view public disputes as signs of the community's political freedom. And neither did they take consolation in anything like the nineteenth-century liberal faith that social harmony could one day result from clashes within the free marketplace of ideas.

Colonials emphasized the need for quick resolution of bitter private and public debates. In the vast majority of cases, no stigma was attached to rulers who curbed licentious expression or to those who sued their neighbors for slander; both were simply carrying out their civic duties.[27] Similarly, most defendants acknowledged the error of their ways and accepted their punishments; few attempted to justify their actions according to higher principles of free expression or even to appeal their cases to higher judicial forums. Therefore, when people adjudged to be slanderers publicly apologized, they were doing more than attempting to restore injured reputations or to reduce chances of continued ill will. Cast in the role of "repentant deviants," they signified that their violations of village norms constituted only temporary lapses from the ideal of harmony and cooperation. They reaffirmed that the community consensus against licentious expression remained intact. The much smaller number of "unrepentant deviants," those who refused to admit their wrongdoing or who defied legal authorities, faced severe sanctions and ultimately even banishment from the community.[28]

A series of cross-national anthropological studies on the "politics of reputation" in European villages, together with a burgeoning number of works on early American society, provide further insights into the problem of defamation law in seventeenth-century America. In particular, modern anthropological investigations suggest that distinctions between political and private defamation were not as clear cut in the legal culture of village societies as in the doctrines of cosmopolitan common law lawyers. These studies also caution against the easy temptation to attribute the large number of slander suits solely to puritanism or to the peculiar tensions of life in English North America.

Summarizing a number of investigations of twentieth-century mountain communities in southern Europe, F. G. Bailey stressed the importance that rural villagers placed upon "small politics"—the everyday maneuvering and infighting to protect personal reputations.[29] In these static villages, after all, people dealt almost entirely with neighbors who possessed a great deal of information—and, quite likely, misinformation—about their characters. Villagers constantly fought to uphold their good names; they also encountered numerous opportunities to downgrade the reputations of potential rivals. In such closed societies nearly every social exchange, nearly every meeting, raised the possibility of conflict over someone's reputation. This was "not just a question of how to do people down; one need[ed] also to know how to influence people and to make friends."[30]

At the same time, Bailey argued, the rough economic and social equality of these communities increased the likelihood of conflicts over reputation. In dealing with their peers, villagers felt equality of reputation was the "reward for constant vigilance." They remained alert to the possible machinations of "upstarts," people who used various stratagems—ranging from idle chatter, to malicious gossip, to outright character assassination—in order to diminish the reputations of neighbors and to elevate their own.[31]

Most of these same considerations also influenced battles over character in the world of "large politics"—conflicts over the reputations of community leaders and the government itself. Village officials, no less than ordinary citizens, were anxious to protect their reputations: "Whether your aim is to protect yourself and remain part of the community of equals, or to cut upstarts down to size or to rise out of the community of equals to a position of leadership, you need the important skill of being able to control information about yourself and others. . . . The would-be leader must cut down the flow of news about him. . . ."[32] At some point, then, both public leaders and private citizens might need to abandon informal and extralegal tactics and to use the law courts as a means of halting the circulation of information they considered harmful to themselves or to the general community.

Viewed against these anthropological studies, both the heavy caseload of "petty" slander suits and the flexible system of criminal restraints in North American villages during the earliest years of settlement comes into sharper focus: both clearly reflect the nature of politics—small and large—in premodern communities. Indeed, long before the era of trans-Atlantic expansion, local and church tribunals in medieval England proscribed defamatory and abusive language, whether directed at village officials or at common folk. Disputes that flared into harsh words required containment and then settlement before they became something worse. If allowed to continue, the abusive language of small politics could escalate into even harsher words and perhaps into violent conflicts within the world of large politics.[33]

As recent histories of seventeenth-century communities in North America have emphasized, these earliest settlements exemplified English rural society at its most traditional. The first English immigrants had grown up in a land undergoing wrenching economic and social change. Many of the leaders saw migration to North America as an opportunity to restore traditional values and institutions, ideals and organizations that seemed to be decaying in England. A desire for order, and the determination to use the legal system to maintain it, ran strong. And, of course, the rigors of survival in a new, often violence-filled environment reinforced this impulse.

Although they recognized the inevitability of conflict, religious and civil leaders still emphasized the need to seek consensus. People were expected to control antisocial impulses and to subordinate self-interest (and self-expression) to the larger public welfare. Community leaders stressed strict conformity to a set of moral and social norms that were intended to promote order and harmony. Transgressions against village values, such as improper sexual conduct or other types of "licentious" behavior, disrupted the social order and violated the law of God. A "good ruler" would not tolerate actions, or even words, that endangered the public order or threatened to bring down God's wrath upon the community. Similarly, ordinary citizens were supposed to watch over their neighbors, to report improper activities, and to seek formal legal restraints whenever necessary. This ideal of a controlled, static social and moral order existed with greatest intensity—and persisted the longest—in Puritan New England, but it provided a general view of the world shared by most white settlers during the early seventeenth century.

In early American communities the notion that "sticks and stones may break my bones but words can never hurt me" would have seemed hopelessly naive. Since geographic mobility was limited, people branded as adulterers, liars, or thieves could not easily move away from their reputations. Neither could they likely expect that today's bad name would vanish tomorrow. Colonials could not escape into the anonymity of a "lonely crowd" or easily join alternative social groups. And gossip or slanders carried over the village's face-to-face communications system undoubtedly had as long, if not longer, an active life than malicious items spread by modern-day systems of mass communications. There were, quite obviously, no newspapers or electronic media to replace one month's notorious celebrities with a new cast of symbolic sinners. Derogatory tags, even if unjustly deserved, could remain fastened to one's name for years unless the legal system offered some sort of ready solvent, such as quick actions for slander, to remove unflattering personal labels.

The readiness of colonial officials, particularly in New England, to control "political" expression, even when it only involved words between neighbors, contrasted with the practice of seventeenth-century common law courts in England. By then, common law judges were trying to discourage private slander suits by setting various procedural and substantive hurdles in front of prospective plaintiffs. In 1624 Parliament attempted, by statute, to decrease the number of small defamation claims in common law tribunals. And the first English treatise on slander, published in 1647, expressed the hope that most defamation suits, which involved "words only of brangle heat and cholor," and which served simply "to promote the malices and vent the spleen of private jars and discontents," would soon disappear so that common law judges could hear more important disputes, especially those involving England's expanding commercial interests.[34]

But across the Atlantic, courts proved more hospitable to cases that reflected the "brangle heat and cholor" of both small and large politics. Legal institutions, legal doctrines, and the legal culture all encouraged citizens to turn to the courts in order to maintain the appearance, if not always the reality, of communal solidarity. Ideals such as mutual love and harmony represented more than utopian standards. They were also very real, and very practical, goals in small societies dominated by continuing face-to-face relationships. The legal system was as open as the system of expression was restrictive, at least as judged by twentieth-century standards. Yet, in terms of the social realities of early seventeenth-century America, a restrictive set of controls over speech was, in many ways, compatible with an expansive system of personal communication. In its broadest meaning, the "right to communicate" involved the freedom to interact with other people. Especially in small village societies, defamatory statements, whatever their source, could interrupt the normal channels of interpersonal communication: persons whose reputations had been besmirched were likely to find their ability to communicate freely with others becoming increasingly restricted. Viewed in this way, operation of the broader system of free communication required some rather clear-cut restrictions on certain types of expression.

From Defamation to Political Libel

Neither an open system of courts nor a restrictive law of defamation survived the colonial era. During two centuries of English rule much of the openness and informality of the earliest legal institutions disappeared. As colonial society "matured," provincial authorities created more sophisticated legal structures, ones that more closely followed common law procedures and doctrines than did their early seventeenth-century counterparts. At the same time, the legal culture changed. With the rise of a more commercialized society, one in which law was coming to be seen as an important instrument for shaping economic relationships and for settling disputes arising out of marketplace transactions, American jurists shifted their priorities and refocused their energies. Early seventeenth-century courts, especially in New England, had tried to concern themselves with nearly every departure from the moral standards of their communities. In Essex County, Massachusetts, for example, nearly 38 percent of the prosecutions for fornication during the seventeenth century involved married couples whose firstborn had arrived suspiciously early. But by the eighteenth century, despite a sexual revolution that saw nearly half of all brides in Massachusetts going to the altar "with child," authorities in Middlesex County concentrated almost entirely on illegitimate births, a decision signifying that legal officials were more concerned about the costs of caring for bastards than about the sin of premarital sex.[35] The same process of reallocating scarce legal resources and shifting priorities can be seen in cases involving expression, especially in private defamation suits and criminal prosecutions for various types of "dangerous" expression.

In England, the heyday of defamation law was the sixteenth century; in colonial America it was the seventeenth. After the earliest years of settlement, most legal authorities began to consider adjudication of ordinary defamation cases a waste of valuable legal resources. This shift in colonial priorities, which paralleled that of English legal officials a century earlier, did not occur suddenly. But the Connecticut statute of 1708 that declared that "defamation and slander is a growing evil amongst us" and mandated both criminal prosecutions and civil suits in response, clearly looked toward the past. In Virginia and Maryland, for example, there was a marked decrease in the number of private defamation actions, civil and criminal, over the course of the seventeenth century. Even in Massachusetts, defamation cases became less frequent during the late seventeenth and early eighteenth centuries. By the late seventeenth century, for instance, the county court of Suffolk, which served the growing commercial center of Boston, primarily reserved criminal prosecutions for defamation on public officials.[36]

Although colonial leaders certainly never encouraged personal vilification among citizens, they adopted measures that made it more difficult for people to sue their neighbors for alleged injuries to reputation. In 1684, for example, New York's legislature imposed money and time barriers in attempts to discourage small slander suits. Following the parliamentary statute of 1624, New York declared that in all cases where jurors awarded less than forty shillings in damages, plaintiffs could receive no more than forty shillings in court costs. This change was not insignificant, for in many cases the court costs far exceeded the actual judgment. Thus potential litigants, even if successful in their suits, could face the prospect of a financial loss. This was intended as a deterrent to taking a defamation case to court. In addition, New York's law of 1684 required plaintiffs to seek legal redress within nine months of the alleged slander.[37]

Lawmakers in Virginia took even more drastic action. Complaining that "oftentimes many brabling women often slander and scandalize their neighbours for which their poore husbands are often brought into chargeable and vexatious suites," legislators provided additional punishment for female slanderers: in addition to payment of damages by their "poore husbands," women were to be punished by ducking. Similarly, legislators sought to tighten the legal definition of defamation because "many vexatious persons do very much trouble the courts and their neighbors for babbling words, sometimes passionately but not maliciously spoken. . . ." As a consequence, the legislature declared that no words would be actionable in county courts unless they charged the plaintiff with a specific criminal offense. Defamation suits involving any other type of verbal abuse were to be "cast out of the court, and the plaintiff to be nonsuited. . . ."[38] In effect, this statute moved Virginia closer to the restrictive common law definitions of defamation that had been framed by English common law courts during the late sixteenth and early seventeenth centuries.[39]

As courts in colonial North America increasingly borrowed from English common law procedures and doctrines—one part of a general process of the anglicanization of provincial life—procedural and substantive barriers against litigation of private disputes involving only "babbling words" grew more sturdy. During the early seventeenth century, courts in Massachusetts, for example, welcomed civil defamation suits by all sorts of citizens and settled most of them without elaborate legal procedures and without the assistance of professional lawyers. A century later, courts in Massachusetts were still hearing defamation suits, but the mechanics of initiating such actions had become more difficult. By 1760, as the legal papers of John Adams reveal, a slander suit could require lengthy preparation by a trained lawyer, who would have to make a fairly extensive (and presumably fairly expensive) excursion through the tangled byways of English defamation law. Entry into the legal game obviously had become more difficult for people who wished formal vindication of their reputations.[40]

The cases collected by Richard Morris from New York City's Mayor's Court also suggest that, even in a tribunal that was always seeking more business, defamation cases involving slanders against tradespeople or of a serious criminal nature received priority over cases growing out of the small politics of neighborhood life. In 1713, for example, Rebecca Drury sued Thomas Husk, claiming he had called her a prostitute and alleging damages of 200 pounds. Although jurors found in Rebecca's favor, they awarded her a mere twenty shillings. In contrast, John Ruston, "a glover and Britches-maker" recovered more than twelve pounds when he successfully sued a man who had charged him with fraudulent trade practices.[41]

By the end of the colonial period, cases involving purely private defamation had settled into the pattern that would continue over the next two centuries. As a number of studies have revealed, cases for private defamation, particularly for slander, became only an occasional concern of nineteenth- and twentieth-century courts. An exhaustive study of cases heard by a trial court in Wisconsin from 1854 to 1954, for example, revealed only thirty-four defamation cases in the hundred-year period—and most of these were libel cases involving newspaper defendants.[42] In contrast, many seventeenth-century courts (which served much smaller populations) would have heard that many defamation cases in a single year.[43] And a study of every reported slander case in the United States during the 1950s found only 184 suits. In contrast to the seventeenth century when plaintiffs usually prevailed, only 31 plaintiffs successfully maintained their actions. "A plaintiff's lawyer having worked all the 184 slander cases for this ten year period on a contingent basis could have worked himself to death, lived in penury and died a bankrupt."[44]

Thus, the civil action for defamation, particularly for slander, has become almost irrelevant to the give-and-take of small politics. According to Professor Leon Green, who devoted most of his seventy years of scholarship to tort law, no "other formula of the law promises so much and delivers so little. No other formula has been so restricted in operation as to make legal the very conduct it seemingly condemns."[45] The law has, in effect, left ordinary citizens to settle controversies over their reputations without any significant help from the judicial system, the end result of a trend that can be traced back to legal and nonlegal changes beginning during the colonial era.

But if the law generally left the common folk to "lump it" or to adopt the remedy of self-help, colonial lawmakers maintained considerably more interest in verbal and printed attacks upon more prominent citizens, particularly upon political authorities. Although the legal system became less involved in the world of small verbal politics, colonial politicians and lawyers sought to retain a fairly strict system of controls, particularly over the press, when it came to "dangerous" expression in the world of large politics. This task, particularly after the middle of the eighteenth century, would not be an easy one.

Chapter Two | Publishers Beware!
Libel Law in Eighteenth-Century America

Though they may have been willing to lower their guard against neighborhood gossips, the colonial elite kept their legal weapons primed and ready for libelers who entered the public field. And during the late seventeenth and eighteenth centuries most colonial officials did not lack for potential targets. If the dominant idea remained one of order and harmony, the clash of factional groups suggested a somewhat different reality. Shifting coalitions of political "outs" formed and reformed in many communities and in most provinces. This intermittent factionalism gave birth to bitter political debates that authorities could not always terminate by the old system of controls.

Most areas of English North America endured severe, sometimes violent, political troubles during the late seventeenth century, and colonial authorities often invoked new controls over political expression. Responding to continued unrest in the Old Dominion, for instance, Lord Effingham's Thanksgiving Proclamation of 1685 warned Virginians that "the Rise and Growth of Sedition and Faction proceeds and encreases by the over lycentiousness of people in their discourses," and his Lordship charged all governmental officials to act resolutely against "seditious discourses" lest they upset "ye Giddy headed Multitude." Disturbed by opposition in Pennsylvania's lower counties to William Penn's proprietary rule, the provincial legislature passed a comprehensive sedition law in 1684. And in the wake of Leisler's Rebellion of 1689 in New York, authorities stepped up prosecutions for "contempt of authority."[1]

By the early eighteenth century, many colonial officials faced a new political threat—the printing press. In New England, for example, introduction of the printing press gave the literate public access to a great deal of information about politics and government; after the first decade of the eighteenth century, pamphlets and then newspapers appeared regularly. Through these publications, citizens could learn about the actions of their political representatives and could read English and colonial political essays, many of which offered alternatives to the views presented by New England's political and religious establishment.[2]

Not everyone welcomed the printing press. Governor William Berkeley of Virginia, for example, once thanked God that in his colony "*there are no free schools nor printing*, and I hope we shall not have these [for a] hundred years; for *learning* has brought disobedience, and heresy, and sects into the world, and *printing* has divulged them, and libels against the best government. God keep us from both!"[3]

However much the colonial elite might have favored Governor Berkeley's ideas about political communication, the press ultimately became a significant force in most provinces. By magnifying the power and preserving the message of individual voices, the printing press threatened to supplant patterns of communication based on face-to-face relationships and to complicate even further the lives of colonial officials.

The "Peculiar Unhappiness" of Colonial Printers

When confronted by charges that their publications threatened political tranquility and individual reputations, ink-stained printers quickly donned the unsoiled robes of gallant defenders of free expression. But most avoided any direct assault on the law of libel in favor of more circumspect strategies; they sought to persuade others of the difficult nature of the printing trade and to popularize definitions of free expression tailored to their specific needs.[4]

Benjamin Franklin's "Apology for Printers" (published in 1731) offered one of the earliest attempts to defend both the cause of free expression and the trade interests of printer-journalists.[5] Responding to complaints about anti-clerical references in a handbill printed at his shop, Franklin adopted several contradictory defense strategies. He began by bemoaning the cruel nature of his trade: "the peculiar Unhappiness" of the printing business. Although "the Smith, the Shoemaker, the Carpenter, or the Man of any other Trade, may work indifferently for People of all Persuasions without offending any of them," the work of printers too often produced dissatisfaction from many different sides. Such discrimination, Franklin also claimed, was unjustified because printers were really indistinguishable from other artisans who served the public. "Printers are educated in the Belief," he claimed, that "both sides ought equally to have the Advantage of Fair Play," and therefore printers should "cheerfully serve all contending Writers that pay them well, and without the least ill-will to the Persons reflected on" in their newspapers, pamphlets and handbills.

Owners of presses, Franklin seemed to argue, should offer a kind of "free forum" for all groups and individuals. If printers granted access only to opinions they found agreeable, "an End would thereby be put to Free Writing, and the World would afterwards have nothing to read but what happen'd to be the Opinions of Printers."

Other colonial printers suggested similar definitions of free expression, ones that relegated them to the role of innocent bystanders, "meer mechanics," who were not really responsible for the contents of their publications.

Although this "trade definition" carried no legal weight—under common law, republication of another person's libelous statements offered no defense in either a civil or a criminal case—the idea that the press served as a common carrier for all ideas promised at least some extralegal protection for printers. If colonials could be convinced of the neutrality of printers, they might also be persuaded to forgo retaliation against the "meer mechanics" who operated the engines of their discontents.[6]

More important for the community at large, had printers been willing and able to operate according to this free forum theory, colonial readers could have sampled a wide array of intellectual products. To be sure, some eighteenth-century libertarians did extol the "free marketplace of ideas." "If Sense and Nonsense are blended" in a writer's work, wrote New Yorker James Alexander in 1733, "by the free Use of the Press, *which is open to all*, the Inconsistencies of the Writer may be made apparent."[7] But in practice, and even in the safer realm of theory, few colonials—particularly printers—ever opted for a truly free and open press.

In his "Apology," Franklin quickly qualified his own free-forum theory. Whatever "might be urg'd in behalf of a Man's being allowed to do in the Way of his Business whatever he is paid for," Franklin argued, "yet Printers do continually discourage the Printing of great Numbers of bad things, and stifle them in the Birth." He specified three types of publications: "anything that might countenance Vice, or promote Immorality"; those "things as might do real Injury to any Person how much soever I have been solicited, and tempted with Offers of Great Pay"; and "such Things as Usually give Offence either to Church or State. . . ." In this last crucial area, the printing of controversial political and religious materials, Franklin boasted that he had been more careful "than any Printer that has followed the Business in this Province before." Reiterating this theme in his *Autobiography*, Franklin flatly rejected the idea that the press, "like a Stage Coach in which any one who would pay had a Right to Place," was a common carrier for all ideas.[8] He suggested, in short, an eighteenth-century version of what would become orthodoxy among twentieth-century journalists: the idea that "a free and responsible" press should exercise some type of self-censorship over what appeared in its pages. A free press, among other things, was free from material that its printer deemed unacceptable for public distribution.

Franklin, then, granted access to a variety of viewpoints in his relatively brief essay, and his "Apology for Printers" presented no coherent theory of free expression. Yet Franklin's inconsistencies do suggest a good deal about the diverse pressures faced by colonial printers. Any consideration of the impact of libel law, as well as any evaluation of the larger system of political communication, must consider these nonlegal restraints upon the colonial press.

First, as Franklin's "Apology" indicates, the occupation of a printer generally produced little wealth or social status. If a printer had aspirations to something better, as Franklin clearly did, opportunities for money and prestige lay outside the print shop. Franklin himself ultimately prospered, branching out into other activities, creating a thriving business empire, and eventually launching an international political career. But few other colonial printers escaped from the font and type box. The vast majority, in fact, could consider themselves successful if they kept their small operations solvent. Printers faced a continual battle that pitted high fixed costs against uncertain revenues; as a business operation, the press demanded the same cost-conscious command of details as any other small capitalistic venture. Even a governmental printing contract might not eliminate the need to secure other business, and printers generally avoided items that might rankle potential customers.

In hopes of augmenting their incomes, of advertising their shops, and of keeping their apprentices busy, many printers eventually entered the newspaper business. Such a decision, however, compounded the pressures upon colonial printers; publication of a weekly journal only increased the chances of printing something considered in some way offensive. Consequently, as Franklin suggested in his *Autobiography*, most colonial printers exercised more rigorous self-censorship over their newspapers than over pamphlets and handbills. Colonial newspapers offered something less than a free forum where citizens could examine controversial issues.[9]

Generally, colonial papers contained little material on local affairs, particularly on politics. Printers employed no journalistic celebrities to make news or investigative reporters to discover other people doing noteworthy things. They waited for events, such as natural disasters or wars, to occur, and then they waited a while longer for adequate information to filter into their shops, usually from newspapers closer to the site of the story. Sometimes printers found themselves left with inadequate supplies of news. Samuel Keimer inaugurated his *Pennsylvania Gazette* in 1728 with this whimsical admission: "We have little news of consequence at present. In the meantime we hope our readers will be content for the present, with what we can give 'em, which if it does 'em no good, shall do 'em no hurt. 'Tis the best we have, so take it."[10] Other printers, finding no news at hand, learned to improvise, even if this meant recycling the old. Satirically defending repetitive journalism, Franklin observed that "'tis not to be always expected there should happen just a full Sheet of New Occurrences for each Week." And in any event, "the oftener you are told a good thing, the more likely you will be to remember it."[11]

England and Europe provided the surest—and politically safest—sources of material for colonial newspapers. Colonial printers republished English political essays, sometimes because they seemed relevant to local disputes but at other times simply to fill the blank spaces between advertisements. Even when printers possessed an adequate supply of "New Occurrences," these were most likely to be reports of European military and diplomatic affairs that had been gleaned from months-old English and continental newspapers. Designed to be retained, reread, and rehashed with friends, colonial newspapers served more as repositories of English essays and as chronicles of recent European diplomacy than as summaries of current colonial events. This format, quite obviously, reduced a printer's chances of running afoul of local political passions or of the law of libel.

As Franklin's "Apology" demonstrates, printers recognized the legal and economic dangers of partisanship. Franklin himself gained valuable firsthand experience when he apprenticed with his brother James in Boston from 1719 to 1723. James Franklin's *New England Courant* kept up a running battle against Massachusetts's ruling establishment until a full-scale legal assault—which included a stay in jail for seditious libel—encouraged James to tone down his rhetoric and eventually entirely shut down his paper. Few other printers, including brother Benjamin, made the same mistakes as James Franklin.[12]

Factional Politics and Seditious Libel, 1700–1750

James Franklin was not the only colonial to discover the reality of legal restraints. During the early eighteenth century, provincial officials attempted to maintain at least the possibility of controls over oral expression and to use English restraints, including the Orthodox Whig version of seditious libel, to bridle the press. Judges could punish people who spoke contemptuously or seditiously about political authority. In 1721 a Pennsylvania court sentenced a man to spend two hours in the pillory and to wear a placard that announced that he had spoken "contemptuously of my Sovereign Lord King George." More than thirty years later, in 1755, another Pennsylvanian was required to don a similar sign; this one announced that he had uttered "seditious words against the Best of Kings." And though the volume of cases declined after tensions from Leisler's Rebellion eased, courts in neighboring New York continued to punish defendants for "contempt of authority" throughout the colonial period.[13]

Colonial authorities could, if the occasion seemed to warrant, also restrain printers and writers. In fact, until well into the eighteenth century, legal controls, especially over printed materials, undoubtedly proved more effective on the western side of the Atlantic than in England. Official licensing, for instance, continued in some North American colonies for several decades after Parliament had lifted prior restraints over domestic publications. Only four days after the appearance of the first American newspaper, Benjamin Harris's *Public Occurrences, Both Foreign and Domestic* (1690), the Governor and

Council of Massachusetts shut it down. Harris, it seemed, had failed to secure a license.[14] Meanwhile, colonial judges fully endorsed the strict libel doctrines used in English common law courts. Indeed, given the deference of colonial judges to all English precedents, it would have been surprising had Leonard Levy discovered that they had made an exception in the area of libel law. More important, as Levy has shown, members of elected legislatures guarded the reputation of the government, and their own good names, with even more zeal than common law judges. Invoking the legislative power to punish breaches of parliamentary privilege, colonial assemblies could humble or even imprison their critics without observing the procedural safeguards required in common law courts.[15]

Legislators and common law judges, however, were not the only English citizens with ideas about libel law, and the Star Chamber–Holt–Blackstonian view generated opposition in both England and America. When directed against isolated or unpopular dissenters, people such as those Pennsylvanians who denounced the monarch, colonial officials easily enforced orthodox legal controls. But when popular support could be rallied behind political critics or printers, the orthodox view of seditious libel met considerable resistance.

Even before the eighteenth century, officials in Pennsylvania faltered when they tried to gag a dissident Quaker sect led by George Keith. After a series of bitter religious and political confrontations in 1692, authorities exhausted their entire stockpile of legal ammunition in an effort to silence Keith. First, the dominant faction, headed by Deputy Governor Thomas Lloyd, secured a conviction against two of Keith's supporters for a technical violation of an obscure licensing act; next, the Governor's Council ordered the Commonwealth's judicial officers to prevent publication of all material that seemed to carry the tendency of "sedition" or merely to encourage "contempt of magistracy." When these moves failed to gag his opponents, Thomas Lloyd procured a formal indictment for seditious libel against Keith and three supporters, including printer William Bradford. Although Lloyd did obtain summary conviction against three of his adversaries, the Lloyd-dominated court chose to impose small fines rather than to risk creation of popular martyrs by exacting jail terms.

In the fourth prosecution, that of William Bradford who demanded a jury trial, Lloyd failed to secure even a symbolic victory. Conducting his own defense, Bradford argued, for the first time in an American libel prosecution, that the jury should be allowed to determine not only the fact of publication but "to find also, whether this be a seditious paper, or not, & whether it does tend to the weakening of the hands of the Magistrate." The court initially overruled Bradford's claim, but perhaps sensing popular resistance, even from the jury box, it did allow jurors to determine "the law of the case." The jury deadlocked, and Bradford ultimately escaped retrial when a new administration secured his release.[16]

Controversy over freedom of press proved much more sustained, and resistance to orthodox libel laws much more intense during the celebrated prosecution of John Peter Zenger in 1735. Zenger's trial for printing allegedly seditious attacks upon New York's Governor William Cosby was only one incident in a larger power struggle between two relatively well-organized factions—an opposition group led by Lewis Morris, the province's chief justice, and the ruling clique led by Governor Cosby. Seeking to broaden their base of support, but denied access to New York's only newspaper, the Morrisites financed publication of the *New York Weekly Journal*, a unique type of colonial paper. Zenger provided the technical know-how—though not very skillfully, complained his patrons—and James Alexander, a talented lawyer-publicist, directed the *Journal*'s assault upon the Cosby administration. Contrary to the familiar style of colonial journalism, Alexander devoted his columns, including bogus advertising notices, to local politics and, more precisely, to the destruction of Cosby's reputation. Not even his Excellency's wife was spared. Judged by the rhetoric of colonial printers and by Alexander's own statements on liberty of the press, the *Weekly Journal* hardly qualified as a "free" press. It made no pretense of being neutral or of being open as a forum for diverse points of view. And measured according to strict common law standards, the paper was clearly an example of "licentiousness" rather than "liberty" of press.[17]

Recognizing that Cosby would not allow attacks against his family and his administration to continue, Alexander assumed more than a theoretical interest in using the *Weekly Journal* to inform New Yorkers about the inequities of "Star Chamber libel laws." A series of essays on libel and free expression ultimately became the basis of Zenger's courtroom defense, conducted by Andrew Hamilton of Philadelphia.

Hamilton readily conceded that Zenger had printed material critical of Cosby and offered to substantiate the charges; Chief Justice James De Lancey (handpicked by Cosby as Lewis Morris's successor) refused to allow any evidence of truth to go before the jury. A loyal member of the Cosby faction and a completely orthodox jurist, De Lancey invoked settled precedents, holding that a libel "is nevertheless a libel that it is *true*." And continuing to follow English precedents, he also ruled that he, not the jury, possessed the power to determine whether or not Zenger's publications were libelous. But in a trial that twentieth-century libertarians continue to showcase, the jury defied De Lancey's instructions and returned a general verdict of not guilty.[18]

The impact of the *Zenger* case was not nearly as immediate nor as obvious as historians have sometimes claimed. Hamilton did not suddenly spring "the

Zengerian principles" on a surprised De Lancey. William Bradford had contended back in 1692 that a jury should determine the law of the case rather than simply the fact of publication, and Zenger's court-appointed attorney, allegedly one of Cosby's stooges, had also argued that De Lancey should admit evidence of truth as a defense in the case. Since De Lancey ultimately rejected both of the defense's contentions, the *Zenger* case, in truth, constituted a precedent for the Orthodox rather than the Opposition Whig view of seditious libel. The significance of the *Zenger* case stemmed from the changes in political culture that it reflected. In particular, Hamilton's oral argument and Alexander's writings demonstrated the growing intrusion of English "country" or "opposition" political ideology into partisan disputes in North America.

Isolated from the sources of effective political power in England, a diverse group of country writers—including radical Whigs such as John Trenchard and Thomas Gordon, and Tories such as Viscount Bolingbroke—condemned the alleged machinations of "court" insiders around the king and in the front benches of Parliament. Opposition literature, especially Trenchard and Gordon's *Cato's Letters*, offered a view of eighteenth-century society and politics that appealed to many American readers. Written at a time of heated debate in England over collapse of the state-chartered South Sea Company and over general political and economic corruption, *Cato's Letters* (1720–21) expressed Trenchard and Gordon's distaste for the social changes that accompanied an expanding commercial economy and their even greater contempt for the Whig aristocrats who dominated the nation's political system. Nostalgic for a simpler and supposedly more virtuous age, most country writers took scant comfort in their nation's economic growth or its new-found political stability. New wealth, country critics believed, would only corrupt English society and upset political relationships. From their perspective, Britain seemed to be approaching a time of political crisis.

This gloomy view of English political affairs shaped *Cato's* libertarian (by early eighteenth-century standards) thoughts on freedom of expression. *Cato's* views offered the most complete, and most often quoted, alternative to the Orthodox Whig position. Although Trenchard and Gordon praised freedom of discussion as a means of advancing knowledge and combatting ignorance, they primarily valued liberty of expression as a means of preventing changes, particularly political change. Because they considered England, despite ominous portents, the freest nation on earth, and because they viewed the nation's constitutional system as the best in the world, political and constitutional innovations could only be changes for the worse. Free expression, they believed, would enable English citizens to detect signs of incipient degeneration in the constitutional balance. Only if citizens retained freedom to expose the corrupt schemes of wicked political leaders could England hope to escape the unhappy fate of so many other once-free nations: a descent into tyranny and despotism. "Freedom of Speech," proclaimed *Cato*, "is the great Bulwark of Liberty; they prosper and die together."[19] Thus, *Cato's Letters* contained a series of essays on free expression and the law of libel, pieces that challenged the position of Orthodox Whigs like Sir John Holt.

James Alexander reprinted *Cato*'s essays on libel in Zenger's *Weekly Journal*, supplementing them with several contributions of his own.[20] In Alexander's pieces, as in the writings of many other colonials, *Cato's* imprint was clear. Free speech and press were the people's great bulwark against tyranny; only citizens who enjoyed free expression could unmask corrupt ministers; publication of the truth, except in rare cases, could never be libelous; even the most licentious falsehoods would not really injure the reputations of virtuous officials; and because truth could be trusted to prevail over falsehood in the end, temporary circulation of licentious nonsense would do less harm to the public interest than restrictive libel laws.[21]

Alexander's views did not go unchallenged, particularly when he attempted to explain precisely what types of restraints were legitimate. In one essay he suggested "that every man of common Sense will judge that he is an Enemy to his King and Country who pleads for any Restraint upon the Press. . . ."[22] Immediately confronted by Cosby's supporters, Alexander retreated from the absolutist implications of this position and admitted the legitimacy of some libel prosecutions. But the problem remained, he continued to insist, of giving the crime of seditious libel a clear definition. "Some people have a Knack of calling any Paper they don't like, that treats of Governours or Magistrates, a libel against the Government. . . ."[23] Similarly, he argued that the libelous construction of controversial passages would likely change according to the particular viewpoints of different readers. Summing up his position, Alexander concluded that existing doctrines raised one particularly serious question about the punishment of political libels: "who shall be the Judges of this Abuse" of free expression?[24] At Zenger's trial, Andrew Hamilton convinced jurors that only they, and not De Lancey or any other magistrate, should possess the ultimate authority to limit political criticism.

Andrew Hamilton's elaborate defense strategy deserves close attention for what it suggests about the relationship between law and political communication. The wily old lawyer from Philadelphia managed to present most of the country critique of orthodox libel law and to make the interests of Zenger's partisan press seem identical to those of the jury. Throughout his defense, Hamilton stressed two basic country themes: the potential for a corrupted executive ("a bad administration" Hamilton called it) to crush individual liberties; and the necessity, therefore, for "the people" zealously to guard their "right to complain" about executive chicanery.

According to James Alexander's account, Hamilton made a dramatic entrance into the Zenger trial, suddenly rising from amongst the spectators and announcing his intention to defend not only the jailed printer, but broader interests as well. Initially, he had dismissed the indictment as the work of an overzealous prosecutor. But after learning "that this prosecution was directed by the Governor and Council" and after seeing "the extraordinary appearance of people of all conditions" in the crowded courtroom, he suspected that something more sinister was afoot. It now seemed "that those in the administration have by this prosecution something more in view and they the people believe they have a good deal more at stake than I apprehended at First."[25] Continually raising the specter of executive usurpation of power, Hamilton emphasized the method of Zenger's indictment, by an information filed by the Cosby administration rather than by an indictment by a grand jury drawn from the people.[26]

Avoiding direct attacks upon Cosby, Hamilton still suggested how a bad administration could endanger the freedoms enjoyed by New Yorkers. He linked, for example, Zenger's cause to the struggle for religious liberty. What dire fate might befall religious freedom, he wondered, if in heterogeneous New York the executive could suddenly begin to prosecute alleged heresies by information? Thus, Hamilton suggested a theme that would be used by future opponents of Orthodox Whig libel doctrines: liberty of expression was indivisible, and any laws affecting political debate could not be separated arbitrarily from the larger system of communication and opinion.[27]

Hamilton also employed the theme of a corrupt administration in his efforts to encourage jurors to defy common law restrictions on their powers. Suggesting the tyrannical measures that a distant executive branch might enforce through appointive judges, Hamilton extolled the superior virtue and wisdom of local juries, of people *"summoned out of the neighborhood where the fact is alleged to be committed . . . because you are supposed to have the best knowledge of the fact that is to be tried."*[28] Embellishing this point, Hamilton played to the packed galleries by reading from the Bible and suggesting how a corrupt judge might construe various Biblical verses as libels on Governor Cosby.[29]

Thus, Hamilton's speech emphasized a basic country theme: no executive officer should be entrusted with vague and unchecked powers, particularly over expression. In this sense, the *Zenger* case reflected the fact that seventeenth-century ideas about the need for obedience to "good" rulers, to political authorities who enforced the law and maintained order, were being challenged by country ideas. Country thought stressed the tendency for political power to corrupt even the best of rulers and to tempt them to infringe upon popular liberties in the name of greater public order.

Most important—and most ironic in light of the importance that journalists would later claim for the *Zenger* case—Hamilton seldom mentioned the rights of the colonial press. He made no ringing appeals about the value of a free press, about the public's need for an opposition newspaper. Instead, Hamilton stressed two other constitutional arguments: the ultimate right to resist a tyrannical ruler, a liberty vindicated by England's Glorious Revolution against James II, and the more immediate right to complain about a bad administration, a liberty that ordinary New Yorkers who disliked Cosby apparently exercised quite frequently. Of what use was the "mighty privilege to resist tyranny," Hamilton asked, "if every man that suffers must be silent? And if a man must be taken up as a libeller for telling his suffering to his neighbor?"[30]

Throughout Hamilton's speech, then, images of neighborhood politics, of face-to-face verbal exchanges, predominated. Hamilton proceeded as if factional politics and partisan newspapers did not exist. In this, his defense of Zenger (and the Morrisite faction) capitalized on the fact that the day-to-day process of oral communication was far less regimented than it had been during the seventeenth century, a time when colonial leaders had tried to monitor closely both private and political defamation. By building his defense around neighborhood politics, Hamilton chose a place where colonial authorities had come to tolerate a good deal of "complaining," especially in the area of small politics. Hamilton's defense strategy assumed that ordinary New Yorkers believed that they enjoyed a right to complain about affairs in the world of large politics as well. Thus, Zenger's victory on behalf of liberty of the press owed a great deal to changes within the everyday system of communication. Recognition of freedom of the press did not, as some scholars have argued, precede acceptance of a similar right for speech; the most famous colonial trial involving freedom of expression suggests precisely the opposite to be the case.[31]

Although jurors defied De Lancey's instructions and rendered a general verdict in favor of Zenger, the case did not mean that legal restraints over expression counted for nothing in New York. Hamilton's intricately constructed argument would have been unnecessary if he could have assumed that any prosecution automatically clashed with the province's legal and political culture. Rather, Hamilton's defense strategy tacitly acknowledged that the jurors were not opposed in principle to punishing people for criticism of political leaders. On other occasions, against other defendants, New Yorkers did, in fact, accept the legitimacy of legal restraints. As we have seen, successful common law actions for "contempt of authority" and legislative actions for "breach of parliamentary privilege" demonstrated that New York's system of political communication possessed limits. But Zenger's acquittal, and the furor surrounding the prosecution, indicated that New Yorkers were unwilling to risk these limits being arbitrarily staked out by representatives of a ruling clique.

The *Zenger* case, then, offers a dramatic example of successful resistance to governmental interference with complaints, here coming from a partisan press, about political affairs. Andrew Hamilton's argument, immortalized in a pamphlet narrative of the trial prepared by James Alexander, quickly became part of popular Anglo-American political culture: throughout the rest of the eighteenth century, Alexander's *Brief Narrative* reappeared in both England and North America, and it provided a central document in an increasingly powerful, popular alternative to the orthodox view of libel and public speech.

The Keith and Zenger controversies demonstrated the difficulty of applying traditional libel laws against organized opposition groups through common law prosecutions. Although colonial factions lacked the cohesion or legitimacy of latter-day parties and pressure groups, they still presented serious challenges to entrenched political elites. Unlike village cranks or political and religious dissenters of the early seventeenth century, factional leaders of the mid–eighteenth century could not easily be induced to repent and accept the direction of their "good rulers." Neither could the prominent merchants and landowners who dominated these factions be expelled from their communities in the name of harmony and order. As time went on, colonial authorities came to face what Governors Berkeley and Effingham of Virginia so feared: organized political factions that, armed with the power of the printing press, sought to reach out to the "giddy headed multitude."

The Limits on Political Communication in Eighteenth-Century America

What, then, were the effective limits on political expression? How broadly based was the mid–eighteenth-century system of political communication? The Zenger controversy suggested the "premodern" character of mid–eighteenth-century political culture and political journalism. To Anglo-Americans schooled in English country ideas, factional politics offered cause for concern: citizens were pursuing selfish private interests rather than the general public good. Although this fear failed to prevent the emergence of factional politics, it did help to restrict the scope of partisan activity, including political journalism. Hamilton's circumspect defense of Zenger indicated that even New York, which possessed the most fully developed system of factional politics in North America, lacked a set of images and ideas to justify the use of the press as a partisan instrument.

Moreover, in the everyday conduct of provincial politics, colonial gentlemen preferred a system based upon deference to a political elite rather than one predicated upon regular popular involvement by the majority of white males. Although aristocratic New Yorkers like Morris and Alexander did use the press and other popular techniques to gain broader support, in neighboring New Jersey, and in many other parts of colonial America, there were no partisan

what [of] dwelling?

newspapers at all. Throughout most of the colonial era, provincial politics generally remained limited to factional clashes between a relatively narrow segment of the population.

In debating political differences, most members of the mid–eighteenth-century elite attempted to limit, not expand, the arena of conflict. In Annapolis, Maryland, for example, an exclusive group of political leaders used a private organization, the Tuesday Club, to express political criticism. Through a series of satirical skits, these gentlemen examined political issues within the safety of their own group. They hoped that such a form of communication would reduce misunderstandings, promote harmony, and eliminate the need for dissenting political leaders to seek a more public forum.[32] As the massive modern editions of the papers of the Founding Fathers attest, even during the Revolutionary era, political leaders relied heavily upon personal correspondence to circulate political ideas and intelligence; as a result, it "is often difficult to distinguish between the private correspondence and the public writings of the Revolutionaries." Similarly, the high-toned rhetorical style of most eighteenth-century pamphlets indicate that they were aimed at an educated elite. Gentlemen used pamphlets to communicate with other gentlemen, not to reach a regular, broad audience.[33]

Nothing like permanent political parties developed anywhere, and newspaper journalism only intermittently included the kind of public debate found in Zenger's journal. Not until the 1740s, for example, did candidates solicit votes through direct newspaper advertisements, and then they limited their notices to simple statements like this one by a candidate for sheriff:

> To the Freeholders of the City and County of Philadelphia
> Gentlemen,
> THO' it has not till this Time been customary to request your votes in Print; yet that Method being now introduced, I think my self obliged in this publick Manner . . . to acquaint you that I intend to stand a Candidate for the Sheriff's office, and request your Votes and Interest at the next Election. . . .
>
> > Your real Friend
> > Nicholas Scull[34]

Printers were equally subdued in most of their political statements. Even John Peter Zenger's career as a partisan printer proved short lived. When New York's factional tensions eased and political winds shifted during the late 1730s, Zenger became the colony's public printer. Not coincidentally, the *Weekly Journal*'s sharp tones mellowed, and some people soon accused the paper of being a tool of the new "court" faction. Thus, the partisan course of the *Weekly Journal* prior to the *Zenger* trial was an unusual one. The vast majority of printers attempted to maintain at least the pretense of neutrality toward partisan political issues; in practice, many followed strategies of non-involvement or safely aligned themselves with the faction in power.[35]

Even in New York, undoubtedly the most "advanced" province in terms of its political culture, prominent members of the colonial elite could not always secure easy and full access to the public prints. During the 1750s, a trio of opposition politicians—John Morin Scott, William Smith, and William Livingston, popularly known as "the Triumvirate"—continually struggled to secure publication of essays critical of the province's ruling clique. After beginning their own journal, *The Independent Reflector*, the Triumvirate found their printer pressured into terminating his contract with them. In order to publish the *Reflector*'s final edition, written prior to cancellation of their printing agreement, they had to lure an elderly printer out of retirement.[36]

The Triumvirate complained bitterly about their lack of access to New York's other papers. In a piece entitled "Of the Use, Abuse, and LIBERTY OF THE PRESS," William Livingston assailed Hugh Gaine, printer of the *New York Gazette*. According to the *Independent Reflector*'s theory of a free press, a printer possessed no right to refuse whatever "was conducive of general Utility. . . be the Author, a Christian, Jew, Turk, or Infidel. Such Refusal is an immediate Abridgement of the Freedom of the Press." Livingston went on to condemn Gaine for making himself "the Tool of the ruling faction," for publishing what Livingston considered slanders on the Triumvirate, and then refusing "to print the Answers or Vindications of the Persons he had abused." And yet, Livingston indignantly concluded, "this Wretch had the Impudence to talke of the Liberty of the Press. God Forbid."

As a theorist, Livingston recognized that printers themselves limited expression when they denied access to particular ideas and writers or when they assaulted the character of others without giving them the opportunity to reply. But as the sponsor of a clearly factional journal, Livingston rejected any suggestion that his own press offer a neutral conduit for all opinions. "A printer ought not to publish every Thing that is offered to him," Livingston conceded, but only items of "general Utility."

Though Livingston both endorsed and practiced a more vigorous style of public debate than Orthodox Whigs would have desired, he had no intention of approving licentiousness. Whenever a printer "prostitutes his Art by the Publication of any Thing injurious to his Country, it is criminal,—It is high Treason against the State."[37] Livingston's model for a system of political communication still included the expectation that the press would not offer certain ideas for public consumption and that officials would apply postpublication penalties against injurious materials. Legal restraints would encourage printers themselves, rather than the state, to apply a system of prior restraints in the form of careful self-censorship.

At mid-century, the possibility of legal restraints remained real. As printers in New York and most other provinces discovered, not even the country line of defense offered much protection when the colonial assembly applied restrictions. Theorists like *Cato* emphasized the danger of vague Star Chamber restraints in the hands of a corrupt executive; they said little about controls applied by elected representatives, the legislative equivalent of a jury drawn from and representing the collective people.[38] And if a legislature were united enough to vote for action against dissident writers and printers, from whom, as a practical matter, could defendants seek support? When faced with indignant assembly members, intent on preserving their own and their institution's reputations, a colonial printer's best strategy was to acknowledge humbly his error and promise to be more careful in the future. Or, as Benjamin Franklin suggested in his "Apology," a printer could adopt an ever safer strategy: exercise rigorous prepublication censorship to avoid so much as the appearance of licentiousness.

Elimination of so-called licentiousness and demagoguery from the public prints characterized what might be called the Moderate Whig theory of a free press. Andrew Bradford, printer of the *American Weekly Mercury*, offered one of the most articulate expositions of this position. An adversary of Andrew Hamilton in Pennsylvania's factional struggles—Hamilton once instigated a legislative assault on his press—Bradford joined the debates surrounding the *Zenger* case. Although he also published several vigorous attacks on Hamilton's defense tactics by Orthodox Whig lawyers, Bradford's own position represented something of a compromise between the libertarian implications of the country view and the restrictionist ones of Orthodox Whigs. Rejecting the notion that all political criticism carried a dangerous tendency, Bradford leaned, instead, toward the country view that meaningful expression included "a Liberty of detecting the wicked and destructive Measures of *certain Politicians . . .* of attacking Wickedness on high, of disintangling the intricate Folds of a wicked and corrupt Administration, and pleading freely for a Redress of Grievances."[39]

But Bradford's approach to political criticism differed significantly from the one suggested by Andrew Hamilton at Zenger's trial and employed by James Alexander in his *Weekly Journal*. Emphasizing the danger from the "Caprice and Fury of a Mobb undisciplined and under no Restraints from Law" and warning that the "Extreams that separate Liberty from License are closer than most Men imagine," Bradford insisted that even when "Lawful Governors . . . behave themselves ill, their measures are to be remonstrated against in terms of *Decency* and Moderation not of Fury or Scurrility."[40] Several years later, an associate of Bradford underscored the elitist implications of the Moderate Whig approach. Even when people were "reduced to the unhappy necessity" of issuing public "remonstrances," he still hoped "that the management might always be reserved for men of skill and address. It is not for every puny arm to attempt to wield the club of Hercules."[41]

Most colonial theorists accepted the legitimacy of criminal restraints over expression. Writers and printers could never entirely discount the possibility of having to justify, in some type of legal proceeding, the fact that their publications remained on the safe side of that shadowy line that divided liberty from licentiousness. In fact, several of the printers who espoused the free forum theory had at one time or another encountered legal restraints, and their professions of neutrality may have been occasioned by this awareness of the reality of legal, as well as extralegal, pressures.[42]

Examples could be multiplied—of self-serving free forum comments from printers, of support for the Zengerian principles, of endorsement of Orthodox Whig doctrines, of *Cato*-like sentiments from opposition politicians, and of nearly universal condemnations of "licentiousness"—but it should be obvious that no single view, and certainly not a Blackstonian one as Leonard Levy once claimed, dominated colonial discussion about free expression. If there were agreement that public officials should, and could, limit political criticism, this consensus shattered when discussion turned to consideration of what these legal limits were, and how restraints should be applied in actual cases. This disagreement carried over into the Revolutionary era, a time when royal officials desired some type of control over criticism of British measures and attacks on provincial officers.

Political Communication and Seditious Libel during the Revolutionary Era, 1750–1776

During the Revolutionary era, fundamental changes in both the form and the content of political expression sharpened disagreements over the proper role of legal restraints. The entire system of communication was becoming more open during the second half of the eighteenth century, a trend that quickened as the colonies approached independence. Both oral and printed forms of communication were affected. The frequency with which citizens mounted popular protest demonstrations in the streets, for example, meant that political dissenters from across the social spectrum could gain access to highly visible public forums. According to recent scholarship, other nonprinted forms of expression, particularly religious revivals, spearheaded development of a less elitist, more spontaneous system of communication; the print media, it has been argued, remained much more closely wedded to the stylistic and rhetorical conventions of the educated elite.[43]

But one need not enter into the debate over the relative contributions of

oral versus printed sources to see that both types of expression reflected—
and helped to accelerate—the "popularization" of all phases of public life.
Whether they looked to the revivalist speeches or to partisan newspapers, both
Orthodox and Moderate Whigs could find numerous examples of licentious
and demagogic appeals to "the rabble." From such perspectives, both legal
and extralegal controls were disintegrating.

Colonial leaders often recognized the futility of invoking orthodox libel
doctrines. In 1765, for example, New York's Council declined to pursue the
question of who had printed the *Constitutional Courant*, a one-shot paper
containing slashing attacks upon government officials. The councillors believed that it would be "prudent at this time to delay making any more
particular inquiry lest it should be the occasion of raising the Mob which it is
thought proper by all means to avoid." Several years later, when the same body
pressed for penalties against Alexander McDougall, at least one councillor
was acting as an *agent provocateur* for the opposition cause. Recognizing that
any move against McDougall, author of a handbill critical of the New York
assembly, would only rebound against New York's ruling faction and British
officials, William Smith pressed for legal action. Prosecution of McDougall,
Smith hoped, would provide "fresh Oil to quicken that expiring Lamp" of
liberty in North America.[44]

Perhaps Thomas Hutchinson of Massachusetts provided the best authority
for the decline of orthodox libel doctrines. "My repeated Charges to Grand
Juries" on the dangerous tendency of attacks on royal officials are "so entirely
neglected," he confessed, that "I have no Hope of the ceasing of this atrocious
Crime." Unable to suppress his critics by legal action, as Massachusetts
authorities would have done a half-century earlier or as officials in late eighteenth-century Ireland were still doing, Hutchinson could only adopt the remedy of self-help. He began a small paper, which appeared irregularly, called
The Censor and futilely tried to beat his opponents at their own game. But
like other Orthodox Whigs, he sadly confronted the evolution of a new system
of political communication and the depletion of the old stockpile of legal
weapons.[45]

Printed criticism of political leaders, as we have seen, did not suddenly
begin during the 1760s, but during that decade unrelenting attacks upon
colonial and British officialdom became a regular part of popular political
culture. In response to internal and external pressures, the old deferential
system was steadily eroding. In most colonies the intermittent factionalism of
the earlier eighteenth century was giving way to more permanent, more clear-
cut political divisions. Extending the techniques used earlier in some urban
areas, opposition leaders used the printing press to reach greater numbers of
people especially of the "middling," but even of the "meaner" sorts. Openly
partisan printers such as John Peter Zenger had once been the exception; now,

partisanship was becoming the rule. And in most provinces, partisan literature observed few boundaries, legal or otherwise. (A similar situation, it should be noted, was developing in England where John Wilkes came to symbolize opposition to traditional controls on political criticism. Thus, English officials had no difficulty understanding the problems of colonial authorities like Thomas Hutchinson.)

As would be expected, older political habits did not disappear entirely. The 1764 provincial election in Pennsylvania, for example, has become justly famous for the "scurillous" publications produced by all sides. But even as writers joined in the vituperative spirit, they felt compelled to condemn the new partisanship and to justify their own efforts as attempts to heal divisions by giving citizens "the truth."[46] False and inflammatory publications by others, it was charged, represented a dangerous departure from the traditional system of communication, a system that sought to limit debate so as not to produce permanent factional divisions or to inflame the "untutored" masses. While heaping slanders upon Benjamin Franklin—including familiar charges about the old printer's alleged fondness for young women—the author of one broadside put to verse his fears about the new journalism and about the rise of dangerous political "Divisions," which "No human Arts on Earth can Stop."

> Each fool manures his Barren Head,
> By Contradictory Papers
> When All the Nonsense that they read,
> But turn to windy Vapours.
>
> Yet tutor'd by the Flying Post
> The Gazettes and the Post-Man,
> Each fancies he can rule a host
> Or steer a Fleet with most Men.
>
> When thus grown Wise in their Conceit,
> And skillful in State Matters,
> They Charge their Fault, when Things don't hit
> Unjustly to their Betters.
>
> Thus every shallow Doat-Head vents
> Some groundless Exclamation,
> And raises Feuds and Discontents,
> To the Mischief of the Nation.[47]

But for those who wanted harsh political language to disappear, time would only bring greater "scurility." The Tuesday Club of Annapolis found it increasingly difficult to discuss political issues through its satirical productions. Even before the onset of controversies involving imperial questions, for instance, local political and social tensions no longer muted, but only sharpened, political divisions, even among the club's elite membership. With imperial grievances being added to local political conflicts, political discourse in most colonies became more, not less, inflammatory.[48]

The Orthodox and even the Moderate Whig theories of free expression ultimately became casualties of the popular journalism of the 1760s. In the rhetoric of opposition publicists like Samuel Adams, British officials and their colonial allies planned nothing less than the destruction of American liberties. Viewed from this apocalyptic perspective, administrative changes and financial innovations—measures such as reorganization of the colonial judicial systems and the Stamp Act—suggested rampant corruption in Anglo-American politics and evidence of incipient decay in the constitutional balance. Defense of free expression constituted the vital first step, it was thought, in the larger battle to defend American liberties.

Controversy over the limits on free expression was particularly heated in pre-Revolutionary Massachusetts where Governor Sir Francis Bernard and Lieutenant Governor Thomas Hutchinson demanded seditious libel prosecutions against their political opponents. At first, much of the two leaders' concerns stemmed from personal considerations. As early as 1763, Boston newspapers contained what Hutchinson considered outrageous attacks—particularly by James Otis, Jr., in the *Boston Gazette*—upon his and Bernard's political and personal reputations. Initially, Hutchinson viewed Otis's bombast more as a breach of good manners than of the law of libel, and he hoped that James Otis, Sr., might intervene and restrain his son. But as opposition criticism became more seditious, aimed at describing the inner-workings of an alleged conspiracy involving Hutchinson and Bernard, the embattled officials came to view Otis's attacks as more sinister. Hutchinson considered printed assaults on Massachusetts officials part of a plot to destroy popular confidence in provincial government and ultimately to overthrow British rule.[49]

On numerous occasions between 1767 and 1771, Bernard and Hutchinson futilely implored legislators and grand jurors to indict several Boston printers for seditious libel. Fulminating against the *Boston Evening Post*, Governor Bernard charged that "the Devil himself" could not have assembled "a greater Collection of imprudent virulent and seditious Lies, perversions of truth and misrepresentations than are to be found in this publication."[50] Instructing grand jurors about their duty to punish such licentiousness, Hutchinson followed Orthodox Whig tenets: any criticism of governmental policies or public officials constituted seditious libel. "Every man who prints, prints at his peril"; to permit "the licentious Abuse of Government is the most likely Way to destroy its Freedom."[51] His view left no room for "true" criticism of "corrupt" officials. But neither grand jurors nor a majority of the legislature would vote to so much as indict opposition writers and printers on the basis of

Blackstonian libel doctrines. Grand jurors, Hutchinson later claimed, wrongly believed that truth could be no libel. "Loose notions of government were now prevailing," he fumed.[52]

Most supporters of royal authority in Massachusetts, however, countered opposition publicists with Moderate Whig rather than with Blackstonian theories of free expression. Most of the writers who confronted Otis, Adams, and company in Boston's newspaper wars conceded that the Orthodox Whig view was too narrow. Hastening to distinguish his views on free expression from "the slavish doctrine of unlimited passive obedience and non-resistance," a supporter of the Bernard-Hutchinson administration concluded that "the persons of rulers [were] sacred no longer than they steadily pursue the whole end of their creation, the good of the community."[53] This statement encapsulated the old Moderate Whig position: liberty of expression must include the right to criticize the failings of bad rulers. Although these Moderate Whigs did not concentrate upon technical legal issues—they were, after all, appealing to Boston's growing political community rather than its narrow, primarily pro-Bernard, legal establishment—their positions implied some protection for publication of the truth. In the end, it would be "the truth" that would help determine whether a ruler was a "bold pretender" who only posed as the protector of the public welfare or a virtuous ruler who safeguarded the people's liberties.

Nevertheless, Boston's Moderate Whigs made it clear that their view of free expression included definite limits. Political leaders did not deserve the kind of vicious criticism that routinely appeared in the *Boston Gazette* merely because they "sometimes err in their judgment in trifling instances." A governor could be considered corrupt only when "all sober and impartial judges" found that "his whole course of conduct" demonstrated hostility to public welfare.[54] Criticism should never "overleap the bounds of decency" but must contain "sober arguments" designed to convince sober citizens.[55] In a free country in which rulers were "circumscribed with positive law," no other form of political argument was necessary. Any attempt to "impose chains and shackles on the people" would be so obvious "as to render all false colouring totally unnecessary to arouse the public attention—a simple narration of the facts, supported by evidence, which can never be wanting in such a case, would convince citizens of their danger."[56] Although such views allowed greater room for political dissent than was offered by the strict Blackstonian approach, the Moderate Whig theory failed to satisfy the more zealous opponents of Bernard and Hutchinson.

To opposition writers, fired with visions of corrupt schemes and wicked officials, rhetorical moderation in defense of American liberties seemed unthinkable. The mere existence of public dissension was a cause for concern. When the chief magistrate was "made the subject of public altercation," it surely indicated that "the body public is some way out of order." Although a magistrate's reputation might suffer unjustly, the "cause of the injured community" ultimately counted far more than "the character of a single man."[57] Even if liberty of expression sometimes veered toward "licentiousness" and writers became overzealous, "the spirit of the people must be frequently roused in order to curb the ambition of the court."[58]

According to opposition writers, most people involved in political affairs, including some administration supporters, agreed that "bad" men and "bad" measures could be criticized freely. The problem, these analysts continued, was determining what people and which policies were bad.[59] Any solution that permitted officials to use libel laws as a means of terminating allegedly abusive attacks would be "giving the court very large discretionary power to punish whatever displeases them."[60] Echoing the position of *Cato* and Andrew Hamilton, opposition writers claimed that it was better to err on the side of tolerance than to wait until "corrupt" magistrates began twisting vague libel doctrines in order to convict legitimate critics. The safest course, these opposition publicists maintained, was to tolerate a certain amount of personal abuse. James Otis, Jr., claimed to be following this course when in 1769 he dropped plans to file a civil libel suit against pro-administration writers and to let them continue their attacks on him if they wished. The only effect of their slanders on his reputation was to enhance it "in the opinions of those with whom I wish to stand well at home and abroad." A libel suit would not make a person's character better; and if it were bad, "no such action can mend it."[61]

A piece in the *Boston Evening Post*, "Observations on Liberty of the Press," offered a fuller analysis, one of the best pre-Revolutionary statements of the anti-Blackstonian position.[62] The writer first sought to show the difference between oral and printed discussion. Even the worst harangues, when disseminated through the press, seemed unlikely to carry the dangerous tendency feared by Orthodox Whigs and certainly not the dreadful consequences that "followed the harrangues of the popular demagogues of Athens and the tribunes of Rome." Although newspapers undoubtedly increased the range over which such agitators could hurl their bombast, the press curiously made their missiles less lethal. "A man reads his newspaper alone. . . . He is not hurried by the force and energy and action." Even when abused, free presses allowed citizens to vent their anger in print rather than in the streets; they also permitted officials to discover popular discontent and to correct the conditions producing dissatisfaction. Just as old fears that religious toleration would lead to conflict had proved groundless, "it is hoped that men being every day more accustomed to the free discussion of public affairs, will improve in the judgment of them, and be with greater difficulty seduced by idle rumour and popular clamor." The effectiveness of public debate would be improved, this essayist concluded, if opposition writers and printers would be willing to grant space to their own critics. "This would indeed be a *convincing* proof to the world of that *impartiality* which publishers so often boast of in their weekly performances."

But impartiality was generally not part of the patriot view of journalism. The goal of opposition writers—to expose the plotters they believed were conspiring against American liberties—determined the form and content of the Revolutionary press. The patriot exposé, which reached its full-blown form in Boston, unmercifully flayed both the public and private acts of colonial officials; to people schooled in country political thought, the private vices of political leaders spread corruption just as surely as their public sins.[63]

Detailed accounts of hitherto-hidden misdeeds carried patriot newspapers to journalistic and legal shores that James Alexander and Andrew Hamilton had only briefly explored in the 1730s. The right to complain that was part of oral communication became preserved and amplified on the printed page. Readers could now reflect upon the patriots' charges of official corruption and could carefully compare the press's vision of political reality with their own. For the first time in America, writers were systematically focusing the powerful lens of the press upon political affairs and continually contradicting official explanations of how local and imperial politics worked. Equally as important, patriot writers elevated Andrew Hamilton's liberty of complaining into the beginnings of the modern liberal theory of the political role, and ultimately the constitutional status, of the press. They took it for granted that the press—a term that still lacked clear definition—facilitated scrutiny of political actions and provided one of the best defenses against the spread of corruption by public officials who considered themselves, in every way, the "best men." The press's liberty of complaining could not, this view of journalism openly asserted, be squared with Blackstonian libel doctrines.

Although later historians have sometimes echoed eighteenth-century royal officials in condemning the paranoid style of patriot writings, the newspaper journalism of the 1760s and 1770s represented a significant breakthrough in the development of a rational public.[64] The basis of Blackstonian libel doctrines, it should be reemphasized, was that any criticism of governmental affairs or public officials, however accurate or rationally structured, created legal liability. "The Greater the Truth, the greater the Libel." Broad categories of political information, then, theoretically remained the exclusive property of a narrow political elite rather than something that could be distributed broadly among the political nation. By shattering old notions of what kinds of information belonged in the arena of public discussion, patriot journalists also delivered a fatal blow to orthodox theories of seditious libel.

Freedom of Expression during the American Revolution

There was, to be sure, a good deal of expediency in the free press views of patriot writers. Once opposition to British policies turned to resistance, patriots recognized their own personal stake in theoretical discussions about free expression. Anonymously arguing the case of Alexander McDougall in the *New-York Gazette*, William Smith underscored the obvious: if British officials could actually enforce Orthodox Whig theories of seditious libel, then "all our Vindications since the Year 1765 are seditious and libelous, if not of a Treasonable Complexion. What if a Door should be opened, to be revenged of the Patriots who have wrote and printed in our Favour?"[65] Thus, supporters of royal authority, as well as some later scholars, have questioned the sincerity of those who courted the goddess of republican liberty.

> To feign a red hot zeal for freedom's cause,
> To mouthe aloud for Liberties and Laws;
> For public good to bellow all abroad,
> Serves well the purposes of private fraud
>
> .   .   .   .
>
> What do we mean by Country and by Court,
> What is it to oppose, what to Support?
> Mere words of course, and what is more Absurd
> Than to pay homage to an empty word!
>
> *Majors* and *Minors* differ but in name,
> Patriots and Ministers are much the same;
> The only difference after all their root
> Is that one is *in* and the other *out*.[66]

Even before the outs had fought their way in, opposition partisans showed little desire to grant liberty of expression to court forces. Consider the fate of John Mein of the *Boston Chronicle*. Turning the patriot technique of the exposé against its originators, Mein obtained lists of prominent opposition leaders who had allegedly broken their own boycott against importation of British goods. Seeking to discredit these people, Mein published their names and hinted at future revelations of perfidy in their personal lives. Boston's opposition mob soon attacked the editor's shop and eventually forced him to flee to England. Several years later, John Rivington of the *New York Gazetteer* suffered similarly rough treatment after patriot leaders branded his press as insufficiently anti-British. A group of New Yorkers forced him to seek refuge on a British warship, and, shortly after he returned, another patriot delegation, this one from Connecticut, sacked his shop.

Once resistance turned to revolution, patriot groups acquired the force of law to coerce "wrong" opinion and encountered the same problem as their former adversaries: how much political criticism could governmental officials safely allow? Before 1776, patriot leaders had agreed that just governments and good rulers could prosecute seditious libels, and during the war, courts and revolutionary "committees of public safety" applied these standards. They prosecuted seditious utterances and publications by loyalists and, in some cases, by people who merely expressed doubts about the patriot cause.

The revolutionaries of 1776 did not see prosecutions of such utterances as repudiations of pre-Revolutionary ideas. The people themselves, it could be argued, through their chosen representatives, were applying the restraints. Unlike easily corruptible magistrates, the agents of a liberty-loving people would never convert necessary legal controls into tools of repression. In some cases, people accused of seditious criticism did secure acquittals or merely suffered reprimands, and there were also instances when committees of public safety sought to restrain the licentiousness of overzealous revolutionaries themselves. But the fact that tens of thousands of loyalists chose to leave the new republic does suggest that many people felt their liberty of expression, not to mention their lives and property, endangered by the revolutionary cause.

The nation's founders, then, adopted much the same approach toward criticism of their military effort as the wartime leaders who have followed them. Although the Revolutionary generation hardly merit praise for muzzling dissent, the lackluster record of their military forces early in the conflict meant that revolutionary leaders confronted a situation far more perilous than those faced by most later advocates of restraints upon criminal criticism. Prior to Lexington and Concord, British officials openly discussed indictments for treason, and when authorities transported captured rebel leader Ethan Allen and thirty-three other prisoners to England in 1775, the possibility that American "traitors" might swing from English gallows seemed real. Throughout the war, British forces occupied large expanses of territory, and the prospects of an American victory oftentimes seemed remote. When dealing with people who failed to embrace the movement for independence, particularly when British troops were nearby, the Revolutionary generation not surprisingly resorted to suppression.[67]

Once the focus is shifted away from people who criticized the war effort itself, and from those who could be labeled Tories, the system of political communication was surprisingly open. Newspaper printers, for example, gained stature. Patriot spokesmen praised them for having alerted citizens to the British "conspiracy" during the 1760s and early 1770s. Printers themselves believed that the Revolution provided them with an opportunity to gain fame and immortality. As defenders of liberty and promoters of republicanism, they were no longer "meer mechanics." According to John Holt of the *New*

York Journal, "newspapers which contain historical accounts of events, as they occur, at such an important era as this, will be esteemed in after ages; they will increase in worth the older they grow, and every succeeding generation, will value them more than the former."[68] Revolutionary political leaders showed less concern about the immortality of printers than about their immediate value in the war effort. With a number of presses, such as those of Hugh Gaine and John Rivington, solidly pro-Tory, Revolutionary officials found it necessary to extend governmental assistance to people who possessed the requisite devotion to the patriot cause and the technical skill to run a printing press.

Yet even with governmental sponsorship, printers continued to claim that the cause of republicanism required them to "write freely of *all* men, and of *all* measures."[69] Patriot newspapers were filled with statements, albeit conveniently vague when it came to legal specifics, about the necessity of free presses. Political officials recognized the popular appeal of such statements. When in 1779 the Continental Congress considered invoking its parliamentary privilege against John Dunlap of the *Pennsylvania Packet* for publishing an anonymous critique of congressional monetary policies, John Penn warned against any move to imprison Dunlap or, if he could be discovered, the author. If "you have the power, which I doubt," he advised, "they would come out [of prison] greater men than they went in. What was it made [John] Wilkes so great and popular a Man, but the imprisonment he suffered. . . ." Congress let the issue drop.[70] Even before the war was over, John Adams observed that "both by law and by practice," Americans enjoyed a wide degree of freedom to criticize political leaders. "There is nothing that the people dislike that they do not attack," he wrote in 1780. "They attack officers of every rank in the militia and in the army, members of congress, and congress itself, whenever they dislike its conduct. . . ."[71]

Political Libel in Eighteenth-Century America

The Revolutionary generation was not united in a Blackstonian consensus, and neither, as Leonard Levy's *Legacy of Suppression* maintained, were opposition ideas simply "in the air." The anti-Blackstonian position, in America as in England, grew out of a popular political and legal culture.[72] To view the opinions of the Orthodox Whig legal elite as the only authoritative sources for American ideas about free expression unduly restricts the purview of legal history. Here, as elsewhere, legal history can help to refute the idea of "unitary law." In liberal political theory, of course, the ability to make law rests solely with the state; in reality, however, the view "that only the state creates law . . . confuses the status of interpretation with the status of political domination." Once the broader legal culture becomes the focus, other versions of legal meaning emerge. Popular ideas about libel law were, in fact, an important part of the legal culture of the Revolutionary era; this popular view of free speech, more than the opinions of orthodox Blackstonians, determined when and how officials could apply legal restraints to political discussion.[73]

Raised on the postulates of country political theory and nurtured in the rough-and-tumble world of small politics, many colonials were much more concerned about the bad tendency of political officials who threatened frequent libel prosecutions than about the supposed bad tendency of every example of political criticism. The increasing political involvement by ordinary colonials made the right to complain an important element in the popular understanding of free expression. Insistence upon the right to criticize bad rulers and upon adoption of the Zengerian principles undercut the value of the law of libel. Political leaders found that they could use controls over expression only with great difficulty and at considerable risk to their political fortunes.

Although some members of the Revolutionary generation did cling to Blackstonian libel doctrines, others embarked on the challenging task of devising theories of free expression that included some postpublication penalties for certain kinds of political expression. Leonard Levy was perfectly correct in maintaining that few, if any, legal writers in Revolutionary America rejected the "core" of seditious libel, the notion that government "may be criminally assaulted by mere words."[74] Similarly, elite theorists never went so far as to contend that political criticism, including libels upon public officials, could never be made the subject of some type of legal redress. But the view that there can be no legal accounting for political expression has never been a widely accepted tenet of liberal political thought in any era. Although their arguments lacked the precision offered by the legal conceptualizers who followed them, members of the Revolutionary generation were trying to do precisely what later generations of lawyers and citizens would attempt to do: decide at what points and under what conditions public officials could legitimately apply legal controls, be they criminal or civil, to what types of political expression.

Despite the vagueness of their alternative formulations, during the last quarter of the eighteenth century, numerous Americans flatly rejected the Blackstonian premises that freedom of press meant merely the absence of prepublication restraints and that any criticism of government and public officials carried criminal liability. Most also insisted that the people's representatives, not the magistracy, possessed the final power to determine which publications and speeches were libelous. Indeed, involvement by citizens themselves, as both grand and petit jurors, retarded the development of a large body of literature that might have anticipated later libertarian ideas. In theory, prosecutions for political libels remained options for political leaders; but as a practical matter, once George III's armies had been defeated at Yorktown, critics of post-Revolutionary governments and political leaders rarely had to worry about law of libel. In the years between 1781 and 1797, American lawyers found no pressing need to develop the kinds of more precise legalistic arguments that would come to characterize free-speech discourse in the last years of the eighteenth century and throughout the nineteenth and twentieth centuries.

Chapter Three | Framing an American Law of Libel, 1781–1797

Independence from British legal institutions brought no sudden clarity to the law of political libel. Although the social-political basis for enforcing Blackstonian doctrines had eroded, events of the early national era demonstrated that most political leaders still argued that libel law, in some form, might check licentious political criticism. Beginning in the late 1780s and continuing through the next two decades, Americans debated the precise nature of libel laws. At the same time, the process of political communication remained as unsettled as the law of libel. Those who saw defamation law, whatever its ultimate shape, as a legitimate restraint on political debate, had to deal with constantly changing, steadily expanding channels of communication. Before we can understand libel law, then, it is necessary to assess, in general terms, the means by which members of the political community received information about public affairs.

Post-Revolutionary controversies over libel law first surfaced at the state level, particularly in Pennsylvania and Massachusetts. In these two states, sustained factional conflict prompted considerable debate about the general limits on political criticism. More important, the constitutions of Pennsylvania and Massachusetts guaranteed liberty of the press, and prominent lawyers in both states discussed the precise relationship between these constitutional safeguards and the law of libel. Evidence from these states, then, offers important clues about the place of libel law in late eighteenth-century political culture.

The System of Political Communication in Post-Revolutionary America

In many ways, the system of political communication, like the larger political culture, continued to become more popular, if not completely democratic, between the end of the American Revolution and the election of Thomas Jefferson. Although printers possessed no legal duty to publish everything offered to them, most did boast that their presses were open to all political opinions. In both Pennsylvania and Massachusetts, political writers sometimes seized upon such claims to demand that their statements appear in print.[1]

Citing the difficulty of gaining access to the twentieth-century mass media, scholars have contended that the small presses of the late eighteenth century offered a remarkably open forum for ordinary citizens and for political outsiders. According to one modern analyst, the post-Revolutionary generation enjoyed "great accessibility to the means of reaching the public with new ideas. No one thought of legislating a 'right of access' to the pages of the newspapers, at least in part, because of the relative ease of access to the presses themselves."[2]

This argument, though not without some merit, can be overstated. In truth, most late eighteenth-century newspapers offered something less than diverse coverage of a full range of issues. Printers in Philadelphia, for example, proceeded carefully when dealing with controversial issues such as the plight of the city's black population. Rather than encouraging truly open public debate on their pages, Philadelphia printers generally operated cautiously and invoked the traditional rhetoric of neutrality in order to avoid decisive stands on controversial subjects. And in Massachusetts, one scholar has argued, printers withheld information on the state government's financial dealings, an omission that allegedly gave urban interests, which possessed their own private channels of intelligence, an advantage over citizens who had to rely on public sources of information. Not everyone, then, enjoyed equal access to the public prints. The private correspondence of prominent political leaders shows that, not surprisingly, they used their influence to secure publication, and often republication, of their views. Less-distinguished political opponents lacked this kind of leverage.[3]

Perhaps the clearest example of this type of bias in the system of communication came in the debates over ratification of the Constitution of 1787 and over election of representatives to the first national Congress of 1789. Most newspapers and printing establishments were located in commercial centers, places that tended to be strongly in favor of the new charter, and anti-Federalist leaders complained of unequal treatment. "Through the influence of the tyrants of Boston," the anti-Federalist writer "Philadelphiensis" charged, "very little information has reached the people; the *press*, generally speaking, was devoted to the *well-born* and their tools. . . ."[4] Modern scholarly studies have generally confirmed many of the anti-Federalist complaints; lack of sympathetic printers, pressure by subscribers and advertisers against those who were anti-Federalists, and interference by pro-Constitution crowds all hindered opponents of the Constitution. Anti-Federalists could never match the volume of printed material circulated by the supporters of the Constitution.

Although the press may not have been as open in 1787–88 as the anti-

Federalists desired, people who opposed popular political trends found late eighteenth-century newspapers far too open. As the volume and bitter tone of political invective increased during the 1780s and 1790s, so did calls for greater deference to the reputations of the best men. Clergymen in New England, for example, often used their election sermons to praise civil authorities and to condemn their critics. According to Chandler Robbins, a prominent Congregational minister from Boston, the "important privilege" of "writing, speaking, and publishing, with decent freedom, our sentiments on public men and measures" was being abused by both disappointed office seekers and by "persons in the lower walks of life." Robbins feared that slanderous attacks upon virtuous officials could result in the rejection of "men of known and tried abilities" and the selection of those "who are destitute of the most essential qualifications."[5]

Others who considered political leadership the prerogative of the elite were similarly upset by the vehemence of political criticism and by the continued growth of popular political forms. During a congressional election in South Carolina, for example, William Smith seemed genuinely amazed when Dr. David Ramsey, his political rival, published a newspaper piece critical of Smith. But faced with the choices of fuming in private or replying through the press, Smith finally issued his own public reply. His broadside criticized Ramsey for violating an unwritten rule of the traditional political culture. "This is the first instance in this country of one candidate publishing to the world in the newspaper the ineligibility of his competitors. In general, *gentlemen* wait the event of the election," Smith complained, "and trust to the good sense of the electors that they will not elect improper men."[6]

Critics of political journalism generally blamed the growth of "scurrility" upon political factions. Writer after writer complained about "the rage of party," or the "obstinate virulence of party scribblers," or "the tools of party" who defamed decent men. "The obstinate virulence of party scribblers," charged a contributor to the *Massachusetts Spy* in 1788, was creating "an obstacle to all free and judicious inquiry, in matters of the highest moment to the people and to posterity." Another person from Massachusetts claimed that factional partisans were "ever ready to disseminate among the people jealousies and suspicions, and thus weaken the public confidence, and prevent the improvement of men best able to serve the country. . . ." Partisan slanders, this writer concluded, were "the *hidden dagger*[s] with which the assassin murders the characters of honest men and weakens the public confidence in their most trusted friends."[7]

Benjamin Franklin, America's most famous printer, also denounced the post-Revolutionary press. He complained that printers "have the privilege of accusing and abusing fellow citizens at their pleasure" or the ability to "hire out their pens and press to others for that purpose." When confronted by the people he had abused, a printer hid behind guarantees of free expression. Because "so much has been written and published on the federal Constitution, and the necessity of checks in all other parts of good government has been so clearly explained," Franklin thought it only logical and fair that citizens enjoy some check upon the power of the press.[8]

Such sentiments had little effect on political rhetoric. Only the most old-fashioned gentlemen remained silent; most political figures adopted the remedy of self-help and struck back at their critics. Many, of course, preferred to write under pseudonyms, and they warned printers to keep their identities secret. (This practice, however, failed to fool political insiders who could usually recognize stylistic "signatures" or learn the identity of popular correspondents from their own sources.) When political leaders did openly confront their critics in print, some, like William Smith, felt the need to justify their actions. A gentleman, after all, should not deign to notice common slanderers. When Robert Morris, the nation's chief financial officer under the Articles of Confederation, finally answered his critics, he disdainfully announced that he had always "look[ed] down with silent contempt on the repeated slanders of my enemies, so far as they can effect myself. . . ." But because some defamatory attacks on his character and conduct were really designed to lower public confidence in the new Constitution, Morris felt compelled to break his gentlemanly silence.[9]

This lofty approach to political debate hardly satisfied Morris's political opponents. Anti-Federalist leader Samuel Bryan—who wrote under the pen name of "Centennial"—ridiculed Morris's view of proper political manners. "Is it slander to call upon a public officer to account for the disposition of millions of public money entrusted to him eleven years ago? Or is it slander to denominate such a man a public defaulter?"[10]

Bryan's approach to political criticism accurately reflected the condition of journalism in most states during the 1780s. In part, heated political rhetoric reflected deep concern over how post-Revolutionary governments would affect American lives and livelihoods. How might tax burdens be apportioned? What type of currency system should be established? How should the legal system be organized? Despite appeals to submerge selfish factional interests in favor of "the public good," political conflict in most states centered on very concrete differences, and these partisan divisions often followed sectional and economic lines. Yet in many cases, writers debated public issues in highly personal terms. After surveying popular sources of information in postwar Massachusetts, for instance, the historian Van Beck Hall concluded that most publications emphasized attacks upon the characters of political leaders rather than factual analyses of particular issues.

Measured by later standards of professional journalism, the political discourse of the Revolutionary and early national eras does seem skewed toward moralistic rhetoric and away from more concrete factual information. But viewed in light of late eighteenth-century political culture, which was still dominated by the imagery and rhetoric of the English "country" tradition, this emphasis upon the virtues and vices of public men seems perfectly natural. In the country view of politics, the health of the political system and the future of individual liberties rested as much upon the character of public persons as upon the logic or wisdom of their particular positions on public issues. If the public could not discover the true character of public officials and candidates, they ran the risk of seeing unscrupulous leaders capture the reins of power, of standing by and watching "aristocratic schemers"—or "demagogic rabble-rousers"—subvert the nation's experiment in republicanism.[11]

This factional and ideological backdrop also helps explain the almost total absence of political libel suits during the turbulent 1780s and early 1790s. On those rare occasions when writers or printers did face the threat of libel prosecutions, they could rely upon the theories of free expression popularized by pre-Revolutionary opposition groups and upon the very concrete power of sympathetic political factions.

In 1782, for example, when Pennsylvania's Chief Justice Thomas McKean tried to prosecute Eleazer Oswald, whose *Independent Gazetteer* opposed Mc-Kean and his political allies, supporters of the obstreperous printer mounted a campaign against traditional libel doctrines. Oswald's political allies not only restated familiar eighteenth-century themes but offered new arguments that presaged the attacks that Jeffersonians would use against the national Sedition Act of 1798. The Revolutionary principle of popular sovereignty, one of Oswald's supporters argued, demanded repudiation of Blackstonian libel doctrines. Another suggested that the law should not punish even false charges of political corruption. And a number of newspaper contributors claimed that Pennsylvania's constitution of 1776—which declared that "the freedom of the press ought not to be restrained" and that "printing presses shall be free to any person who undertakes to examine the proceedings of the legislature, or any part of the government"—barred any legal proceedings based upon the common law doctrines of political libel.

As pro-McKean papers made clear, not all Pennsylvanians approved these claims, but the issue of libel law never reached the law courts. Instead, Oswald and his supporters adopted the pre-Revolutionary tactic of appealing directly to the people. Openly lobbying with grand jurors, they successfully blocked any indictment against Oswald. As a result, no Pennsylvania court entered the popular conflict over the meaning of Pennsylvania's constitutional guarantee of free expression.[12]

During the 1780s, a similar situation prevailed in Massachusetts, another state with a constitution that guaranteed freedom of press. Nine years after adoption of Massachusetts's constitution of 1780, two of the commonwealth's most learned lawyers, John Adams and William Cushing, remained uncertain about the exact meaning of "freedom of press," particularly about the precise effect of the new constitutional guarantee on the old law of political libel. And arguing against inclusion of any free expression clause in the national constitution of 1787, Alexander Hamilton ridiculed the provisions in various state charters. "What signifies a declaration that the liberty of press shall be inviolably preserved? What is the liberty of the press? Who can give it any definition that would not leave the utmost latitude for invasion?"[13]

Adams's uncertainty and Hamilton's skepticism were understandable: absence of political libel prosecutions eliminated the need, and the opportunity, for lawyers and judges even to begin to settle complex legal issues involving defamation law. But absence of any definitive analyses of libel and free expression during the 1780s did not mean that Americans, including leading politicians and lawyers, entirely ignored the issue. In Pennsylvania and Massachusetts, at least, factional politics provoked considerable, oftentimes searching, legal discussions about the limits on free expression.

Libel and Politics during the 1780s: The State Background of the First Amendment

Debates in Pennsylvania focused upon the law of libel; these same discussions clearly illustrated a fundamental lack of agreement over the nature of the post-Revolutionary political and constitutional systems. Pennsylvania's Constitutionalists, for example, rallied behind the state's "democratic" constitution of 1776, a document that expressed in many of its provisions (such as a single-house legislature and a weak executive branch) some of the more radical impulses of the Revolutionary era. The constitution of 1776 also contained two clauses guaranteeing freedom of expression. One clause, placed in the "Declaration of Rights," provided that "the people have a right to freedom of speech, and of writing, and publishing their sentiments; therefore the freedom of the press ought not to be restrained." Obviously, this language left wide range for interpretation. The second clause, located in the main body of the constitution, was even more vague: "The printing presses shall be free to every person who undertakes to examine the proceedings of the legislature, or any part of government." To people such as Eleazer Oswald, this latter provision, which might be read merely as a constitutional exhortation in favor of open access or as a prohibition of any type of stamp tax, seemed both an invitation to take on governmental leaders and a constitutional safeguard against their retaliation through the law courts.[14]

The constitution of 1776 became the subject of controversy in Pennsylvania. As their attempt to "gag" Eleazer Oswald suggested, Republicans wanted—and in 1790 secured—revision of this constitution. They contended that a stable republic required strict legal and political controls as well as popular deference to the leadership of the best men.

Events of the late 1780s—the decisive response in Massachusetts to Shays's Rebellion, attempts in many states to bolster the judicial branch, and the drive for a new national constitution—demonstrated that people in other states shared the fears of Pennsylvania's Republicans. In this view, which predominated among people involved in commercial enterprises, America's republican revolution was getting out of hand; liberty appeared to be degenerating into licentiousness. As opposing political groups expressed their differences in ever-increasing numbers of newspapers, pamphlets, and broadsides, a number of prominent people suggested the need to crack down on the purveyors of scurrility. Benjamin Franklin offered two suggestions. If people were determined to support absolute freedom for the press, he facetiously suggested, the legislature should authorize persons whom the press had abused to reply by means of "the liberty of the cudgel" (including moderate tarring and feathering). But if people "thought that this proposal of mine may disturb the public peace, I would then humbly recommend to our legislators to take up the consideration of both liberties . . . and by an explicit law mark their extent and limits. . . ." Thus, Franklin urged legal controls, including the law of libel, to check the growing political role of the popular press.[15]

Other Pennsylvania political leaders, including Thomas McKean and Dr. Benjamin Rush, had the same thought. In 1789 McKean and Eleazer Oswald tangled once again; but this time the chief justice emerged victorious, and Oswald ended up in jail. The printer's legal problems began with an ostensibly private libel suit brought by Andrew Browne, former editor of the *Federal Gazette*. Oswald alleged, however, that his political enemies, particularly Dr. Rush, had instigated the lawsuit in order to hamstring Oswald's opposition to the new national constitution. When Browne refused to drop his suit in exchange for a retraction, Oswald revived his strategy of 1782: through his paper, he denounced the "Federalist conspiracy" against him and appealed for public support.

McKean immediately hauled Oswald before the state supreme court. Oswald's article on a pending lawsuit, charged prosecuting attorney William Lewis, constituted a contempt of court and should be punished summarily by a jail term and by an attachment against his printing business. Oswald's attorney, Anti-Federalist leader William Findley, raised numerous constitutional objections, including the claim that the whole summary proceeding violated freedom of the press. Since the alleged contempt occurred outside the courtroom, Findley argued, the case really amounted to a prosecution for political libel and required a jury trial.[16]

Not surprisingly, McKean refused to allow a jury trial, which would likely have meant Oswald's acquittal. McKean also took the opportunity to lecture Oswald and Findley on the law of libel. The state's constitution of 1776 gave no one, especially newspaper printers, the right to defame other citizens or to disrupt the workings of republican government. A slanderer possessed a heart "more base and black than that of the assassin" or the arsonist. A libeler was even worse than a slanderer: dissemination of defamation "in the public prints must render it impractible to apply the antedote as far as the poison has been extended." Could anyone, McKean asked, really believe that Pennsylvania's constitution rendered defamation "sacred" when spread through "the more permanent and diffusive medium of the press?"[17]

McKean quoted liberally from Blackstone, but he also conceded that Pennsylvania's constitution guaranteed citizens more than liberation from prior restraints. Under Blackstonian rules, it will be remembered, any critical publication, no matter how accurate or well intentioned, carried a bad tendency and created criminal liability; in contrast, opposition Whig doctrines proscribed only false attacks against good rulers. Although he said nothing about the issue of truth, McKean borrowed from both of these approaches and offered, in effect, a neo-Blackstonian rendition of opposition Whig ideas. Courts should not punish all critical statements; rather, they should examine the motives and intentions of political critics in order to distinguish between statements "which are meant for use and reformation, and [published] with an eye solely to the public good and those which are intended merely to delude and defame."[18] Applying this test to Oswald, McKean quickly decided that the printer's article had a "bad tendency" and therefore must have stemmed from "bad motives." The publication, McKean ruled, clearly carried "the tendency which has been ascribed to it, that of prejudicing the public (a part of whom must hereafter be summoned as jurors) . . . and of corrupting the administration of justice." He sentenced Oswald to pay a fine of ten pounds and to serve a jail term of one month.[19]

The first successful legal assault on a partisan press since the Revolution, the *Oswald* case anticipated the conflict that would erupt during the 1790s over freedom of press and the law of libel. Oswald kept his cause alive by petitioning the Pennsylvania legislature and demanding impeachment proceedings against McKean and the other members of the Supreme Court. Although Oswald's supporters lacked the will and the votes to take this action, they did use the occasion to attack McKean's view of free expression. During three days of debate, pro- and anti-McKean forces reprised and expanded the arguments presented at Oswald's hearing. Technically, of course, Oswald had been convicted of contempt; but everyone involved in the dispute believed that it also involved other legal issues.

Expanding his earlier argument before McKean, William Lewis stressed the larger legal questions raised by the Oswald affair. He wished to illuminate "the inestimable character of true liberty, which is equally endangered by tyranny on the one hand, and by licentiousness upon the other." He also wanted to rescue Sir William Blackstone "from the stigma of being a courtly writer" and to show that the common law, and particularly Blackstone's version, offered appropriate principles for a republic. Blackstone's basic approach to freedom of press, Lewis argued, outlined the wisest policy: citizens could publish whatever they pleased, but the government still possessed full authority to punish them for "any thing which violates the rights of another, or interrupts the peace and order of society." Even under Pennsylvania's (democratized) constitution of 1776, he concluded, "the right of publication, like every other right, had its natural and necessary boundary; for, though the law allows a man the free use of his arm, or the possession of a weapon, yet it does not authorize him to plunge a dagger in the breast of an inoffensive neighbor."[20]

Oswald's supporters vigorously challenged McKean's neo-Blackstonian views on freedom of expression. William Findley, in a bitterly sarcastic reply to Lewis's lengthy (three-day) oration, reiterated his view that both the letter and the spirit of Pennsylvania's bill of rights banned any summary punishment for statements made outside judicial chambers. But his argument carried much broader implications. Appealing to popular understanding as against the "technical learning" of the bar and "the jargon of the law," Findley ridiculed the legal and constitutional principles of the Republicans. An eighteenth-century democrat from western Pennsylvania, Findley dismissed the arguments of the Republicans as appeals to "the dark and distant period of juridical history" and invoked, instead, the "rights and immunities which formed the great object of the revolution. . . ." Everyone "who possessed a competent share of common sense, and understood the rules of grammar" could see, by "a bare perusal" of the state's bill of rights that McKean had improperly denied Oswald a jury trial. Findley denounced any lawyer who would use "the sophistry of the schools, and the jargon of the law to pervert and corrupt the explicit language" of constitutional guarantees. It would be "fatal to the cause of liberty if it was once established, that the technical learning of a lawyer is necessary to comprehend the principles" of the constitution, "this great compact between the people and their rulers."[21]

The controversies of the 1780s carried over into the Pennsylvania constitutional convention of 1790, when some of the young republic's best lawyers tried to weave the tattered threads of eighteenth-century libel law into a new tapestry. After rejecting both a general declaration, similar to the one in the constitution of 1776, and a simple clause allowing all defendants in any libel prosecution to plead truth as a defense, delegates weighed numerous, and highly technical, alternative proposals. During debates that sometimes cut across Republican-Constitutionalist lines, the convention tried to resolve disputes about truth as a defense and about the power of juries. Finally, Alexander

Addison and James Wilson—attorneys who were strong Republicans, soon-to-be staunch Federalists, and ultimately advocates of the frequent use of libel law—suggested that defendants could plead truth as a justification in prosecutions where the alleged libels involved the conduct of public officials and the "men in public capacities" or "matters proper for public information." McKean, Lewis, and other Republican delegates finally accepted the Addison-Wilson formula, but only after adoption of severe restrictive amendments. One limited the clause on public men to attacks on their "official conduct," and another deleted the words "in justification" from the guarantee of pleading truth.[22] As finally amended, Section 7 of the Pennsylvania Bill of Rights provided

> That the printing-presses shall be free to every person who undertakes to examine the proceedings of the legislature or any branch of government; and no law shall ever be made to restrain the right thereof. . . . In prosecutions for the publication of papers investigating the official conduct of officers, or men in a public capacity, or where the matter published is proper for public information, the truth thereof may be given in evidence. And, in all indictments for libels, the jury shall have a right to determine the law and the facts under the direction of the court as in other cases.[23]

Despite—or perhaps because of—the presence of so many learned lawyers, the convention drafted a clause that raised as many problems as it solved. At first glance, Pennsylvania's bill of rights incorporated the Zengerian principles for prosecutions involving public libels; but, in truth, the amendments of McKean and Lewis created the opportunity for the type of neo-Blackstonian interpretations that McKean had used in Oswald's contempt hearing. The term "official conduct" obviously implied less legal protection than the original Wilson-Addison term, "conduct." And though delegates guaranteed defendants the right to present evidence of truth, deletion of the phrase "in justification," the lawyer's equivalent of the layperson's "complete defense," permitted judicial imposition of additional requirements for acquittal, such as McKean's prerequisite of good motives and upright intentions. Finally, a majority of the 1790 convention members also took a stand against calumniation and in favor of the right of reputation when they declared, in the same article that contained the freedom of expression clause, that "every man, for an injury done him in his lands, goods, person or reputation, shall have remedy by the due course of law . . . without sale, denial or delay."[24]

The Pennsylvania convention, then, bequeathed an ambiguous constitutional approach to the law of libel. Read literally, the free expression clause of 1790 clearly assumed the validity of prosecutions for libelous criticism of the government. Even so, delegates also acknowledged the popular political culture and formally broke with Blackstonian orthodoxy. And for the first time in Anglo-American jurisprudence, they elevated the rules in criminal libel prosecutions to the status of written constitutional principles.

Shortly after adoption of Pennsylvania's new charter, James Wilson mounted an even more pointed challenge to the Blackstonian position. Unveiling his ideas during a series of highly publicized lectures—the first of which attracted the belles of Philadelphia society as well as President Washington—on the nature of American law, Wilson offered an original analysis of the relationship between libel law and republican constitutional principles. Orthodox Whig libel doctrines, he warned, could be used to limit legitimate dissent; in addition, Wilson complained that the popular odium attached to them helped to deprive the entire community, private citizens as well as public officials, of "the benefits of that law, wise and salutary when administered properly. . . by proper persons."[25] America's libel laws needed to be reconstituted so they could serve the useful purposes for which they were intended.

A republican legal order, Wilson proposed, should tear down old principles of defamation law, build new doctrines, and use them to shelter the reputations of virtuous citizens. The right to reputation was a fundamental, natural right, "the enjoyment of which is the design of good governments and laws to secure and enlarge." Sound public policy demanded that republican governments, even more than monarchical ones, guard the reputations of their citizens. The natural desire to possess a good reputation, Wilson theorized, exerted a powerful influence toward correct behavior. Thus, in a "government of which virtue is the principle and vice the bane, the right to individual reputation ought to receive from all its institutions, the just degree of favor and regard."[26]

In Wilson's view, any rational legal system would consider truth a complete defense to a charge of criminal libel: the law could give people no better reputation than the one that they themselves had earned and therefore deserved. The old maxim, "the greater the truth the greater the libel," ignored the obvious fact that only falsehoods, never the truth, could injure someone's character. In addition to admitting truth as a defense, Wilson endorsed the other basic demand of eighteenth-century Zengerians. In a republican society, the question of whether or not a particular statement was actually libelous could only be decided by a jury drawn from the community at large.[27]

Wilson did not want liberation from Blackstonian doctrines to lead to elimination of legal restraints over political expression. In fact, his intention was precisely the opposite: liberalization of the standards of criminal liability should be the prelude to more frequent prosecution of both public and private libels. When circumscribed by proper rules, frequent prosecutions were perfectly compatible with constitutional guarantees of free expression. Clearly, Wilson wanted to discourage libelous calumny of public officials. In meting out punishment, courts should consider political libels even more reprehensible than private ones. "Other things being equal," he argued in his lectures, the law "ought to incline the beam, if the libel refer to . . . official character or conduct; because an officer is a citizen and more."[28] But, Wilson continued, some libels against private citizens could "certainly be more atrocious, and of example more atrociously evil, than a libel of another kind against a publick officer." Once they recognized that the "love of reputation and the fear of dishonour," which were "implanted in our breasts" by God "for purposes the most beneficient and wise," operated as bulwarks to republicanism, jurists would see the necessity of stringent legal protection for both public and private reputation.[29]

After the initial enthusiasm for Wilson's lectures, his ambitious work attracted surprisingly little attention from American lawyers. Few other members of the American bar, for example, shared Wilson's enthusiasm for using criminal prosecutions as a means of discouraging purely private defamation. Although state laws and judicial precedents did not prohibit prosecutions for libels upon private citizens, most American lawyers and judges viewed criminal libels as a political offense against governmental leaders, against the best men.

But though American lawyers did not rush to adopt James Wilson's specific proposals, most did join him in rejecting the Orthodox Whig–Blackstonian position. Few were willing to speak in favor of the rule that limited jurors to finding only the fact of publication. And not even Thomas McKean was prepared to argue that every piece of political criticism should subject authors and publishers to criminal liability. But the lengthy controversy over Pennsylvania's libel laws revealed that even lawyers who rejected the orthodox Blackstonian position would still not agree upon the precise shape of legal doctrines or upon the more basic issue—the degree of dissent that a republican polity might safely allow.

The type of disagreement evident in Pennsylvania also prevailed in Massachusetts, the only other state where libel law became a prominent issue before the late 1790s. In an exchange of views in 1789, John Adams and William Cushing readily agreed that Blackstone should not be the final authority for interpretation of their state's constitutional guarantee of free expression, but they differed over where to draw the line against licentious political criticism. Reiterating many of the policy arguments offered by country writers, Cushing contended that if free governments were to flourish, the law could impose no criminal liability for truthful political statements.[30] The press, Adams acknowledged, played a vital role in a republic—providing citizens with information upon which to make intelligent choices at the polls—and deserved more legal protection than in a monarchical system. But Adams personally favored a more restrictive legal standard, one similar to that adopted by Thomas McKean during Eleazer Oswald's contempt hearing. The law, Adams argued, should allow defendants to present evidence of truth; but only if it were determined that they had published the truth "for the public good," could they secure an acquittal. He feared that any rule that allowed publication of truth, "without any honest motive" and "merely from malice," would provide an insufficient check against slanderers.[31]

During post-Revolutionary Massachusetts's first political libel prosecution, the 1791 trial of Edward Freeman of the *Herald of Freedom*, members of the state supreme court also disagreed upon a republican alternative to Blackstonian orthodoxy. Indicted for allegedly accusing a state senator of being a drunk and a murderer, Freeman mounted no broad constitutional assault against political libel prosecutions involving the press. Instead, his attorney argued that this particular indictment must fail because Freeman's article never identified the senator by name. Pleading for leniency, he also stressed Freeman's inexperience in the newspaper business. Although this defense strategy made it technically unnecessary for the court to rule upon the relevance of truth as a defense, several of the justices did suggest, during oral arguments and in their separate charges to jurors, that evidence of truth would have been admissible had Freeman tried to justify his charges. The judges also unequivocally broke with common law orthodoxy and allowed the jury to determine whether or not Freeman's publication was libelous. After deliberating overnight, jurors returned a verdict of not guilty.[32]

Despite the ambiguity of state constitutional guarantees, many people disputed Alexander Hamilton's view of their uselessness. Especially in Pennsylvania, where the threat of state libel prosecutions had already become an issue, Anti-Federalists denounced the absence of any protection for a free press in the new national constitution. Proponents of the charter, such as James Wilson, ridiculed such charges, but Pennsylvania's Anti-Federalists persisted. Writing in Eleazer Oswald's *Independent Gazetteer*, "An Old Whig" attacked Wilson's claim that national power could never touch the press. According to this essayist, the Federalist claim that fears about free expression were groundless suggested an ominous point: that supporters of the constitution believed "that the common people need no information on the subject of politics. Newspapers, pamphlets and essays are calculated only to mislead and inflame them by holding forth to them doctrines which they have no business or right to meddle with, which they ought to leave to their superiors."[33]

Other Anti-Federalists from Pennsylvania focused on the danger of libel prosecutions in federal courts, prosecutions that would make their own state constitutional protections useless. The new constitution must explicitly protect free expression, claimed William Findley, because "the powers of Congress are fully adequate to its destruction as they are to have the trial of *libels* or pretended libels against the United States. . . ."[34] "A Democratic Federalist," writing in the *Pennsylvania Herald*, joined the general doubts of "An Old

Whig" to Findley's specific fears about libel prosecutions. Experiences such as the Zenger prosecution suggested that "corrupt and wicked judges," when "not restrained by express laws," could twist legal doctrines to restrain the press; history also indicated, "A Democratic Federalist" continued, "how displeasing the liberty of the press is to men in power. . . ." Finally, pointing to the judicial article of the new constitution, this essayist argued that national courts "may claim a right to the cognizance of all offences against the *general government*, and *libels* will not probably be excluded."[35]

Such fears were not limited to Pennsylvania. During the constitution-ratifying convention in Maryland, a delegate warned that in "prosecution in the federal courts, for libels, the constitutional preservation of this great and fundamental right [of free expression] may prove invaluable." And the essay of "One of the Common People," published in the *Boston Gazette*, asked if it were not clear that national leaders would have "the power to prosecute any printer for a pretended libel against the United States? Will not a printer be triable for a pretended libel against any foreign minister or consul, or for a libel against any of the individual states, by a federal tribunal?" A free press, wrote "The Federal Farmer," is the "channel of communication as to mercantile and public affairs; by means of it the people in large countries ascertain each others sentiments; are enabled to unite, and become formidable to those rulers who adopt improper measures." Although newspapers did often contain abusive language and false accusations, "these are but small inconveniences, in my mind, among many advantages" of a free press.[36]

Responses to the absence of any free-press guarantee in the national constitution, then, suggested how far—and how little—the debate over free expression had proceeded. First, fears about the inauguration of national libel prosecutions clearly showed that a sizable body of Americans rejected the Blackstonian view that liberty of press meant only liberation from prior restraints. Second, the vagueness of Anti-Federalist arguments—none spelled out any specific formula for detecting unprotected expression—also indicated that the legal arguments had yet to be joined. Yet, even though Anti-Federalists wrote largely about theoretical dangers, events of the 1790s would show that their fears about libel laws were not frivolous. Soon after establishment of the new government, as we shall see, Alexander Hamilton was urging the kind of prosecutions dreaded by William Findley, and several foreign ministers were attempting to use federal courts for the type of libel actions predicted by "A Democratic Federalist."[37]

After the Revolution, writers and speakers still quoted Blackstone when discussing liberty of the press, but they did so primarily in order to offer textual authority for the common view that this right was not unlimited. Even the conservative legal elite, people like Wilson and McKean, abandoned the old Blackstonian position on libel. By 1791 the views of *Cato*, Zenger, and the

Revolutionary opposition—not the strict Orthodox Whig position—showed what Americans generally understood as the legal limits on political debate. Any more elaborate legal definition would have to await adjudication of concrete cases. By 1791, Americans had simply not seen enough political libel suits to debate legal boundaries at any great length.

Of what help, then, are state discussions in discovering the elusive "original understanding" of the First Amendment? Designed to calm fears of the Anti-Federalists, this amendment, like the entire Bill of Rights, was adopted rapidly, leaving scant evidence of what even its supporters intended by the phrase "Congress shall make no law . . . abridging freedom of speech, or of the press." When read against the fairly extensive, yet inconclusive, debates over state guarantees, the legislative history of this phrase becomes more, not less, murky. At one point during congressional debates, for example, the Senate rejected an amendment which provided that freedom of expression should be protected "in as ample a manner as hath been *at any time* secured by the common law." Was this proposal an effort to incorporate the Holt-Mansfield-Blackstone definition? Or was it, rather, an attempt to enshrine the opposition Whig view that, until corrupted by Star Chamber, the true common law offered defendants the protection of the Zengerian principles? Given the inconclusive nature of eighteenth-century legal debates, it is very likely that some senators would have favored the former interpretation and others the latter.[38]

The final version of the First Amendment offers similar interpretive difficulties. Without any doubt, the evidence shows the desire to prohibit Congress from applying the traditional types of prior restraints to the press. But does this provision, as some historians and Justices Hugo Black and William O. Douglas have insisted, also constitute an "absolute" prohibition against *any* regulation of expression by Congress?[39] Or as supporters of the Sedition Act of 1798 and most later scholars have argued, does not the language, the logic, and the history of the free expression clause indicate a clear intention of leaving Congress authority over at least some kinds of political expression?[40] It might be noted, for example, that delegates to Pennsylvania's constitutional convention of 1790 rejected a proposal very similar to the First Amendment—"No law shall ever be made abridging the freedom of speech or the press." Delegates best described as neo-Blackstonians, such as Thomas McKean, supported this measure and more libertarian delegates (including William Findley) rejected it, presumably because they considered it too vague.[41]

The paucity of evidence on the drafting of the First Amendment itself, together with the abundance of evidence attesting to the absence of precise agreement on state libel laws, points to one conclusion: even the relatively small group of people who framed and ratified the First Amendment shared no common original understanding about its precise meaning or implications for the future. Moreover, the architects of the First Amendment undoubtedly desired an ambiguous guarantee: a broad statement compatible with a number of precise legal formulas would facilitate ratification and leave future political options open. The experience of delegates to the Pennsylvania convention of 1790 suggested that lengthy debates over specific language only delayed matters without, in the end, clarifying all the complex legal and political issues.[42]

Toward the Sedition Act: Political Debate during the 1790s

The opportunity to discuss further the meaning of the First Amendment came fairly quickly. Development of national political factions and partisan newspapers during the 1790s provided the background for fierce debates over the proper limits on political speech and for more frequent use of political libel prosecutions. As early as 1789 Alexander Hamilton helped establish John Fenno's *Gazette of the United States*, and Fenno's paper soon became identified as the organ of George Washington's administration and of Hamilton in particular. In the fall of 1791, as Thomas Jefferson and James Madison emerged as leaders of an anti-Hamiltonian coalition, the poet-journalist Philip Freneau began to edit the rival *National Gazette*. Although Jefferson maintained that he never wrote for the *Gazette*, he helped sponsor Freneau's paper and viewed it as a necessary means of alerting citizens to Hamilton's "anti-republican" and "crypto-monarchical" policies. After various financial difficulties killed Freneau's paper, the *Aurora*, edited by Benjamin Franklin Bache and later by William Duane, proved a more adequate replacement.

The number of newspapers increased dramatically throughout the decade— from approximately 100 papers in 1790 to about 250 ten years later. Actually, journalistic activity was even greater than these figures would suggest. Publishing a newspaper was a risky financial venture; many over-eager printers and editors, particularly in less populated areas, quickly succumbed to monetary realities. In all, more than 500 different newspapers appeared at some time, perhaps only for a day or two, during the decade. Meanwhile, handbills and pamphlets offered relatively inexpensive mediums for providing information on specific issues.

Not every printer or editor was as blatantly partisan as Fenno, Bache, and Duane, but factionally aligned papers attracted the most attention and set the tone for political journalism. Some prominent editors ridiculed the old trade theory of neutrality and championed the value of steady partisan allegiance. Pro-Federalist editor William Cobbett denounced those "lifeless" printers "who may be counted as a fort of blanks: creatures that have nothing of humanity about them . . . and that are . . . as perfectly logs as if they had been cut out of timber." Neutrality in politics, according to the *Baltimore American*, was as much a delusion as neutrality in religion; "Every party will have its *printer*, as well as every sect its preacher. . . ." And, of course, the claim of neutrality provided no guarantee of real impartiality. The first issue of Bache's fiery *Aurora*, for example, even reiterated the old theme that a free press was, among other things, a neutral one.[43]

Between 1791 and 1794, prominent supporters of the Washington administration, who would soon coalesce as the leaders of the Federalist party, viewed the efforts of Bache and other opposition writers with mounting alarm. They feared that newspaper attacks represented something more sinister than the misguided "babblings" of a few deluded "scribblers." Attacks on Hamilton, upon Federalist policies, and upon President Washington threatened the viability of the new constitution and perhaps the well-being of the republic. At first, many believed that disagreement with Hamilton's domestic policies portended a revival of scattered localist opposition to the idea of a strong national union.

Western Pennsylvania's opposition to the federal excise tax on whiskey especially worried Alexander Hamilton. The secretary of treasury vented his outrage against a petition, which was printed as a broadside, drafted by an antitax meeting in August of 1792. "We think it our duty," the tax protestors announced, "to persist in our remonstrances [against the tax] to Congress, and in every other legal measure that may obstruct the operation of the Law, until we are able to obtain its total repeal."[44] Upon learning of the meeting and the broadside, Hamilton asked Attorney General Edmund Randolph for an opinion on whether or not the petitioners had committed "an indictable offense," criminal libel on the United States government. Hamilton considered the claim that the protestors could adopt "legal measures" to block collection of the tax "a contradiction in terms." He "therefore entertain[ed] no doubt, that a high misdemeanor has been committed."[45] But Randolph rejected Hamilton's attempt to use the law of libel. The petitioners had done or said nothing that was illegal. "To assemble to remonstrate, and to invite others to assemble and remonstrate to the Legislature, are among the rights of Citizens," Randolph reminded Hamilton. And even though the broadside-petition "indicates a hostile temper . . . when we advert to the strictness, with which criminal Law is interpreted, and the latitude allowed in drawing a meaning from a libel so as to favour the accused, I must pronounce that the law will not reach" the Whiskey protestors.[46] In arguing that the petition was protected speech, Randolph adopted both a distinction between speech and action, and an early version of the "clear and present danger doctrine": "Thus, Sir, you discover my opinion to be against an attempt to a prosecution *at this moment*, when the malignant spirit has not developed itself in acts so specific, and so manifestly infringing the peace, as obviously to expose the culpable persons to the censures of the Law. My maxim," he informed Hamilton, "is to examine well; to forbear a doubtfull power, and to enforce one, dearly rightfull."[47]

Randolph reemphasized his position several years later, when in 1794, Hamilton suggested that the government might prosecute members of the Democratic-Republican Society of Washington County, Pennsylvania, for a "seditious" petition. The remonstrance, sent to the president for transmittal to Congress, attacked the national government for not taking bold enough action to break Spain's control over the Mississippi River.[48] The society's complaint enraged the president; according to Randolph, who was now secretary of state, Washington thought it "in every view inadmissible" to acknowledge the existence of the group or its standing to petition the government. Seeking further advice from his cabinet, Washington himself suggested either contemptuously ignoring the petition or returning it with a statement declaring "that the President receives no application from a body, as such, whose constitution is not known to him in the laws. . . ."[49]

Randolph advised the first alternative, "silent contempt," but Hamilton unsuccessfully suggested a third course of action—"that the Paper should be referred to the Atty General to examine carefully if it does not contain criminal matter & that if it does it ought to be put in a train of prosecution." Henry Knox, the secretary of war, curtly rejected any thought of a prosecution for seditious libel. "No prosecution—but no answer of any sort," he noted at the bottom of Randolph's request for advice. Randolph's successor as attorney general, William Bradford, concurred and spelled out his reasoning for the president.[50]

Bradford based the case against a libel prosecution on both legal principle and political expediency. Although he thought the petition "exceedingly reprehensible and improper in its language," Bradford doubted "whether it would be considered *per se*, as a proper subject for a criminal prosecution, without some *extrinsic* proof of a seditious intention." Bradford, like Randolph, apparently thought that the crime of sedition could not be committed by words alone. Moreover, he reminded the president, the First Amendment specifically guaranteed the right of petition, and the general public would likely consider any prosecution "as an attack upon the right itself." Many people obviously viewed sharply worded political statements "as excrescences which it is dangerous to touch. More exceptionable matter appears frequently in the public prints; but these abuses are endured from a fear of injuring the freedom of the press." In assessing the understanding of free speech in the mid-1790s, then, Bradford emphasized both the technical requirements of the law and popular attitudes toward political debate. Finally, Bradford alluded to the political realities surrounding any libel prosecution. "An unsuccessful prosecution for seditious writings generally does harm; and independent of any legal doubt, this does not seem to be a case that will *certainly* ensure a conviction."[51] Thus,

Bradford did not reject the legitimacy of libel prosecutions by the national government; but he did recognize a variety of legal and practical impediments to successful application of libel doctrines.

The trend that worried Hamilton—the increasing stridency of attacks upon the national government and its officials—did not disappear. By the summer of 1794, many Federalists linked newspaper "lies" to the growth of "seditious" political organizations—the nuclei of what would become Jefferson's Republican party—and to the spread of incendiary political ideas from revolutionary France. Indeed, important Federalist leaders viewed Jefferson's supporters as advance agents of French Jacobinism. Western Pennsylvania's Whiskey Rebellion of 1794, the short-lived climax to the antitax movement, seemed to confirm some of these suspicions.

Federalists continued to blame opposition publications and partisan activists for the antitax movement in Pennsylvania. After collapse of the Whiskey Rebellion, President Washington sent Congress a message that traced the violence to the publications of the Democratic-Republican societies, diverse groups of anti-Federalist militants whose activities between 1794 and 1796 helped give the Jeffersonian opposition considerable vitality and organizational support. Broadening Washington's attack, Federalist members of Congress condemned the publications of these societies for undermining republicanism by defaming the nation's leaders and by misrepresenting their policies. History and common sense, Federalist leaders argued, demonstrated that no government could tolerate such licentious criticism.[52]

The Democratic-Republican societies quickly condemned these Federalist statements as dangerous attacks upon the right of free expression. "Good rulers will not shrink from public enquiry," resolved the Democratic-Republican Society of Pennsylvania. Only "a corrupt administration" would threaten to limit criticism. In an "Address to Fellow Freemen," another Democratic-Republican Society challenged the president to show where the Constitution prohibited criticism of the national government. The Pennsylvania society implicitly challenged the Washington administration to prosecute it. If members of the society had violated any law, the government should bring them before "a jury of their fellow-Citizens. To the security of such a tribunal, we are willing to submit: but no other department of Government" has any power to interfere with political speech, the society proclaimed.[53]

Three members of Washington's cabinet—Randolph, Bradford, and Knox —had already advised against prosecutions in similar circumstances, and the administration took no legal action against any of the Democratic-Republican groups.

Significantly, then, Federalist lawmakers proposed neither common law prosecutions nor a national criminal libel law in 1794. Although Federalist representative Samuel Dexter believed restrictive measures would be constitutional, the representative from Massachusetts advised that legal action was not "necessary or expedient" at this time. Instead, Federalists sponsored a resolution that blamed the Whiskey Rebellion on the propaganda of the Democratic-Republican societies. "The gentle power of opinion," claimed Fisher Ames, would provide "the proper remedy." Federalists had no desire to attack "the right of a free press," argued William Vans Murray. They only wanted "to excite a judicious and salutary inquiry . . . respecting the just and true limits within which a virtuous and enlightened well-wisher to our country would think it safe to exercise this right."[54]

Thus, in 1794, advocates of restriction faced a dilemma. Though the black-letter law of political libel seemed on their side, the realities of political life were not. Those who wanted to halt the spread of licentious sentiments acknowledged the difference between their own condemnation of libelous publications and the successful prosecution of these infractions of the law. In September 1794, for example, the Washington administration continued to follow the same cautious policy as Federalists in Congress. Attorney General William Bradford advised Edmund Randolph that a piece in John Greenleaf's *New York Journal* clearly libeled the British minister to the United States; abandoning the narrower view he had expressed when libels involved the government, Bradford saw no legal obstacles to a federal prosecution for a libel upon an individual, under the common law of libel. But Bradford qualified his professional judgment with a political caveat: "I confine myself strictly to *legal* considerations, and waive any discussion of the prudence of commencing a prosecution for publications of this kind."[55] Legal action against a prominent opposition paper, Bradford recognized, would likely increase, rather than decrease, the volume of political criticism. Other members of the administration recognized the wisdom of Bradford's approach: they secured an indictment against Greenleaf, thereby asserting the attorney general's theory of libel law, but they also acknowledged his pragmatic political advice by never bringing the case to trial.[56] Other political leaders acknowledged this same reality, and, like General James Lloyd of Maryland, found themselves forced to reply to alleged libels through newspapers and pamphlets rather than to seek redress through the legal system.[57]

The cautious approach of Federalists in Congress and the Washington administration demonstrated a reluctance to appear as the enemies of free expression or even as too vigorous opponents of licentiousness. Their actions in the early 1790s suggest the absence of any deep "legacy of suppression" to which opponents of domestic dissent could readily appeal. Since the Revolutionary era, Americans had had much more experience with political invectives than with legal restraints.

But evidence from the 1790s also suggests a growing desire among some people, especially those of "the Federalist persuasion," to substitute libel laws for rhetorical denunciations of licentious publications. In their charges to grand juries, for example, Judges Alexander Addison of Pennsylvania and James Iredell of the United States Supreme Court steadily escalated their attacks upon political journalism and ultimately pressed for criminal libel indictments.

Addison, president of the courts of common pleas of Pennsylvania's fifth circuit and one of the chief architects of the state's constitutional provision on libel, repeatedly lectured grand juries on the correct principles of republicanism and on the necessity of checking popular passions. Although Addison believed that a portion of the electorate lacked the good sense to elect the best men, he thought that this could be "corrected by extension of knowledge and a decent respect for wisdom and experience." There existed, however, a much more serious threat to republicanism. The greatest source of political evil, Addison claimed, "arises from those parties, divisions and distinctions, which our weakness or wickedness excite among us, and which factious, disappointed, and intriguing men lay hold of to promote their base and malignant views, and raise themselves to consequence."[58]

In most of his published grand jury charges, Addison warned that licentious criticism from factious writers and speakers could corrupt public opinion and thereby undermine popular confidence in good officials and in good governments. In June 1792, he first alerted grand jurors to the "dangerous tendency" of libels "against public officers or authority." In 1794, he recommended that grand jurors consider indictments against the persons who had erected "liberty poles" prior to the outbreak of the Whiskey Rebellion. "It is not *acts* of violence alone which constitute offences," he instructed. "Offences may be committed by writing, by words or by other signs of an evil purpose. The mere act of raising a pole is, in itself, a harmless thing; the question is, what is the meaning of it." The following year, he condemned "the set of people known by the name of *electioneering men*," those who tried to corrupt public opinion by stirring up "some public grievance" or by falsely agitating on "some popular subject of discontent." "Let us [also] put out of fashion," he urged, "the practices of candidates running around the country soliciting votes and interests for their election." In March 1797 he singled out newspaper printers whose objective was "not so much to inform the judgment by just knowledge as to excite passion and curiosity, and support the party that will best support their custom."[59] Thus, Addison's impassioned (and oft-reprinted) defense of the Sedition Act of 1798 rested upon his long-standing conviction that under a republican system of government, one that included constitutional protection for free debate and for political criticism, public officials could still legitimately proceed against "libelous" political publications.[60]

James Iredell's jury charges, like those of Addison, anticipated many of the arguments used by Federalists between 1798 and 1801 to defend the Sedition Act. Iredell shared Addison's fears about the corruption of public opinion by licentious political partisans. Especially in a large republic, Justice Iredell warned in 1796, "there will be always ill disposed men, ready to take advantage of opportunities to do mischief" by misrepresenting political personalities. In May of 1797 at Richmond, Virginia, Iredell delivered a grand jury charge that even his sympathetic biographer considered an "animated, perhaps too warm" attack on the critics of John Adams, the Federalist who had assumed the presidency only two months earlier. Public officials, Iredell maintained, possessed the clear "right to expect that their conduct would not immediately be condemned merely because some persons are ready to find fault with it." Before attacking the policy of a public official, he claimed, critics "ought be very sure that a better [policy] could be adopted."[61] Any person who would "indulge in atrocious calumny" without giving an officer a fair test, must "stand in the view of his fellow-citizens as a slanderer. . . ." Alluding to the nation's internal divisions at a time of increasing foreign dangers, Iredell warned that "if we suffer differences of opinion to corrode into enmity, jealousy to rankle into distrust, weak men to delude by their folly, abandoned men to disturb society by their crimes, we must expect nothing but a fate as ruinous as it would be disgraceful. . . ."[62]

Iredell's charge produced a minor political tempest when grand jurors returned an indictment, under national common law, against Congressman Samuel J. Cabell of Virginia for criminal libel. Jeffersonians immediately protested Iredell's charge and the indictment, but Justice Iredell defended both his own conduct, claiming he had not intended to target Cabell for prosecution, and the action of the grand jury. The following year, shortly before his death, Iredell reiterated his views on the desirability of libel prosecutions in the course of a lengthy defense of the Sedition Act.[63]

Addison and Iredell were both strongly partisan Federalists, but support for some type of legal restraint on the press was not limited to members of the party of Washington, Hamilton, and Adams. Thomas McKean, one of Pennsylvania's leading Jeffersonians, was already on the record as favoring libel prosecutions, and in 1797 and 1798 he began to pursue William Cobbett, an arch-Federalist editor, with every bit as much zeal as he had harassed Eleazer Oswald a decade earlier.

When Cobbett was accused in 1797 of libeling Spain's minister to the United States, who was about to become McKean's son-in-law, the chief justice reiterated and reemphasized the position he had taken in Eleazer Oswald's contempt case. The level of Pennsylvania's journalism, McKean urged, was "so scandalous to our government, and detestable in the eyes of all good men," that the situation cried "aloud for redress." Libels against public officials, he charged grand jurors, were even more heinous than defamation of private individuals. Political libels carried "a direct tendency to breed in the people a dislike of their governors, and incline them to faction and sedition." Nothing in Pennsylvania's constitutional guarantee of free expression, he ruled, automatically exempted publishers from criminal penalties, even if they had published the truth. Suggesting a kind of "truth-plus" test for criminal libel prosecutions, McKean argued that writers "must take care in their publications, that they are decent, candid, and true; that they are for the purpose of reformation and not for defamation; and that they have an eye solely to the public good."[64]

Cobbett answered McKean in a bitter pamphlet entitled *The Democratic Judge*. The fiery editor, who called himself "Peter Porcupine," claimed that McKean's view of libel law emasculated guarantees of free expression. According to Cobbett, McKean's emphasis upon the dangers of political libels violated the spirit, if not the letter, of Pennsylvania's constitution of 1790. And Cobbett sarcastically argued that McKean's truth-plus test—his requirement that critical statements be "decent, candid," and with "an eye solely to the public good"—belied any claim that, under a republican constitution, the truth could be no libel. McKean's legal formula, Cobbett complained, left "a pretty latitude for quibble and contestation! Not only the *facts* are to be established and the *manner* and *stile* approved by the court, but even the *motives* of the writer are to be enquired into, and may be construed into a ground for punishing him!"[65] Even in Pennsylvania, with its constitutional provision, the legal definition of free expression, Cobbett concluded, seemed so vague that the liberties of speech and press were really no safer in the United States than in Great Britain.[66] Despite his personal fears about the American law of libel, however, Peter Porcupine escaped McKean's legal guns, at least temporarily, when grand jurors rejected the chief justice's prompting and refused to return an indictment for criminal libel.[67]

In 1798, however, the major push for legal restrictions on political expression came not from Jeffersonians but from those who favored the cause of Federalism. Throughout the 1790s, many people who found themselves drawn to the Federalist political position gradually came to accept the necessity for some type of legal restraint on partisan debate. Thus, the Sedition Act of 1798 represented more than a sudden partisan move against Jeffersonians or a hasty attempt to meet a "foreign" threat. The decision to use libel law culminated a lengthy public debate about the wisdom of having a system of political communication that provided no legal checks upon "licentious" expression.

Between 1798 and 1800, Federalist speakers and writers continued to argue the issue of libel and freedom of expression with their political opponents. An examination of this debate—generally ignored by historians, who have assumed that Federalists had little of substance to offer and who have therefore concentrated upon the views of the Jeffersonian "libertarians"—can provide a broader framework with which to examine the familiar controversy over the Sedition Act.[68]

Chapter Four | The Era of the Sedition Act
and First-Amendment Thought

Although leaders of the Washington administration did not believe that the First Amendment prevented them from prosecuting political speech, only Alexander Hamilton was prepared to brave the political storms that national libel prosecutions would produce. But as partisan passions intensified, prominent Federalists urged an end to the cautious approach of the Washington administration.

The Sedition Act of 1798

Alexander Hamilton again led the way, but other Federalists were no longer far behind. Hamilton's celebrated "Reynolds Pamphlet" of 1797, in which the former treasury secretary denied charges of public wrongdoing but admitted an extramarital affair with one Mrs. Maria Reynolds, began with a scathing attack upon the Jeffersonian press. "The spirit of jacobinism," Hamilton claimed, menaced the republic. "A principal engine, by which this spirit endeavors to accomplish its purposes" was a carefully calculated assault on the reputations of prominent public leaders. The "most direct falsehoods" were invented; lies that had been "often detected and refuted" were "still revived and repeated, in the hope that the refutation may have been forgotten or that the frequency and boldness of accusation" would fool the public; the "most profligate men" were bribed with money and political favors "to become informers and accusors"; and when all these tactics failed, the agents of Jacobinism continued "in corroding whispers to wear away the reputations which they could not directly subvert." These "conspirators against honest fame," against the well-deserved reputations of high public officials, considered nothing sacred. "Even the peace of an unoffending and amiable wife is a welcome repast to their insatiate fury. . . . Even the great and multiplied services, the tried and rarely equalled virtues of a WASHINGTON;" could not escape this "conspiracy of vice against virtue. . . ."[1]

Two years later, in 1799, Hamilton successfully urged the attorney general of New York, Josiah Ogden Hoffman, to prosecute *Greenleaf's New Daily Advertiser* for repeating rumors that Hamilton had tried to suppress William Duane's *Aurora*. Expanding upon the analysis of the "Reynolds Pamphlet,"

Hamilton argued that "public motives" compelled him to abandon his once-settled policy of not invoking libel laws against his critics. His Jeffersonian adversaries, Hamilton charged, had "of late acquired a degree of system which renders them formidable." He continued: "One principal Engine for effecting the scheme is by audacious falsehoods to destroy the confidence of the people in all those who are in any degree conspicuous among the supporters of the Government: an Engine which had been employed in time past with too much success, and which unless counteracted in the future is likely to be attended with the very fatal consequences. To counteract it is therefore a duty to the community."[2]

By 1799, the Federalist leadership had already joined Hamilton and mounted a full-scale legal attack against their critics. Accompanying the enactment of the Sedition Act of 1798 and a series of highly publicized libel prosecutions, Federalist leaders also orchestrated an extensive public relations effort in order to promote their views about the legal limits on political expression. Between 1798 and 1801 Federalists and Jeffersonians fought both legal and rhetorical battles over the role of libel law in a republican polity. The United States' first experience with prosecutions for political speech and its initial attempt to find the legal meaning of free expression began under ominous circumstances.

Between 1796 and 1800 partisan political differences produced a full-scale constitutional crisis, one that ultimately focused on the issue of free speech and the law of libel. Controversies over the direction of foreign policy widened congressional and popular divisions; Washington's retirement removed a formidable obstacle to the development of an opposition faction; the rising prestige of Thomas Jefferson, despite his loss to John Adams in the presidential contest of 1796, provided a focus for the Democratic-Republican coalition; and the vehemence of newspaper rhetoric embittered the entire political atmosphere. Conflict threatened to spill over traditional channels, bringing more and more white males into the political maelstrom and "democratizing" politics in a nation where the political elite feared democracy. Events and issues came to be framed in apocalyptic terms. All previous republics, jeremiads warned, had ended in disaster; the new American republic, many people feared, was headed for a similarly unhappy fate.

Emergence of interstate factions or parties so soon after creation of the constitutional system of 1787 appeared to be a particular reason for concern. The mainstream political culture of late eighteenth-century America did not include the idea of a permanent party system, one in which organized groups regularly competed for political power. Anglo-American political thought emphasized the need for harmony and consensus, not organized contention. Even as they were building and maintaining political organizations, state and national leaders continually insisted that their efforts really aimed at the ex-tinction of partisan divisions. They saw themselves organizing temporary groups, composed of like-minded patriots, in order to defend the republican revolution against its domestic enemies. When victorious, their partisans would disband.

Thus, few Jeffersonians and even fewer Federalists considered their rivals to be members of a legitimate political organization that was committed to republicanism and the Constitution of 1787. Jeffersonians viewed Federalists as supporters of an antirepublican cabal, and their publications condemned the measures of the Washington and Adams administrations as the machinations of pro-British, pseudo-aristocratic regimes. Rallying around the Constitution, Jeffersonians justified their opposition as a desperate defense of basic constitutional principles. They attacked Federalists for "violating" the fundamental law of 1787 and called for strict construction of the powers of the national government in order to preserve basic liberties, including the right of free expression. Ever since the establishment of the new national government in 1789, claimed Abraham Bishop, "freedom of the press and of opinion had been restrained; federal measures have been presented to the people, *highly colored and embellished with cuts.*" By limiting and manipulating the terms of political discourse, Bishop charged, Federalist leaders had tried to keep citizens in "a state of peaceful submission to the constituted authorities."[3]

Federalist writers cited statements like Abraham Bishop's as proof of their thesis that Jeffersonians were appealing to people's passions by gross exaggerations and outright falsehoods. As the jury charges of Alexander Addison and James Iredell suggested, Federalists liked to picture Democratic-Republican leaders as demagogic Francophiles, wild-eyed mobocrats whose libels and slanders threatened the safety of republican institutions.[4]

By the summer of 1798 Federalist leaders believed that a dangerous situation had become desperate. Overseas, the United States appeared headed for war with France; at home, the rapidly expanding Jeffersonian political machine promised a serious challenge in the elections of 1800. In response, the Federalist-controlled Congress, with the assent of President John Adams, passed a series of measures that they claimed would protect the republic from its foreign and domestic enemies. The program included higher taxes, reorganization of the armed forces, a new Naturalization Act, and the infamous Alien and Sedition laws. (General James Lloyd of Maryland, the same man who had used the press as a means of fighting political libels back in 1794, introduced the Sedition bill.)[5] Jeffersonian publicists viewed the Alien and Sedition measures, particularly the latter, as the primary weapons in the Federalist arsenal.

Section II of the Sedition Act made it a crime to utter or disseminate "any false, scandalous and malicious" comments about the government, members of Congress, or the President "with the intent to defame" them or to excite against them "the hatred of the good people of the United States." (Several days later, Congress passed another measure, which supplemented the Sedition Act; it provided for imposition of good behavior bonds as an additional means of controlling people who had been convicted of making seditious utterances.) After rejecting a one-year limitation and not even considering a period coextensive with a time of actual national emergency, the Federalist majority extended the measure until 3 March 1801, the end of John Adams's first term as president.[6]

Despite the act's obviously partisan features, such as its length of enforcement, the law's Federalist supporters (and some later historians) stressed the foreign danger and the government's "natural" right of self-protection, including its right of punishing "licentious" criticism. "It is so essential to regular society to restrain and prevent" libels upon government and upon political leaders, argued Charles Lee of Virginia, "that in all ages and all countries and under all forms of government, they are forbidden and punished." Another Virginia Federalist, Thomas Evans, maintained that the Sedition Act spelled out offenses that were "*evil in themselves*, and therefore not only prohibited by common law, but by the law of nature, and the original principles of society." Referring to Virginia's own wartime sedition act of 1776, Evans asked "what would the spirit of '76 have said or done" if troublemakers had criticized this law in the same scurrilous manner that Jeffersonians were attacking the Sedition Law? "Let those who remember that period decide."[7] By the time Federalist leaders began to apply the law, however, few suggested parallels to the Revolutionary era. The wartime analogy, of course, became largely inoperative after John Adams opened peace negotiations with France in early 1799.

A Firmness of Faith: Federalists and the Law of Libel

Although the brief war scare of 1798 helped to justify the Sedition Act, the desire of many Federalists to prosecute Jeffersonians for political libels had its roots in the political conflict of the 1790s. This same desire continued after the French threat had passed and during the period when Jeffersonian political fortunes were rising. Despite clear evidence of the Sedition Act's unpopularity, many prominent Federalists underscored their commitment to its basic principles. On several occasions, Federalists in Congress urged extension of the Sedition Act, and in January of 1800 Senator James Bayard sought a declaratory resolution that would have proclaimed that all the offenses specified in the Sedition Act "shall remain punishable at common law" after the act's demise. All the while, Federalists argued that whatever the precise source of legal authority, the country needed more, not fewer, prosecutions for political libel.[8]

Adapting arguments from the 1780s and 1790s and following the same legal paths as James Wilson and Alexander Addison, Federalists took their case to the public. Frequent use of political libel prosecutions, they contended, conflicted neither with general principles of republicanism nor with specific constitutional guarantees. They were not enemies of free expression, Federalists claimed; their libel prosecutions aimed at enhancing enlightened expression and improving political knowledge. Even a cursory look at the public prints, Federalists maintained, showed that a portion of the press was not really "free." A number of newspapers and printers had fallen under the domination of a selfish faction whose leaders were trying to mislead voters into rejecting the best men and their policies.[9]

Most Federalist writers and speakers took considerable care to distinguish their views from the old Blackstonian theory that all political criticism endangered the body politic and was therefore illegal. When citizens used the right to criticize public officials "temperately, rationally and amicably," argued Henry Lee, "it may affect much good and can produce no mischief." But there was considerable difference, he continued, "between the candid censure of a friend, and the malignant aspersions of a vindictive foe." A Federalist pamphleteer from New Jersey expressed a similar theme: Jeffersonians were perverting the right of free expression by puffing undoubted mistakes by Federal office holders into examples of one vast and sinister conspiracy. "The *delinquency* of a petty *officer* becomes an *offence* in the *government*; and the accidental preference of an unworthy candidate for a subaltern appointment, is charged against it as a premeditated wrong!" Even casual conversations and satirical remarks, he charged, were being "exhibited as proofs of treason, of confessions of corruption."[10]

Jeffersonians often invoked the Revolutionary principle of popular sovereignty in their attacks on the Sedition Act, but Federalists could appeal to the same doctrine. Libels on public officials—the men who were merely the agents of the sovereign people—really amounted to attacks upon the people themselves. Just as citizens possessed a personal interest in their individual reputations and a "natural right to an adequate remedy" of libels against their personal characters, so the "people of the United States" possessed "a common interest in their government, and sustain[ed] in common the injury which affects the government" as a result of libelous attacks on public officials. "The people of the United States therefore have the right to the remedy for that injury," continued a prominent Virginia Federalist, "and are substantially the party seeking redress" in political libel prosecutions.[11]

The law of political libel, Federalists often emphasized, provided necessary stability in a republican polity. Adapting one of the central themes of eighteenth-century "country" literature, the dangerous consequences of unchecked corruption, Federalists argued that libel prosecutions prevented the destruction of one of the central pillars of republicanism—public opinion. Prosecutions against political defamation, contended James Iredell, were even more necessary in the United States than in a monarchy "because in a republic more is dependent upon the good opinion of the people . . . as they are, directly or indirectly, the origin of all authority. . . . Take away from a republic the confidence of the people, and the whole fabric crumbles to dust." The national government, James Bayard argued, "is immediately bottomed on public opinion. . . . The Government is bound not to deceive the people, and it is equally bound not to suffer them to be deceived." Public officials possessed a duty to defend the public "against deception, and when they are rightly informed, there is no doubt but, in their turn, they will defend the government."[12]

As they defended the necessity for the Sedition Act, Federalist jurists like Iredell and Addison found themselves trapped within their republican world view. They simply could not understand critics who denounced their ideas on "free" expression as antirepublican, because they considered their own position in perfect harmony with republican principles. Throughout the 1790s Judges Iredell and Addison used grand jury charges as means of instructing citizens on the "true" meaning of republicanism. Both thought that the constitutional framework of 1787 embodied the best political forms and processes that human minds could ever devise. And as partisan Federalists, they also believed that the "wise and virtuous" men who had held office during the decade of the nineties consistently demonstrated their commitment to the maintenance of this system. So, when the results of day-to-day political life seemed increasingly at odds with their visions of consensus, republican harmony, and elite rule, they could not help but despair for the future of the republic.[13]

Unable to imagine a future beyond the present they saw crumbling, Iredell and Addison retreated to one of the most orthodox tenets of republican thought: the idea that the fate of all republics ultimately rested upon the character, spirit, wisdom, and virtue of the citizenry. As they viewed the events of the 1790s, the crucial divisions were not between different socioeconomic groups, or between different political factions, or even between people with disparate visions of republicanism. Instead, it seemed to them that conflicts pitted the worthy and virtuous against the unworthy and the vicious. The "system of slander" against governmental leaders, argued Addison, represented the natural strategy of unworthy schemers. "How can men without virtue or talents," he asked, "rise into consequence but by slander? . . ." Similarly, Iredell traced "libels" against the nation's best men to the base characters of their detractors. "A virtuous conduct will ever be hated by vicious men," he told grand jurors in Charleston.[14]

A wise and virtuous people, who could produce an informed public opinion, became the main focus of these Federalist jurists who defended the Sedition Act. In the view of Judges Iredell and Addison, vicious, lying, and sinister men were intentionally misusing the organs of mass communication for the systematic misrepresentation of public measures and public officials. "The liberty of the press is indeed valuable," proclaimed Justice Iredell. "A pen in the hand of an able and virtuous man may enlighten a whole nation," but the "same pen in the hands of a man equally able, but with vices as great as the other's virtues, may, by arts of sophistry easily attainable, and inflaming the passions of weak minds delude many into opinions the most dangerous, and conduct them to actions the most criminal."[15]

In defending the use of libel prosecutions to end the corruption of political criticism, these Federalists rejected the idea that the marketplace of ideas contained some sort of self-regulating mechanism that guaranteed that truth would ultimately triumph over falsehood. According to Alexander Addison, "truth has but one side: and listening to error and falsehoods is indeed a strange way to discover truth." Certainty in politics, as in religion, could be obtained without having to suffer the voices and the pens of heretics.[16] Other Federalists were less dogmatic on this point than Addison, but they also questioned the claim that truth would always drive falsehood from the battlefield of ideas. Libelous falsehoods, argued George Taylor of Virginia, would always find believers, especially when slanderers touched the more talented members of the community; this type of defamation could do all sorts of mischief "before the truth could arrive to detect and protect" both individuals and the public. Falsehood, Taylor theorized, "was light and volatile," spreading its "mischiefs with inconceivable velocity. . . ." In contrast, "truth was the child of experience, and the companion of time; she scarcely ever outstripped, and rarely kept pace" with falsehood.[17]

At one point, Federalists were even able, at least to their satisfaction, to demonstrate the insidious nature of political falsehoods. During debates in 1801 over an attempt by Federalists to extend the operative date of the Sedition Act, an ill-informed Jeffersonian member of Congress claimed that a printer from Massachusetts had died in prison after being convicted under the Sedition Act. Federalists gleefully pointed out that the defendant had, in reality, been convicted under state common law and, more important, that he was alive, well, and circulating new "slanders" against Federalism! Although Jeffersonians in Congress might have used this exchange to show that, in fact, free debate could expose falsehoods, Federalists seized the initiative. According to Harrison Gray Otis, the incident demonstrated that "outrageous falsehoods" could even "sink deep into the minds of men in high stations, and bear directly upon the measures of this House and government." What, then, might happen when such inflammatory libels infected "the gaping and promiscuous crowd who delight to swallow calumny?"[18]

In part, such fears were self-serving. They grew out of the accurate assessment that pro-Jeffersonian newspapers were more partisan in tone and much more closely tied to Republican leaders than the numerous pro-Federalist papers. Federalists doubted, with some good reason, that all the people who had been exposed to Republican "lies" would secure equal access to Federalist "truths."

Yet many Federalists raised a question that still troubles observers of the media: how can citizens be certain that, largely freed from public controls, a private system of communication will throw up a countervailing truth for every innocent or deliberate political lie? In 1801 Samuel Dana of Connecticut, for example, conceded that, "upon general principles, truth may be said to be an antidote to falsehood." In practice, however, "truth does not always make its appearance in time," particularly when political partisans deliberately spread malicious lies. Few political newspapers granted people they had criticized any chance to reply. "How often," asked Dana, "are calumnies and falsehoods published against the Government; but when is a contradiction of these falsehoods seen in the same paper?" As a result, he and other Federalists charged, even the most intelligent citizens could be deceived by clever slanderers. "When falsehoods are stated in newspapers as facts, and remain uncontradicted," argued James Bayard, "what chance is there for their not being believed?" Criminal penalties should apply only "when known falsehood is maliciously published," Bayard proposed. But prosecutions under such a standard of liability were needed, he believed, to purify the channels of communication and to ensure an enlightened public opinion.[19]

In addition to their theories on the formation and the corruption of public opinion, prominent Federalists emphasized a theme, first raised during newspaper debates during the 1780s, that has long remained the key justification for political libel suits: without a rational system of controls over political debate, a republican nation could not be assured of enlightened leadership. According to Alexander Addison, the nation's "wisest and best public officers"—undoubtedly a reference to, among others, Alexander Hamilton—"have had their lives embittered, and have been driven from their stations by unceasing and malignant slander." Effective libel laws prevented scurrilous newspaper writers and pamphleteers from robbing upright citizens of their reputations and, more important, from depriving the nation of the services of the best men.[20]

The Sedition Act's champions could also cast themselves as defenders of republican values by emphasizing how the law departed from the orthodox rules of seditious libel. In its final form, the act had incorporated the Zengerian principles: a defendant could "give in his defense, the truth of the matter contained in the publication as a libel," and the jury could "determine the law and the facts under the direction of the court, as in other cases."[21] According to the act's chief congressional architect, Robert Goodloe Harper of South Carolina, a jury could convict someone of political libel only after determining that the publication was false, scandalous, malicious, and published with criminal intent. "If in any one of these points, the proof should fail, the man may be acquitted." And, he added, proof of truth would be a complete defense to any indictment.[22] Outside of Congress, Federalist interpretations of the Sedition Law seemed equally libertarian in nature. Judge Addison claimed that juries must be satisfied that the actions of the government or of public officials had been legitimate and that the criticism of them had been both "false and malicious." Justice Iredell advanced a standard of liability even more favorable to defendants: "If the writing be false, and yet not malicious, or malicious and not false, no conviction can take place." Such a construction, he suggested, would protect "any publication arising from inadvertency, mistake, false confidence, or anything short of a wilful and atrocious falsehood." And in the trial of James Callender for defamation of President Adams, Justice Samuel Chase claimed the jurors could acquit the defendant if they found the publication in question to be true, or if they believed it was made without malice and without any intent to defame the chief executive.[23]

Although most Jeffersonians immediately realized the limited practical value of the Zengerian principles, others hoped that popular opinion, ultimately in the form of enlightened juries, would frustrate execution of the Sedition Act. American citizens, George Nicholas told a crowd of Kentuckians, would never use such an unconstitutional measure "to enslave their country."[24]

In practice, however, neither legal rules nor popular opinion proved of much use to Jeffersonians who were prosecuted for libel. Between 1798 and 1800 Federalist officials instituted at least eighteen libel prosecutions—three under state common law and fifteen under the Sedition Act—against Jeffersonians. Several defendants in state prosecutions even went to trial under Blackstonian rules.[25] In 1799 the Supreme Court of Massachusetts rejected the *dicta* of the *Freeman* case, and state authorities prosecuted Abijah Adams of Boston's *Independent Chronicle* under the traditional rule "the greater the truth the greater the libel." That same year, a New York court declined to hear evidence of truth at the libel trial of David Frothingham and tried the defendant, a journeyman-foreman who had set the type for an article critical of Alexander Hamilton, under common law rules. Both were convicted. Directed by Secretary of State Timothy Pickering, the series of national prosecutions was clearly tied to the 1800 elections. Grand juries handed down indictments against four of the leading Jeffersonian papers and against several prominent Republicans, including Congressman Matthew Lyon of Vermont and Dr. Thomas Cooper. In theory, the Sedition Act's stricter standards of liability gave these defendants more protections than Adams or Frothingham, but the results of their trials were no different. Only one acquittal was recorded under the Sedition Act or state common law between 1798 and 1800.[26]

In one sense, the very nature of late eighteenth-century political rhetoric—with its heavy emphasis upon emotional appeals, moralistic judgments, and stereotyped villains—defeated much of the value of pleading truth. What facts could a Jeffersonian defendant offer to support the contention that President Adams dined with the "ridiculous pomp" of an aristocrat? And no attorney could even begin to find evidence to justify all the fantastic charges hurled by the roguish James Callender of the *Richmond Examiner*.[27]

The rulings of Federalist judges did not make the task of defense lawyers any easier. To the layperson, the Sedition Act guaranteed defendants the clear right to present proof of truth to the jury; but common law rules of pleading and evidence were not this simple. In the Callender prosecution, for example, Justice Samuel Chase refused to allow the defendant's lawyer to question John Taylor of Caroline about the truth of specific facts at issue. Justice Chase ruled that it would be improper to put defense witness after defense witness on the stand in hopes of scoring one small point after another; such a technique, he held, might fool jurors into believing that justification of one or two trivial points of fact satisfied the defendant's burden of substantiating every charge in its entirety. As Chase ruled in the prosecution of Dr. Thomas Cooper, common law precedents required that defendants justify every allegation "to the marrow."[28]

Finally, the political culture of the 1790s, including the new forms of political organization, negated the main line of defense used by defendants earlier in the eighteenth century—the hope that a jury would be able to decide more than the act of publication and to return a general verdict of guilty or not guilty. In the older political culture, which had framed most contests as a struggle between the liberties of the collective "people" and the powers of magistrates, most partisans and printers (though perhaps not isolated and unpopular dissenters) could vindicate their liberty of expression through a jury trial. Or like Eleazer Oswald and William Cobbett they could safely trust that grand juries would not hand down a libel indictment. From a very real standpoint, the constitutional right of free expression had been coextensive with the right to a trial of a jury of one's peers; it had not seemed necessary to move beyond the Zengerian position.

The new political culture undermined the protection of a jury trial. First, even though many members of the political community continued to view politics as a battle between the people and the magistrates, and even though Federalists and Republicans denounced one another's factions as illegitimate bands of ambitious schemers and deluded followers, national political conflict clearly revolved around competing parties or "proto-parties." Despite the powerful hold of older antiparty ideas, political leaders found themselves, as we have noted, building new types of political organizations. Although the Federalists of 1798–1800 do not quite fit William Nisbet Chambers's model of modern parties—"formations that exhibit developing consciousness and ideology, continuing organization or structure, and active appeals to a substantial electorate"—they could mobilize sufficient popular support to defeat Jeffersonian claims that a corrupt government was destroying the people's freedom of expression. No previous American political leaders had established such deep-rooted organizations. Equally as important, Federalists of the late 1790s displayed considerable organizational skill when managing the national judicial system. Federalist judges and marshals had little trouble in producing juries of hard-core Federalist partisans, men unlikely to be convinced by any type of Jeffersonian appeal. In his classic defense of John Peter Zenger, Andrew Hamilton did not have to face the kind of obstacles encountered by Jeffersonian attorneys like George Hay when he attempted to defend James Callender.[29]

The "New Libertarianism": The Jeffersonian Response

Even before the first prosecutions, some Jeffersonians explored new lines of defense. Most denied the authority of Congress to pass a seditious libel law or to undertake common law prosecutions. The Constitution itself granted national officials no such powers, and the First Amendment specifically reaffirmed the absence of congressional authority. The case against national authority for the Alien and Sedition Laws, of course, was presented most dramatically in the Virginia and Kentucky Resolutions of 1798 and 1799, documents secretly drafted by Madison and Jefferson. Historians have generally seen these resolutions as reflecting the Virginians' fervent devotion to states' rights and to strict constructionism. More recently, however, as scholars have come to appreciate the persistence of country ideas in American political culture, the documents seem to express a more general defense of individual liberties, one which opponents of Federalism had been developing throughout the 1790s. The principles of states' rights and strict constructionism, one historian has argued, can best be viewed as "necessary parts of a systematic defense of republican liberty against a conspiratorial [Federalist] threat," rather than as the essence of their political thought. In the view of these country-Republicans, Federalists were advocating a broad interpretation of national authority as one tactic in a larger strategy of overturning republican government.[30] Disputing the constitutionality of the Sedition Act, for example, Congressman John Nicholas of Virginia invoked *Cato*'s ideas about the potential danger of all governmental controls over speech and press. Recognition of any national authority over political expression, Nicholas claimed, would lead to greater and greater restraints and eventually to "unlimited power" over political criticism. Such fears were not illusory, he warned; history showed that "the Governments which have exercised control over the press have carried it the whole length."[31]

Jeffersonian writers also employed eighteenth-century country themes to bolster their second line of defense: the claim that freedom of expression was essential to the survival of other liberties. Although Jefferson and Madison failed to explore the meaning of free expression in the Virginia and Kentucky Resolutions, other Republican writers focused directly on the dangers of seditious libel prosecutions. Through the efforts of Leonard Levy, students of the First Amendment have been introduced to these once obscure works and their little-known authors—George Hay, Tunis Wortman, and John Thomson. In addition, Madison, though never Jefferson, joined the ranks of what Levy called the "new libertarians" when Madison authored the "Report on the Virginia Resolutions" in 1800. St. George Tucker's edition of *Blackstone's Commentaries* contained a lengthy appendix that rejected English libel doctrines.[32]

Many of the arguments in these tracts reframed and elaborated positions tentatively advanced by Jeffersonian members of Congress during debates over enactment of the Sedition Law. With Federalists occupying the traditional libertarian ground, Republicans moved on to stake out other legal positions. A few writers attacked the basic eighteenth-century formula for analysis of free expression cases—the distinction between liberty and licentiousness. Such a vague formula (the eighteenth-century analogue of the "clear and present danger" test) really defined nothing, claimed John Nicholas and John Thomson; it merely cloaked suppression of unpopular views under the thin veil of licentiousness. And these Republican publicists, all too aware of the limited value of pleading truth in Federalist-controlled courts, argued that political critics could rarely supply evidence to support all of their contentions. There were "many truths important to society," claimed George Hay, that were not "susceptible to that full, direct, and positive evidence, which can be exhibited before a court and jury." Criticism of public officials, argued Madison, was rarely framed in terms of facts alone, but invariably consisted of a mingling of facts with unprovable opinions and inferences. No one, suggested Albert Gallatin, could demonstrate the validity of most political opinions to nonbelievers. Thus, the mere existence of a sedition law, according to Nicholas and Hay, would have a chilling effect on free expression. Inevitably, cautious printers and writers would over-censor themselves, withholding information and ideas they considered difficult to justify in a court of law.[33]

At least two Jeffersonians, Tunis Wortman and John Thomson, went beyond these arguments and rejected entirely the idea of seditious libel, the notion that the government could be attacked, and its security threatened, by words alone. Wortman's *Inquiry*, "the book Jefferson did not write but should have," broke with eighteenth-century orthodoxy and offered the distinction, so central to later libertarian analyses, between speech and action. "Criminal prosecutions for libels," he argued in contrast to the Orthodox Whig view, "can never be necessary to preserve public tranquillity; the coercion of Violence is abundantly sufficient for that purpose." Criminal penalties interrupted the search for truth in all areas of human experience; in the case of political speech, they inhibited the public debate so necessary for the survival of republicanism and freedom. Wortman disputed the claim of Federalist judges like Samuel Chase (and Democratic-Republican ones like Thomas McKean) that citizens could trust the courts to determine in a criminal prosecution whether false statements had been intended to inform or to mislead, to offer legitimate criticism or simply to vilify. "Nothing can be more difficult," Wortman argued, "than to pronounce with certainty upon the sincerity of the man who may have misstated the transactions of Government. How can it be ascertained what portion of actual Malevolence and how much of mistaken Zeal, existed within his mind? Shall I be imprisoned for credulity, or fined upon account of my imbecility of understanding?" Criminal restraints upon criticism of governmental measures, argued Wortman, were far more dangerous than publication of the most scurrilous political lies. Libel prosecutions were "invariably more formidable than the evil they are intended to prevent."[34]

The arguments of the new libertarians were not entirely novel. Most, for example, drew a familiar analogy and claimed that the broad liberty to discuss religious matters applied in the political realm as well. Freedom of discussion, these writers argued, was indivisible. And much as Andrew Hamilton had done in the *Zenger* case, George Hay suggested that Jeffersonian views about freedom of the press merely represented the necessary and logical extension of a broad popular understanding about freedom of speech. "It is obvious in itself and it is admitted by all men," claimed Hay, that only the law of defamation, insofar as it protected individual reputations, limited the right of citizens to speak their minds. On political issues, Hay insisted, people had become accustomed to unfettered speech; they should, he argued, enjoy the same type of freedom with printing presses. "A man may say every thing which his passion can suggest; he may employ all his time, and all his talents, if he is wicked enough to do so, in *speaking* against the government matters that are false, scandalous, and malicious. . . . If the freedom of speech means . . . the privilege of speaking *any thing* without control, the words freedom of the press . . . mean the privilege of printing *any thing* without control."[35] The Jeffersonians' claim that their published views did nothing more than articulate a popular understanding of free expression may have been a self-serving position, but it may also have been an accurate one. Certainly their contention that political libel prosecutions had virtually disappeared in the 1780s and early 1790s was correct.[36]

Similarly, the views of Jeffersonian pamphleteers on libel law were not entirely new. In opposing criminal prosecutions, for example, Tunis Wortman relied heavily on policy arguments from *Cato's Letters*. Though prior to 1798, few, if any, lawyers had used *Cato*'s broad themes in order to press beyond the Zengerian standards of liability, the Jeffersonians were not the first to recognize the potential limits of these guarantees. Andrew Hamilton was defending powerful critics of an unpopular administration in the *Zenger* case, and he was perfectly content to rest his case upon the argument that "*Truth* ought to govern the whole affair of libels." But he also suggested that "the party accused runs risk enough even then; for if he fails to prove every title of what he has wrote, and to the satisfaction of the court and Jury too, he may find to his cost, that if the prosecution is set on foot by men in power, it seldom wants friends to faun it."[37] Similar doubts existed among ordinary citizens. In 1782, when Eleazer Oswald was facing the threat of prosecution, some of his supporters pointedly argued that the defense of truth really offered insufficient protection for political critics. "Even mistakes in matter of fact, not proceeding from design, and malice, ought to escape punishment," one contributor to Oswald's paper suggested. If courts displayed "too much severity toward such mistakes," they would make the right of free expression "a nullity." "Restrain the licentiousness," Oswald himself bitterly complained, "and you in effect demolish the liberty of the press." And in 1798, before the Jeffersonian lawyers issued their written protests, popular meetings in Kentucky adopted resolutions that advanced ideas similar to those found in the tracts by the new libertarians.[38]

Finally, the Jeffersonian libertarians stayed within the confines of familiar eighteenth-century ideas when they discussed the whole process of political communication. Tunis Wortman's lengthy analysis, for example, glossed over the new realities of political life, particularly the emergence of competing factions and party presses and generally treated the whole issue of free expression in an anachronistic, nonparty context. In the best antiparty tradition of republican thought, he maintained that a truthful and open government, an administration devoted to virtue and the public good, could easily combat the misrepresentations of divisive individuals; such a government, in fact, would prevent the growth of political factions. "There can be no room for jealousy and suspicion where nothing is mysterious and concealed. Faction is confounded and appalled by the powerful lustre which surrounds a system of Virtue."[39]

Wortman's discussion failed to confront Federalist charges that partisan presses were maliciously slandering the government and corrupting public opinion. In Wortman's analysis, "the Press," like "the people," was a corporate entity. It was the "natural" ally of the cause of "the people" and the cause of public liberty. When unfettered by libel prosecutions and freed from corrupt officials, the "natural direction" of the press "will always be towards Truth and Virtue. It is by no means surprising that Ambition should always be jealous of so formidable and discerning an Opponent."[40]

Despite the obvious fact that he and his fellow Jeffersonians were themselves organizing partisan newspaper–presses, Wortman emphasized the role of individual republican citizens in the opinion-making process. Out of the exchange of individual views—exchanges facilitated by the printing press—came truth, a commodity that Wortman tended to identify with public opinion. A good and virtuous government would never seek to suppress public opinion. "As the guardian of Public Liberty," public opinion would "lose its powers and its usefulness the moment it is rendered dependent upon the Government. The stream must flow in the direction to which it naturally inclines. . . . [T]he infliction of Penalty, instead of being a wholesome corrective of Falsehood, will . . . infallibly destroy that censorial jurisdiction of Society which is the only salutary preservative of Public Liberty and Justice. . . ."[41]

Although the Jeffersonian libertarians considered the Sedition Act unconstitutional, they did not quite endorse absolute freedom of political expression. In most of their writings, they shifted the focus from protection of government as an institution and from concern about attacks on governmental policies to protection for reputations of public officials and to slanders upon the good names of the best men. In summarizing his argument, Tunis Wortman carefully specified the limits of his analysis. "As far as the interests of Government, in its collective capacity are concerned, it has been a principal object of this work to prove, that no necessity can exist for the criminal suppression of Libel." But Wortman made it clear that the good name of public officials still possessed some value in the marketplace of ideas.[42]

Wortman and the other new libertarians rejected Federalist doctrines of seditious libel; they did not, by this, advocate an end to all political libel cases. In language not much different from James Wilson's, St. George Tucker decried attacks on the reputations of leading political figures. "The right of character is a sacred and valuable right," wrote the American Blackstone, "and is not forfeited by accepting a public employment."[43]

Jeffersonian theorists disagreed on how public officials could protect their reputations. Although they denied national officers any power to prosecute libels in national courts, James Madison and St. George Tucker suggested that officials of the central government might seek remedies, including, apparently, criminal ones, in state courts. A libelous attack on public officials, claimed Tucker, constituted "a crime against the community as well as against the individual." Madison and Tucker would have personally advocated acceptance of at least the Zengerian standards in state prosecutions, but no authoritative precedents would have barred trials under Blackstonian rules in their own state of Virginia. Although George Hay went beyond his fellow Virginians to reject state as well as national libel prosecutions, he suggested civil libel suits as a means of protecting the reputations of public officials and of controlling political scurrility. In his pamphlet of 1799, Hay concluded that constitutional guarantees allowed an individual to publish "what he pleases *provided he does no injury to any other individual*."[44] Political writers, like other citizens, were subject to civil liability if they defamed anyone, including persons who held political office.

Tunis Wortman's views were less clear. Much of his book, as a young Federalist reviewer named Daniel Webster noted, was repetitious, and his grasp of legal issues (including some very basic ones) often shaky. It might be argued, for example, that Wortman even approved, under some circumstances, criminal libel prosecutions by individual politicians. He made it clear that public officials who became the targets for libelous attacks on their "private character" should "be placed upon the same footing with a private individual." Presumably, this would include the right to seek criminal action against anyone who attacked their good names. Moreover, when Wortman specifically endorsed legal action against personal defamation, he constantly referred to such cases as prosecutions rather than as civil lawsuits. The threat of such prosecutions was real: the most famous Jeffersonian libel prosecution, that of Federalist Harry Croswell in 1804, involved alleged libels against the private conduct of President Jefferson.[45]

Despite the ambiguity of Wortman's prose, it does seem likely that he simply misused the term prosecution and meant to offer civil libel suits as the appropriate protection against scurrilous writers and as the most effective "check upon the licentiousness of the Press." He argued that "private prosecutions, at the suit of the injured party," provided "a real compensation for the injury" to reputation and were "much less likely to be rendered a dangerous weapon in the hands of a prevailing party, or an aspiring administration," than criminal prosecutions.[46]

Civil suits did, in fact, offer an alternative to criminal libel actions. And in Pennsylvania, civil libel law had already done what criminal prosecutions had not—shut down the presses of the notorious "Peter Porcupine." In 1797, it will be remembered, William Cobbett had escaped the snare of criminal libel when a grand jury refused to heed Thomas McKean's plea for an indictment. But the Porcupine's escape proved only temporary. In the summer of 1797, Dr. Benjamin Rush, the prominent Philadelphia physician and political figure, sued Cobbett for civil defamation. When the case finally came to trial two years later, Cobbett, anticipating that he would face a partisan jury, had already fled Philadelphia for New York. Indeed, the jury awarded Rush $5000, a crushing judgment, which ultimately helped persuade Cobbett to return, with his venom-dipped quills, to England.[47]

Rush's civil suit was, in fact, only part of Cobbett's problems with McKean and with Pennsylvania's libel laws. In August 1797, before the judicial determination that Cobbett's publications were libelous, McKean imposed good-behavior bonds totalling $4000 against Cobbett and his two sureties. When Cobbett continued to print stories that the chief justice and his son, now Pennsylvania's attorney general, considered defamatory, the state sued Cobbett and his sureties for recovery of the peace bonds. At the trial, which finally took place in 1800, Cobbett was represented by William Lewis, the former attorney general who had prosecuted Eleazer Oswald in 1789. Now an ardent Federalist, Lewis argued that Pennsylvania's Democratic-Republicans were violating the state's constitutional provision on freedom of expression.

The whole procedure binding Cobbett to good behavior, Lewis correctly charged, amounted to a subterfuge. Under it, the McKeans could, in effect, charge and try Cobbett for libel without having to secure a grand jury indictment. Attorney General McKean defended both the proceeding's legality—this suit, he claimed, was "merely a civil action" to recover Cobbett's debt to the state on his forfeited bond, which still required a trial by a petit jury—and its political propriety. Cobbett's publications, McKean continued, were "replete with gall and wormwood, without an atom of useful information to the public mind." Unable to resist a partisan gibe, McKean wondered why William Lewis, who had argued that neither a grand nor a petit jury was needed in the *Oswald* case, had suddenly become such a defender of free expression. In any event, McKean added, the Democratic-Republicans were showing no partiality: the faction led by Thomas McKean was preparing to use a similar proceeding against the *Aurora*'s William Duane, a dissident Jeffersonian "radical."[48]

Although the Pennsylvania Supreme Court accepted the theory that this suit for recovery of a debt did, in reality, amount to a trial for libel, it rejected Lewis's objections and authorized the trial to proceed. The justices quickly dismissed the issues of libel and freedom of expression, and they left no doubt about what they thought the verdict should be.

> The jury in this case have the constitutional right of determining the law and the facts under the direction of the court whether the publications of the defendant are libels; and if they view them in the light we do, they will have no hesitation in pronouncing them to be such. Libels are destructive both of public and private happiness, manifestly tend to breaches of the peace, and are good causes for forfeiture of a recognizance to keep the peace or of good behavior. They merit every discouragement, to which they may be legally subjected by a court and jury.[49]

The jurors apparently agreed; they returned a verdict against Cobbett and in favor of the Commonwealth of Pennsylvania.

It is difficult to believe, given the prominence of Peter Porcupine, that Hay and Wortman were unaware of the use of civil libel law in Pennsylvania. Moreover, as lawyers versed in at least the rudiments of defamation law, they would have known that civil suits were conducted under rules of liability analogous to the standards of guilt in the Sedition Act: defendants were exempted only for "libels" that they could prove to be true. Despite the potential threat of civil suits by political figures, those Jeffersonian critics of the Sedition Act who offered private defamation suits as "non-partisan" alternatives to criminal prosecutions did not even consider the issues raised by Cobbett's problems. These prominent Jeffersonian libertarians limited their critique of truth as a defense to criminal prosecutions.

Other Jeffersonian writers offered even more cautious discussions of the right of free expression. James Sullivan of Massachusetts, for example, advanced a view of libel law similar to, but even more severe, than James Wilson's. The "bands of society," Sullivan warned, would seriously be weakened if important individuals who served as "examples to virtue and goodness" could have their reputations injured by libelers and slanderers. Because no man was "without his failings," argued Sullivan, the law of libel should reject any defense of truth when libels touched a person's "foibles" or merely "weakness of character." Similarly, he claimed that there could be "no man of any consideration, who will sacrifice his own reputation, by advancing it as a principle, that the press shall be free to abuse and slander a man, merely because he holds a public office. . . ." Truth should not be a consideration in political libel prosecutions for publications containing "a charge of corruption, for which a magistrate, or public officer, may be removed from his office, or punished *criminaliter*, for fraud or corruption; or be displaced for weakness, incapacity, or impropriety of conduct in his official capacity." Proof of truth, however, should be a justification when writers were examining the officer's official conduct (except where the charges involved allegations of "gross immoralities, corruptions or frauds") or the qualifications of candidates for office. In the case of civil libel suits, a public official "sues in his private capacity . . . and can make no use of any public official character he may sustain, *excepting merely in aggravation of damages*."[50] Thus, Sullivan left no doubts about his position: a meaningful system of free expression should include specific, and rather severe, penalties for misuse of the printing press.

Most Jeffersonian writers, however, were much less forthright in expressing their views about limiting political expression. They were, after all, presenting a strongly partisan case against the Sedition Act. But, significantly, most of the Jeffersonian tracts did contain language that qualified any broad, absolutist-sounding rhetoric. John Page of Virginia, for example, could denounce Federalists for their attempts to stifle free expression and could announce his own support for "the most *unbounded liberty of the press.*" But Page also tacitly, though clearly, accepted the legitimacy of at least some prosecutions for libel under the Zengerian principles. Thus, he rejected the claims of Federalists that the Sedition Act had given the American people the right to plead truth; citizens in a republican nation, he believed, already possessed this fundamental liberty. The right "to prove the *truth* in defense against such prosecutions must be a right which Congress need not give and take away; it must be allowable, and meritorious, as it may be the means of preserving the constitution from violation" and of correcting mistakes by public officials.[51]

It would, of course, be unfair to focus only on the various inconsistencies in the writings of the new libertarians; but their theories of free expression rested upon views of political communication and public opinion that had at least as much (if not more) in common with Federalist theories as with the beliefs of mid–nineteenth-century libertarians.[52] Despite their criticism of the Sedition Act, Jeffersonians also expressed fears about the impact of an uncontrolled press. St. George Tucker, for example, set forth his own maxims of responsible journalism, principles which almost every Federalist would have endorsed. "Whoever makes use of the press as the vehicle of his sentiments on any subject, ought to do it in such language as to shew he has a deference for the sentiments of others. . . . In his statements of facts he is bound to adhere strictly to the truth; for any deviation from the truth is both an imposition on the public, and an injury to the individual it may respect." State courts, Tucker warned, were "always open, and may afford ample, and competent redress" for departures "from any of these maxims."[53] Thus, Tucker favored a process of public debate characterized by a good deal of self-restraint; and this self-censorship would be encouraged and, when necessary, reenforced by state libel laws.

The exception among the new libertarians was John Thomson, an obscure lawyer from New York City and a member of the radical democratic wing of the Jeffersonian coalition. Thomson restated many of the arguments used by other critics of the Sedition Act and added two propositions of his own. First, he argued that because public officials enjoyed complete freedom of expression, citizens should enjoy equal liberty: "It is absurd to suppose the people divested of that which their public agents enjoy." In addition, Thomson contended that people lacked control over their own minds and their own opinions. And because "man individually has no control over his mind, so it must follow that he could never have delegated that to a government which he did not himself possess." Thomson argued that people should be allowed to express their thoughts with complete freedom. "In other words—speak, or publish, whatever you believe to be the truth." Thomson did not condone "personal invective and abuse." But he maintained that even the worst scurrility "ought never to be adduced as a proof of the licentiousness of the press; nor used as an argument for the necessity of infringing its Liberty."[54]

Thomson placed complete faith in the results of unfettered discussion, even when the discussants were clearly publishing falsehoods, and even when they were partisan political writers. Unrestrained debate, Thomson conceded, would undoubtedly parade "many errors" "before the public eye; but, even these will not be without their use. When detected by accurate reasoning, the truth will appear with increased lustre." "Let the whig and tory, the royalist and aristocrat, the republican and democrat, or by whatever other name the partisans of political parties are designated . . . be allowed to express their opinions . . . with the same unconstrained freedom with which men of science discuss their subjects of investigation."[55]

Thomson also broke, as the other Jeffersonian libertarians did not, with the idea that some type of restraints were necessary to protect the reputations of the "best men." In fact, Thomson criticized the Sedition Act precisely because it was "less intended for the maintenance of public tranquility, than for the defence of certain individuals." In this sense, argued Thomson, political libel prosecutions violated "that great principle of all law"—"That of operating equally upon all, whether it protects or punishes."[56]

Similarly, Thomson condemned the notion that ordinary citizens should not presume to criticize public officials. "Notwithstanding all that has been said to the contrary, the poor man has as much at stake, and is as much interested in the stability of the government, as the richest man in the community. And if he thinks that any observations of his may be of advantage to his fellow-citizens, he has an equal right to communicate them."[57]

Thomson suggested only one mechanism to frustrate the efforts of malicious slanderers: whenever writers levied particular charges against specific individuals, they should affix their names to the publications. Such a practice would enable readers to identify writers whose previous publications had been proven unreliable. Once the marketplace had revealed a particular writer to be unreliable, he "would forever after be deprived of giving currency to his calumnies." But Thomson cautioned that the government should never interfere with political debate. "The laws of society . . . are fully sufficient to the purpose. . . . Let characters who have been unjustly accused, vindicate themselves by pointing out the falsehood of the charges; and let foul language be treated with that contempt it so justly merits. *In no case whatever use coercive measures.* Truth is at all times sufficiently powerful."[58]

Federalist speakers and writers did not let the Jeffersonian libertarians go unchallenged. Charles Lee, for example, argued that all of the "false" and "demagogic" misrepresentations of the Sedition Act only confirmed the need for such legislation. Objections to the law, he claimed, should be expressed in "decent and simple language," not by inflammatory rhetoric that was intended "to create discontents among the people at large with the national government." Similarly, Lee charged that suggestions that national officials must prosecute seditious libel in state courts demonstrated the Jeffersonians' hostility to the Constitution. If the national government were forced to rely upon state tribunals to protect its officials and enforce its laws, the national union would "depend entirely on the pleasure of the state judiciaries." Finally, Lee assured his fellow citizens that national judges would never allow "any law to be perverted to the vexation or oppression of any of us." He condemned criticism of the value of a jury trial as an "indecent and unjust" slander upon the whole idea of a government based upon the rule of law.[59]

The Era of the Sedition Act and First-Amendment Thought

What did events from 1781 to 1800 suggest about the history of libel and free expression? The series of convictions in 1799 and 1800 failed to shut down the Jeffersonian presses, and there is little evidence to suggest that prosecutions encouraged much self-censorship either. The Sedition Act gained the Jeffersonians much more in campaign ammunition than it ever cost them in editorial firepower. Tales about the harshness with which Federalists enforced their "gag law" and about their "reign of terror" quickly became part of popular political folklore. Throughout the nineteenth century, most politicians and lawyers condemned either the Sedition Act itself or, more commonly, the manner in which Federalists applied its provisions. Because the efforts of embattled Federalists backfired, enforcement of the Sedition Act seemed to demonstrate that national prosecutions for libel, in the absence of more vigorous suppression of dissent, offered ineffectual weapons against an organized opposition press.

If Federalists feared that the leaders of the Jeffersonian coalition intended to upset the national judicial structure, overthrow the rule of law, and implement the theories of radical Jeffersonian democrats, they had little cause for alarm. Those who rallied behind Jefferson between 1794 and 1800 possessed disparate views on legal issues, including the question of free expression. As historian Richard Ellis has argued, most Jeffersonian leaders advocated a moderate approach to the broad issue of legal change.[60] And as this chapter has shown, even the most advanced Jeffersonian libertarians advocated a similarly moderate revision of defamation laws. The ideas of John Thomson were as abhorrent to Jeffersonians like Thomas McKean as to Federalists like Charles Lee.

Some lawyers and scholars have recently contended that the language of the First Amendment, read very carefully and precisely, mandates special protection for the mass media; the amendment, it has been argued, protects not simply "freedom of press" but "freedom of *the* press." According to Justice Potter Stewart, the press was the only business whose interests received express constitutional protection.[61] Whatever the contemporary wisdom of granting the modern mass media rights and privileges not enjoyed by private citizens and other institutions, to political leaders of Jefferson's generation constitutional guarantees did not require toleration of everything published in the press about the conduct of the best men. Rather, political leaders from both major factions endorsed a quite different proposition: government, if not at the national then at the state level, had a positive responsibility to monitor—and, when necessary, to step in and to moderate—political communication. People differed over how far government action should extend and over what types of remedial steps could be taken; but those in prominent political positions agreed on the ultimate legitimacy of some types of controls.

After 1800, the free-speech views outlined by the Democratic-Republicans during the 1790s would be put to the test when partisan Federalist presses, in the style of Peter Porcupine, hurled all sorts of quills at the reputations of people whom Jeffersonian leaders considered their best men. Their patience and tolerance would also be tested by other Jeffersonians when members of the radical democratic wing, in the tradition of Eleazer Oswald and John Thomson, would attack mainstream interpretations of free expression as too restrictive.

Chapter Five | The Law of Libel and Early Nineteenth-Century Political Culture

The triumph of Jeffersonism did not end controversy over the law of libel. During the War of 1812, it is true, the administration of James Madison sought no sedition act, a decision that reflected Jeffersonian awareness of how enactment of a controversial libel law, during a very divisive war, might assist the resurgence of Federalism. Experiments with national prosecutions for seditious libel, except for several abortive efforts, would not be revived until World War I.

Yet libel law remained an important political and legal issue in the early national era. The celebrated 1805 impeachment trial of Supreme Court Justice Samuel Chase, for example, involved not only questions about the nature of the impeachment power and the role of an independent judiciary, but issues relating to the law of libel and free expression. Several of the charges against Chase rested upon differing views of defamation law and upon partisan disputes over how the arch-Federalist judge had conducted some of the trials under the Sedition Act.[1] More important, the rise of the Jeffersonians, a political coalition that had closely identified itself with opposition to the Sedition Act, did not mean an end to political libel cases. Without any spectacular national libel prosecutions, there were no constitutional conflagrations similar to the one over the Sedition Act, but the bitter political conflicts of the early nineteenth century sparked a number of legal brushfires over defamation law.

The Law of Libel and Partisan Politics

The partisan passions of the late 1790s persisted into the first decade of the new century. Federalist leaders refused to concede that citizens had rejected their policies or candidates; lying Republican scribblers, Federalist chieftains reassured one another, had poisoned public opinion and fooled voters into rejecting the best men. If Federalists changed their tactics, they could reverse the defeats of 1800. Consequently, Federalists worked to create a string of partisan newspapers, especially in New England, that could effectively challenge the vigorous Jeffersonian presses.

The invigorated Federalist presses contributed to what the historian Frank

Luther Mott called the "Dark Age of Partisan Journalism." Displaying little self-censorship, editors freely assaulted the reputations of opposition politicians and political writers. These early editors were the journalistic descendants of Tom Paine rather than the cautious printer-mechanics of the colonial era. And their battles did not always remain verbal; an editor's ability to fight could be nearly as important as his ability to write.

Yet the age of partisan journalism was not all dark—at least not in terms of development of new forms of popular political communication. If the imperial crisis before the American Revolution gave birth to political journalism, the factional battles of the Jeffersonian era brought political newspapers into a new age. As factional instruments, newspapers disseminated some useful information, stimulated voter interest, and provided plenty of amusement for the political community. Partisan editors also inaugurated significant technical innovations in political communication: regular editorial columns, eye-catching headlines, and cooperative news gathering. This new journalism contributed to, and in turn reflected, the continuing changes in American political culture.

But even after 1800, American political culture still exhibited older notions and forms of political conflict. Many people, even those in public life, never quite accepted all of the new developments. The first national party system never evolved into a truly nationwide structure, and ideas about deference and about the dangers of factions persisted into the Jacksonian era. Most Jeffersonian and Federalist leaders treated political office as a duty, a responsibility of gentlemen, rather than a profession. Running for office generally seemed an unpleasant chore for the candidate himself, and many voters distrusted men who pursued political office too actively.

Jurists and political leaders often complained about the vituperation that accompanied most elections. Partisan writers eagerly exposed ambitious office seekers and corrupt public officials. Both Jeffersonian and Federalist lawyers condemned the prevalence of such libels against members of their respective parties and blamed these attacks upon the evil influence of political factions. The press has lost "its character for veracity," claimed a New York attorney. "The demon of party has forced it to become a prostitute in the service of licentiousness."[2]

The Jeffersonian victory of 1800, then, failed to end disputes over the law of libel. Even before the House of Representatives had determined that Jefferson rather than Aaron Burr should become the new chief executive, the lower house became embroiled in a fight over the future of the Sedition Act. For a variety of reasons, most Federalists wanted to extend the act, which was due to expire on 3 March 1801. Some Federalist leaders, particularly Robert Goodloe Harper, had so closely identified themselves with the law that they felt honor bound to defend both its constitutionality and its value to any system of republican government. Although Jeffersonians maintained that no president of their political persuasion would ever use—or ever need—such a gag law, Federalists persisted. If they could maintain control of the national judiciary, they might even be able to employ the law against Jeffersonian writers.

Several Federalist members of Congress also argued that they, and the citizens who supported their principles, might need the protections afforded by the Sedition Act. Without the libertarian guarantees included in that law, they charged, Federalists would be left to the common law mercies of Jeffersonian prosecutors. Alluding to attempts by Republicans in Pennsylvania to silence William Cobbett through criminal prosecutions and civil lawsuits, Federalists insisted that their apprehensions were fully justified. "I wish to interpose this law between the freedom of discussion and the overbearing sway of that tyrannical spirit, by which a certain political party in this country, is actuated," Harper charged. The Jeffersonian spirit, "arrogating to itself to speak in the name of the people, like fanaticism arrogating to itself to speak in the name of God, knows neither moderation, mercy, nor justice." It would, Harper feared, sweep down "with relentless fury, all that dared to detect its follies, oppose its progress, or resist its domination."[3]

Although Harper exaggerated his opponents' antipathy toward dissent, few prominent Republicans endorsed the libertarian principles of 1798–1800 once their forces had gained political power. Even after his victories in 1800 and 1804, Jefferson himself retained fears about the corrosive effects of "corrupted" Federalist presses. He agreed with his Federalist opponents that the value of public presses could be destroyed by popular "licentiousness" as surely as by official prosecutions for libel. He also questioned the ability of truth to erase effectively all falsehoods. And he joined Federalist defenders of the Sedition Act in endorsing libel law as a legitimate tool for purging the press of licentiousness and lying and for encouraging credibility and integrity among the nation's printers. In short, Jefferson believed that libel prosecutions, if conducted under proper standards of criminal liability, would not endanger freedom of press but would, in reality, make the American press a true bulwark of republican principles.

Running through all of Jefferson's public and private statements on freedom of press was one dominant theme: if his administration decided to forgo libel prosecutions, it would be conducting an "experiment" based upon expediency rather than embracing a policy founded upon firm libertarian conviction. Jefferson clearly recognized the practical obstacles to a series of prosecutions against Federalist partisans. A party that had denounced the Federalist prosecutions of 1799–1800 would obviously encounter some difficulty justifying their own indictments. Even more important, Federalists had achieved little and apparently had lost much as a result of their own barrage of prosecutions. Thus, Jefferson believed that too many partisan prosecutions would prove counterproductive. In March 1802 he advised his attorney general that prosecutions would be "impracticable until the body of the people, from whom juries are to be taken, get their minds to rights; and even then I doubt its expediency. . . . I would wish much to see the experiment tried," the president concluded, "of getting along without public prosecutions for libels."[4]

Jefferson's ideas about his experiment in freedom of expression received considerable attention in his second inaugural address of March 1805. He complained bitterly that "the artillery of the press has been leveled against us, charged with whatsoever its licentiousness could devise or dare"; these "abuses of an institution so important to freedom and science, are deeply to be regretted." Jefferson now suggested that both criminal actions and civil libel suits might provide appropriate remedies. Anyone "who has the time, renders a service to public morals and public tranquility, in reforming these abuses by the salutary coercions of the law." But Jefferson ended his remarks on a more libertarian note, claiming that his "experiment" had resulted in the correction of "false reasoning and opinions, on a full hearing of the parties," through the power of public opinion rather than through the force of libel laws.[5]

Although Jefferson continued to refer to an experiment in free expression, by early 1807 he was prepared to try a different type of experiment—national common law prosecutions for political libel. Following expiration of the Sedition Act, Republicans lacked any statutory authority for prosecutions in national courts, and federal indictments under unwritten common law raised an unsettled constitutional issue. Although the Supreme Court had never decided the question, lower federal courts had invoked a national common law of crimes during the 1790s. But in their arguments against the Sedition Act, most Jeffersonians had contended that the national government lacked any authority to prosecute libels under common law. Nevertheless, in 1803 Jeffersonians in Kentucky indicted, under the Logan Act, a Federalist writer for criticizing Jeffersonian policy toward France. And in 1807 Jefferson himself defended the indictment of a number of important Connecticut Federalists in the federal District Court as a justifiable response to libel actions against Connecticut Republicans in Federalist-dominated state courts. As long as the defendants had the right to offer truth as a defense, Jefferson advised Republican leaders in Connecticut, common law prosecutions could not destroy "the once useful freedom of the press."[6] But when one of the defendants threatened to subpoena some prominent Virginians in order to prove that Jefferson had, indeed, once attempted to seduce a married woman, the president hastened to abort the prosecutions. The district court subsequently dropped several of the indictments, and in 1812 the Supreme Court quashed the final two, against the publishers of the *Connecticut Courant*.[7]

In this landmark ruling, *U.S.* v. *Hudson and Goodwin*, a divided Court held that the Constitution granted no common law criminal jurisdiction of any type.

According to William Johnson of South Carolina, who had been Jefferson's first appointee to the High Bench, the case against a common law criminal jurisdiction had "been long since settled in public opinion" and had been confirmed by the "general acquiescence of legal men. . . ."[8]

These cases in Connecticut were the only indictments of Federalists in national courts, but Republicans initiated a number of prosecutions in state tribunals. During debates over the Sedition Act, it should be reemphasized, Jeffersonian lawyers had suggested state indictments as alternatives to national prosecutions; after 1800 calls for state action increased. Jefferson himself had no objection to state prosecutions, and in 1803 he agreed with Pennsylvania's governor—none other than Thomas McKean—about the desirability of indicting a few "licentious" Federalist editors. Several "prosecutions of the most prominent offenders," Jefferson advised McKean, "would have a wholesome effect in restoring the integrity of the presses."[9] Republicans in Pennsylvania did file a number of criminal actions against Federalist writers and against printers who supported rival Republican factions. Likewise in New York and in Massachusetts, Jeffersonian political leaders used libel prosecutions against their Federalist critics. In 1812, for example, Massachusetts's Republican governor Elbridge Gerry, claiming that his attorney general had found no less than 236 libels in Federalist papers during a six-month period, urged more vigorous action against "the depraved and profligate part of the community" whose slanders threatened the reputations of the better members of society. At least ten indictments followed Gerry's message.[10]

Jeffersonians also encouraged civil libel suits as a means of restricting licentious publications. Because plaintiffs in civil suits could claim that they were merely vindicating their personal reputations and not restraining the press, this course avoided some of the odium attached to criminal indictments. In 1800, for example, the New York Senate tried to prosecute James Cheetham of the *American Citizen* for charging that rampant corruption had secured passage of a controversial banking bill. After the state's attorney general failed to secure a grand jury indictment and Cheetham continued to print his claims, several members of the state senate sued for damages. Thomas Tillotson recovered two substantial judgments against Cheetham, one for $1400 and another for $800. Civil suits offered continual threats and imposed financial burdens upon the more outspoken political editors.[11]

Several prominent Jeffersonian leaders suggested even more restrictive controls over the press. In 1803 George Hay, author of one of the libertarian critiques of the Sedition Act, became embroiled in a controversy over use of "prior restraints" against James Callender of the *Richmond Recorder*. Stung by criticism of his efforts to silence Callender, whom he had earlier defended against a prosecution under the Sedition Act, Hay reissued his pamphlet of 1799 but with significant additions. He now recommended that state officials

take a firm stand against political libels: sometimes government had to intervene in partisan debates in order to prevent the scurrilous pitch of political
rhetoric from shattering the fragile electoral process.

The "spirit of party," Hay argued, was producing too many defamatory
attacks against illustrious political leaders. The public's interest in the preservation of republican government demanded new restraints, particularly when
slanders affected those who ran for "the *great* offices of the state and federal
government. . . ." Candidates for these positions were "generally men who
are advanced in age, who have been long in public service, and whose
characters, whatever they may be, are well understood." Given this elitist
view of electoral politics, Hay found it difficult to believe that the marketplace
for political criticism would contain anything other than partisan slanders; "the
expectation of any public good or any great political effect, from discussions
of this kind is childish and absurd." Since 1789, he claimed, there had not
been "a single instance" in which a partisan writer had dealt fairly with either
the conduct or the character of political adversaries.[12]

It would, therefore, be disastrous, Hay believed, if the state did not impose
firm restraints upon "the venal writers for a desperate party." Although he still
opposed seditious libel prosecutions for general criticism of governmental
policies, he urged individual political figures to seek criminal or civil recourse
whenever malicious falsehoods injured their "private character." Constitutional guarantees of free expression, he maintained, "ought never to be inter-
posed" in private libel suits.[13]

More significant, Hay also proposed revival of a traditional form of control:
justices of the peace, upon a proper complaint, should impose a security bond
for good behavior upon anyone, including newspaper editors accused of libel.
Publication of any additional libels would result in forfeiture of the bond. Hay
insisted that this requirement of security for future publications, before any
judicial determination of the dispute, did not constitute a prior restraint.
Echoing fears raised by Federalist supporters of the Sedition Act, he worried
that, on the eve of closely contested elections, last-minute slanders could not
be corrected. Circumventing the slow process of formal libel proceedings,
imposition of these good behavior bonds would prevent corruption of the
electoral process. There was no reason, he argued, that members of the press
deserved special exemptions enjoyed by no other citizens; if judges could bind
to good behavior violence-prone people who seemed a threat to the lives and
property of other citizens, why could they not do the same to writers and
printers who threatened the political process with violent language?[14]

Some Republicans agreed with Hay's ideas. Pennsylvania's governor
Thomas McKean warned that it was time "that the good sense of our fellow
citizens, aiding the authority of the magistrate, should interpose to rescue us
from a tyranny, by which the wicked, and the obscure, are enabled to prey

upon the fame, the feelings, and the fortunes of every conspicuous member of the community." In 1806 he formally proposed that the Pennsylvania legislature adopt a system of good behavior bonds similar to the one proposed by Hay.[15]

But other Republicans, hesitant to identify themselves with such draconian measures, joined Federalists in rejecting the proposals of Hay and McKean. John Taylor of Caroline, who had attempted to testify for Hay in behalf of Callender in 1800, urged the Virginia legislature to repeal any law that might justify imposition of good behavior bonds on the press. A court composed of five Federalists and three Republicans found no statutory authority for Hay's position, and the justices refused to bind Callender to good behavior. In Pennsylvania, where the most bitter political conflict waged within the Jeffersonian ranks, a rival Republican faction led by the *Aurora*'s William Duane joined with Federalists to block McKean's proposal.[16]

Even so, attempts by prominent Jeffersonians to silence Federalists and rival Republicans brought charges of hypocrisy. Federal writers pictured Republicans as the real enemies of free discussion. Jeffersonians had condemned the "libertarian" Sedition Act but were now advocating much more harsh measures themselves. Federalists were quick to label every Jeffersonian libel prosecution and every civil suit part of a systematic plot to muzzle the opposition press.

Although they criticized Jeffersonian actions, Federalists used the law of libel themselves. William Coleman's *New York Evening Post* urged Federalists to file civil suits against Republican papers, claiming that "federal officers of integrity and talents have been completely lied out of the confidence of the people." It applauded Federalists who had already begun lawsuits and predicted that this practice might effectively counteract Jeffersonian slanders. In Massachusetts, Federalists indicted a number of Republican printers for criminal libel, including Andrew Wright of the *Republican Spy* who was convicted of libeling Governor Caleb Strong.[17]

During the first decade of the nineteenth century, then, political editors in states where party rivalry remained intense faced the threat of libel suits. James Cheetham of the *American Citizen* encountered thirteen libel cases during his first two years of operation. William Duane, editor of the *Aurora*, accumulated so many libel suits, one critic claimed, that a reputable lawyer could offer only one defense to any new suit: Duane's own reputation was so bad that his slanders could no longer injure his targets.[18] Although few editors suffered as many defamation suits as Cheetham and Duane, libel suits were a concern to many printers and editors.

The Law of Criminal Libel, 1800–1815

The prevalence of political libel suits kept alive many of the issues raised by the Sedition Act. Despite all the opposition to Blackstonian libel doctrines before and after the Revolution, a few lawyers and state judges tried to resuscitate the common law rule that barred any evidence of truth in criminal prosecutions. In 1811, the Federalist-dominated Supreme Court of South Carolina rejected the argument that the ancient common law had admitted evidence of truth as a defense. According to Justice Thomas Waties, Blackstonian-like doctrines antedated the Court of Star Chamber and rested upon valid precedents. Furthermore, he argued, sound public policies supported retention of the Blackstonian view. To permit evidence of truth as a defense would undermine the very reasonable policy of encouraging libel prosecutions as alternatives to violent retaliation; relaxation of the old rule would allow libelers the freedom to expose "the secret infirmities of their neighbors" or "imprudencies, long since committed and repented. . . ." François Xavier Martin, a leading Jeffersonian jurist, announced the same rule for the territory of Louisiana.[19]

Such rulings, however, clearly represented a decidedly minority position. A republican nation, most Federalist and Jeffersonian lawyers agreed, needed more libertarian standards than a monarchy. In the United States, St. George Tucker argued, the "people, not the government possess the absolute sovereignty"; as a result, freedom of the press meant more than liberation from prior restraints. Similarly, Abraham Van Vechten, a Federalist from New York, contended that the nature of American government demanded repudiation of British libel laws. All governmental officers were merely the "servants" of the people, and their conduct should be open to broad public scrutiny.[20] Despite the broader libertarian implications of the theory of popular sovereignty, American judges and lawyers invariably rejected suggestions that the doctrine justified unrestrained criticism of public officials. Unless the law offered some restraints upon political invective, the men who shaped early American libel laws agreed, the principle of popular sovereignty could lead to the worst kinds of demagoguery and to a political system in which voters could no longer distinguish between virtuous and corrupt officials and candidates.

In Pennsylvania, where Jeffersonians were deeply split between a group supporting Governor McKean and a "radical democratic" faction led by Duane and Dr. Michael Leib, political warfare did produce a temporary ban on most criminal libel prosecutions. After the Duane-Leib faction in the legislature blocked McKean's proposal for authorization of good behavior bonds, Leib and Duane moved to eliminate the threat of political libel prosecutions against the *Aurora*. The common law of libel, Leib told the Pennsylvania legislature, was far too harsh, and he introduced a bill that forbade any criminal indictments for publications that examined the actions of public officials or the proceedings of the legislature.

In support of his proposal, Leib offered a bitter denunciation of the entire common law. It "was high time the people should be governed by laws they understood—by the *lex scripta* instead of the *lex non scripta*. . . . It was time that monument of feudal origin, the common law, which rose out of the mists of barbarity and ignorance, should be fitted to the days of improvement and the institutions of a free people." Because the common law of criminal libel was one of the most noxious examples of a generally oppressive legal system, it should be abolished without delay. Freedom of press could never be safe in the hands of common law courts.[21]

Enacted by a small margin and limited to a trial period of three years, Leib's bill nullified a conviction against Duane for libeling McKean. Pennsylvania's chief justice William Tilghman, a staunch Federalist and a firm opponent of McKean, ruled that the state's constitution did not forbid abolition of libel prosecutions for political criticism. And even though the legislature had enacted the law after Duane's trial, he also held that the court should apply the measure retroactively.[22]

Clearly, the battle over Pennsylvania's libel laws was only part of a broader political struggle over the role of the judiciary and the nature of American legal practices. In several states, radical democrats like Duane and Leib continued the post-Revolutionary crusade to make substantial revisions in the entire fabric of American law, not just in criminal libel doctrines. In virtually every state, however, moderate Jeffersonians allied with moderate Federalists to repulse attacks on the common law and on the power of the judiciary. In Pennsylvania, for instance, Leib and Duane's coalition of urban and rural radicals achieved a few victories, such as Leib's libel bill and an act providing for inexpensive arbitration of some legal disputes. But commercial-minded supporters of a structured, professionalized, and independent judicial system ultimately prevailed. In Pennsylvania, the Duane-Leib faction lost control of the legislature after the 1808–9 session. Among other things, this meant that Pennsylvania's experience with formal abolition of political libel prosecutions ended when the law automatically expired. A report of Jared Ingersoll, the state's attorney general and a moderate Federalist, contended that the 1809 legislature had extended freedom of press much too far, denying the protection of libel prosecutions to "those who, for especial merit, have been selected from among their fellow citizens to administer the offices of the commonwealth." The act barring criminal libel prosecutions was not renewed.[23]

Resistance to change proved strongest in New York and Massachusetts, states where political conflict produced a number of libel prosecutions and where influential lawyers rejected the Zengerian standards of liability as too liberal. In New York, for example, the prosecution of Federalist Harry Croswell in 1803 offered the opportunity for a full-scale legal debate over most of the issues raised, but left unsettled, by the controversy surrounding the Sedition Act.

Croswell became the first, though not the last, journalist to become ensnared in the intense rivalries in early nineteenth-century New York politics. Ambrose Spencer, a leading member of the state's Republican faction, secured Croswell's indictment for republishing James Callender's claim that Jefferson had once paid him to slander President Washington. Croswell's attorneys, some of New York's most prominent Federalists, sought a delay so that Callender might come to New York and verify the charge. Anxious to stop further circulation of Callender's story, the trial judge, Republican Morgan Lewis, denied the motion for a continuance; he then applied Blackstonian libel rules at Croswell's trial. Lewis instructed the jury to decide only the fact of publication, and they quickly returned a verdict of guilty.[24]

When Croswell appealed his conviction to the New York Supreme Court, Alexander Hamilton, who had been monitoring the case, donated his considerable legal talents. Although some historians, notably Richard Buel, have argued that the triumph of Jeffersonianism marked a victory for a new, libertarian approach to free speech, Hamilton and other Federalists assessed the situation (with considerable justification, as we have seen) quite differently.

In coming forward to argue the *Croswell* case, Hamilton saw himself fulfilling one of the highest callings of the republic's best men: explaining the nature of great constitutional causes. Hamilton hoped to convince lesser minds of both the need for permitting political criticism against public leaders who merely pretended to possess republican virtue and of the necessity for limiting defamatory attacks against the reputations of truly virtuous public figures. Drawing upon his legal learning and his experience in the art of statecraft, Hamilton sought to establish a set of propositions about the law of libel and about how political critics should behave toward the reputations of the nation's leaders.

Hamilton's appearance as an advocate for liberty of expression was not without irony. As a member of the Washington administration and as a private citizen, Hamilton had always stressed the need to protect the reputations of political leaders; he had urged that the Washington administration prosecute several allegedly libelous publications, had called for vigorous enforcement of the Sedition Act, and had instigated one common law prosecution (under Blackstonian rules) himself. And few leaders of the Revolutionary generation were more sensitive—with good reason—about their own reputations. Thus, Hamilton's defense of Croswell and liberty of the press also acknowledged the need to maintain effective libel laws. "In speaking . . . for the Freedom of the Press," Hamilton emphasized that he did not mean "there ought to be an unbridled license; or that the characters of men who are good, will naturally tend eternally to support themselves." To allow the "spirit of abuse and calumny" to go unchecked was unthinkable; if calumniators were permitted to destroy the reputations of the nation's leading citizens, it "would be to put the best and the worst on the same level." The United States "will be an ill-fated Country," Justice James Kent's notes quote Hamilton as saying, "if this Doctrine [of an unchecked Press] prevails."[25]

But Hamilton saw this particular prosecution as a sinister perversion of libel law and the legal process. As Hamilton framed it, the underlying issue in the *Croswell* case was how to prevent a power-hungry group—i.e. the Jeffersonians—from using libel laws to halt political criticism and to hide the possible misdeeds of a man Hamilton despised, Thomas Jefferson. Although Hamilton's discussion, of necessity, focused on technical legal questions and various constitutional issues, he could not resist the opportunity to chide an old political foe. "It ought to be distinctly known whether Mr. Jefferson be guilty or not of so foul an act as the one charged. It is in every view interesting."[26] Hamilton's primary political focus remained the allegedly sinister motives actuating this prosecution and other Jeffersonian actions, including the campaign to impeach Justice Samuel Chase. Viewed in its totality, Hamilton's speech was not simply a discourse on libel and free expression; it was also a plea for maintaining the integrity of an independent judiciary and of the rule of law.

Despite its broad context, Hamilton's argument still had to begin at the beginning: the Blackstonian view of libel law adopted by the New York Jeffersonians. Rejecting this approach as too restrictive and the formulation contained in the Sedition Act as too liberal, Hamilton offered a definition of libel law that he claimed rested on both common law and common sense. "The liberty of the Press consists, in my idea, in publishing the truth, from good motives for justifiable ends, though it reflect on government, on magistrates or individuals." According to Hamilton, Blackstonian doctrines based upon the supposed bad tendency of all political criticism made neither good sense nor good law. Surely, he argued, "a man may go far in the way of reflecting on public character, without the least design of exciting tumult. He may only have it in view, to rouse the nation to vigilance and a due exertion of their right to change their rulers." The essence of the crime of libel, like any other offense, was the malicious intent of the defendant. Evidence of truth helped determine the vital elements of intent and malice. Publication of a defamatory falsehood, Hamilton was satisfied, fully demonstrated malicious intent, but he did not believe that truth always constituted a complete defense. Hamilton could imagine cases in which people published injurious statements, though true, for purely malicious motives and without any intention of advancing the public good. In such cases, no amount of evidence about the truth of such publications would amount to a legal justification. Thus Hamilton's formulation of a "truth-plus" test, the kind of criminal libel formula advanced earlier by the Jeffersonian Thomas McKean, was more restrictive, at least in theory, than the ones employed in trials under the Sedition Act of 1798.

Hamilton did follow the Zengerian position on the role of juries. The crime of libel was "a complicated matter of fact and law," he observed, and determination of guilt depended upon "time, manner, and circumstances." No judge could formulate a "specific and precise definition of facts and circumstances" to cover all situations. The safest and most logical course was to empower a jury of the defendant's peers to return a general verdict of guilty or innocent.

In Hamilton's view, the highly complex relationship between judge and jury in criminal trials should reflect the more general blending and mixing of legal and constitutional powers within the broader polity: judges should act as "constitutional advisors of the Jury" in matters of law; and though jurors should never "lightly or rashly" disregard judicial advice, they could still vote their consciences on questions of law and fact when they had "a clear conviction that the charge of the court is wrong."[27]

This blending of judicial and juror authority, Hamilton insisted, was especially crucial in political libel cases. He warned that judges—"a permanent body of men appointed, by the executive, and, in some degree always connected with it"—could not be trusted with the exclusive power of deciding "what shall constitute a libel on our rulers. . . ." With Jeffersonians in control in Albany and in Washington, Hamilton displayed a newfound faith in "the people." Although judges "may be inclined to lean over towards party modes" in deciding political libel cases, juries "selected, as they now are, by lot" would be far less likely to defer to partisan pressures and "to make the most innocent publications libelous." Hamilton argued that denial of the Zengerian principles in political libel prosecutions would unwisely remove much of what eighteenth-century proponents of balanced government called the "popular" element from the American constitutional system. Countries could be called "*free*," he maintained, only when "the People have a representation in the government so that no law can pass without their Consent" and only when "they have a Trial by Jury."[28]

In developing this line of defense, Hamilton had to frame his arguments with considerable care. He was urging citizens not to accept passively the legal pronouncements of Jeffersonian judges (not only in this case but in any future cases with partisan overtones) and exhorting juries to serve as counterweights to judicial authority. But, on the other hand, Hamilton's claim that judicial decisions tended to follow prevailing political winds could not go so far as to cast doubt upon the Federalist view of the rule of law or to support Jeffersonian charges that Chase, then facing the threat of impeachment, had misused his judicial authority during prosecutions under the Sedition Act. The solution to Hamilton's dilemma was to emphasize that his view of libel law squared with ancient common law principles and to appeal to historical tradition. Citing Roman and medieval precedents, Hamilton contended that truth had always been a relevant consideration in libel prosecutions; contrary doctrines, he insisted, represented corruptions of the "true" common law that had originated in the Court of Star Chamber.[29]

By adopting this position, one used extensively by opposition Whigs during the eighteenth century, Hamilton could dismiss the Mansfield-Blackstonian doctrines of the New York Jeffersonians as perversions of common law orthodoxy. More important, the discovery of the "correct" principles in the ancient common law allowed Hamilton to argue that the *Croswell* case carried a political message highly valuable in a period of partisan strife and (in his mind) constitutional danger: adherence to the rules of the common law, which were "natural law and natural reason applied to the purposes of Society," provided the only means of safeguarding Federalist principles, the Constitution of 1787, and republicanism itself.[30]

Correctly interpreted, Hamilton maintained, common law served the nation admirably. It offered, for example, the only reliable guide to the meaning of general constitutional provisions, such as the free expression clause of the First Amendment. Hamilton also suggested that acceptance of common law as the basis for constitutional interpretation would vindicate Samuel Chase's handling of the sedition trials of 1800. The threat that Chase's impeachment offered to an "independent" judiciary, Hamilton warned, "admonishes us, to use with caution, these arguments against common law. To take care how we throw this barrier which may secure the men we have placed in power; to guard against a spirit of faction, that great bane to community, that mortal poison to our land." In addition, he pleaded that the Constitution itself "would be melted away or borne down by Faction, if the *Common law* was not applicable." If the nation were to jettison common law, as radicals like Dr. Michael Leib suggested, "we degenerate into Anarchy & the Transition from Anarchy is to despotism—to *an armed Master*."[31]

Finally, in an argument clearly directed against Jeffersonian political power, Hamilton implored citizens to guard against efforts to corrupt the common law. Alluding to long-standing Jeffersonian charges that he had plotted to destroy American liberties by use of the provisional army during the Alien and Sedition crisis, Hamilton scoffed at the idea that "tyranny [could] be introduced into this country by arms; these could never get rid of a popular spirit of enquiry. . . ." It was "only by the abuse of the forms of justice that we can be enslaved," Hamilton claimed. Only "by a pretence of adhering to all the forms of law," while subtly corrupting their substance, could the enemies of liberty prevail. Thus, this dispute over libel law, Hamilton concluded, reflected a much larger issue: the struggle over the fate of the common law and the role of the judiciary within the American political system. "Sacrificing & crushing individuals by the perverted Forms and mask of law," Hamilton pleaded, "is the most dangerous & destructive tyranny."[32]

Although Harry Croswell himself escaped legal liability when the New York Supreme Court, divided along partisan lines, could reach no decision and the prosecution was halted, the *Croswell* case remained a *cause célèbre* for a number of years. Almost thirty years after the prosecution, during a debate in the United States Senate, Ambrose Spencer still faced jibes about his role in the case.[33] More immediately, a number of Federalists from New York, who had criticized the prosecution's tactics and Morgan Lewis's Blackstonian rulings, found themselves facing civil libel suits.[34] And throughout the country, Federalists took up Croswell's cause, citing his indictment as a prime example of Jeffersonian hypocrisy. In his cantos satirizing Republicanism, Thomas Green Fessendon, a lawyer and newspaper editor from Vermont, wrote in reference to the *Croswell* case:

> I'll search in Democratic annals
> Elicit truth from dirty channels
> Describe *low* knaves in *high* condition
> Though *speaking truth* be deem'd sedition.[35]

Generally, however, Federalist lawyers offered arguments in favor of free expression that were more cautious than the views suggested by many Jeffersonian opponents of the Sedition Act. Truth alone, under the Hamiltonian test, would not amount to a complete justification. When James Kent's opinion in the *Croswell* case finally appeared in 1812 (it was not needed to settle Croswell's fate when the prosecution was dropped), it pointedly denounced Madison's *Report* to the Virginia legislature for its criticism of the common law. "Against such a commentary upon freedom of the American press," wrote Kent, "I beg leave to enter my protest." Instead, Kent fully endorsed the Hamiltonian position.[36]

In the creation of early American libel doctrines, Hamilton's arguments, even in their truncated pamphlet form, proved far more important than the writings of the Jeffersonian libertarians. Hamilton's lofty reputation among the legal elite gave his views on libel considerable weight, and adoption of his basic position by influential judges (such as Kent and Theophilus Parsons of Massachusetts) provided additional support. Most important, early nineteenth-century legal and political leaders saw the Hamiltonian or truth-plus position as providing greater protection for the right of reputation—and their own good names—than the old Zengerian position.

While Hamilton was arguing before the Supreme Court of New York, the state legislature was considering a bill designed to clarify New York's libel laws. In 1804 it enacted a statute providing that truth could be given in evidence in all prosecutions involving public officials or candidates. The

Council of Revision, a body which under New York's constitution of 1777 could review all legislative acts, vetoed the measure because it made no distinction "with respect to the nature, tendency or intent of the libel. . . ." The council argued that the act would allow distorted charges against the private character of public officials and permit "factious, turbulent or discontented individuals to awe and humble the spirit of the officers disposed to discharge their duty faithfully. . . ." At the next session of the legislature, both Republicans and Federalists supported a bill which contained the Hamiltonian modifications of the Zengerian position. This New York law of 1805 became the model for most nineteenth-century libel provisions.

> . . . in every prosecution for writing or publishing any libel, it shall be lawful for the defendant, upon the trial of the cause, to give in evidence in his defence, the truth of the matter contained in the publication charged as libellous: *Provided always*, That such evidence shall not be a justification, unless on the trial it shall be further made satisfactorily to appear, that the matter charged as libellous, was published with good motives and for justifiable ends.[37]

During these same years, lawyers in Massachusetts were also debating the issue of libel law. In 1804, however, the legislature rejected a bill that would have permitted introduction of evidence of truth in libel prosecutions. Although judges held common law doctrines applicable in the Bay State, they often relaxed the English rules in criminal libel prosecutions.[38] Finally, in 1808 the state supreme court reexamined the whole issue in *Commonwealth v. Clap*, a prosecution for an alleged libel against an auctioneer. Representing the defendant, Harrison Gray Otis argued for libel doctrines similar to those proposed earlier by the state's former chief justice, William Cushing: whatever the common law rule had been prior to 1780, the Massachusetts constitution gave "the citizens of a free elective republic [the right] to speak and publish respecting the characters of men in public office, and of candidates for office." Because the auctioneer had been appointed by the state, Otis argued, the public had "an interest in his integrity" and "a right to be informed" about his performance in office. "It is of much greater importance that this high constitutional privilege should be preserved unimpaired, than that a libeller should now and then go free." Moreover, Otis argued, to allow truth as a justification to a criminal indictment would align civil and criminal defamation rules. Is there "any justification in good sense for a distinction between a justification in a civil action and an excuse in a criminal prosecution," he asked?[39]

Chief Justice Theophilus Parsons and other members of the Supreme Court of Massachusetts believed that there was. The state prosecuted libels, Parsons argued, not because of the injury to reputation but because of the bad tendency of all libels, whether true or false, "to inflame the passions, and to excite revenge. . . ." The court therefore rejected Otis's claims that truth should be a justification, but it also refused to embrace Blackstonian orthodoxy. Although Parsons cited no authorities in his opinion, his view of criminal libel resembled the truth-plus position suggested earlier by John Adams, Thomas McKean, and Alexander Hamilton. Publications of the truth, "with the honest intention of informing the people," about candidates for elective office could not be prosecuted as libels. "For it would be unreasonable to conclude that publication of truths, which it is in the interest of the people to know, should be an offence against their laws." The same rule applied to criticism of an office holder. Reelection was "the only way his constituents can manifest their approbation of his conduct," and "it is to be presumed that he is consenting to a re-election, if he does not disclaim it."[40]

Publication of falsehoods—and even some truths—about political figures, Parsons warned, remained "an offense most dangerous to the people. . . ." Massachusetts's version of the truth-plus test, he concluded, amply protected the state's legitimate interests in maintaining the purity of the electoral process and in encouraging election of only the best citizens to public office. The same considerations did not apply, however, in the case of appointive officers.[41]

The actual use of criminal libel prosecutions continued to produce controversy in Massachusetts. Republican governor Elbridge Gerry began waging his crusade against Federalist papers in the fall of 1811, and at about the same time, Federalist Isaac Parker of the state supreme court was encouraging a Suffolk County grand jury to seek out libels in Jeffersonian newspapers. In his charge to grand jurors Parker endorsed Parsons's theory in the *Clap* case: sound public policy—the need for the press to discuss with accuracy and fairness the merits of elective officials—justified only a limited departure from common law orthodoxy. Seeking to take advantage of the position of the two Federalist judges, Gerry sent the legislature a special message that argued that appointive officials, including judges, should come under the same libel rules as elected officers. If "the conduct of a judge is to be exempt from the press," Gerry charged, the judiciary might "establish an unconstitutional and dangerous influence" within the state. In response to Gerry's blast, Republican members of the Massachusetts senate adopted resolutions that denounced the Federalist-dominated judiciary for intruding into the province of the legislature and for limiting the right of defendants to plead truth in libel cases. But the Jeffersonian majority did not rouse itself to change the libel laws. Meanwhile, Federalists also took up the cause of free expression; they condemned Gerry's investigation of alleged libels as an unconstitutional invasion of the authority of the judiciary and as a dangerous precedent for the rights of a free people.[42]

Thus, the political battles of the Jeffersonian era kept the issue of criminal libel law alive, particularly in Pennsylvania, New York, and Massachusetts. By 1815, judges or legislators in these and most other states had finally rejected Blackstonian libel doctrine. Only South Carolina and Louisiana still formally adhered to the Orthodox Whig position. Yet, most lawyers and political leaders showed no desire for any sweeping revision in their state's libel laws. Many believed that even the provisions of the Sedition Act—the old Zengerian position—represented too radical a departure from the common law. Clearly, Alexander Hamilton and Theophilus Parsons—and not Tunis Wortman, George Hay, or James Madison—would provide the classic statements of this new orthodoxy.

Criminal Libel and Politics, 1815–1827

Six of the nine state constitutions drafted or revised between 1815 and 1827 included specific provisions to cover criminal libel prosecutions. All of these authorized juries to determine both law and fact. But their clauses on the pleading of truth varied. Although only New York's constitution makers adopted the Hamiltonian rule, no convention unequivocally declared truth alone to be a complete defense.[43] Because of the declining number of indictments in most states and because of widespread belief that truth should be a consideration, controversy remained limited in most conventions. In the Maine constitutional convention, for example, the only discussion of the free-press guarantee concerned the precise meaning of the section on the role of the jury. The most extensive debates over the rules of criminal libel occurred, once again, in New York and Massachusetts, two states in which bitter and well-organized political conflict continued long after Federalism had faded as a national political force.

Delegates to the 1821 New York constitutional convention accepted the Hamiltonian doctrine for all libel prosecutions after rebuffing efforts either to broaden or to narrow the rule. Erastus Root, a nineteenth-century democrat who urged abolition of special privileges in every area of public life, endorsed abolition of political libel prosecutions. Root never formally presented this proposal to the convention, but delegates did defeat a motion that would have made truth alone a justification. On the other hand, the convention also turned back Chancellor James Kent's attempt to restrict the application of the truth-plus doctrine. Defendants should not be allowed to offer evidence to the jury, Kent argued, unless they first established to a judge's satisfaction that all alleged libels had been published with "good motives" and for "justifiable ends." He claimed that this procedure, which would have guaranteed considerable judicial discretion in libel prosecutions, would keep courts from becoming forums for "dragging before the public gross indecencies, which ought not to be made the subject of investigation, *whether true or false*."[44]

Critics of Kent's position opposed giving judges such power in cases involving freedom of expression. Widespread popular disenchantment with the New York judiciary contributed to this sentiment. A majority of the convention members disliked not only the over-centralization and the lethargy in the state's judicial system but also the Federalist lineage of most judges on the state supreme court. A pending civil libel suit by Justice William Van Ness against the editors of the *New York American* may also have influenced the decision to reject Kent's amendment. The "best security for the freedom of the press, and the best security against its licentiousness," argued one delegate, was to vest the ultimate authority in libel prosecutions with juries.

On the issue of criminal libel, as on most other questions in the New York convention, moderate delegates led by Martin Van Buren triumphed over democrats such as Root and traditionalists such as Kent. By an overwhelming majority, the convention adopted a clause that guaranteed the right of all libel defendants to plead truth as a defense, but that made the Hamiltonian rule the measure of liability in all prosecutions for defamation.[45]

Controversy over the precise meaning of the Hamiltonian rule persisted in Massachusetts as well. In 1820 a few members of the state constitutional convention attempted to incorporate some type of libel provision into the new charter. George Blake, a venerable Republican attorney who had argued against the constitutionality of all libel prosecutions back in 1798, claimed that liberty of press and the law of criminal libel were "intimately connected" and that defamation doctrines must be specified in the commonwealth's fundamental law. Freedom of press, he maintained, should not rest upon judicial decisions alone. But delegates disagreed upon the precise standards to be incorporated into the constitution, and they ultimately abandoned any effort to include a provision on libel. The rule in *Commonwealth* v. *Clap* remained intact.[46]

The differences evident in the constitutional convention of 1820 eventually spilled over into the political arena. Two years later Judge Josiah Quincy, Jr., a Federalist, reopened the issue of libel law when he allowed Joseph Buckingham of the *Boston Galaxy* to offer evidence of truth in a prosecution for libel upon a Methodist revivalist.[47] Quincy's ruling and Buckingham's subsequent acquittal angered some members of the Massachusetts bar. Harrison Gray Otis, another veteran of the libel law debates of 1798–1800, finally issued an open letter challenging Quincy's position.[48]

Otis insisted that restrictive libel laws did not infringe upon freedom of expression. To denounce English libel doctrines as products of Star Chamber, he protested, was an appeal "to passion and prejudice without proper investigation." English libel doctrines remained basically sound. And by endorsing the ruling in *Commonwealth* v. *Clap*, most lawyers and judges had already recognized that the "genius and nature of our government" required some modification of English law in prosecutions on behalf of elected officials and candidates. But not even the Revolutionary principle of popular sovereignty, Otis insisted, justified wholesale rejection of traditional defamation rules. Otis defended the need to protect personal reputations. If, "because of the visionary, insubstantial, impracticable notions of imaginary public good which have possessed or may possess the brains of a few enthusiasts," newspapers could freely drag prominent men's past misdeeds and personal indiscretions into public scrutiny, both private citizens and public officials would see their prestige and influence diminished. Otis favored a procedure similar to the one proposed by Chancellor Kent: in most cases, defendants could offer evidence of truth only after judges determined that alleged libels had some justifiable purpose. By allowing revelation of damaging information without any prior judicial inquiry into the authors' motives, Otis charged, Judge Quincy had undermined the social value of libel law.

Otis considered most political criticism purely mischievous. Although he approved permitting defendants to plead truth in order "to justify remarks made on a public officer, or candidate for office in their official capacities," he denounced the continual publication of "*injurious truths* of public men which have no relation to their fitness for public stations." Otis contended that unfortunately, public and private virtue did not always go together; many great public leaders led less than exemplary private lives. But the community's interest in good government might suffer if fear of scandalmongers kept talented people out of public service. Common sense, argued Otis, suggested that, in 999 instances out of 1000, attacks on public officials stemmed purely from malicious motives and from "love of gossip" rather than from any real desire to inform the public. In most libel cases, therefore, Otis believed that defendants could offer judges no valid reason for allowing evidence of truth to be presented to jurors.[49]

Although most lawyers in Massachusetts apparently accepted the truth-plus doctrine, they were unwilling to allow judges such broad authority to reject evidence in libel prosecutions. Replying to Otis, a younger member of the Massachusetts bar, Edmund Kimbull, claimed that he personally saw little harm in adopting the rule that truth alone constituted a complete justification. In a free nation, citizens had much more reason to fear the evil of "tyrannical restraint" than the threat of a licentious press. Honest politicians and good governments could both withstand the most scurrilous comments about their activities. There was no need, however, to make truth a complete defense in libel prosecutions. Allowing defendants in every prosecution to present evidence of truth as one means of establishing their good motives and justifiable ends protected both the right of free expression and of personal reputation. To clarify the confusion raised by the Quincy-Otis dispute, the Massachusetts legislature should enact a comprehensive libel law. In 1826 the legislature finally did pass a measure that provided that any defendant could offer evidence of truth to the jury but still had to demonstrate good motives and justifiable ends in order to secure acquittal.[50]

Thus, during the first three decades of the nineteenth century, criminal libel law remained an issue, especially in highly politicized states such as Massachusetts, New York, and Pennsylvania. When it seemed likely to work to their advantage, political leaders, including those from the Jeffersonian ranks, tried criminal libel prosecutions, even invoking (as in the *Croswell* case) doctrines stricter than those used in the Sedition Act prosecutions. As a result, the connection between libel law and constitutional guarantees of free speech remained a close one, and American defamation law continued to be a topic of general legal debate. Although in this era, as in others, the exact state of American libel law defied easy generalizations, two clear legal trends emerged. First, in approaching most issues, judges and lawyers looked much more to the views of Hamilton and Chancellor Kent than to those of the libertarians of 1798–1800. And, increasingly, civil suits brought by politicians and other public figures replaced criminal prosecutions as the most common, and hence the most controversial, aspect of defamation law.

Politics and Civil Libel Suits, 1800–1830

The use of civil libel suits in political disputes after 1800 represented a new departure in American political life. Until the nineteenth century, public officials and candidates had initiated very few civil libel actions. Such forbearance, of course, did not mean that members of the eighteenth-century political elite were unconcerned about their reputations or that political leaders were exempt from attacks that fell within the traditional bounds of civil defamation law. Why, then, did eighteenth-century political figures, especially those active during the Revolutionary era, avoid use of the law of civil defamation to erase aspersions on their characters?

Institutional and doctrinal considerations were clearly involved. Between 1776 and 1790 the unsettled nature of most judicial systems and the uncertain state of the common law itself would have discouraged initiation of civil suits for defamation. Nonlegal factors were also involved. As the historian Douglass Adair suggested, when political leaders of the Revolutionary era considered their "reputations," they primarily thought about what they called "fame"—their stature in the annals of history—rather than the current estimation of their characters in the minds of other citizens. To display excessive personal concern about what appeared in the public prints, it seemed, violated the code of conduct that distinguished public leaders from ordinary members of the political community. Most public men, as has already been noted, at least claimed they would not stoop to notice their detractors, especially when personal considerations might seem in conflict with popular views of free expression. In 1786, for instance, Thomas Jefferson and John Jay agreed that public men should simply suffer attacks on their personal characters. Jay wrote that freedom of expression should not "be restrained for the sake of personal Considerations . . . for altho Slander may prevail for a while, yet Truth and consistent Rectitude will ultimately enjoy their Rights. While I possess the Esteem of those who merit Esteem, the Effusions of unmerited Malevolence will give me no greater Concern, than what naturally results from the various other Evils to which we are liable."[51] When, during the 1790s, people such as Hamilton, Alexander Addison, and James Iredell called for legal action to restrain licentiousness, they emphasized public considerations—such as the purity of the electoral process and the general impact of political libels—over personal ones. Private suits for damages during the 1790s by George Clinton and Dr. Benjamin Rush were exceptions to the eighteenth-century norm.

By the early nineteenth century, however, civil libel cases, ostensibly private cases, came to replace criminal prosecutions as the most prevalent restraint on political expression. All the furor surrounding prominent criminal libel prosecutions made civil suits seem an attractive alternative, one that avoided some of the stigma that attached to politicians who used criminal sanctions against political critics. In addition, the bitter nature of political conflict in states such as New York and Pennsylvania contributed to the increase in civil libel cases. The new realities of partisan politics and the proliferation of caustic political newspapers forced most public leaders to reevaluate, on a regular basis, the market value of their reputations. Unless they preferred to leave public life entirely, a course that some aristocratic and tradition-bound Federalists actually followed, officials and candidates could not ignore criticism, especially from a public press, that might affect their political reputations. Concern about one's immediate political name became a more pressing concern than thoughts about one's ultimate fame.

Although politicians who sued for libel were not averse to collecting monetary damages—thus swelling their own pocketbooks while depleting the always-limited purses of political editors—most partisan libel suits seem mainly to have been a way to escalate political conflict into another realm and to underscore the message that political criticism, at least in theory, should respect some sort of bounds. Very quickly, this reality affected the way in which the legal system handled civil libel suits brought by political figures. Both the politician-lawyers who argued early nineteenth-century cases and the politician-judges who decided them constantly emphasized that these seemingly private suits for defamation really involved the weighing of a number of competing public issues. Although common law courts had long recognized proof of truth as a complete justification in civil suits, other issues could become every bit as complex and controversial as those raised in criminal libel prosecutions.

Some courts began to acknowledge that the right of free expression required a special privilege, in a limited number of circumstances, for defendants who had been sued by public officials or candidates for office. New York, for example, permitted special or "struck" juries in cases that involved libels against an officer's "official conduct." This procedure authorized the impaneling of a separate list of jurors and granted each side a greater number of challenges than in ordinary cases. Presumably, use of struck juries would reduce the danger of litigants facing twelve hostile jurors, all of whom belonged to the other party.[52]

More important, courts in several states began to liberalize the requirement of proving the truth when charges of political corruption were contained in official complaints directed to proper public officers. Reasoning that corrupt officials must be accountable to the sovereign people, judges held that citizens who prepared legitimate petitions should not be held strictly liable for all defamatory falsehoods. False allegations about misconduct in office would not justify damages without further evidence of wrongdoing such as malice, lack of good faith, or improper inquiry into the facts. William Tilghman, chief justice of Pennsylvania, for example, ruled that even if a defamatory complaint against an officer proved erroneous, defendants could still escape civil liability as long as they had acted "altogether from mistake, and with the most perfect of good faith."[53]

In other libel trials, however, defense attorneys failed to win recognition for a similar type of privilege for general political criticism. In only one unusual case, *Mayrant* v. *Richardson* (1818) did an appellate court extend the type of privilege granted for official petitions. Here an unsuccessful candidate for Congress from South Carolina sued the brother of his victorious rival for both slander and libel. The defendant had told several potential voters that a recent illness had left Mayrant mentally unqualified to serve in Washington. In response to Mayrant's petition, Richardson's attorney filed a general demurrer, which the trial judge granted.

A unanimous South Carolina Supreme Court affirmed dismissal of Mayrant's suit, and its opinion contained a number of unique arguments. According to Justice James Nott, when a man became a candidate for public office, he "makes profert of himself for public investigation. All of his pretensions become proper subjects of enquiry and discussion. He makes himself a species of public property. . . ." The "ordeal of public scrutiny," he continued, was "the necessary attribute of every free government, and is expressly guaranteed to the people of this country by the Constitution."[54] Justice Nott bolstered this assertion of broad constitutional protection—which South Carolina courts did not recognize in criminal prosecutions—with a long quotation, unattributed, from Madison's *Report* of 1800. He also adopted another argument used by Madison and some other opponents of the Sedition Act: Richardson's observations about Mayrant's mental faculties, Justice Nott maintained, were not stated as "facts" but merely as "opinions," and libel laws did not reach such critical opinions. Seeking to justify this theory, one not recognized by common law precedents, Justice Nott suggested that an election was analogous to a proceeding in a court of law. Just as a witness could not be sued for libel on account of testimony given before a judge, neither could a citizen be held liable for giving political opinions to the ultimate judges of political candidates, the sovereign voters. The privilege was not unlimited—critics had no "right in such a case to impute to one infamous crimes or misdemeanors"—but "talents and qualifications for office are mere matters of opinion, of which the electors are the only competent judges."[55]

Although many early nineteenth-century jurists agreed that critical political statements enjoyed some type of constitutional protection, no other court even approached the sweeping implications of Justice Nott's theories. Few, if any, judges, for example, would have agreed that the First Amendment to the U.S. Constitution—South Carolina's constitution said nothing about freedom of expression—had any direct binding effect on the way in which state courts conducted either civil or criminal libel trials. Similarly, no other court invoked Justice Nott's analogy between the absolute privilege accorded to witnesses in courts of law, where judges monitored the introduction of evidence, and any type of general privilege for political critics. And even had the common law recognized a distinction between facts and opinions, Richardson's written assertion that Mayrant possessed a "frequently affected mind" and his verbal claims that "Dr. Irwin said his mind was impaired, weakened, and could never be depended on," both seem much more like statements of fact than expressions of opinion.[56]

The difficulties in Justice Nott's decision, it seems apparent, did not stem from ignorance of the law; neither was his opinion a clumsy attempt to adapt Jeffersonian libertarianism to civil libel suits. Rather, his somewhat tortured discourse makes it fairly clear that he agreed with Richardson's view of Mayrant's mental incapacity and that he sought some way to keep painful facts out of the courtroom. Richardson, it should be remembered, did not publish his charges in the public prints but circulated them in private correspondence and in private conversations. Richardson's letter, Justice Nott suggested, "might have been calculated to excite a compassion, but not hatred, ridicule, or contempt" toward Mayrant. In the end, the court ruled that Mayrant's claim must ultimately fail not because Richardson possessed some constitutional privilege to state opinions, but because his statements did not meet the legal definition of defamation. They did not bring Mayrant into shame or disgrace or hold him up to hatred, ridicule or contempt. His problem "was a misfortune and not a fault."[57] Thus, from a strict legalistic perspective, *Mayrant* v. *Richardson* can be read quite narrowly, and Justice Nott's statements about a constitutional privilege dismissed as dicta. Certainly other jurists ignored its reasoning and holding.

Before 1830, no other court adopted anything like the approach of *Mayrant* v. *Richardson*, particularly when libel suits involved political statements in the press. Even in New York, where partisan passions ran deep, judges of both major political persuasions generally agreed upon the necessity for a firm stand against political calumniation and upon the application of this general principle to the precise case at hand.

A leading case from New York, once again involving Morgan Lewis, illustrated the hard line that most courts took against attempts to claim some privilege for defamatory falsehoods circulated in the public prints. In 1807 opponents of Lewis published a series of resolutions, framed at a public meeting, which condemned his conduct as governor. Alleging damages of $10,000, Lewis sued William Few, chairman of the gathering. Few countered that the governor's complaint stated no cause of action and entered a demurrer. On appeal to the state supreme court, Few's lawyers argued that magistrates were only the people's agents and that "the people should be at liberty, *bona fide*, to express their opinions of any public officer, or candidates for office." A public assembly had been called to urge removal of a public servant, and the press offered the best means of making the grievances generally known. In such a situation, a plaintiff must show "malice, or evil intention," not simply falsehood, in order to recover damages for libel.[58]

Justice Smith Thompson, a Republican who had accepted the Hamiltonian position in the prosecution of Harry Croswell, rejected this argument. Thompson simply ignored the defense's contention that malice rather than falsity should be the basis of liability and asserted that Few's attorney was claiming an unlimited right to slander public men. Branding this as a "monstrous doctrine," Thompson concluded that both candidates and voters had rights and that "those rights and privileges must be so guarded and protected as to harmonize one with the other." The fact that the publication conveyed the sentiments of a public meeting changed nothing.

The court also rejected the defense's other contention, that the relationship between voters and public officials was analogous to that between masters and domestic servants, a situation in which common law courts exempted nonmalicious falsehoods from any civil liability. The analogy between public officials and domestic servants, which defense lawyers would employ frequently later in the nineteenth century, attracted few judges during the early national era. In civil libel cases, courts granted no privilege for defamatory falsehoods published in the press.[59]

In other libel cases that raised issues of importance to the press, judges also generally showed little desire to grant newspapers any relief from strict common law principles. Although most civil libel cases trapped appellate courts in lengthy debates over complex rules of pleading and evidence, judges did not automatically transfer English precedents into American law books. Invoking the "instrumental" style evident in other areas of early nineteenth-century decision making, judges carefully considered how their libel decisions might affect the operation of the American press. In these judicial deliberations, one policy goal, one theme, predominated: in establishing rules for civil libel cases, courts should take care to circumscribe a "licentious" press by the "rule of law." The law of libel, judges almost universally believed, should encourage publishers to exercise rigorous scrutiny and self-censorship of their copy, particularly when it contained libelous charges against the character of public officials and candidates for office.[60]

This was the unequivocal view of the Connecticut Supreme Court of Errors in *Stow* v. *Converse*, a libel suit brought by a member of a debating club called the *Ethosian* Society. Converse published his libels in a pamphlet, but the court also considered its decision's probable impact upon portions of the newspaper press. It conceded that the law could not reasonably require defendants in civil libel cases to prove "the *letter* and *form*" of every libelous statement; but neither could courts allow defendants to escape liability merely by showing that libelous charges against public officials were more or less true. Defendants must provide, the court held, "full proof of the essential facts charged. . . ." Courts that authorized standards of liability that "sink below this standard, would deserve nothing short of public censure." Even if the charges had been framed in broad and general terms, judges should never relax rules requiring proof of truth. "Were it otherwise, the press, which now often teems with gross licentiousness, might easily be made the vehicle of the most wanton approach and vile calumny, without the possibility of correction; and this palladium of liberty would thus become a hateful curse."[61]

In bolstering their decision, the Connecticut court relied upon an earlier New York case, *Foot* v. *Tracy*, a lawsuit that grew out of partisan debates over the Croswell prosecution. Rejecting appeal of a $200 judgment against Tracy, editor of the *Lansingburgh Gazette*, Justice Brockholst Livingston rejected the claim that the trial judge, James Kent, had improperly excluded evidence about the plaintiff's generally poor reputation. Insistence upon strict rules of evidence, Justice Thompson held, merely required "those who choose to publish their animadversion on the crimes or failings of others, which occupy so great a portion of our public papers, the task of proving by particular facts, the truth of what they assert. . . . Those who sport with the feelings of others, under the professions of zeal for the public good, on no other basis than that of common fame . . . cannot complain, if courts require from them, on these, as on most other occasions, some better proof of their calumnies than general opinion." To hold otherwise, Justice Livingston argued, would be disastrous "in a country where the liberty of the press is so much perverted and abused. . . ."[62]

Most judges were no more sympathetic to the press than Justice Thompson. The growing distinction between editors and printers brought little rise in the professional status of journalists—at least in the eyes of most members of the legal profession. Newspapers, judges often complained in their opinions, devoted far too much space to abusing public figures and tearing down the reputations of people who entered the public forum.

Thus, early nineteenth-century courts invariably rejected legal formulae designed to relax some of the restraints libel laws imposed upon the press. In a suit against an editor who had published someone else's libelous letter, James Kent overruled the editor's claim that he had merely provided access for the author's views and was, therefore, not personally liable for damages. Kent pointedly noted that a responsible publisher would have been alerted to the dangerous content of the letter; the text itself admitted that one paper had already refused to print an earlier version. Clearly on notice, the defendant could not be "an object of sympathy as an inadvertent, ignorant, or heedless publisher. . . ." More important, Kent ruled that the defendant's whole theory, that newspaper editors and publishers were not liable for all that appeared in their columns, was as "repugnant to the principles of public policy" as it was "destitute of foundation in law."[63]

In another early New York libel case, judges rejected the suggestion that the law should adjust old doctrines to the new realities of political journalism. Appealing a judgment of $800, James Cheetham of the *American Citizen* contended that evidence about a previous suit—in which the same plaintiff, Thomas Tillotson, had recovered $1400 against Cheetham—should help to mitigate damages. The second suit did involve a separate publication, Cheetham's attorney acknowledged; but "they were all a connected *series* of numbers relating to the same subject, containing the same charge, and published in the same gazette. The plaintiff in this suit is certainly not entitled to the same damages, as if he had not already recovered a heavy sum for the same cause of action."[64]

The New York Supreme Court, and its chief justice James Kent, rejected Cheetham's appeal. "Miserable would be the condition of civil society," Kent warned, "if those who had once broken the law, by attacking the peace, or wounding the character of their neighbors could thereby acquire a valid plea for a future relaxation of its wholesome severities." The supreme court also rejected the contention that the trial judge, the same James Kent, had erred in charging the jury to consider awarding "exemplary damages."[65] Cheetham's libels, Kent had told jurors, not only wrongfully injured Tillotson's reputation but, because of his political position, also produced a "pernicious effect" upon society. On appeal, Kent reaffirmed the view that judges should press for an increase of damages in civil cases—similar to what James Wilson had called "inclining the beam" in criminal prosecutions—if libels damaged the reputations of public officials. "Surely," Kent argued, "this is the true and salutary doctrine. . . . It is too well settled in practice, and is too valuable in principle, to be called in question."[66]

In other libel cases, involving different issues, early nineteenth-century judges usually underscored the same basic concern: to frame libel doctrines that encouraged self-censorship by newspaper editors. In 1814 the New York Court of Errors reversed the supreme court after it had dismissed a suit on the grounds that the *Albany Register* had not specifically charged Justice Ambrose Spencer with "pecuniary corruption" but had merely left it for the reader to infer such financial skullduggery. A majority of the court of errors held that such a ruling had left the reputation of Spencer, a member of the supreme court, at the mercy of the press. To allow the *Albany Register* to escape liability because of cleverly constructed stories, complained Martin Van Buren, would produce considerable "mischief." The decision of the state supreme court, when "added to the acknowledged licentiousness of the press, would form a rampart, from behind which the blackest scurrility and the most odious criminations might be hurled on private character with impunity, and would, indeed, render the press both a public and private curse. . . ."[67]

Most important, in cases where the issue of a privilege for libelous political falsehoods was raised, courts quickly rejected any departure from the doctrine of strict liability. During the 1820s, courts in New York fully considered the issue of a privilege for defamatory political falsehoods when Erastus Root— the same person who had opposed all criminal libel prosecutions at the 1821 constitutional convention—sued the editors of the *New York American*. The paper claimed that Root, as the state's lieutenant governor, often presided over the senate while intoxicated. The trial judge charged the jury that Root's official position entitled the paper to no "favor," and that only proof of truth could sustain a verdict for the defense. Any malice required in a libel action was to be inferred from the falsity of the publication. When the jury returned a judgment of $1400 in favor of Root, the *American*'s editors appealed. The supreme court unanimously upheld the award, but the editors appealed again to the court of errors, then the highest tribunal in the state of New York.[68]

Reuben Walworth, who had succeeded Kent as chancellor of New York, wrote the majority opinion upholding the award. To depart from the ordinary rules of civil libel simply because the case involved criticism of a public servant by the press would produce "deplorable" results, Walworth argued. Recalling the old Blackstonian bromide, he suggested that by censuring licentiousness, courts were actually promoting liberty of the press. If "an editor could publish what he pleased against candidates for office, without being answerable for the truth of such publications," the chancellor claimed, no "honest man" would edit a paper. Courts had to protect the press from itself. Even more important, any grant of legal protection for false charges against political leaders threatened the integrity of the electoral process. If newspapers possessed any immunity for defamatory falsehoods, no man "who had any character to lose would be a candidate for office under such a construction of the law of libel."[69]

The Law of Libel and Early Nineteenth-Century Political Culture

The years between 1800 and the early 1830s repesented a transitional period in American political culture—an "elitist-participant" period that preceded the age of mass party politics.[70] Despite the continued popularization of politics and the emergence of new forms of political organization and communication, eighteenth-century political ideas and practices never quite disappeared.

Viewed most broadly, libel decisions such as *Root* v. *King* represented part of a general effort by most courts to take a stand against some of the more popular, antielitist tendencies in this transitional political culture. After the Revolution, for example, governmental officials generally sought to limit the role of extralegal political assemblies, what eighteenth-century constitutional theorists had called the "people out of doors." Although they conceded that popular political protests and extralegal bodies had provided valuable checks against the misuse of power by monarchical governments, political authorities now claimed that these activities served no such function in a free republic. When citizens possessed recourse to the electoral process, it was argued, the "people out of doors" only encouraged the growth of a licentious, and ultimately antirepublican, political spirit.

Similarly, early nineteenth-century libel doctrines announced that the conspiratorial rhetoric that had characterized early American political debates now represented an illegitimate, antirepublican form of discourse. When factional partisans tried to "inflame" the people with allegations about dark political schemes and wrongdoing by seemingly honest men, warned judges like chancellors Kent and Walworth, they were encouraging political licentiousness. In 1800, for instance, when William Duane publicly denounced the Federal Circuit Court of Pennsylvania for its handling of a libel suit against him, Judge Edward Tilghman censured Duane's criticism as contempt of court and disputed the editor's broad theories of free expression. Duane's published attacks on the bench, Judge Tilghman argued, threatened the operation of the national judiciary. The American constitutional order, he implied, represented the best of all possible worlds. "If you seek for anything more perfect, it will be necessary to bring down judges from the skies."[71] In a free republic, the broad theory of pre-Revolutionary patriots—that citizens enjoyed the right to criticize the corrupt acts of evil officials—required some rather precise legal qualifications. Toleration for circulation of libelous falsehoods or even for the spreading of many injurious truths, most early American courts declared, served no legitimate political purpose.

Libel decisions such as *Lewis* v. *Few* and *Root* v. *King*, then, were designed to help maintain the balance of democratic and elitist impulses in American political life. Although judges and lawmakers rejected the Blackstonian doctrine that the law should proscribe virtually all political criticism, they still hoped to protect the reputations of public officials, using civil rather than criminal libel as their main line of legal defense.[72]

Chapter Six | The Law of Libel
in the Age of Mass Politics

Despite the partisan conflicts of the Jacksonian period, the law of libel seldom became the prominent issue it had been during the earlier era of elitist-participant politics. Though writers vigorously assaulted the reputations of public figures—the vicious slanders against Rachel and Andrew Jackson and the sharp barbs flung at Abraham Lincoln were conspicuous examples—both critics and conductors of political presses considered libel law a minor legal issue and an insignificant restraint upon rhetorical ingenuity. During a brief return to the journalistic battlefront in 1834, the old Jeffersonian warhorse William Duane immediately noted the absence of the frequent suits that he had faced earlier in the century. Editors "are not incarcerated, nor are the courts and lawyers arrayed against the press—they will not prosecute each other—'dog will not eat dog'—for they have all the slander to themselves, and enjoy a plenary indulgence."[1]

Mid–Nineteenth-Century Libel Suits: A Survey

Some nineteenth-century jurists and later historians attributed the declining significance of libel law to relaxation of strict common law rules. But during the first two-thirds of the nineteenth century, virtually every jurisdiction still followed some version of the Hamiltonian "truth-plus" test in criminal prosecutions and traditional common law doctrines for civil suits. Before the 1870s, only New Hampshire formally extended any significant legal protection to libelous falsehoods published in the press. The infrequency of partisan libel cases in mid–nineteenth-century America reflected basic changes in the general legal culture rather than significant alterations of substantive libel doctrines.[2]

Framers of mid–nineteenth-century constitutions generally incorporated the Hamiltonian truth-plus standard into their states' charters. In those constitutional conventions where the issue of a more libertarian standard was raised, most delegates finally supported the Hamiltonian rule. Significantly, however, few emphasized the old rationale of the need to protect the reputations of the best men; instead, most now argued that the good-motives and justifiable-ends tests protected private persons who had once committed some indiscretion but had later become model citizens; no one, especially newspaper editors, should be allowed to expose past misdeeds without some valid purpose. Similarly, advocates of the truth-plus test defended it as a sort of protection for personal privacy; it could prevent persons from entering the sanctity of homes and of private life and holding up embarrassing facts to public gaze.[3]

When suggesting changes in libel law, Joel Parker of New Hampshire and Thomas Cooper of South Carolina, two of antebellum America's most prominent jurists, also moved very cautiously. Writing for the Supreme Court of New Hampshire in *State v. Burnham* (1837), Parker did concede a conditional privilege for at least some libelous political falsehoods. On certain "lawful occasions," Parker argued, a court might excuse libelous falsehoods if a judge determined that the defendant had made an innocent mistake—i.e. published a libel without any "bad motives." Though such a doctrine was more liberal than either the Blackstonian or Hamiltonian formulas, it still left judges with full authority to restrict any claim of privilege. Moreover, Parker's test rejected the theory that this qualified privilege should depend upon whether or not a defendant had "probable cause" to believe in the truth of a statement that turned out to be false; instead, Parker's doctrine focused on the much more speculative issue of the defendant's motives, a result much less favorable to political critics than the probable-cause test.[4]

In his *Treatise on the Law of Libel and the Liberty of the Press* (1830), Thomas Cooper was willing to grant more power to jurors than Justice Parker. He argued that in criminal libel prosecutions, "the whole matter in issue, with all the circumstances of truth or falsehood, intent, motive, and design," was "within the right of the jury to decide upon, after hearing all the evidence, and the charges of the court." In addition, Cooper suggested that defendants not be held to strict proof of truth but should be able "to offer evidence of public notoriety or public rumor" in support of libelous charges. But, when modified with changes such as these, the Hamiltonian position still formed the core of Cooper's analysis of libel law. And though he preferred civil lawsuits to criminal prosecution, this former victim of the Sedition Act agreed with his old Federalist rivals that the state possessed full authority to prosecute libelous political statements.[5]

Appellate court judges usually took an even tougher position than the ones outlined by Parker and Cooper. In *Hunt v. Bennett* (1859), the New York Court of Appeals rebuffed every attempt to overturn a $1000 judgment against James Gordon Bennett of the *New York Herald*. The justices rejected, for example, Bennett's claim that the doctrine of privileged publications, by now firmly established in libel suits involving official petitions, should cover newspaper criticism of a nominee for appointment as a New York City police judge. The court considered the press an improper forum in which to discuss the qualifications of candidates to appointive offices and held that Bennett's *Herald* had no greater privileges than a private citizen. The paper would have been exempt from strict liability only if it had formally petitioned the city council, the body that selected police judges. Publication of serious charges in a newspaper, especially one of "wide circulation," was "unnecessary and offered no basis for a claim of qualified privilege."[6]

Judges in New York also took a consistently firm stand against allowing the press any special privileges. In *Hotchkiss* v. *Oliphant* (1842), for example, Chief Justice Samuel Nelson (who would soon become an associate justice of the United States Supreme Court) followed Chancellor Kent's holding in *Dole* v. *Lyon* (1812) and denied newspapers any qualified privilege for libelous statements reprinted from other papers. An attorney for the *Oswego County Whig* had argued that the law should grant some qualified privilege "in favor of editors, on the ground of the peculiarity of their occupation." Editors were in the business of publishing "such matters relating to the current events of the day happening at home or abroad, as fell within the sphere of their observations, and as the public curiosity or taste demands," and it seemed "impracticable for them at all times to ascertain the truth or falsehood of various statements" reprinted from other papers. If the judiciary did not act, the attorney warned, the legislature would. Judge Nelson was neither persuaded by the defense's policy arguments nor bothered by the threat of legislative intervention. In part, he turned back the defense's position on the basis of settled precedents, especially *Dole* v. *Lyon*. But he also countered the defense's policy argument with one of his own: the law of libel, Nelson insisted, should encourage rigorous self-censorship by the press. A contrary policy, one that tolerated republication of libelous falsehoods, he argued, would be acceptable only if lawmakers wished "to pamper a depraved public appetite or taste, if there be any such. . . ." The policy of allowing no privilege for republication, he concluded, "will greatly tend to the promotion of truth, good morals and common decency on the part of the press, by inculcating caution and enquiry" among the publishers of newspapers.[7]

Most courts outside of New York endorsed similar doctrines in cases involving newspaper publishers and editors. In 1859, for example, the supreme court of Wisconsin refused to accept the idea that newspaper publishers possessed any special immunity for political criticism. In *Lansing* v. *Carpenter* the publishers of *The Daily Wisconsin Patriot* contended that charges of official misconduct by a court commissioner were not libelous. But the trial judge rejected this claim, and the state supreme court affirmed his decision. Imputations of corruption by a judicial officer, the court argued, "have a natural tendency, so far as the influence of the press extends, to diminish public confidence in his official integrity, and thus injure him in the business of his office."[8]

Similarly, appellate courts reiterated the rule of *Root* v. *King*, the doctrine that newspapers merited no exemption from strict liability in political libel cases. In an 1841 libel suit brought by a federal postmaster, for instance, the supreme court of Maine upheld a lower court ruling that required the defendant, a Whig newspaper editor, to prove the truth of his charges against a Jacksonian appointee. The high court accepted the argument of the postmaster's attorney:

> Carelessness or negligence is no excuse. An editor has no greater privilege than an individual. If he takes the responsibility of publishing what is not true, he cannot avoid it. He cannot assume the prerogatives of a judicial tribunal, and decide upon the character of individuals, and consign them to infamy, and then shield himself from harm by saying he was an editor and believed it. His position furnishes no excuse for the publication of falsehood.[9]

In 1864 the supreme court of Minnesota adopted the same position in a lawsuit brought by a candidate for the United States Senate. Admitting that the state bill of rights guaranteed "liberty of the press," the court held that this provision gave the press no privilege to publish libelous falsehoods about political officials or candidates. The court refused to apply the doctrine of privileged communications to such cases. Could it be argued, the court asked, "that every household visitation made by itinerant politicians poisoning the minds of electors with libelous and slanderous charges against candidates, every public harangue filled with similar matter, every clubroom discussion in which such charges are bandied about with licentious freedom and exaggeration, are privileged communications," and require plaintiffs to show "express malice? . . . We have never supposed that the freedom of speech even in this country could legally be carried to such an extent," the court answered. It held that public discussions of political issues by the press stood on no higher legal ground than purely private slanders by individuals.[10]

Insistence upon strict liability for libelous falsehoods, even in newspaper stories about public officials and candidates, constituted a significant exception to the general trend in nineteenth-century tort law. In other areas, such as the law of industrial accidents, courts generally rejected strict liability in favor of less stringent standards such as negligence.[11] In a few types of defamation cases, particularly ones arising out of business dealings, some courts did reject strict liability, but virtually every American court refused to concede any privilege when newspapers and periodicals published libelous falsehoods about political leaders or private citizens.[12] When it came to the reputations of the best men, the press remained an inherently dangerous instrument.

Although the libel doctrines applied in this period tended to be some form of the Hamilton truth-plus formula, the most significant trends in libel law were, in fact, the increasing resistance to political defamation suits and the growing recognition of libel law's limited effectiveness as a political weapon. During a celebrated murder trial, in which a political official was charged with killing the publisher of a Missouri newspaper, for example, attorneys ridiculed the notion that defamation law was an effective remedy for political slanders. Neither criminal nor civil sanctions, defense attorneys claimed, offered any real answer, especially in newer states like Missouri. Joseph Crockett, who edited the *St. Louis Intelligencer* and later served as an associate justice of the supreme court of California, mocked the claim that the press operated under legal restraints. "The very idea of sending the sheriff in pursuit of a man who has abused you in the newspaper . . . is preposterous in the extreme." And in the unlikely event that a criminal prosecution were successful, argued another defense attorney, the convicted editor "becomes a martyr" and the libeled victim "a persecutor." Civil libel suits, it was claimed, offered even less of a remedy. The litigation process only forced people who had been libeled to open their past lives and characters to "searching scrutiny" on the witness stand.[13]

Debating the Law of Libel

Despite the obvious hyperbole in the arguments of Joseph Crockett, his critique of the efficacy of libel law was essentially accurate. The prosecution of P. T. Barnum in 1832, for example, dramatized the conflict between libel doctrines framed in the early nineteenth century and the changing legal culture. A popular legal extravaganza, the Barnum affair highlighted the questionable value of libel actions, even successful ones.

Entering the newspaper business as a supporter of Andrew Jackson, Barnum aimed his exuberant prose at Connecticut's Christian Party, a small group of former Federalists who urged exclusion of all non-Christians from state politics. These attacks soon embroiled the twenty-one-year-old Barnum in several libel actions, the most serious being a criminal prosecution for libeling a leader of the Christian Party who was also a deacon in the Congregational Church. The case was tried before David Daggett, an old-line Federalist with little tolerance for Barnum's Universalist religious views or his Jacksonian political sentiments. According to Barnum's account of the trial, the judge heard the case with "no less than eight" Congregational ministers sitting nearby, and he gave the jurors a highly emotional, anti-Barnum charge. In addition to spiritual support, Judge Daggett had legal authority on his side. Following his own ruling in an earlier case, he held that Barnum's religious apostasy barred his testimony in a court of law. And because Barnum's article had charged the deacon with a serious moral offense, usury, Daggett ruled that proof of truth, by itself, would not justify the libel. After the jury dutifully returned a guilty verdict, Daggett sentenced Barnum to pay a small fine and spend sixty days in jail.

Displaying his gift for showmanship, Barnum dominated the stage that Daggett had erected for him. He continued to edit his *Herald of Freedom* from jail, while his supporters carpeted and wallpapered his cell. In a letter to another Jacksonian editor, Barnum confided that his prison stay was intended to garner maximum publicity. Following Barnum's cue, his Jacksonian supporters mounted an extravagant coming-out party on the sixtieth day when, promptly at noon, Barnum emerged from jail. Jacksonian papers claimed that 1500 cheering spectators celebrated the editor's liberation with a gala that recalled the rituals of the Revolutionary War and anticipated the promotional efforts that Barnum himself would later stage. The crowd feted Barnum with an ode "composed especially for the occasion"; a procession through the streets of Danbury; a dinner punctuated by numerous toasts to Barnum and "liberty of the press"; and an emotional *Oration on the Freedom of the Press* by Theophilus Fisk, editor of the *New Haven Examiner*.[14]

Theophilus Fisk's oration epitomized what historian Major Wilson has called the "federative view" of freedom: citizens of a nation that had been conceived in liberty, Americans must shoulder the clear, though not always easy, task of preserving the freedoms that the Founding Fathers had bequeathed them. Freedom of expression was a legacy of the Revolutionary era and protecting it from encroachments was a patriotic duty. Thus, Fisk saw the First Amendment as a kind of religious text, its free-press clause a kind of holy inscription that knew no temporal bounds. The amendment had "been published to the world. It is read in foreign lands, by him who groans beneath the accumulated weight of unnumbered years of bondage and oppression." Americans owed the rest of the world—and themselves—the duty either to withdraw such a promise or to respect it to the fullest. Fisk's choice seemed unequivocal: "Let there be no fetters upon the human mind—no shackles upon the press— no barriers in the pathway of knowledge."

Barnum's experience, Theophilus Fisk warned the crowd, should alert Americans to the threats against free expression. Even though these enemies of freedom had to resort to stealth and cunning, the danger was still very real. In time, Fisk claimed, the enemies of freedom might be able to exclude certain ideas from the press so that it would be "open only to those of OUR faith—to those who pronounce Shiboleth with OUR grimace and contortion of face. . . . Such a press is not free."

Fisk's argument assumed that Barnum's supporters were well aware of a legacy of press suppression in Connecticut, one that included a series of libel suits during the first decade of the nineteenth century. Thus, Fisk recalled the "ungodly persecutions and proscriptions of former years" and recited the names of suffering printers. He had fondly hoped that the persecutions of the press had ceased forever, but the prosecution of Barnum indicated that "we have been doomed to be disappointed."

Fisk expressed outrage that the law of libel could still be a threat. If common law authorized the jailing of P. T. Barnum, he thundered, "I trust in God that such laws will not be COMMON much longer." Common law courts and judges, Fisk complained, represented a corrupt past; they had no place "in a land where liberty has reared an everlasting home" or in a "new era" in which institutions, "now venerable by age, are falling into decay" and in which prejudice, "held sacred through the longer period of the past, are becoming a proverb and a byword."

In the end, then, Fisk could dismiss his worst fears about the future of liberty and of free expression. The forces of history had already propelled the United States far along the path of progress. "Our progress in all that ennobles human kind," he proclaimed, "is without parallel in the annals of creation!" And America—"proud symbol of salvation! its stars shall be un-dimmed through ages yet untold"—could credit much of this progress to its "FREEDOM OF THE PRESS."

Fisk's *Oration* flaunted the political style that so frightened traditionalist lawyers like David Daggett. There was no careful weighing of language, let alone of competing legal positions; no mention of social order or the right of reputation; and no sense of the "necessary" legal restraints that, according to all prudent lawyers, should limit "free" expression.

The *Barnum* case showcased egalitarian political styles and popular ideas about freedom of expression; and despite Barnum's conviction, the prosecution also showed the limited effectiveness of libel actions. Shortly after leaving jail, Barnum renewed his attacks upon the Christian Party and his prosecutor. Avoiding the epithet "usurer," he now denounced the deacon as a "notorious note-shaver." In addition, Barnum leveled new accusations, charging that the deacon publicly posed as a supporter of temperance while secretly seeking a liquor license. Although the deacon still enjoyed the protection of Hamiltonian legal doctrines, this time he chose to let Barnum's press remain unchecked.[15]

Theophilus Fisk's direct challenge to the law of libel was not unique. In 1838, for example, Joseph Whitmarsh of Boston, a defendant in a libel prosecution, claimed that the Revolutionary generation intended to deprive their public servants of the "power of persecution." Liberty of press, he argued, encompassed the "right to express any opinion upon any subject, whether true or false, right or wrong," without fear of criminal penalties. Though admitting that licentious publications might be dangerous, Henry Geyer of Missouri warned that, "for obvious considerations, legislative inter-ference is dangerous." Legal controls raised the "danger of an infraction of the constitution—none can tell at what point it could stop. . . . It is, therefore, better that the press not be shackled by law . . . leaving its licentiousness to the rebuke of public opinion" and, in extreme cases, violent retaliation by injured citizens.[16]

Other prominent libel trials demonstrated the difficulty of applying early nineteenth-century doctrines. Three political cases in New England—two criminal prosecutions in Massachusetts and a civil suit in New Hampshire— during the formative years of the second party system found defense attorneys denouncing Hamiltonian doctrines as hostile to republican principles and popular attitudes toward free expression. Any legal rule requiring writers to demonstrate the literal truth of political statements infringed upon guarantees of a free press. Although judges in these trials joined David Daggett in upholding the Hamiltonian position, all of the defendants escaped liability, two of them when jurors failed to agree upon a verdict. Several decades later, New York City's mayor George Opdyke tried to overcome popular resistance to political libel suits by offering to donate any damages he might collect against Thurlow Weed to charity. Jurors awarded Opdyke—and his charities— nothing.[17]

The Opdyke suit gave Thurlow Weed little worry because he had already triumphed over nineteenth-century America's most determined libel plaintiff when he and other New York editors outlasted James Fenimore Cooper, the celebrated novelist and political essayist. Between 1837 and 1843, Cooper conducted his own war of libel suits against several Whig party editors; he initiated numerous civil and criminal cases. Cooper took on both large and small: a verdict for $400 did drive the tiny *Ostego Republican* out of business, but leading Whig journalists like Weed and Horace Greeley easily outlasted the squire of Cooperstown.

The unprecedented legal crusade, unmatched until the chain libel suits against Drew Pearson by United States Representative Martin Sweeney in the 1930s and 1940s, grew out of concern over personal slanders, but gained momentum from Cooper's baleful view of larger political issues. Initially, Cooper's anger at the press stemmed from hostile reviews of his literary works by journalists who disliked his political ideas, and from critical newspaper coverage of a controversy involving public access to land owned by the Cooper family. After bitterly partisan reviews of *Home as Found* (1838), a novel that fictionalized some of the issues involved in his own land dispute, Cooper's rage took the form of a series of libel actions. As Whig newspapers denounced both Cooper's use of libel suits and his literary talents, the novelist linked his cause to what he considered ominous tendencies in American life. In a series of letters to various editors and in his famous work, *The American Democrat*, Cooper assailed the power of the American press and called for invocation of traditional restraints.[18]

An old-style paternalist cast adrift on the stormy seas of the Jacksonian era,

Cooper believed that a corrupted public opinion threatened to overturn republican government and the rule of law and to substitute a tyrannical system that respected neither the right of property nor the right of reputation. The "entire nation, in a moral sense," Cooper claimed, "breathes an atmosphere of falsehoods. . . ." Although Cooper sometimes feared that a hopelessly debased public opinion had itself spawned a demagogic press, he most often blamed "interested political adventurers" and partisan newspaper editors for the nation's troubles.[19] Thus, Cooper could still hope that the republic's descent into tyranny might be halted if, among other things, the landed gentry—Cooper's version of the best men—regained political power; this could only happen, he believed, if strict defamation laws prevented the press from destroying the characters and reputations of these worthy citizens.

Claiming that his libel suits could alert public opinion to the dangers of a corrupted press, Cooper vowed that he was ready to devote the rest of his life to unmasking the people he considered most responsible for the decay of republican ideals. Those who were misleading "the publick mind, as regards facts, characters or principles" were "corrupting all that is dear to society as its source, opinion being the fountain whence justice, honors, and the laws, equally flow." It was a "matter of indifference," he wrote, "whether he who wishes to tyrannize over men, be a prince by birth, claiming to make me his slave by inheritance, or a blackguard who edits a newspaper, who aims at effecting his purpose by drawing on the sympathies of other blackguards—I resist the tyranny I find in the country. . . ." The right of reputation, like the rights of property, must be protected by clear, tough, and easily enforceable laws. In all of his libel suits, Cooper claimed that the basic issue was simple: "whether the press of this country, or the laws of this country are the strongest. There can be neither political nor personal liberty, in any society, where there is not perfect protection of character. . . ."[20]

Cooper found himself forced to devote nearly his full energies during 1840 and 1841 to his libel suits; in the end, though, Cooper's short-run successes worked against his long-term goals. Sympathetic juries in upstate New York awarded Cooper $3060, enough to finance continuation of his suits, and the novelist did force two editors to retract offending statements. At several points in his crusade, Cooper even claimed his lawsuits were having a positive effect on journalistic content and on public attitudes. In reality, it became increasingly evident that Cooper's use of libel law was actually working against the causes he championed: mobilizing popular sentiment against the press, and creating greater respect for the law of libel.

Cooper's courtroom victories handed his opponents several popular issues, ones that they used to good advantage. The novelist's newspaper adversaries, for example, employed the issue of his damage awards as a multi-purpose weapon. On the one hand, editorialists could parade small awards against large publishers like James Watson Webb as proof that Cooper's claims were essentially frivolous; on the other hand, they could also accurately argue that even relatively small judgments threatened the survival of struggling rural papers and journals of opinion. In May 1839, William L. Stone, who himself was about to be sued by Cooper, suggested establishment of a general fund for payment of all damage claims awarded to Cooper.

Critical journalists also cited the frequent lawsuits as proof positive that Cooper misunderstood fundamental American values, including fair play and freedom of expression. In February 1839, for example, the *New-Yorker* condemned Cooper for rejecting legitimate criticism of ideas first advanced in his own writings; did not Cooper's critical comments on American life, the *New-Yorker* charged, make his remarks "a fair subject of comment?" Moreover, the *New-Yorker* argued, Cooper's resort to the law courts—instead of his chosen weapon, the pen—demonstrated a lack of confidence in his own abilities and in the wisdom of the American people. For a person like Cooper to "carry a controversy from the press into the law is to acknowledge either his own incompetency to wield his proper implement or the superiority of the courts of judicature to the high court of Public opinion in which he is by right a practitioner."[21]

Cooper's libel suits led to criticism of the traditionalist nature of New York's defamation laws. First, newspaper editors condemned New York's definition of libel, which was based upon Alexander Hamilton's argument in the *Croswell* case, as too narrow. More important, they criticized the state's complex pleading laws, provisions that, in the tradition of Chancellor Kent, sometimes prevented defendants even from offering evidence of truth or good motives. Those who were steeped in the byways of pleading and evidentiary rules might support such results as compatible with precedent; but to many others, Cooper's victories over mute opponents seemed to represent classic examples of the triumph of common law over common sense and simple justice. The tough, restrictionist decisions also allowed Whig editors and politicians to argue that they were not seeking immunity from all libel rules, only liability under reasonable restraints. "We are quite willing to be held to a rigid responsibility for all we say," argued Thurlow Weed, provided that "we may be allowed, with proper restrictions, to give the truth in evidence. But we are not willing to have the Courts standing between us and a Jury." If courts persisted in such restrictionist rulings, Weed warned, Cooper's opponents would "appeal to the People for relief."[22]

Weed and other Whig leaders made good their threat to take Cooper's suits to the court of public opinion and make the law of libel a political issue. The Cooper lawsuits were especially important to Horace Greeley, who hoped to boost his *Tribune*, then a fledgling daily, into a prominent organ for Whig reformism. Thus Greeley and his allies quickly assumed the forefront of the anti-Cooper efforts. In widely reported defense arguments by William E. Seward, one of New York's most prominent Whig leaders, and in a series of *Tribune* articles, Greeley and others hammered away at the view of libel espoused by Cooper and some New York judges.[23]

This counterattack induced Cooper to rethink his whole campaign. Cooper's suits had hardly stopped attacks on his literary works and political positions; judgments had proved even more difficult to collect than to obtain; and, most important, the suits threatened to politicize the entire libel issue. It was quite obviously in the interest of all political editors, not simply Whigs, to oppose court decisions that limited the ability to plead truth in defamation cases. Only a handful of New York papers supported Cooper's efforts. And in fighting the larger political battles, ones that his opponents sought to bring inside the courtrooms themselves, Cooper found both the judicial system and defamation law coming within the range of fire. His adversaries did not confine themselves, Cooper complained, to arguments "out of doors"; they tried to pack juries. Similarly, attorneys did not limit themselves to debating the technical definition of libel or complex pleading points; they argued, instead, that the very theory of libel law conflicted with the spirit of American institutions.[24]

Cooper had intended that his lawsuits substitute legal adjudication for political conflict; instead, the novelist found himself, and the legal restraints he sought to vindicate, caught up in heated popular debates. There was, as the address of Theophilus Fisk suggested, a strong popular tradition of opposition to politically motivated libel suits. Perhaps most important, Cooper found his view of libel law in conflict with that of many important people, especially the influential northern elites who were creating powerful new political and informational organizations. The men who owned the leading papers and those who operated the new political machines possessed a powerful series of arguments that provided the basis for a view of free expression considerably different from the more traditional view of James Fenimore Cooper and old-line jurists like Joseph Story.

The Press, Mass Politics, and Free Debate

Although defenders of a free press sometimes dressed their cause in the white robes of the Revolutionary Goddess of Liberty, they spread their message with power from grimy nineteenth-century steam engines. A number of important technological innovations—such as improved hand-operated presses and, ultimately, steam-driven presses—helped distinguish mid–nineteenth-century newspapers and periodicals from the papers and journals of the Jeffersonian era. Advances in printing technology were only one part of a general revolution in communication. By mid-century, miles of telegraph lines and railroad track speeded the flow of information across most parts of the country. In 1799, for example, it required seven days for news of George Washington's death to travel from Virginia to New York; in 1830, fifteen years before the telegraph, Andrew Jackson's State of the Union Address reached New York in less than sixteen hours.

Meanwhile, in the urban northeast, a new generation of publishers created the "penny presses," papers that eschewed the familiar diet of political and financial affairs in favor of "news" from America's vibrant cities. The penny presses of the 1830s inaugurated the use of regularly paid reporters, and they competed with one another to gather the freshest and most exciting happenings from their sprawling localities. Replacing backyard gossip and even personal experience as validators of reality, the new papers, according to Michael Schudson, "saw news in ordinary events where no one had seen anything noteworthy before."[25]

The antebellum communications revolution, which primarily affected the northern states, did not escape the notice of people who analyzed society, politics, and law. In his *Notes on New York* and various political speeches, William Seward offered a view of the press that differed significantly from the ideas of an earlier generation of politician-lawyers like Chancellor Kent. Seward epitomized the modernizing thrust of antebellum Whiggery. Confident that the United States was on the threshold of fundamental social and techno-logical changes, Seward championed use of governmental power to hasten the arrival of modern life. But there was no need to fear that governmental authority would extend its coercive force to the press; indeed, Seward claimed that the press, as one of the primary mediums of popular enlightenment, could smooth the transition to a new society by helping to create an intelligent public opinion, a progressive sentiment in harmony with the new technologies and social institutions. Thus, to "modernizers" like Seward, a vigorous press, one free from governmental controls, was an essential aid to national progress.

Seward praised the technological changes that had expanded the reach and social impact of the American press. Commercial newspapers, for example, recorded "with accuracy every occurrence and every indication which affects trade; and the advertising columns are indispensible auxiliaries in every opera-tion of commerce or finance." Taken together, the various branches of the American press gathered information from all over the globe and from all segments of American society; a powerful instrument for homogenization, the press left "no portion of the community without information concerning all that can engage their curiosity or concern their welfare." Seward also com-mended the press for its brashness. The press "no longer fears the odious *information*, or the frowns of power; but dictates with boldness to the govern-ment, and combines and not infrequently forms the public opinion which controls everything."[26]

In contrast to liberal political leaders of an earlier era, Seward discounted fears about the social impact of an unrestrained press. Despite the persistence of licentiousness, the press was not a despotic, antirepublican institution. Where James Fenimore Cooper saw danger, William Seward saw hope. The press did sometimes trample individual reputations, Seward admitted, but it also armed those assaulted with "equal weapons of defence, and yields redress for injuries it inflicts." And even if the ignorant and vulgar could not "be deprived of its weapons," the press "never generally, nor long, withholds its resistless influence from truth, wisdom, justice, and virtue." A free press, Seward concluded, "was at once the chief agent of intellectual improvement and the palladium of civil and religious liberty."[27]

Newspapers of the Jacksonian era also drew praise for aiding the growth of political democracy. Changing ideas about the role of the press, and ultimately about libel law, can be traced, in large part, to emergence of "mass parties" and to development of a new intellectual rationale for organizing political conflict. Libel doctrines framed during the elitist-participant era clashed with some of the most basic forces in mid–nineteenth-century political culture. Relying heavily upon the press, the architects of the second national party system assigned important duties to political editors. Supporters of Andrew Jackson took the lead in establishing a newspaper network that was far more extensive than any which had existed during the elitist-participant era. Prior to the election of 1828, Old Hickory's backers sponsored pro-Jackson sheets in most states; following the victory over John Quincy Adams, party newspaper editors helped turn Jackson's political machine. Democratic party editors produced a steady stream of partisan literature, informed leaders about local electoral prospects, and some—such as Thomas Ritchie, Isaac Hill, Amos Kendall, and Francis P. Blair—rose to important posts in the party hierarchy.

Opposition groups adopted these practices more slowly. The disparate anti-Jackson forces initially criticized "King Andrew's" frequent appointments of editors to political offices, and at the 1832 National Republican Convention Daniel Webster complained that the policy of rewarding editors was a "vital stab at the purity of the press." These appointments extended the executive power over the press "in a most daring manner" and undermined its "independence, by addressing sinister motives to it." In 1832 a coalition of anti-administration senators rejected several Jacksonian editors whom the president had nominated for federal positions.[28] But despite complaints about the Democrats' use of the press, National Republicans and then Whigs ultimately adopted similar tactics. By 1840 political newspapers blanketed much of the nation. Almost every hamlet in America, Alexis De Tocqueville claimed, had at least two party papers.

Editors were not required to toe the line on every issue, but they were expected to support major goals and basic programs. When the *New York*

Evening Post criticized President Jackson's monetary policies, another party paper denounced this example of freedom and independence. Although it was "most natural" for opposition sheets to abuse "worthy public officials," it represented the "extreme of folly" for a Democratic organ to attack the party's leader. Thomas Hart Benton considered it perfectly understandable that Francis P. Blair's *Globe* replaced the *United States Telegraph* as the "faithful, fearless and incorruptible" Democratic paper in the capital city after Jacksonian supporters suspected the *Telegraph*'s editor of disloyalty to the president.[29] Except for some of the old-line commercial papers and the new penny presses, both of which were primarily limited to the larger cities of the northeastern seaboard, most American newspapers remained closely tied to political organizations from 1824 to about 1870.

In truth, few political papers matched William Seward's effusive comments about the American press. A political editor's primary journalistic task was to rally the party faithful, not to provide the larger community with access to diverse sources of information. Party papers were also supposed to serve as the headwaters for torrents of partisan writings; carefully managed party organs provided views and information that partisans could use in their own debates with friends and neighbors. In an age of firm party allegiance, a voter's favorite newspaper undoubtedly indicated his political affiliation. Certainly, most newspaper writers assumed this to be the case. The staunchly Democratic *Memphis Commercial Appeal*, for example, printed the following capsule report of an 1855 political debate: "Cols. Tilman and McLanahan, the Democratic candidates came fully up to the expectations of their friends, defending their cause and explaining their principles with clearness, eloquence and ability. . . . Mr. Holmes (Know Nothing) defended his weak cause with considerable ability."[30] The letters to the editor in the *Appeal* followed the same partisan pattern. On one occasion, the *Appeal* apologized for printing a letter critical of Democrats to a typesetter's oversight; rushing to fill a blank space, the editor claimed, the harried typesetter grabbed the first available copy. Party newspapers routinely accused their rivals of circulating false and defamatory information. John Cooper's *Chambersburg* (Pennsylvania) *Valley Spirit* characterized the *Philadelphia Press* as "a reaking pest-house of personal defamation—a filthy sewer of stinking slander—a noisome receptacle of rancorous abuse. Its editor's propensity to libel the great and good is not displayed occasionally but every day. . . ."[31]

Politicians thus generally operated on the principle that one good libel deserved another. Enjoying easy access to party or factional newspapers, political leaders could quickly meet opposition slanders with denials, countercharges, or libels of their own. In the constant rounds of mudslinging, neither side hurled "mountains at each other, in the style of Milton's warring angels," observed one Whig partisan, but there was always enough dirt to "make at least one good sized mountain, and some half-dozen hills besides, under which numerous unfortunate candidates lie buried." Some office seekers, this Whig writer concluded, never rose again, but "others either crawl, or are at least dug out by their friends; when after a little recollection, refreshment and breathing, they re-engage in the contest, with unabated spirit and undiminished fury."[32] Party competition provided mass popular entertainment, and heated rhetoric became the centerpiece of political conflict. Debates attracted large and enthusiastic crowds, and the new political presses amplified and preserved the furor. Immortalizing debates in newspapers and pamphlets, the political press allowed the party faithful to replay furious battles at their leisure.

The way in which antebellum politicians viewed their own roles also contributed to the tone of political debate. As historian George Forgie has suggested, many mid–nineteenth-century political leaders operated in the shadow of the Revolutionary generation and came to doubt their own place in the nation's history. The great issues and the heroic political roles appeared to have been played out; politics seemed to have been reduced to a "pot-house squabble," to the building of hills rather than mountains. To be able to see political life as a noble and heroic enterprise, then, became important to antebellum politicians. One of the places they could display heroism was on the battlefield of political rhetoric. By manfully facing the verbal bullets of opposition publicists, by enduring the slanders of pamphleteers and newspaper writers, politicians could demonstrate their courage and test their mettle. Vilification of their public names only strengthened their true characters and demonstrated that they possessed the republican virtues of the Founding Fathers. Actions for libel, claimed William Seward "are now at least comparatively unnecessary. A virtuous and humble life carries with it its own vindication."[33]

Accompanying the emergence of mass politics was a new rationale for the value of organized, ongoing competition between permanent political parties. Although the antiparty ideas of earlier eras never entirely disappeared, a new generation of theorists and political writers, people such as Frederick Grimke and Francis Leiber, began championing the virtues of party politics. Not only were permanent parties inevitable in a free and pluralistic society, it was argued, but they supported rather than undermined the operation of republican government.

Party politics supposedly guaranteed truly effective popular participation in government. According to defenders of mass parties, a party's program rested upon the wishes of its own members, and regular party competition greatly increased the likelihood that this popular opinion would be translated into public policy. While one party controlled government institutions, the loyal opposition was supposed to serve as a vigilant public watchdog, seeking through its own partisan publications to expose dishonesty, corruption, or deviation from the dictates of public opinion. In this new political culture, politicians could no longer hope to equate most activities of their opponents with "sedition" or label all of their critics as licentious. Party conflict and partisan debates were phenomena to be welcomed, not unpleasant distractions to be condemned.

As the new system of mass political parties became closely identified with the health of republicanism itself, party presses gained new stature. The idea that even the most partisan presses should be free from most legal restraints seemed a necessary and logical extension of the whole new theory of political competition. In this calculus, the presses of the nation were not dangerous weapons, always about to wound some individual's reputation or halt the march of political truth; even at their bombastic worst, they remained vital parts of the process of free government. For if, as the defenders of party claimed, the new system was supposed to ensure popular participation, in both party and governmental decision making, then party presses could not suffer too much outside interference. Without party organs to help formulate and give some definite shape to the sentiments of individual citizens, the whole idea that mass parties advanced the cause of popular sovereignty would have lost considerable credibility.

Thus, both Democratic and Whig leaders came to have a vested interest in championing the freedom of party presses, even those of the opposing party. Restrictive defamation laws and fears about attacking personal reputations should not be allowed to impair the formation of public opinion—or the boisterous dissemination of partisan litanies. The idea that popular opinion was supreme, a proposition rejected by legal writers and political thinkers of the Revolutionary generation, became a central tenet, and the necessity of a free press a vital corollary, in the mid–nineteenth-century political litany.[34]

Mid–Nineteenth-Century Libertarianism: Public Opinion and the Marketplace of Ideas

A jurist and political theorist from Ohio, Frederick Grimke, provided one of the most articulate justifications for the mid–nineteenth-century system of free expression. After a career as a lawyer in South Carolina and a member of the Ohio Supreme Court, Grimke turned his attention to political analysis in the mid-1840s. His *Nature and Tendency of Free Institutions* lauded the American press as an integral part of the entire system of free government. "If the press were extinguished, the great principle on which representative government hinges, the responsibility of public agents to the people," would be largely lost.[35]

Previous generations of Anglo-American libertarians—including John Milton, "Cato," and Tunis Wortman—had placed considerable importance upon free expression, and some of Grimke's discussion merely embellished familiar themes. But, in contrast to all of these earlier writers, Grimke endorsed freedom of press in a *party* context. Eighteenth-century opposition writers and Jeffersonian opponents of the Sedition Act, it will be remembered, had warned against the "corruption" of the press and of public opinion; they urged libel prosecutions and civil lawsuits in order to prevent factional "scribblers" from destroying the reputations of individual politicians and from debasing the whole process of public discussion. Grimke, on the other hand, went to great lengths to argue that, in the "modern" era of party politics, even the most scurrilous party publications created no serious public danger. Extensive legal restraints were both unwise and unnecessary.

Nineteenth-century libertarians such as Frederick Grimke attributed almost magical healing powers to an essentially self-regulating marketplace of political ideas. Grimke advanced the marketplace of ideas as an alternative to exclusive reliance upon the political process. Through a free press, citizens could fully evaluate the merits of prospective governmental policies. Lengthy public discussion thus afforded "a sort of lesser experience which supersedes the necessity of actual experiment as a means of testing the utility" of proposals; Americans could enjoy the benefits of innovative policies without having to fear unwise governmental measures.[36]

Seeing the press as an important part of the new political system, Grimke argued that party newspapers helped to extend the benefits of organized political competition. Through the political press, for example, all sorts of "very obscure men in the inferior walks of life" could gain access to the channels of public opinion. In the best antebellum traditions of romantic reform and popular democracy, Grimke suggested that this supposed openness would produce remarkable results. These hitherto "mute Miltons" would "often suggest hints and anticipate improvements which men of cultivated understandings, and more intent upon past history than upon the character and genius of their own age, would not have the boldness to adopt. Perhaps it would not be too much to affirm that almost all the great revolutions in human affairs may be traced to this source."[37]

In addition to throwing out new ideas from "the inarticulate masses," Grimke argued that party presses would help bring together the nation and its diverse people. Party newspapers would help eliminate the "great advantage which the towns formally possessed over the country" because of "their superior intelligence and greater ability to combine for any public purpose." Now, "the dispersion of knowledge by means of the public journals," Grimke claimed, "has placed the city and the rural population on nearly the same footing—another example of the influence of the press in producing an equal distribution of both knowledge and power throughout the community." Similarly, by providing "the men who occupy a lower position in society" outlets for their ideas, party presses helped to bridge class lines, "to form substantially one class, and to create a system of opinions and interests which shall be common to the whole population." The press, then, operated as an aid to other egalitarian forces, "the principal function which the press performs in a political view is to equalize power throughout all parts of the community."[38]

Whigs initially expressed less enthusiasm for free-swinging political debate than Democratic writers, and Grimke sought to convince his political allies that even the most vituperative political newspapers were unlikely to threaten the survival of the republic. Since the United States possessed so many political newspapers and journals, he first argued, party debates did not really involve "the terrific assaults of two hostile combatants upon one another." The power of the American press was broken "into small fragments, and we have only a war of skirmishes."[39]

More important, Grimke could reject the need for strict legal controls because he simply did not believe that popular debate was likely to produce far-reaching changes in American society. Confident that the nation was firmly set on its proper liberal course, he could not really envision political agitation diverting the country from its progressive path. A vigorous marketplace of ideas would, in fact, eventually strengthen the bourgeois consensus. By providing "the men who occupy a lower position in society" with outlets for their ideas, party presses helped "to form substantially one class, and to create a system of opinion and interests which shall be common to the whole population."[40]

By relegating a good deal of popular debate to a nonpolitical status, Grimke's analysis actually discounted the legitimacy of the most angry political voices. A "great part of what we term public discontent is in reality only private discontent in disguise." Much of the undoubted scurrility in the public prints, Grimke claimed, merely reflected the happy absence of an overly coercive state, one which would have sought legal solutions for every petty neighborhood dispute. Because the law did not tightly control what one modern anthropologist has called the world of "small politics"—what Grimke called "all those private discontents which originated in envy, personal animosity, neighborhood bickering, the finding of one's self placed in a false position to the rest of society"—the nation must simply endure intermittent forays into the realm of "large politics" by disgruntled citizens who felt their own reputations had been unjustly injured. Delving into popular anthropology, Grimke argued that most Americans ordinarily avoided bringing private disputes over reputation into public view. Instead, private feuds were generally "deposited among the secrets of the human heart." But when controversial political issues agitated the community, all of these "private discontents" could give "a bitterness and vulgarity to public disputes which do not properly belong to them." At such times, people threw "the mantle of politics over their faces" and fought each other "in masks." Even though, on such occasions, American newspapers produced more scurrility page-for-page and column-for-column than the presses of any other nation, all of this bombast hardly threatened social or political stability. What, Grimke asked, "in its vulgar form is party politics but backbiting reduced to a system?" Political differences, he reassured his readers, were not nearly as great nor party debates as bitter as they might seem.[41]

If the presses were left open for freewheeling political discussion, Grimke emphasized, there would be no need for extensive governmental controls over political slander. The papers of one party could effectively answer and refute misrepresentations and libels published in opposition publications. "There is a real and formidable censorship on the press in America," Grimke claimed, "but the institution is in and not of the press." The existence of organized party debate meant, then, that the government need not exercise the type of post-publication "censorial" powers which most earlier libertarians had endorsed.[42]

Throughout his argument against strict legal controls, Grimke returned to one basic theme, to one firm faith: the clash of party politics, the bombast of party newspapers, and the furious exchanges between political partisans would inevitably lead to political consensus and social stability. Despite all of the bitter character assassination, political battles in the United States effectively cut across geographic and class lines, Grimke argued. "Society is divided into parties, but they are parties of the people." Political battles were not feuds between "distinct orders of men," but "the quarrels of members of one and the same family."[43] Thus, the political contention in party publications, Grimke claimed, did not indicate the existence of deep-seated political differences, the kind of fundamental disputes that many Federalists and Jeffersonians believed divided them during the 1790s. And to the extent that enfranchised Americans did differ over political issues, Grimke contended, a system of free expression, not an extensive system of legal controls, offered the best hope for moderating the clash of ideas and principles.

> The mixture of so many opinions, causing light to be shed upon each, contributes to moderate the tone of party spirit. However irreconcilable the views of parties may appear to be, a free communication cannot be established between them without producing a visible influence of each upon all. The press in its efforts to widen the breach and to make one opinion predominant is compelled to make all opinions known and creates the very process by which all are sought to be rectified.[44]

In this process of homogenization, even "absurd and preposterous opinions," even outright political lies, could be valuable because they often led citizens "to a clear sight of the truth."[45]

The views of Frederick Grimke were not unique; *The Nature and Tendency of Free Institutions* simply offered one of the most articulate mid–nineteenth-century statements about freedom of expression. Despite differences over a wide range of issues, both Whigs and Democrats endorsed the kind of free-ranging public debate that characterized antebellum politics. In the inaugural edition of the *Democratic Review*, the official oracle of the Jacksonian party, John L. O'Sullivan praised "Young America's" presses for democratizing politics, for undermining the notion that ordinary citizens must defer to the superior wisdom and judgment of the best men. "The general diffusion of education . . . [and] the freedom of the press, whose very licentiousness cannot materially impair its permanent value, in this country at least, make the pretensions of those self-styled 'better classes' to the sole possession of the requisite intelligence for the management of public affairs, too absurd to be entitled to any other treatment than an honest, manly contempt."[46] Another contributor to the *Democratic Review* unequivocally argued for unrestrained party debate and for no controls over allegedly licentious publications. Restraints over "licentiousness," he argued, merely "convert men into secret hypocrites or hostile malcontents." Restrictive laws could never do any real good, and "they ever must do harm." Writing that same year, 1848, a Whig essayist joined Grimke in stressing the value of the political press as a safety valve for both public and private discontents. Political partisans, he observed, "spend their fury in ink, instead of bloodshed, and content themselves with *speaking* daggers, in place of using them—as was the more ancient and approved method. . . ."[47]

Although legal restraints rarely affected publicists for the major political groups in the country, not everyone could write or speak so freely. To white Americans who either supported slavery or feared the social impact of anti-slavery agitation, abolitionism represented a dangerous force of dubious legitimacy. Fearful that their states might be overrun by abolitionist activists and their lives threatened by slave uprisings, Southern political leaders claimed to have discovered a "conspiracy" against the liberties of white people in the slave states. The language and imagery of Southern antiabolitionist literature often paralleled the Federalist jeremiads that had warned against jacobin conspirators during the late 1790s. According to the *Charleston Mercury*, the abolitionist editor was "a foreign enemy, creeping about in disguise, and demanding for malice and treachery the protection due to honest and good faith." In short, the abolitionist-antislavery conspiracy seemed to demand legal action similar to the Sedition Act of 1798.[48]

Libel suits hastened the demise of one of the first prominent abolitionist papers, *The Genius of Universal Emancipation* (coedited by young William Lloyd Garrison), and proslavery forces wanted to rattle similar legal sabers against Garrison's *Liberator* and other Northern abolitionist papers. In 1831 a number of prominent white Southerners urged Harrison Gray Otis, then Boston's mayor, to seek legal restraints upon Garrison's press. But the old Federalist remembered the lessons of 1798. Any attempt at formal legal action, Otis advised his Southern friends, would only alienate moderate Northerners and allow abolitionists to "justify themselves with the prejudices and arguments that abound against sedition acts."[49]

Southerners and their allies in the North also appealed to Northern state legislatures for new legal weapons against abolitionist presses. They rested their case upon the supposed bad tendency of abolitionist literature. A committee of the legislature of South Carolina demanded that officials in the free states recognize the difference "between the freedom of discussion and the liberty to deluge a friendly and coterminous state with seditious and incendiary tracts." Invoking the old eighteenth-century formula for seditious political literature, restrictionists also claimed that legislation against seditious and incendiary publications did not infringe upon the liberty of the press but merely restrained its licentious excesses.[50]

Although support for restrictive legislation was evident in some Northern states, abolitionists successfully linked their cause with the far more popular one of free expression. In every state that considered restriction, legislative majorities eventually rejected antiabolitionist legislation. Meanwhile, Garrison's unhappy experience with libel suits was rarely repeated; only a handful of antislavery crusaders ever confronted the law of defamation.[51]

In their confrontations with other types of restrictions—including direct pressure by hostile mobs—abolitionists often joined the banner of free expression to that of antislavery. Drawing upon free-speech traditions largely developed out of earlier battles over the law of libel, antislavery spokespeople urged protection of free expression as essential to the ultimate preservation of all other fundamental liberties. Using many of the same arguments he had employed in his *Oration* for P. T. Barnum, Theophilus Fisk warned Northern citizens to opppose even the slightest encroachment upon the abolitionist press. "Modern despots," he advised the readers of the *Liberator*, must proceed by stealth; direct legal controls "would arouse the people to rebellion—as they well know." "Let this freedom, guaranteed to every citizen of the United States by the constitution, be once destroyed on this point," advised another antislavery writer, "and it will be an easy work to destroy it on every other point."[52]

Thus, antislavery speakers could make the existence of free expression a test case of the general state of liberty. A dramatic confrontation between Theodore Dwight Weld and a group of the leading citizens of Painesville, Ohio, vividly illustrated how deeply the cause of free expression had become imbedded in Northern political culture. Told by a grandson of Painesville's founder that he must stop his antislavery lectures, Weld challenged his audience, correctly assuming that they would not passively accept limitations on his free speech—and, more important, on their own right to listen. "The issue is fairly made. I must not lecture any more and you must not come to hear me. Friends when I came here I came to lecture among A FREE PEOPLE. I assumed that I was speaking to the FREE *people* of Painesville. Is the assumption made by the Gentleman who has intruded himself upon our meeting warranted by the facts as they exist here? Is that, my friend, your master? Ladies are you the wives of slaves?"[53] With the issue baldly drawn, with the rights to speak and to listen linked to freedom from any type of outside domination, the people of Painesville sided with Weld and rejected his suggestion that they were no better than Southern slaves. A sizable crowd returned the following day, and Weld continued his lectures.

In the end, outright suppression of antislavery publications in the South and efforts to silence abolitionists in the North helped to strengthen Northern support for the liberal, marketplace view of free expression. Even though he denounced abolitionism as a "seditious and inflammatory" doctrine that incited its opponents to violence, William Leggett counseled use of the marketplace of ideas, rather than legal restraints, as the best solution. This Jacksonian Democrat advised opponents of abolitionism to convene public meetings and frame "temperate but firm resolutions" against antislavery agitation, and he called for greater use of the press to expose "the absurdity and impracticality" of abolitionism. Most important, Leggett rejected any suggestion that legal controls be used against antislavery publications. The call for governmental restraints, Leggett argued, ignored the important safety valve of free expression. "Fanaticism has ever flourished most exuberantly in the most intolerant countries; nor are there many minds . . . so ignorant of the history of nations as not to know, that, whether in religion or politics, enthusiasm gains strength and numbers the more its dogmas are opposed."[54] Like Frederick Grimke, Leggett saw imposition of governmental controls as a last resort, as something to be used only when political activists turned from inflammatory agitation to illegal action.

The Law of Libel in the Age of Mass Politics

During the antebellum era, then, an important change occurred in the way in which influential American liberals conceptualized the issue of free expression. Those who made the republican Revolution and established the nation's legal-constitutional framework, as we have seen, had placed great importance on the use of libel law to protect the reputations of the best men. The law of libel not only safeguarded the reputations of individual political leaders but served larger goals: in theory, restrictive libel laws helped to ensure that virtuous men would seek governmental position, that voters would not be fooled into selecting knaves and fools, and that public opinion itself would not become corrupted. Thus, the guarantees of free expression did not extend to licentious publications; most libels on the reputations of the best men, as well as other types of licentious utterances, lay outside the bounds of protected expression. Such ideas, of course, never disappeared, and most appellate court decisions still invoked them. But increasingly, the ideas of Alexander Hamilton and Chancellor Kent and the liberty-licentious formula came under attack as relics of a less confident age. At the same time, nearly everyone concerned with defamation law recognized that neo-Blackstonian doctrines could be applied only in the face of considerable resistance and with even less effectiveness than before.

Instead of viewing issues involving libel and free expression in terms of protecting the best men and fighting the "licentious corrupters" of public opinion, liberal jurists like Frederick Grimke and William Seward rejected the liberty-licentious equation. Rather than emphasizing the need to protect the public from libelers, they stressed the necessity of promoting a relatively open system of free expression. At the very least, as William Leggett suggested, free expression acted as a safety valve for popular discontents. More hopeful analyses—such as those of Seward, Grimke, and (as we shall see) Thomas Cooley—took account of the changes in the ways Americans fought political battles and received information on public affairs; the machinery of mass politics and the institutions of popular communication, these antebellum libertarians claimed, made it unnecessary and unwise to retain traditional controls for protecting the reputations of leading citizens. As long as the entire system were free to operate, it would produce a largely self-correcting popular opinion. Public opinion was "not the opinion of any one set of men, or of any particular party, to the exclusion of all others," argued Frederick Grimke. It was "the combined result of a great number of differing opinions"; some "portion of truth often adheres to views and speculations which are apparently the most unreasonable, and it is the true side which they present that goes to swell and to make up the sum of public opinion."[55]

Chapter Seven | Beyond Hamiltonianism: Libel Law Debates, 1840–1880

Mid–Nineteenth-Century Libertarianism: A Critique

In many ways claims that ordinary citizens contributed, through the channels of popular communication, to the formation of public opinion rang hollow. Even before the major wire services contributed to the standardization and industrialization of political reporting, the partisan newspaper networks exerted similar pressures toward uniformity. As early as 1826, Andrew Jackson's supporters had begun to fill smaller pro-Jackson papers with extracts from leading journals and newspapers. According to one of the closest students of nineteenth-century political journalism, the party presses produced "a manufactured or synthetic public sentiment."[1]

Similarly, the noisy penny presses, such as James Gordon Bennett's *New York Herald*, preached a social-political view that ultimately squared with the interests of powerful elites. Although the penny presses liked to laud their political independence and feature bombastic exposés of public corruption, they still (in the words of one of their most perceptive historians, Dan Schiller) "assumed the institutional legitimacy of the republic" and used the cause of universal social justice "as a means to [their own] ever-enlarging circulation and profits." All the while, the penny-press operators could offer considerable deference to the best men. "We ought to guard the reputation of our great men—to whatever party they belong—better than to make them the sport of other nations, by revealing every little thing, by a forced construction to their discredit," advised James Gordon Bennett. The reputation of men such as Daniel Webster "ought to be cherished, encouraged, and taken care of."[2]

The mid–nineteenth-century marketplace of free expression contained other "distortions."[3] Most obviously, it did not extend to the Slave South where the law of human bondage prohibited the enslaved from questioning their statuses, and where both law and custom effectively quashed criticism of the peculiar institution by whites. Even in the North, blacks encountered much more difficulty than white abolitionists when they spoke out on racial issues. In addition, the ongoing struggle to obtain political equality, including an equal right of free speech, involved women as well as blacks. Even Theodore Dwight Weld's libertarian speech to the citizens of Painesville acknowledged that women possessed an inferior position in the marketplace of ideas. "Ladies," he asked, "are you the wives of slaves?" The ability to participate fully in a truly open system of public debate requires that speakers and writers enjoy equal status as citizens and freedom from at least some of the time-consuming tasks of the household; in mid–nineteenth-century America, few women possessed this kind of freedom.[4]

In addition to distortions grounded in race and gender, there were growing ones based on class. The kind of free speech favored by nineteenth-century liberals was hardly neutral in its social and economic orientation. As historians such as Edward Pessen and Paul Johnson have argued, for example, the moral tone of nineteenth-century newspapers and the messages of evangelical preachers helped to pave the way for a new system of industrial discipline. This new order ultimately resulted in substantial limitations upon what could be said or what publications could be circulated within the workplace. Beginning in the mid–nineteenth century, the traditional workplace milieu, one in which there had always been a good deal of conversation on a wide range of issues, was being transformed. A new generation of capitalists insisted that the free marketplace of ideas stop at the workplace door. "The Rules and Regulations of the Matteawan Company of Rockdale, Pennsylvania," for instance, contained the following restrictions.

No talking can be permitted among the hands in any of the working departments, except on subjects relating to their work. . . .

Those who take jobs will be considered as overseers of the persons employed by them, and subject to these rules.

Should there exist among any of the persons employed, an idea of oppression on the part of the company, they are requested to make the same known in honorable manner, that such grievances, if really existing, may be promptly considered.

If the right of free expression was a much-discussed issue in the public domain, it was a liberty absent from the new industrial workplace.[5]

Similarly, the kinds of religious-ethnic tensions that cut through mid–nineteenth-century politics affected members of groups who fell outside the political-cultural mainstream. Assaults against the religious practices and political expression of Mormons and Catholics, for example, were hardly unknown events in the antebellum era. Indeed, the emphasis on the free marketplace of ideas and the supremacy of public opinion could be used against those—such as Catholics, Masons, and Mormons—who desired to create their own self-contained, closed societies. The refusal of such groups to operate by open, marketplace principles, their critics argued, demonstrated their sinister, anti-American nature. Those who wanted to live by rules other than those endorsed by the custodians of proper public behavior, the historian Paul Murphy suggests, sometimes discovered that they had also "surrendered the right to play by their own."[6]

Finally, there is the very difficult issue of how to evaluate nineteenth-century libertarianism itself. If one were to measure this body of thought—and ultimately practice—against egalitarian standards of free expression used by critics of twentieth-century corporate-dominated informational systems, significant limits are evident. Though they broke with the neo-Blackstonianism of the Revolutionary generation and with the cautious libertarianism of the Jeffersonian era, mid–nineteenth-century libertarians never really envisioned free expression leading to fundamental debates over the nature of the American society and economy or even to the kind of passionate discussions pioneered by republicans like Thomas Paine. Writers such as Frederick Grimke, William Seward, and Thomas Cooley could so enthusiastically embrace the liberal marketplace of ideas because they were convinced that, outside the Slave South, threats to the liberal-capitalist order were insignificant and because, as Grimke explained, they felt confident that angry dissent represented isolated examples of sociological distempers or individual pathologies. (Grimke, it will be remembered, dismissed most heated political rhetoric as the result of personal pique rather than as the expression of legitimate political commentary.)[7] And though nineteenth-century libertarians did denounce traditional controls on the basis of fundamental legal principles, they also believed, on the basis of political expediency, that resort to legal controls would, in any case, either be useless or counterproductive. When later in the nineteenth century, liberal fears overwhelmed liberal hopes, doubts about the efficacy of legal controls over political speech faded and legal visions of the limits on free speech once again narrowed.[8]

Yet this somewhat baleful perspective should not obscure the libertarian impulses, in both theory and practice, that did emerge during the early nineteenth century. Although one should not invent a golden age of free expression—even after admitting all the qualifications with respect to race, class, and gender—nineteenth-century theory and practice did, in many ways, represent a democratization of political communication.

Even penny presses, despite their limitations, brought new approaches to popular journalism. Borrowing much of their rhetoric and at least some of their political viewpoints from the artisan republicanism of the workingmen's papers, the penny presses championed the principle that all citizens had an equal right to knowledge and information. Thus the penny presses joined the labor papers in denouncing the party organs for failing to delve into political misdeeds within their own ranks and the commercial papers for refusing to look critically at the emerging industrial order. And as Dan Schiller has pointed out, the popular presses' emphasis on criminal reporting represented something more than a desire to cash in on the public's appetite for sensationalism. By closely examining how the criminal justice system worked in concrete legal cases, the penny presses could test how well the entire system of civil liberties operated in the United States.

Moreover, as historian Christopher Lasch has noted, the nineteenth-century system of political communication, for all of its obvious limitations, still compares favorably to that of the twentieth century. As Lasch argues, for example, the bitterness of nineteenth-century political debates "testified to an underlying agreement about the nature of political communication"; participants and listeners "assumed that political actions had to be justified by an appeal to a body of moral principles accessible to human reason and subject to rational discussion." This approach to political speech, Lasch and other critical historians maintain, was more open and participatory than the highly manipulative, corporate-dominated modes that have dominated post-1900 political communication.

And, to return to the central focus of this study, nineteenth-century libertarian thought also eventually bolstered efforts to overturn the Hamiltonian libel doctrines of appellate courts and to align defamation law more closely with both the idealized and real nature of nineteenth-century politics. In this new political culture, as historian Sean Wilentz suggests, party professionals "stood for the orderly pursuit of office, in which loyalty, merit, talent, and hard work for the party—not honor, reputation, and family connections, and certainly not the pursuit of larger ideological goals—brought preferment and power."[9]

A New Law of Libel?

Changing ideas about the organization of political competition, the contributions of the American press, and the benefits of a liberal system of free expression ultimately affected the law of political libel. First, as we have already seen, public officials and candidates found it very difficult to sustain a successful civil suit or initiate a criminal prosecution. During the decade from 1865 to 1876 there were fewer than twenty reported libel prosecutions in the entire country.[10] Even in New York, with its tough libel laws, criminal prosecutions disappeared almost entirely.

Second, the theories undergirding civil libel suits came under increased scrutiny, and arguments for liberalizing political libel doctrines gained some important supporters. Some lawyers came to apply the ideas about politics and journalism articulated by writers like Frederick Grimke directly to the issue of libel law. The very fact that restrictive legal doctrines diverged so significantly from popular attitudes and journalistic practices provided a potent argument for change. If the law of libel were to remain any sort of restraint—and virtually every nineteenth-century legal writer agreed that defamation law should still apply to the grossest political slanders—there would have to be adjustments in the older rules. The legitimacy of the whole concept of defamation suits, it appeared, could be undermined by popular contempt for neo-Blackstonian doctrines.

The persistence of debates about the relationship between defamation law and guarantees of free expression during this period needs special emphasis. For many years, First-Amendment scholars have claimed that no significant discussion of free-speech issues occurred before about 1919; it was renewal of restrictionist legislation by the national government during World War I, according to this traditional thesis, that produced the first real analysis of the legal meaning of freedom of speech and liberty of the press.[11]

The reality, however, was quite different. As we have seen, the nineteenth-century record is filled with discussions about the meaning of free expression. These debates, of course, took place in a legal culture significantly different from the one in which twentieth-century scholars have contested issues relating to free expression. Post-1919 debates became part of a highly specialized legal culture, one in which law reviews that were aimed at the legal *illuminati* provided the major outlets for participants. But the people who analyzed legal topics, including free expression, in the nineteenth century lacked these types of forums. Although there were some nineteenth-century law journals, they were quite different from their twentieth-century counterparts, and there were comparatively few scholar-writers to fill their pages. Thus, an 1845 article on libel law by William Seward was simply a reprint of his defense of Horace Greeley in one of the *Cooper* lawsuits.[12] When the true forerunners of the twentieth-century law review appeared during the Gilded Age, these journals did contain a number of pieces that analyzed defamation law and other issues relating to freedom of expression.

During most of the nineteenth century, treatises and practical manuals offered more important sources than law reviews for guidance on legal matters. Virtually all of these works, from the magisterial treatises of Kent and Story to the unpretentious guides for ordinary practitioners and laypeople, continued to link the legal definition of free expression to the law of libel.[13] If defamation law was irregularly applied, its rules of procedure and standards of liability remained central to legal guarantees of free speech, and the dominant forms of legal literature reminded Americans of the connection. Thus, the popular treatise of Thomas Cooley, *Constitutional Limitations*, deserves special attention because it contained a lengthy discussion of libel law and freedom of expression; Cooley's analysis, as we shall see, provided an important legal bridge between the political culture of the antebellum era and the legal debates over libel law during the Gilded Age.[14]

Probably the most popular forum for debating freedom of expression and libel law was the nineteenth-century courtroom. But, as in the case of law reviews, a view of nineteenth-century legal battles based upon the perspectives of twentieth-century legal culture can obscure the importance of the earlier debates. In contrast to recent times, when legal arguments only rarely attract public attention, debates in nineteenth-century courtrooms were widely disseminated, especially before the Civil War. Antebellum political culture, as historian Daniel Walker Howe has suggested, lacked rigid divisions between elite and popular levels. In an age when American popular culture was in its infancy, political speeches offered one of the few "games" in town; they were a central—perhaps *the* central—form of entertainment. And legal-constitutional arguments represented one of the standard forms of popular political speech rather than an esoteric genre directed at the tastes of legal and political elites. If readers or listeners could not fathom all the legal nuances, they could still appreciate the rhetorical and intellectual virtuosity of their favorite champions. Thus, William Seward in his defense of Horace Greeley could alternate between opaque analysis of ancient defamation doctrines and popular appeals aimed at the potential tyranny of overly complex common law rules. In addition, as the controversy surrounding the *Cooper* lawsuits demonstrated, newspaper writers extended courtroom debates into their own journalistic domain. Horace Greeley and other Whig editors, for example, tried to synthesize the arguments of attorneys like Seward and to popularize legal debates over defamation law.[15]

In the public debate over libel law and free expression, proponents of liberalization of the law stressed some familiar themes, such as the press's role in spreading useful information and political democracy. Defending Horace Greeley at a libel trial in 1861, I. F. Williams argued that newspaper readers now "demanded" all the news their money could buy and that editors consequently owed customers a public duty to disseminate rapidly all the information they could gather. Courts should not allow outdated defamation laws to interfere with this buyer-seller relationship. In a Massachusetts libel prosecution against the editor of the *Boston Daily Chronotype*, Richard Hildreth argued that newspapers were "no longer considered as nuisances but as a necessary article of life; the daily bread of the public." In seeking to cover rapidly unfolding events or "exciting causes," editors were sometimes forced to "act upon slight evidence. . . . In the performance of their duty to the public, they are therefore entitled to some indulgence" when they discussed issues of general concern. "Prosecution for libel against editors ought not to be encouraged." William Seward claimed that citizens could not—and would not—allow libel laws "established in the worst of times in England" to burden the daily operations of the modern press. Defamation rules, he maintained, must be updated so that they separated "harmless invective, or that temperate and discreet censure or ridicule," which actually promoted public morals, from truly vicious defamation.[16]

The cause of democratic government, as well as the needs of a rapidly growing society, also pointed toward liberalization of libel laws. An anonymous reviewer for the *American Law Magazine* maintained that the new, democratic political culture required abandonment of older libel doctrines. Any person whose public conduct or private character could not "abide the ordeal of the most searching scrutiny ought not in these days of the supremacy of public opinion, to solicit the suffrages of that opinion, either with a view to fortune, fame, or station." The public press, contended attorney William Gardiner, was "the only tribunal in which to combat libelous statements." William Seward endorsed a similar position, arguing that the self-regulating marketplace of ideas offered its own antidotes to the poisons of political slanderers. The very licentiousness of some papers, for example, had made libel suits against them "comparatively unnecessary"; their own recklessness had impaired their power to defame. Libel laws that failed to take account of new social and political developments, Seward concluded, could never be executed. "Whatever may be the course of the courts of justice, the press will go on to perform its high and imperative duties, sustained by the free people, whose liberties it maintains and defends."[17]

A Connecticut law of 1855, upheld by the state supreme court, took account of demands for changes favorable to the press. Although the statute did not change standards for determining liability, it did make it more difficult for public officials to collect large damage awards. The law provided that "in every action for an alleged libel the defendant may give proof of intention, and unless the plaintiff shall prove malice in fact he shall recover nothing but his actual damage proved and specially alleged in the declaration." According to the Connecticut Supreme Court, the act was intended to relieve newspapers from the threat of "heavy punitive damages for articles which contained rumors, so generally circulated and credited as to constitute a part of the current news of the day, or proper and just criticisms upon public men, public measures or candidates for office, or other matters of public interest." In such instances, plaintiffs could recover punitive damages only if they could show that the newspaper had published libelous falsehoods from an "improper and unjustifiable motive."[18]

Ironically, advocates of more liberal libel rules also began to look toward England for support. Earlier in the nineteenth century, American lawyers who advocated greater protection for free expression had condemned English law. By mid-century, however, English courts were beginning to modify some traditional doctrines, and American critics of strict liability could draw upon this trend. In the 1843 edition of an English libel treatise, John Wendell, the American editor of *Starkie on Slander and Libel*, went beyond the limited role of annotator and urged courts to broaden the legal definition of free expression and to align our libel laws with recent English decisions.

John Wendell was a well-connected member of the Democratic party of New York and a lawyer familiar with defamation law. In 1828 he had appeared before the state supreme court, unsuccessfully urging modification of the Empire State's tough libel laws. Fifteen years later, in his edition of *Starkie*, Wendell renewed his argument. Writing at the time of James Fenimore Cooper's controversial libel suits, Wendell acknowledged popular demands for changes in New York's defamation laws. But any legislative action, he claimed, was "unnecessary and inexpedient." Existing doctrines, "correctly understood and wisely administered," protected liberty of expression. Seeking to demonstrate this, Wendell devoted the bulk of his discussion to an analysis of the complex pleading problems raised in many of Cooper's lawsuits.

Wendell also considered the issue of political libel. He quickly dismissed criminal libel, noting that popular opinion had largely blunted this threat to political discussion, and concentrated upon the chilling effect of civil lawsuits. Wendell's inconsistent analysis reflected the gap between his own view of the law and the holdings of leading state court precedents. Thus, in his introduction Wendell praised the English doctrine of "privileged communications" and regretted the fact that it was "scarcely known" in the United States. But elsewhere, he suggested that it was doubtful "at this day" whether American courts would recognize a case of defamatory falsehood by a candidate or a public official "without proof of *express malice*." In political libel cases, he contended, there should be no liability for libelous falsehoods without independent proof of malice; courts could not imply malice from the mere fact of falsity.[19]

To sustain this view, Wendell could cite only two American cases, neither of which supported his view of privileged communications. *Mayrant* v. *Richardson*, the 1818 South Carolina case, said nothing about any privilege for falsehoods. And in *Commonwealth* v. *Clap*, it will be remembered, Theophilus Parsons not only rejected any privilege for falsehoods but applied the truth-plus test only to elective officials.[20]

American precedent may not have supported Wendell's interpretation of existing law, but a reviewer for the *American Law Magazine* immediately endorsed his theories. In an age of free institutions, "rapidly expanding ideas" of political and personal rights, and "the predominating influence of public sentiment," the anonymous writer argued, "liberal principles" of free expression were of "paramount importance." People unwilling to endure rigorous scrutiny of their characters and activities should stay away from public life. Thus, the *American Law Magazine*'s reviewer endorsed Wendell's view that the issue of truth or falsehood was not the important consideration in political libel cases. Moreover, the same principle applied in all situations where citizens possessed a legitimate interest in statements made by defendants in libel cases. In trials that involved political or other public matters, the crucial legal issue was not the factual accuracy of the publication; rather, the ultimate question of legal liability, which was solely an issue for jurors, depended upon the defendants' good-faith belief in the truth and their motives for making the libelous publication.

Going beyond Wendell's position, the reviewer also claimed that writers and publishers needed broad legal protection in order to discuss the personal character of politicians and literary figures. In both political and literary discussions, he argued, "we associate the ideal of personal excellence and purity of character with all our conceptions and illustrations of Scott, of Irving, of Wordsworth, of Hamilton, of Jay, or of Marshall. . . ." The law could not ignore the obvious realities of public debate and insist upon sharp distinctions between public actions and private character. There were still, though, some limits to such discussion. The privilege of examining a public person's private character, the reviewer suggested, did not give anyone the "right of penetrating into the recesses of his household gods, or of investigating his private pursuits of business or of pleasure."[21]

Thomas Cooley and the New Law of Libel

The views expressed by the *American Law Magazine*'s commentator closely paralleled those of Thomas M. Cooley, the nineteenth century's most illustrious critic of neo-Blackstonian libel laws. Cooley's views merit special attention because he approached the problem of libel and free expression from two vantage points. As a writer of a number of popular legal treatises, Cooley served as one of the nineteenth century's most widely read—or at least widely cited—conceptualizers and glossators. One of the American legal profession's first prominent lawyer-academicians (he taught at the University of Michigan Law School from 1859 to 1884), Cooley sought to derive and then to articulate justifications for prevailing legal rules, and to formulate and then advocate modifications that he deemed necessary and appropriate. As a member of the supreme court of Michigan from 1864 to 1885, Cooley also had the opportunity to argue with his skeptical colleagues about the viability of his approach and to apply the theories of the treatise writer to the concrete problems of the appellate judge.[22]

American liberals, Thomas Cooley included, have always placed great importance on a series of supposedly self-regulating marketplaces. Cooley's *Constitutional Limitations* (1868), his earliest and most influential treatise, became famous for its implicit endorsement of the glories of a free, largely self-adjusting, economic marketplace. But Cooley's legalistic version of marketplace theology was not simply a set of arbitrary doctrines that cynically sanctified the growth of capitalism and the profits of the robber barons. In *Constitutional Limitations*, as well as in his other writings, Cooley also glorified several other liberal marketplaces, including the intellectual and the political. In Cooley's view, maintenance of these three marketplaces—the economic, the intellectual, and the political—provided the essential framework for the continued development of a liberal republic.

Writing in *Constitutional Limitations* about freedom of expression and American journalism, Cooley often used analogies from the expanding economic marketplace to bolster arguments about similar benefits that would result from the free flow of ideas and from the unhindered clash of rival political forces. If political ideas and political aspirants could freely compete for attention and for supporters, Cooley believed, Americans would enjoy the steady advance of social and political wisdom. America's culture, government, and economy would thrive. The state's intrusion into the marketplace of ideas by means of laws was as ill advised as its intrusion into the economic marketplace with mercantilistic regulatory measures. The task of lawmakers was to see that legal institutions released, rather than restricted, the flow of individual ideas into the intellectual marketplace. Both as a treatise writer and as a judge, Cooley sought to develop legal principles that would promote intellectual and political development by removing illiberal restrictions from public debate and the primary channel of communication, the American newspaper press.

Traditionally, the law of libel had offered the most significant legal check upon political discussion and upon the press, and Thomas Cooley thus devoted considerable attention to eliminating what he considered the antiliberal features of defamation law. In *Constitutional Limitations*, Cooley began to question the wisdom of Hamiltonian libel doctrines.

An advocate of free soil, free trade, and free public education, Thomas Cooley found traditional libel doctrines in direct conflict with his support of free expression. Devoting an entire chapter of *Constitutional Limitations* to "Liberty of Speech and of the Press," he took direct aim on English and early American authorities. After a quick review of English constitutional history, Cooley concluded that Sir William Blackstone's famous definition, equating liberty of expression with liberation from prior restraints, was woefully inadequate. "Mere exemption from previous restraints cannot be all that is secured by constitutional provisions, in as much as of words to be uttered orally there can be no previous censorship, and the liberty of the press might be rendered a mockery and a delusion . . . if, while every man was at liberty to publish whatever he pleased, the public authorities might nevertheless punish him for harmless publication."[23]

Post-Revolutionary adaptations of English doctrines also failed to satisfy

Cooley. He contended that the Sedition Act of 1798, although it departed from common law orthodoxy by permitting truth as a defense, still violated the First Amendment. He argued that it was "impossible to conceive at the present time . . . the passage of any similar repressive statute." Cooley conceded that public debates might become impassioned and that some people would call for criminal libel prosecutions. But "the evil likely to spring from the violent discussion," he counseled, "will probably be less, and its correction by public sentiment more speedy, than if the terrors of the law were brought to bear to prevent this discussion."[24] Cooley believed that civil suits for damages could also infringe upon liberty of expression. He insisted that courts become more sensitive to complex issues raised by libel suits in which political leaders sued their critics for defamation.

A one-time editor and an active political partisan before becoming a judge, Cooley drew upon the ideas and the spirit of mid–nineteenth-century political culture to bolster his critique of existing libel doctrines. He, like William Seward and Frederick Grimke, praised free-swinging political debates and extolled the rationality of most voters and the ultimate integrity of the free marketplace of political ideas. Commenting on the Sedition Act, Cooley attributed its passage to the apprehensions of an earlier age, a time when "the fabric of government was still new and untried" and "when many men seemed to think that the breath of heated party discussion might tumble it about their heads."[25]

Fears about the bad tendency of party polemics could no longer justify such limitations on the right of free expression. Constitutional guarantees, Cooley argued, insured "every citizen at any time" the liberty to "bring the government and any person in authority to the bar of public opinion by any just criticism upon their conduct in the exercise of the authority which the people have conferred upon them." Repressive libel laws only frustrated translation of public opinion into public policy and undermined the operation of the new system of popular politics. Traditional common law restraints could even become direct tools of political repression. In "times of high party excitement," Cooley feared, "the party in power" might be tempted "to bolster up wrongs and abuses and oppressions by crushing adverse criticism and discussion." On the basis of both republican principles and political expediency, then, Cooley urged elimination of outdated libel laws. Citizens should recognize that enlightened "public sentiment" would provide a safer and even more effective remedy for libelous publications than the old system of legal controls. Anyone who entered public life could be expected to submit his actions and his character, Cooley believed, to searching and sometimes even libelous criticism.[26]

Cooley also argued that the American newspaper press merited liberation from the burdens of traditional defamation law. His views about American newspapers, like his ideas about politics, paralleled those of mid–nineteenth-century jurists such as Grimke and Seward. Cooley included a glowing sketch of the American press in *Constitutional Limitations*. Breaking sharply with earlier treatise writers like Kent and Story, he argued that the political press was "gradually becoming more just, liberal, and dignified in its dealings with political opponents, and vituperation is much less common, reckless, and bitter now" than earlier in the century. The daily newspaper, he continued, "may be said to be the chief educator of the people; its influence is potent in every legislative body; it gives tone and direction to public sentiment on each important subject as it arises. . . ." He also praised journalists for reporting events from "every civilized country" and for scrutinizing the conduct of politicians and anyone else "sufficiently interesting or notorious to become an object of public interest."[27] In his *General Principles of Constitutional Law*, Cooley went even further, assigning the press quasi-constitutional status. The press, he argued, certainly operated as "a public convenience, which gathers up the intelligence of the day to lay before its readers, notifies coming events, gives warning against disasters, and in various ways contributes to the happiness, comfort, safety, and protection of the people." And, he continued, "in a constitutional point of view," the press enabled "the citizen to bring any person in authority, any public corporation or agency, or even the government in all its departments, to the bar of public opinion. . . ."[28]

On the question of a free press, Thomas Cooley was a thoroughgoing consequentialist. With considerable passion, he argued that a variety of beneficial consequences would result from a healthy marketplace of ideas. Thus, Cooley did not justify his view of free expression solely on what has been called "the marketplace theory of truth," the Mills-Holmesian notion that the marketplace should provide the battleground for the contest between truth and falsehood. In Cooley's view, the marketplace of ideas, in conjunction with several other marketplaces, provided the foundation for a prosperous and progressive liberal republic. Seen in these terms, the emergence of a free marketplace of ideas, and a free press, becomes part of a larger historical process.[29]

Evidence that the nation's presses were prospering buoyed Cooley's liberal-romantic faith that the mid–nineteenth-century press offered a medium of mass communication that would bind together people in diverse places and from different socioeconomic circumstances. The new mass media, Cooley hoped, could provide a noncoercive, largely self-regulating means of tempering the possessive individualism that was at the heart of liberal society. He also anticipated that the press would help to combat difficulties raised by the great size of the American republic. Through specialized publications, the press would enable people with similar occupations and interests, such as merchants and spiritualists, to communicate with one another over ever-greater distances. In short, Cooley praised the mid–nineteenth-century press as a prime force in the expansion and improvement of almost every aspect of American life. Outdated laws that unnecessarily hampered the flow of ideas and opinions threatened to slow the United States' march into the modern world.

In Cooley's view, supporters of neo-Blackstonian libel doctrines ignored the value of the marketplace of ideas and the important role of the modern press. In other areas of law, he complained, courts and legal theorists had acknowledged the reality of technological and economic progress. "The railway has become the successor of the king's highway, and the plastic rules of the common law have accommodated themselves to the new conditions of things," he observed. Yet, "the changes accomplished by the public press seem to have passed unnoticed in the law. . . ." Except for a few minor modifications made by legislators and constitutional conventions, he concluded, "the publisher of the daily paper occupies to-day the position in the courts that the village gossip and retailer of scandal occupied two hundred years ago, with no more privilege and no more protection."[30]

Cooley argued that American courts must bring the law of libel into line with new political and social realities. He claimed, for example, that the rapid development of America's system of mass communication made it unreasonable to hold newspaper publishers legally responsible for all libelous falsehoods in their papers. Strict liability ignored the essential dynamics of the journalistic marketplace—the buyer-seller relationship. Readers, the sovereign buyers of information, "demanded of the newspaper publisher . . . a complete summary of the events transpiring in the world, public or private, so far as those readers can reasonably be supposed to take an interest in them," and the journalist "who does not comply with this demand must give way to him who will." The reading public, Cooley continued, "demand and expect accounts" about a wide range of events; it was impossible, the newspaper-editor-turned-jurist argued, "that these shall be given in all cases without matters being mentioned derogatory to individuals. . . ."[31]

In cases where libelous material related to the activities of governmental officials and other public citizens, Cooley believed, courts could easily invoke common law principles in order to relieve the press, as well as ordinary citizens, from some of the burdens of strict liability. Because criminal libel prosecutions occurred so infrequently, Cooley was most concerned about civil defamation suits. He was particularly critical of the leading American precedent, *King* v. *Root*, the 1829 New York case that imposed strict liability for libelous falsehoods, even when they appeared in newspaper stories about the official conduct of governmental officers. Such a rule, he complained, was not "very satisfactory to those who claim the utmost freedom of discussion in public affairs." In deciding the *Root* case, he argued, the New York Court of Errors wrongfully assumed that "no public consideration had in any way been involved" and erroneously decided that there was "no middle ground between absolute immunity for falsehood and the application of the same strict rules which prevail" in purely private libel cases. Cooley took some solace in his belief that "the general public sentiment and the prevailing customs allow a greater freedom of discussion" and hold a newspaper publisher "less strictly to what he may be able to justify as true." But he also urged acceptance of doctrines that could bridge the gulf between these prevailing customs and the law of libel.[32]

Thomas Cooley, of course, became most famous and remains best known for his jeremiads on the dangers of governmental power. Even though he had supported the antislavery cause before 1860 and abolitionism during the Civil War, for example, Cooley saw ratification of the Fourteenth Amendment in 1867 as the end of the crusade for the rights of black people. By purging slavery, the war had secured equality for all Americans, including blacks. In Cooley's view, the Fourteenth Amendment merely confirmed this reality and granted the national government no new powers that could be used to assist black people. Similarly, his concern about firm legal protection of political speech was intended not so much to activate the engine of government, but primarily to provide further obstacles to governmental activity.

Thus, Cooley's ideas on the importance of free expression nicely dovetailed with his larger emphasis upon minimizing the use of governmental power. As historian David Potter has observed, "the marked American reliance on endless discussion as a means of finding solutions for controversies reflects less a faith in the powers of rational persuasion than an unwillingness to let anything reach a point where authority will have to be invoked."[33] Although Professor Potter's sweeping thesis is too broad, it does capture an important tenet of Cooley's view of free expression. Like many other nineteenth-century liberals, Cooley placed great value upon the marketplace of ideas as a safety valve for public and private tensions, allowing citizens to release their anger in words and in print rather than in clashes that might require mobilization of governmental power to restore public order.[34] Similarly, if political leaders had to wait until the people and the party presses had debated every political issue at full length, the engine of government would generally be at a slow idle. Finally, of course, it seemed axiomatic that abuses of governmental power would be detected more readily and remedies found more easily in a political culture that allowed broad freedom of public discussion than in one where restrictive laws limited the power and range of political criticism. In a variety of different ways, then, enlightened libel laws helped to limit the powers of government and to expand the self-correcting mechanisms of the political and intellectual marketplaces.

In his attempts to reshape the law of libel, Cooley constantly swore allegiance, in both his treatises and in his judicial opinions, to existing common law doctrines. The changes in the black-letter law that he proposed, Cooley insisted, were not simply necessary judicial responses to external pressures; his new doctrines were logically consistent with the nation's common law heritage. Properly defined, Cooley asserted, freedom of the press meant not only liberation from prior restraints, but "complete immunity for the publication, so long as it is not harmful in its character, when tested by such standards as the law affords." And where would Cooley find these legal standards? "For these standards we must look to the common law rules which were in force when the constitutional guarantees were established."[35]

If Cooley's approach to libel law showed both instrumentalist and formalistic styles of legal reasoning, his formalism was, by his own admission, not based upon slavish devotion to earlier libel decisions. For Cooley, the common law of defamation consisted of general principles and logically related rules. Common law doctrines, he insisted, were not fixed in stone: the common law was plastic. This metaphor, however, also suggested some limits to Cooley's instrumentalism: old legal rules could be reworked and remolded, but they were not supposed to be broken arbitrarily or bent in any convenient direction. Even though Cooley's laudatory sketch of American journalism included the suggestion that the press should be allowed to print, without fear of liability, reports from other papers, he also conceded that established precedents barred judicial adoption of such protection. But in other areas of libel law, Cooley did not restrict himself to such a formalistic approach. Judges, he argued, possessed considerable latitude to interpret established doctrines in more libertarian directions than those taken by jurists of the Revolutionary era. More important, Cooley believed, courts possessed a constitutional responsibility to offer firm legal protection for the right of free expression. In his view, adoption of the old common law rule of conditional privilege offered the means by which judges could fulfill their responsibilities to common law orthodoxy, to constitutional commands, and to the needs of an expanding liberal democracy.

Defining a Conditional Privilege

The common law doctrine of conditional privilege, Cooley believed, would give new vitality to the guarantees of free expression that had been included in virtually every state constitution, as well as in the First Amendment to the national charter. These provisions, he contended, were meant to stop "those in authority from making use of the machinery of the law to prevent full discussion of political and other matters in which the public are concerned."[36] They should not be interpreted narrowly. But if Cooley was not a neo-Blackstonian restrictionist like Chancellor Kent, neither was he an early advocate of the "absolutist" position championed by Justices Hugo Black and

William O. Douglas a century later. Cooley's doctrine of conditional privilege was not designed to eliminate the law of political libel; it was intended to give more concrete meaning to the phrase "liberty of expression": "The term 'privileged,' as applied to a communication alleged to be libelous, means generally that the circumstances under which it was made were such as to rebut the legal inference of malice, and to throw upon the plaintiff the burden of offering some evidence of its existence beyond the mere falsity of the charge." Cooley would have placed this burden upon all libel plaintiffs who were public officials or candidates for public office. Equally as important, because he believed that most readers demanded that the press critically discuss a wide range of public issues, he would have extended the rule of conditional privilege to *"all cases where the matter discussed is one of general public interest."*[37]

In Cooley's view, conditional privilege was more than a common law rule; in liberal America, it had become part of the constitutional guarantees of free expression. There were, he argued, "special cases where, for some reason of general public policy, the publication is claimed to be privileged, and where consequently, it may be supposed to be within the constitutional protection." In these constitutionally protected situations, a plaintiff could not maintain a suit for civil libel "without proof of express malice." The right of free expression required a conditional privilege because of a public "duty" to speak out (such as the obligation of lawyers to inform their clients openly and candidly), which justified departure from the principle of strict liability in any subsequent libel suit. For libels made on such "lawful occasions," the law would "throw upon the plaintiff the burden of offering some evidence . . . beyond the mere falsity of the charge" that defamatory statements had been made "maliciously." In order to effectuate the right of position, for instance, courts granted a conditional privilege to official remonstrances, and persons who sent petitions to proper authorities would not be liable in civil suits "unless it be shown" that the libels were "both false and malicious." The same type of privilege, Cooley reasoned, should apply to all citizens, including newspaper people, when they fulfilled their duty to speak out on political issues.[38]

The key issue in Cooley's formula, then, became the legal definition of "malice." Despite a good deal of effort, Cooley failed to delineate a consistent view of malice in either *Constitutional Limitations* or in his *Treatise on Torts.* (And, as we shall see, his colleagues on the Michigan Supreme Court thought his judicial opinions equally inconsistent.) Although Cooley emphasized that he used the term malice in a legal sense rather than in its popular meaning of "ill will," this did not settle the ambiguities. In *Constitutional Limitations* he praised recent English decisions on the privilege of "fair comment"—a defense that could protect expressions of pure opinion but not any libelous misstatements of fact—and suggested that the privilege to criticize public officials was limited only "by good faith and just intention. . . ." In determining whether or not the privilege had been breached, a jury could take into "account the nature of the charges made, and the reasons which existed for making them." And in his *Treatise on Torts*, first published in 1879, he suggested a general rule designed to soothe the potential sting of political defamation suits while maintaining some legal restraints over libelous attacks. Libel defendants, he argued, should not be liable for civil damages when they discussed "in good faith, the character, the habits, and mental and moral qualifications of any person presenting himself, or presented by his friends, as a candidate for public office. . . ."[39]

Although Cooley's language might be read as nothing more than a version of the English rule of fair comment, he clearly wanted broader protection than allowed under English decisions. He specifically argued that the English doctrine, which limited criticism about private matters, was "not sufficiently comprehensive," and he intended that his defense of conditional privilege apply to libelous misstatements of fact.[40] Despite their ambiguities on the meaning of malice, Cooley's treatises, especially *Constitutional Limitations*, emphasized the expansive nature of both constitutional provisions on free speech and the common law doctrines that supported such guarantees.

Cooley believed that a rough approximation of the law of conditional privilege had already been absorbed into the marketplace of ideas and that this marketplace, rather than the law courts, would correct most libelous statements and comments. In its publications "upon public events and public men," the American press "proceeds in all respects as though it were privileged . . . and the man who has a 'character to lose' presents himself for the suffrages of his fellow citizens in the full reliance that detraction by the public press will be corrected through the same instrumentality, and that unmerited abuse will react on the public opinion in his favor."[41]

But what about those occasions when the courts, not the marketplace, would be called upon to correct breaches of conditional privilege? Could common law doctrines and principles provide wise judges with clear and consistent answers? Thomas Cooley, like other members of the late nineteenth-century legal elite, believed (in the words of legal historian G. Edward White) that law "was a science, governed by axioms; one discovered the axioms, articulated and synthesized them, then applied them to resolve controversies. Solutions were evident, lines could be drawn, rules could be made." The common law scholar, Cooley told the Georgia Bar Association in 1887, could bring certainty to American jurisprudence.[42] Cooley's discussion of the liberal theory of free expression did not break new ground; most of what Cooley said, Grimke had said better, and Cooley's discussion of the social role of the mid–nineteenth-century press read as if it had been borrowed from

Seward's *Notes on New York*. Cooley's genius lay in his efforts to show how courts could go about the job of relating liberal theories of free expression to common law doctrines.

The work of Thomas Cooley, especially on libel law, exemplified some of the fundamental themes in late nineteenth-century legal culture. Cooley, like his contemporary glossators, was trying to resolve some of the basic dilemmas of liberal politics: how to circumscribe and mediate conflicts between individuals by a system of rational, known, and equitable rules that the state would administer; and, *then*, how to limit the power of the state so that powerful and cunning individuals could not corrupt its officials or abuse its mechanisms in order to destroy, in practice, the rights and liberties that, in theory, the state was obliged to protect. In contrast to those twentieth-century legal writers who would come to see law as pluralistic, Thomas Cooley believed in a single, overarching common law of constitutional principles, fundamental propositions about liberal society, government, and human nature that, in the end, took precedence even over particular constitutional texts. In this sense, Cooley's writings on libel and free expression provided a good example of what legal scholar Patrick Gudridge has called "the classical style," an approach to law that offers "decided preferences for clarity, order, or balance, and the appearance of universality." Thus, late nineteenth-century theorists such as Thomas Cooley viewed the legal world as a comprehensive, rational structure of substantive rules that demarcated clearly bounded rights and powers. This view of law, which later critical scholars have called "boundary theory," held that properly trained, conscientious judges could objectively determine—by applying "objective" common law and constitutional rules—the legal boundaries to bring both order and justice to American life. As long as individuals and governments stayed within their proper boundaries, the legal system would protect their rights from invasions by others or uphold their actions as legitimate. In the case of defamation law, Cooley could defend the common law rules as not only rational, objective doctrines that adjusted private conflicts over individual reputation, but as clear definitions of legal rights that marked off the constitutional boundaries of protected public speech.[43]

Thomas Cooley labored in the tradition begun by Sir William Blackstone in his *Commentaries* and carried on by Kent and Story: he sought to "prove" that the common law could be seen as a unified system and that the careful jurist could demonstrate how various common law rules protected rights deemed fundamental in a liberal polity. Cooley's great faith in self-regulating marketplaces appeared to make his task that much easier. With a smoothly functioning system of free expression, courts would play an essentially minor role, only occasionally deciding when publishers had entered forbidden legal territories. The rules of libel law, including the doctrine of privileged communications, would not have to be invoked frequently.

But as a judge on the Michigan Supreme Court from 1864 to 1885, Cooley found that the task of bringing certainty to the law of libel and to constitutional guarantees of free expression was not a simple one. Cooley's jurisprudence, with its faith in the ability of trained legal minds to capture complex social and political realities in the language of law and to draw clear and firm legal boundaries around many-sided conflicts over reputation, would confront numerous challenges. Moreover, it was one thing for the treatise writer to rationalize and then align rules and doctrines—legal principles extracted from old cases involving abstract plaintiffs and unknown defendants. But Thomas Cooley eventually discovered that the attempt to decide real controversies, involving real newspapers that had libeled flesh-and-blood defendants was a different matter. It was at this point that Thomas Cooley really confronted both the social and the legal meaning of the law of political libel. And it was during this time that the contradictions in his marketplace liberalism and the problems with his jurisprudence became fully apparent.

A survey of reported cases and law review articles from the two decades following publication of *Constitutional Limitations* reveals considerable debate over the issues raised by Thomas Cooley—the revision of traditional libel doctrines and the alignment of defamation laws with the realities of late nineteenth-century journalism and evolving ideas of free expression. Lengthy and complex arguments before appellate courts, especially in libel cases where trial judges had initially ruled against politician-plaintiffs and for critics from the press, belies the claim that the legal limits of free expression were not debated in the late nineteenth century.

Moreover, strenuous judicial efforts to devise formulas for handling political libel cases refutes the notion—at least in the case of defamation law—that courts "rarely went beyond the facts of a particular case to articulate 'fundamental principles of interpretation.' "[44] In fact, a number of judges, including Thomas Cooley, went to considerable lengths to develop such fundamental principles. Although most of these juristic efforts have been found wanting by scholars who use the Holmesian-Brandeisean or the *New York Times* v. *Sullivan* tests as the height of legal sophistication and the measure of libertarian rectitude, such critiques ignore the extent to which some late nineteenth-century libel decisions went beyond the neo-Blackstonian jurisprudence of earlier eras. According to one careful study of public-official libel cases decided between the Civil War and 1900, twenty-eight states had appellate court decisions on the law of political libel; in twenty-five of these states, courts granted some type of privilege, albeit limited by twentieth-century standards, for libelous political criticism.[45]

The case of *Negley* v. *Farrow* (1882) helps to illustrate the point. Here, a newspaper article charged that a Republican state senator had dishonored his constituents and turned "traitor" to his party by collaborating with the Democratic caucus in defeating a bill in the Maryland senate. A jury awarded the senator $3000 in damages, and the paper appealed. The newspaper's theory of defamation law followed the position outlined by Thomas Cooley. Guarantees of free expression protected even libelous discussions of the acts of public officers and examinations of other matters of public interest. "On such occasions there is a qualified privilege," which required libel plaintiffs to prove malice. A majority of the Maryland Supreme Court rejected this reasoning, but Justice John Mitchell Robinson's opinion did set forth a standard of liability that went beyond the old, early nineteenth-century position.

Justice Robinson viewed the right to criticize public officials as a fundamental constitutional liberty of all free citizens. The right "to discuss and criticize boldly the official conduct" of public officials was "a right which, in *every* free country belongs to the citizen, and the exercise of it, within lawful and proper limits, affords some protection at least against official abuse and corruption." In this case, however, the newspaper had exceeded its right of "fair and legitimate discussion" by claiming that "base and corrupt motives" had occasioned the plaintiff's vote switching. Thus, the defense of "fair comment" was not available; the newspaper bore the same burden as any other libel defendant—supplying evidence of the truth of its charges against the senator.[46]

The majority opinion provoked a vigorous dissent by Justice Frederick Stone who contended that the publication was protected by Maryland's constitutional provision on freedom of press. Justice Stone's theory closely followed that of Thomas Cooley: the plaintiff's votes in the state senate were "the proper subjects of the fullest criticism"; journalists possessed a "duty to the readers of their paper" to inform them fully about the conduct of public officials; and only proof of malice would create liability for this type of newspaper story.[47]

Justice Stone's argument, that the defense of fair comment did not satisfy constitutional standards for protecting free expression, was heard throughout the 1870s and 1880s. Debates over the precise meaning of free expression could become quite pointed. In supporting the positions of Justice Stone's dissent and Thomas Cooley's *Constitutional Limitations*, for example, George Chase of Columbia Law School ridiculed Justice Robinson's claim that the defense of fair comment established "a full and free right of criticism. To call it 'full and free,' " as did cases such as *Negley* v. *Farrow*, "would seem a mockery."[48]

One of the preeminent law teachers of the late nineteenth century, Chase insisted that jurists should view the law as a system of principles and not as a mere aggregation of cases decided by the courts. His own broad approach to defamation law followed this precept; it also continued the antebellum tradition of viewing cases and issues in light of a broader system of free expression. Chase's article on public officials and defamation, published in the *American Law Review* in 1889, restated many of the positions taken in Cooley's first edition of *Constitutional Limitations*, and criticized appellate decisions that did not accord with a very broad theory of public debate. In particular, Chase argued for acceptance of the Cooley qualified privilege rather than the more limited fair-comment rule. When courts viewed guarantees of free expression "to sanction only the expression of such imputations and opinions as can be proved to be true, it is absurd to speak of it as a special right pertaining to public men" because "even private men may be so discussed."[49]

Chase argued both from an appeal to first principles and from a policy position that reflected a late nineteenth-century mugwump's jaded view of political life. "The basic purpose of constitutional guarantees of free speech—advancement of public welfare through the enlightenment of public opinion concerning the characters and qualifications of public men"—demanded abandonment of strict liability and fair comment as standards in political defamation cases. Moreover, Chase believed that the corruption of Gilded Age politics strengthened the case for broadly interpreted libel laws. "No evil is more insidious, more dangerous to the public welfare than official corruption." Yet he feared that journalists would quite naturally hesitate to investigate political corruption if they had to defend their exposés under standards such as those embraced by the majority in *Negley* v. *Farrow*. "From its very nature," political corruption "is conceived in darkness, and though sometimes openly consummated in defiance of public opinion, yet usually it is executed with all possible secrecy." Anyone seeking to uncover this type of chicanery could rarely find "all its hidden links. . . . Nothing is seen but the overt acts, which, more or less plainly, suggest the presence of corrupt designs." Not to allow the press and citizens to criticize public officials based upon their "honest, fair, and reasonable judgment" of the entire affair "would prove a greater peril to the public interest than a benefit."[50]

Thomas Cooley and Conditional Privilege: The Michigan Supreme Court Experience

Thus, George Chase agreed with Thomas Cooley that advancement of the larger public interest in maintaining a system of free expression sometimes required public persons to suffer libelous criticism without having any legal remedy. "But the interest of the public in knowing the character of its servants is of infinitely higher importance" than absolute protection for the reputations of political officials.[51] As a member of the Michigan Supreme Court, Thomas Cooley authored two notable opinions—in *Atkinson* v. *Detroit Free Press* (1881) and in *Miner* v. *Detroit Post & Tribune Co.* (1882)—which argued for a broad view of the qualified-privilege doctrine. In *Atkinson* v. *Detroit Free Press*, the Supreme Court of Michigan reversed a verdict in favor of the press and sent the case back for retrial. Atkinson was an attorney who represented a member of the Detroit Board of Trade. The *Free Press*'s story had alleged various fraudulent activities by both the plaintiff and his client. Atkinson employed at least four other lawyers who raised no fewer than forty-one assignments of error on evidentiary questions alone. In addition to attempting to unravel all of these claims, the court's majority opinion also considered the issue of qualified privilege. Justice James Campbell curtly held that the *Free Press*'s article was not "connected with any matter concerning which it could be regarded as privileged." Only proof of truth could be a sufficient defense.[52]

Justice Cooley issued a vigorous dissent, his most famous judicial statement on behalf of free expression.[53] After tilting with his colleagues over some of the evidentiary issues, he declared that their whole theory of this case was "radically erroneous." The *Free Press*'s story and the *Atkinson* case did not involve "only private considerations" but also raised public issues in which "all consideration of mere technical accuracy becomes irrelevant." The law must extend a qualified privilege to such a story, he argued, because of the public's interest in Detroit's commercial health, which depended, in large part, upon the honesty of members of the Board of Trade. Thus he urged the court to treat stories about quasi-public institutions the same as those about governmental institutions and public officials. "It is as important to the city of Detroit that it should have an honorable and trustworthy board of trade . . . as it is that it should have a trustworthy mayor or controller, or police authorities or other public functionaries."

Although Justice Cooley never raised the issue of balancing public benefits against public evils, he apparently thought that the story itself, though intemperate, carried no legal malice. The newspaper possessed a duty to investigate rumors of wrongdoing by members of the board and to report their findings, particularly to readers from the business community. The *Free Press* "would have been unworthy of the confidence and support of commercial men if its conductors had shut their eyes to such a transaction." The paper "might have used more carefully-guarded language, and avoided irritating headlines," but Justice Cooley could excuse such indiscretions as examples of "honest indignation." He appeared, then, to endorse rough-and-tumble political journalism as inseparable from a liberal system of free expression. All of "the beneficial ends to be subserved by public discussion would in large measure be defeated if dishonesty must be handled with delicacy and fraud spoken of with such circumspection and careful and deferential choice of words as to make it appear in the discussion a matter of indifference." Even if the plaintiff were wholly innocent, Justice Cooley argued, "it was his misfortune that it was impossible to deal with the case without bringing him into the discussion." The principled balancing inherent in Cooley's view of conditional privilege had already taken place.

The circumstances of the *Atkinson* case, Justice Cooley concluded in his dissent, demanded that the *Free Press*'s story be protected. "If such a discussion of a matter of public interest were *prima facie* an unlawful act, and the authors were obliged to justify every statement by evidence of its literal truth," Justice Cooley argued, "the liberty of public discussion would be unworthy of being named as a privilege of value."

Justice Cooley believed that his dissent announced a wise public policy that stood on firm legal and constitutional grounds. It was the majority opinion, he claimed, that departed from common law traditions of liberty and from constitutional guarantees of free speech. "In what I say in this case I advance no new doctrine, but justify every statement of principle upon approved authorities." His colleagues might cite many cases "from which a different argument may be constructed," but these precedents were "no longer deserving of credit if they ever were." Regrettably, Justice Cooley suggested, the privilege of discussing issues of public interest had never received enough recognition in the law courts. "Perhaps the privilege would have seemed to stand out more boldly and appeared more sacred if the provisions deliberately incorporated for its protection and perpetuation in every American constitution had been collated and given prominence. . . ." But even though his ideas might, at first glance, seem a novel interpretation of state constitutional guarantees, he concluded, they still had support in the common law. Citizens could find the guarantee of free expression "embodied in the good sense of the common law, where it has constituted one of the most important elements in the beneficent growth and progress of free states."

The following year, 1882, Justice Cooley briefly did carry a majority of the court for his views of free expression. In *Miner v. Detroit Post & Tribune Co.*, the paper accused the plaintiff, a police judge, of several violations of judicial ethics.[54] The *Post*'s attorneys did not attempt to prove the truth of the charges and argued instead that the article "related to matters of public interest and importance, and was for that reason privileged." The trial court accepted the claim of privilege for charges about the judge's failure to enforce liquor and gambling laws, but it rejected any privilege for allegations of false imprisonment of a "Chinaman." The trial judge held, in effect, that a newspaper could claim a privilege for general expressions of opinion about the actions of public officials—what most American courts would eventually accept as the right of fair comment—but not for specific charges of "an act nearly amounting to a crime" or imputations of "specific moral delinquency." For libelous statements of fact, only proof of truth would be a defense.[55]

The jury found for the plaintiff, but the supreme court overturned the judgment. Justice Cooley felt that the trial judge had erred by permitting portions of the story that he himself had declared privileged "to be made subject of comment [by the plaintiff's attorney] to the prejudice of the defendant." But Cooley further argued that a qualified privilege should attach to the entire story, not simply to the portions about liquor and gambling. "A much more serious and more dangerous error," stated Cooley, "is found in that part of the article which concerned the proceedings in the case of the Chinaman."

Relying upon his lengthy dissent in *Atkinson*, Justice Cooley only briefly discussed the issue of conditional privilege in *Miner*. The trial judge, Justice Cooley bristled, erroneously "put the case upon precisely the same footing with publications which involved merely private gossip and scandal." A story about alleged judicial corruption clearly involved a subject of genuine public interest: "When a judge orders a man into confinement without a charge against him, he deprives him of liberty without due process of law; and in doing so violates the earliest and most important guarantee of constitutional freedom. . . . There must be some great and most serious defect in the administration of the law when such things can take place, and the matter is one which concerns every member of the political community. . . ."

The *Post*, then, was properly exercising its duty "to challenge public attention to official disregard of the principles which protect public and personal liberty." The theory of the trial court and of Justice Campbell's dissent—that there was no privilege for libelous misstatements of fact—could be valid only if there were "no difference in moral quality between the publication of mere personal abuse and matters of grave public concern. . . ." The common law, Justice Cooley concluded, could never justify such an absurd conclusion, one which would place "the reckless libeller . . . in the same company with respectable and public spirited journalists. . . ."[56]

Justice Cooley's opinion reiterated his clear break with Hamiltonian libel doctrines and his conviction that even the defense of fair comment restricted free discussion too tightly. But his majority opinion in *Miner* also made it clear that he was not prepared to tolerate all libelous falsehoods.

Cooley now emphasized that his ideas on libel were intended to do more than protect freedom of the press; they would also help to isolate journalistic renegades and to place them under proper legal restraints.

> I know of nothing more likely to encourage the license of a dissolute press than to establish the principle that the discussion of matters of general concern involving public wrongs and the publication of personal scandal come under the same condemnation in the law; for this inevitably brings the law into contempt and creates public sentiment against its enforcement. If a law is to be efficiently enforced the approval of the people must attend its penalties and there must be some presumption at least that an act which it punishes involves some elements of wrong-doing.[57]

Only carefully crafted libel doctrines—ones that attempted to distinguish between stories in the public interest and sensationalist accounts that pandered to popular tastes, doctrines that separated legitimate journalists from gossipmongers—could gain enough public support to provide effective restraints. Cooley still endorsed libel laws that encouraged vigorous discussion of "legitimate" public issues.

Beyond Hamiltonianism: Libel Law Debates

The law of political libel, then, was a matter of sharp legal debate during the late nineteenth century. The case law in the majority of states upheld doctrines that had been framed during the early nineteenth century. But as the new political culture emphasized robust, even free-swinging debate, older ideas about proscribing falsehoods and protecting the best men seemed anachronistic. Contrary to most accounts, American lawyers did discuss the question of free speech, particularly as it related to political libel cases, during the years between the Sedition Act of 1798 and World War I. Indeed, some argued that in a political system based upon public opinion and popular sovereignty, voters needed diverse sources of information in order to make an informed choice. Like Thomas Cooley, they proposed no absolute privilege for the press; they believed, however, that a qualified privilege for false statements would encourage political debate without unduly sacrificing individual reputations or driving honest men from public life. The paucity of political libel cases prevented most state courts from confronting the issues in any detailed way, but there was enough discussion to develop a comprehensive opposition argument to the earlier views of Hamilton, Kent, and Walworth.

Chapter Eight | Legal Science and Hamiltonian Principles: Libel Law, 1880–1920

Although there was vigorous debate during the 1870s and 1880s over liberalization of political libel doctrines, the libertarian impulses, so evident in Cooley's *Constitutional Limitations* and his *Atkinson* dissent, eventually met stiff resistance. Decisions such as the majority opinion in *Negley* v. *Farrow*— which contained extravagant praise for free expression alongside legal rulings that were less libertarian than Cooley's doctrines—were as far as most courts were willing to go. By the end of the nineteenth century, in fact, the strongest current of legal opinion favored enshrinement of early nineteenth-century, neo-Blackstonian libel doctrines. Alexander Hamilton, not Thomas Cooley, became the leading late nineteenth-century oracle on libel law.

To begin to understand the forces that turned back the libertarianism of the mid–nineteenth century, we should return to the judicial career of Thomas Cooley. There was, as we have already seen, the libertarian Justice Cooley, the vigorous dissenter who insisted that the Michigan Supreme Court squarely face the free-speech issues he found lurking in cases such as *Atkinson*. But a full appraisal of the judicial record reveals another, more cautious Thomas Cooley. This Thomas Cooley's view on free speech, rather than the libertarian Cooley's view in *Constitutional Limitations* and *Atkinson*, was closer to the positions that would prevail in most American courts. Only with the rather sudden reversal of libel doctrines in 1964, when the United States Supreme Court adopted its own version of Cooley's "qualified privilege" rule as a national constitutional standard, did the libertarian Cooley reemerge. But any attempt to draw a straight libertarian line from Cooley's treatises and *Atkinson* dissent to the libel decisions of the Warren Court must detour around the tangled history of defamation law in the late nineteenth and early twentieth centuries.

Mr. Justice Cooley Retreats

Thomas Cooley did not suddenly liberalize Michigan's libel laws. For a number of years, in fact, he had few chances to review any libel cases. During Cooley's first twelve years of judicial service, the Michigan Supreme Court heard only two libel appeals. More important, his colleagues, particularly Justice James Campbell, resisted efforts to write Cooley's ideas about political libel into the case law of Michigan.[1] Justice Campbell acknowledged the press as "one of the necessities of civilization," and he agreed with Cooley that laws affecting its operation "should not be unreasonable or vexatious." But "the reading public are not entitled to discussion in print upon the character or doings of private persons, except as developed in legal tribunals or voluntarily subjected to public scrutiny." In Justice Campbell's view, newspaper publishers owned a dangerous weapon, and they owed the public a special duty "to reduce the risk of having . . . libels creep into their columns to the lowest degree which reasonable foresight can assure." The doctrine of strict liability, he insisted, should remain in force.[2]

Ultimately, though, between 1878 and 1884, Cooley did hear a number of defamation appeals, many of them involving James E. Scripps, the flamboyant publisher who brought "popular journalism" to Michigan in 1873. During his earlier experiences with the *Chicago* and *Detroit Tribunes*, Scripps became disenchanted with the traditional large sheet–small type format and the staid content of most middle western newspapers. Using the "penny presses" of the cities along the Atlantic seaboard as his models, Scripps offered his *Evening News* at two cents and aimed it at Detroit's growing working class. Many Detroiters, he believed, could not afford the city's other papers, which sold at five cents, or digest their immense helpings of political and financial doings. Scripps argued that the old political papers had left the field of popular journalism "entirely unoccupied."[3]

The *Evening News* initially found little support, particularly from Detroit's financial community. In time, though, it caught on, apparently with many people who had not previously purchased papers. The *News* featured exposés about supposedly respectable people who, the paper claimed, actually lived quite different types of lives and about political skullduggery in high places. This kind of journalism produced numerous threats of libel suits, particularly after James's youthful half-brother, E. W. Scripps, became city editor in 1875. The eventual founder of the huge Scripps newspaper chain, E. W. proudly boasted that he gave his reporters one basic order: "to raise as much hell as possible."

The Scripps style of hell provided the Michigan Supreme Court with several opportunities to clarify the broad theoretical issues that Thomas Cooley had raised in his treatises. In *Foster* v. *Scripps* (1878), a lawsuit arising from a story alleging that a city physician had been criminally negligent in vaccinating children, Justice Campbell rejected the contention that the doctor's public position should render the story privileged. The supreme court overturned a directed verdict in favor of James Scripps. Although Justice Campbell disapproved of granting a qualified privilege to any type of political criticism, he argued that the court could decide *Foster* v. *Scripps* on narrower grounds: because the plaintiff occupied an appointive rather than an elective office, there could be no possible argument for the existence of any privilege. Because his colleague's *dicta* about privileged communications clashed so loudly with his own views as developed in his treatises, Justice Cooley issued a concurring opinion asserting a broad conditional privilege, but concluding that Scripps had abused his privilege in this particular case.

To reach this result, Justice Cooley ignored most of the ambiguous ideas presented in his treatises; instead, he adopted a new "ad hoc balancing" test. As he tacitly acknowledged, Cooley had always grounded his general theory of public libel law upon the "principled balancing" of a private individual's right to reputation and the public's interest in the free discussion of vital issues. This obviously meant that "individuals whose characters or actions are impugned may suffer without remedy." Because the "plainest principles of justice" required courts to grant such a privilege only "on reasonable grounds," Cooley urged judges to examine carefully the nature and subject matter of libelous publications. In most lawsuits involving a claim of conditional privilege, courts would have no difficulty; the public's interest would clearly outweigh the individual's right of character. In some instances, however, the publication itself would carry a "bad tendency," and courts would have to reactivate their scales. During this second balancing, they should weigh the "public benefits of free discussion" against (1) the individual right of reputation and (2) the potential "public evils" arising from the publication.[4]

Justice Cooley concluded that *Foster* v. *Scripps*, which involved an official who was not elected by the voters, required two trips to the scales. Certain appointed officials, Cooley now claimed, were not covered by his marketplace principles. The public's confidence in "an officer whose duties are such as to render confidence extremely important to the continuous useful discharge of his duties," Cooley feared, had been "weakened or destroyed unjustly when it ought to have been supported and strengthened."

This reasoning, which required scrutiny of a publication's supposed tendency and which rested on a highly elitist view of political criticism, departed so radically from Cooley's general views in *Constitutional Limitations* that he felt compelled to issue a disclaimer: "In assenting to the conclusions of the court I confine my concurrence to the exact case before us." Had the doctor been a candidate for appointment rather than an incumbent city physician, Cooley suggested, his decision would have been different, a policy position that seemed to imply that the public had more to fear from an incompetent who wanted to become a city physician than from one who already held the job.[5]

Despite the appeal to a modified bad-tendency test, Cooley's concurrence in *Foster* v. *Scripps* did foreshadow his complete break with the rest of the court in *Atkinson* and his majority opinion in *Miner*.[6] In both of these cases, it will be remembered, Cooley wrote opinions that generally followed the views he had outlined in *Constitutional Limitations*. But despite its libertarian overtones, Cooley's majority opinion in *Miner* also announced that he was not prepared to tolerate all libelous political falsehoods.[7] Cooley still rejected strict liability in cases involving discussion of "legitimate" public issues; but it was becoming clear that his views on conditional privilege would focus more upon the character of the publication, and the supposed motives behind its appearance, and less upon the more objective circumstances that preceded the decision to publish libelous items that later proved to be false.

A year after the *Miner* opinion, Justice Cooley underscored his belief that courts should attempt to assess the motives of newspaper publishers. In *Bathrick v. Detroit Post & Tribune Co.* (1883), the paper had reported the indictment of a physician charged with seducing a young patient, having sexual relations with her, and performing a criminal abortion. Significantly, Justice Cooley rejected the defense's challenge to the trial judge's interpretation of the doctrine of privileged publications. The article—a typical example of how many late nineteenth-century urban newspapers reported crimes—did not pretend to be "a mere recital of the proceedings which had taken place in a court of justice," complained Justice Cooley. The newspaper writer had brought in other facts and "assumed himself to be the judge, and to pronounce guilt and suggest a probable punishment unknown to law."[8] There could be no privilege for such a sensationalized story.

Cooley's judicial experience soon found its way into the fifth edition of *Constitutional Limitations*. Cautioning readers that the libertarian opinion in *Atkinson* (the author of which he modestly left unidentified) represented only *dictum*, he still devoted nearly four pages of the new edition to his own dissent. He suggested that the press should enjoy a qualified privilege for stories that discussed "matters of government in all its grades and all its branches," the "performances of official duty by all classes of public officers and agents," and "all means of transportation and carriage, even when in private hands and management." And, he went on, this privilege should also extend to discussions of "all schemes, projects, enterprises and organizations of a semi-public nature, which invite public favor, and depend for their success on public confidence," including the activities of banks, insurance companies, private asylums, and public fairs.

But in contrast to his earlier musings, Cooley now emphasized that such a privilege implied no special legal status for the press. In fact, he categorically denied that the institutional press possessed any special legal protection under the common law. "The publisher of a newspaper," he concluded, could freely open his columns to sharp, critical examinations "so long as they are restricted within the limits of good faith, not because he makes the furnishing of news his business, but because the discussion is the common right and liberty of every citizen."[9]

Finally, the fifth edition of *Constitutional Limitations* reiterated Cooley's policy argument in *Miner*: libel doctrines that protected "good faith" criticism actually helped to differentiate important journalistic pieces from trivia; they distinguished information the sovereign people needed to know in order to act as intelligent citizens from items they merely wished to discover in order to satisfy their curiosity. Thus, Cooley confidently drew a sharp boundary between "the mere publication of items of news in which the public may take an interest as news merely, and the discussions of matters which concern the public because they are their own affairs." Moreover, he clearly distinguished between libelous stories involving "public characters" and ones dealing with "private individual(s)." In Cooley's view, a "private individual only challenges public criticism when his conduct becomes or threatens to be injurious to others; public characters and public institutions invite it at all times."[10]

In 1883, Justice Cooley and his colleagues heard *MacLean* v. *Scripps*, a case involving a member of the faculty of the University of Michigan School of Medicine and, once again, James Scripps. The *Evening News* had carried a story alleging that the doctor had taken sexual liberties with one of his patients, and the physician-professor had successfully sued for damages. With only one justice dissenting, the Michigan Supreme Court affirmed the award. Most of the issues before the court concerned the trial judge's refusal to allow Scripps and his managing editor to testify as to the absence of malice. The judge had rejected their testimony on this point, and Justice Campbell, with Cooley's support, reaffirmed the ruling. The court invoked a good-motives test, borrowed from Michigan's constitutional provision on criminal libel, against Scripps and the *Evening News*. According to Justice Campbell, the constitutional language—which provided that in criminal libel cases truth was a justification only if published with good motives and for justifiable ends—was "only another form of saying that malicious publications are not *privileged* from criminal prosecution, even if true." Thus, in civil libel suits, he ingeniously argued, there should be no analogous privilege for falsehoods if publishers lacked good motives. The theory that "a person may publish falsehoods of another who occupies a position in which his conduct is open to public scrutiny and criticism, without any reference to the object to be secured by the publication, is a doctrine which had no foundation that we have been able to discover."[11] In short, a newspaper could sustain the defense of privilege in civil suits only if the motives behind libelous stories could pass judicial scrutiny.

Justice Campbell's new construction of Michigan's libel law produced a sharp dissent, one that followed Thomas Cooley's earlier dissent in the *Atkin-*

son case. A story alleging immoral and unethical conduct by a professor at a state university, the dissent maintained, raised important public issues and testimony from Scripps was perfectly relevant to the issues of malice and conditional privilege.

> The charge concerned a public man in a high public position, in charge of most important public interests; those in which all the people were interested. He was a public servant, paid from the public funds; and the article concerns his conduct while in that service . . . and I think the article was privileged within the law as expounded by this court.

"Certainly it must be so," the dissent pointedly added, "if charges against a member of the board of trade is (sic) within the protection as held in *Atkinson v. Detroit Free Press* . . . in which opinion upon the subject I fully concur."[12]

Despite the strong endorsement of Cooley's opinion in *Atkinson*, this dissent was not written by Thomas Cooley but by Justice Thomas Sherwood, who had joined the court in 1883. Justice Cooley not only concurred in Justice Campbell's majority opinion, but he stated his own position when Scripps petitioned for a rehearing. "No court has gone further than has this in upholding the privileges of the press, and very few so far," Justice Cooley boasted. The court would continue to rectify any violation of free expression, Cooley argued, but there had been none. The need for evidence of malice had been satisfied by "proof from which the jury might infer that the publication was made in entire disregard of the plaintiff's rights, and from interested motives."[13]

In *MacLean* v. *Scripps*, then, Cooley announced yet another definition of malice. Apparently, the publication of libelous falsehoods with a reckless disregard of a plaintiff's reputation—with "entire disregard" for his or her rights—might show legal malice. But without a doubt, evidence of bad motives—in the form of sensationalism and search for monetary gain—satisfied Cooley's definition of malice. In other words, courts need not even probe a journalist's state of mind in order to find whether or not there had been an entire disregard for the right of reputation. "A false and injurious publication made in a public journal for sensation and increase of circulation," Cooley ruled, "is unquestionably in the legal sense malicious."[14] Justice Cooley's efforts to realign Michigan's libel laws, when judged even by his own standards, ended in failure. Chaotically mixing rule-bounded jurisprudence and ad hoc balancing, Cooley produced neither doctrinal clarity nor consistent judicial policy making.

Cooley's opinions in *Bathrick* and *MacLean* showed a new approach to the conflict between libel law and constitutional guarantees of free expression. In contrast to his *Atkinson* dissent and his even more cautious opinion in *Miner*, for instance, Cooley was now unwilling to adopt a broad, instrumentalist interpretation of common law precedents. Moreover, as the additions to *Con-*

stitutional Limitations indicated, he expressed a new hostility toward at least some segments of the press and a new caution about granting publishers like James Scripps the benefit of the doubt—or the privileges of the law—in public libel cases.

Mr. Justice Cooley and the Popular Press

Thus, Justice Cooley's final libel opinions for the Michigan Supreme Court offered his judicial response to developments in urban journalism and in the general system of public communication. During the late eighteenth and early nineteenth centuries, the names of the cases themselves—*People* v. *Croswell*, *Root* v. *King*, or *Hunt* v. *Bennett*—suggested an important point: the institutional press of that era was not made up of a series of large corporations, heavily capitalized enterprises that manufactured, marketed, and profited from a highly popular commodity—news. As the titles of these libel cases suggest, most early nineteenth-century newspapers remained inseparable from the persons, personalities, and political preferences of their owners and editors. As a pioneer student of the history of journalism once argued, the party newspapers essentially "took over the function of the political pamphlet. The opinion that had formerly found expression in a broadside was now expressed in the form of editorial leading articles." Although this generalization ignores some other aspects of political journalism, most partisan libel suits did grow out of political editorializing rather than out of straight-news stories that happened to contain libelous misstatements of fact. Political papers dealt almost exclusively with the activities and characters of public men. Not surprisingly, these were the people most likely to complain about, and seek legal redress for, the libelous excesses of licentious writers. By the mid–nineteenth century, then, when public men generally avoided the use of libel suits, the law of defamation was bound to remain a minor concern to journalists.

When Thomas Cooley wrote *Constitutional Limitations* in the late 1860s he clearly recognized some of the changes in American journalism, but he could not foresee all of the new developments. Most important, he could not predict the tremendous expansion of popular journalism or the impact of the broader phenomenon Daniel Boorstin called the "Graphic Revolution." In most parts of the country, the full impact of these journalistic trends, which had been launched with the penny presses of the 1830s, only came with the arrival of popularly oriented evening newspapers during the Gilded Age.

Exponents of popular journalism, such as Detroit's James Scripps, embraced the same marketplace liberalism as Thomas Cooley. The test of a successful newspaper depended upon the number of readers who could be persuaded to purchase its daily offerings. The old political and commercial papers, it can be argued, offered a fairly well-defined service to a certain group of political partisans or merchants. In contrast, the popular papers of the late nineteenth century marketed a product to a general and expanding readership; then, in turn, they sold this readership to their advertisers. As a result, neither newspaper readers nor special patrons underwrote the costs of gathering, processing, and distributing the news. Instead, it required revenues gained from a wide group of advertisers to keep the presses rolling.

Relying upon the image of the marketplace, popular journalists lauded their products as thoroughly democratic. James Scripps argued that "there should be papers in which only such things are published as are of interest to the great mass of their readers. . . . [T]hey will be useful to all classes of people who desire to keep up with the news of the day. . . . Popularity and usefulness are our only aim: the wants of the great public are our only criteria in the choice of matter for our columns." In this statement of editorial purpose, contained in the inaugural issue of the *Detroit Evening News*, Scripps promised that his paper would serve two separate, and not always compatible, purposes. First, the *Evening News* would be useful: it would provide readers with helpful advice on surviving, and perhaps even prospering, in urban America. But above all, it would be entertaining, offering readers all the dazzling and frightening features of late nineteenth-century city life.[15]

Serving as both "use-papers" and as in-home entertainment centers, ventures like the *Detroit Evening News* attracted working class readers and advised them on how to handle the rigors of late nineteenth-century life. In one sense, the popular evening papers benefited from the undoubted improvements in the lives of workers. Enjoying shorter working hours, improved urban transit, and better lighting, more workers could now turn to the evening newspaper upon their return from the job. On the other hand, the success of popular journalism also owed a good deal to the burdens that late nineteenth-century capitalism placed on the working class. Exhausted from a work pace generally brisker than that in other industrial nations, and oftentimes lacking enough money to enjoy urban popular culture on a regular basis, many workers had to rely upon the daily paper for vicarious excitement and spiritual uplift. A good newspaper, through its help-wanted columns, could even offer workers some hope for a better future. In these and other ways, the popular newspapers provided an escape from workplace cares and an inexpensive window into public life.

Novelist Theodore Dreiser, one of the sharpest observers of the late nineteenth-century urban scene, highlighted the importance of the evening newspaper to urban workers. When the heroine of Dreiser's *Sister Carrie* comes to Chicago to live with an older sister, she discovers her brother-in-law too tired from cleaning refrigerator cars and too worried about the small balance in his savings account to chase the bright lights of the city. Instead, Sven Hanson spends his nights poring over the evening paper, interrupting his reading only when it is time for dinner or bed or when the crying of the baby breaks his concentration. (The new papers, Dreiser thus suggests, may have stifled rather than increased communication within the family.) Later, when Sister Carrie runs off to New York with a married man, George Hurstwood, Dreiser charts Hurstwood's decline from a solidly middle-class businessman to a derelict in the Bowery by means of his reading habits. Trapped in New York, with Carrie's star ascending and his rapidly falling, Hurstwood can find both refuge and solace in only one way.

> He buried himself in his papers and read. Oh, the rest of it—the relief from walking and thinking! What Lethean waters were these floods of telegraphed intelligence! He forgot his troubles, in part. Here was a young, handsome woman, if you might believe the newspaper drawing, suing a rich, fat, candy-making husband in Brooklyn for divorce. Here was another item detailing the wrecking of a vessel in ice and snow off Prince's Bay on Staten Island. A long, bright column told of the doings in the theatrical world—the plays produced, the actors appearing, the managers making announcements. Fannie Davenport was just opening at the Fifth Avenue. Daly was producing "King Lear." He read of the early departure for the season of a party composed of the Vanderbilts and their friends for Florida. An interesting shooting affray was on in the mountains of Kentucky. So he read, read, read, rocking in the warm room near the radiator and waiting for dinner to be served.

In time, Hurstwood's retreat into his newspapers becomes nearly total. "Oh how this man had changed!" thought Carrie. "All day and all day, here he sat, reading his papers." Finally, on the brink of suicide, Hurstwood is reduced to scavenging "some old paper lying about" until "he noticed that his eyes were beginning to hurt him, and this ailment rapidly increased until, in the dark chambers of the lodgings he frequented, he did not attempt to read."[16]

Late nineteenth-century urban publishers used a variety of techniques to hold the attention of the real-life counterparts of Sven Hanson and George Hurstwood. They found, for example, that they could advertise their products—by various stunts such as Pulitzer's famous crusade for the Statue of Liberty—without changing basic content. More important, creators of the Graphic Revolution improved upon the methods of the old penny pressmen. They added corps of ambitious reporters to dig out stories of everyday tragedy and triumph, introduced regular sports columns to hold the attention of male readers, and added features on domestic life to attract a loyal corps of female customers. Newer technologies eventually allowed for inexpensive reproduction of photographs, an innovation that helped bring immigrants with few or no reading skills in English into the reading public. And new styles of story construction made newspaper reading easier for everyone. James Scripps, for example, believed that a good paper could be measured by the number of stories, preferably brief ones, that it contained; the more items that could be crammed into a single issue, the better the paper. Of course, this practice, by itself, increased the possibility for libel suits.

The colorful content of popular journalism created more than the chance for greater numbers of libel suits; it also produced new types of defamation cases. By opening all kinds of areas of hitherto private life, including family affairs and sexual morality, to constant newspaper scrutiny, the popular press sought to expand the definition of what issues were in the public domain. Carried to its logical conclusion, popular journalism on the marketplace model implied that whatever appeared in the papers—and was purchased by the sovereign readers—was a public matter. But plaintiffs who were not public people in the traditional sense, governmental officials and political candidates, did not always accept marketplace logic. If they followed the example of the allegedly immoral Professor MacLean and sued for libel, their suits could raise the tricky public-private distinctions that bedeviled the Michigan Supreme Court in the 1880s.[17]

For Thomas Cooley, these new journalistic developments raised havoc with his earlier views about libel and free expression, ideas that evolved from his larger vision of marketplace liberalism. With the rise of large-scale publishing and the invention of mass-mediated news, his liberal faith that the private channels of mass communication could offer neutral conduits through which citizens could freely exchange ideas and information became a romantic myth.

Even more important, trends in the newspaper industry undermined Cooley's liberal faith that the mechanisms of the intellectual marketplace would eventually spread common values and shore up bourgeois institutions. Despite the constant claim by radicals that "the capitalist press" failed to present stories of class conflict, developments of large media institutions did not produce a harmonious, one-dimensional view of social reality. As sociologist Alvin Gouldner has argued, "a *capitalist* news-producing system, like the capitalist system more generally, has its own internal *contradictions*." Needing to attract the widest possible audience, publishers like the Scripps brothers and Pulitzer found it necessary to shock readers with articles that exposed perfidy in high places and with stories that dramatized social conflict and deviations from bourgeois morality. As conservative social critics have long noted, stories dramatizing the limitations, rather than praising the accomplishments, of major social and political institutions prove attractive to readers and profitable to publishers. What sells newspapers, Gouldner concluded, "is not always identical or even consistent with the *publisher's* property interests." To many prominent citizens, the late nineteenth-century journalistic marketplace, like so many other areas of late nineteenth-century life, appeared in need of serious reordering and reform.[18]

The "system" of free expression, then, seemed neither systematic nor self-regulating. The type of state intervention that seemed necessary, as the case of Thomas Cooley shows, required modification of liberal ideas.

Thomas Cooley espoused the liberal faith that the economic, political, and intellectual marketplaces operated in conjunction with yet a fourth market-place—a moral one. Indeed, one of the basic justifications for the liberal devotion to all of these marketplaces was the claim that they allowed good and honest people (as well as good and honest ideas) to get ahead. The best products, the best people, and the best ideas supposedly reached the front shelves on their intrinsic merits, rather than because of some artificial and often governmentally conferred advantage. Conversely, the largely self-regu-lating mechanisms of the marketplace caused evil and dishonest schemers to stay in the background. In a truly free marketplace, all types of "rotten apples," both people and ideas, would be left to wither and decay on the back shelves.

In his treatises, Cooley confidently combined the various marketplaces. He invoked the moral marketplace along with the intellectual, for example, when in *Constitutional Limitations* he insisted that a qualified privilege could apply to libelous stories about even the private lives of public people. The notion, he argued indignantly, "that a judge who is debauched in private life may be pure and upright in his judgments" was "false to human nature," and (Cooley added in a later edition) "contradictory" to the liberal faith that, in the race for success in business or in politics, victory went not simply to the swiftest and sharpest but also the "best."[19] A liberalized intellectual marketplace, in other words, would also ensure proper functioning of the moral realm.

Although Cooley's liberal, boundary jurisprudence claimed to view law as an objective, neutral mediator of conflict, Cooley generally made it evident that his judicial decisions also accorded to his own view of the proper settle-ment of the competing moral issues in the particular controversy. In all but one of his important libel opinions, Cooley confidently included moral judgments in his written decisions. (The exception was *Foster* v. *Scripps*, in which Cooley adopted his intricate balancing test in order to weigh the supposed social impact of the story.) Dissenting in *Atkinson*, Cooley obviously consid-ered the conduct of the plaintiff, an attorney, and of his client-friend, a member of Detroit's Board of Trade, morally and ethically reprehensible. To "any disinterested business man," Cooley fumed, the machinations of the attorney and the official, on their face, "would have been suspicious." And as Cooley recited the "facts," he observed that no honest attorney could "under-take to justify such conduct . . . [i]n morals. . . ." In *Miner* he was equally forthright in denouncing as immoral and unethical the conduct of another member of the legal profession—a police judge in Detroit. In Cooley's view, the morals of a judge must be above suspicion. "When a judge orders a man into confinement without a charge against him . . . there must be some great and most serious defect in the administration of the law. . . ." And, he concluded, any legal theory that did not provide some protection for stories revealing allegations of judicial misconduct ignored the moral quality of such journalism.[20]

In the *Miner* case, Cooley praised the "respectable and public spirited" journalist; but in subsequent cases Cooley obviously found the moral scales tilting against the press. In *MacLean*, Cooley was uninterested in testimony about the state of mind of James Scripps or that of his managing editor. From the content and tone of the story itself, Cooley could confidently conclude that the motives of the *Evening News* had been immoral—and, therefore, equivalent to legal malice. Cooley was not content to rest his finding of liability on the fact that Scripps's paper had exceeded its qualified privilege by publishing a libelous falsehood with entire disregard for the rights of the plaintiff. By seeking sensationalist stories to increase the profits of his paper, James Scripps threatened the fundamental principles of the moral marketplace. To allow such stories to escape legal liability, simply because they touched the reading public's fancy—because they "got ahead" in the intellectual marketplace— was to subvert Cooley's view of the benefits to be gained from the moral marketplace.[21]

The sanctity of the moral marketplace was particularly important to people like Thomas Cooley. As historian Burton J. Bledstein has argued, the new middle-class professionals who came into prominence and power during the mid–Victorian era placed great importance on their reputations—both personal and professional. This concern for reputation was not simply a matter of dollars and cents. To professionals, success and the esteem that followed represented measures of individual moral worth, of personal as well as professional qualities. Moreover, the mechanisms of the moral marketplace did not operate simply to aggrandize members of the new professions. Professionals passionately argued that their own ascending careers—be they in law, medicine, or some other area—also advanced the general public interest, especially because professionals could offer their private talents to public service. Those who would wrongfully tear down the reputations of professionals—as James Scripps did with the good names of Doctors Bathrick and MacLean—were attacking the whole mechanism of middle-class mobility, and of national growth.[22]

The Renewed Faith in Legal Restraints

Thomas Cooley was not alone in his doubts about the direction of American journalism. Publishers like the Scripps brothers created more than a new style of journalism; they also produced a thriving counter-industry that specialized in decrying the dangers of irresponsible journalism. Critical commentaries began to appear during the 1880s, and the volume of material increased markedly during the two decades that followed. Attacks on the popular press resembled the diatribes hurled against popular television in the mid–twentieth century: because of the vivid portrayal of immoral themes and because of the supposedly direct relationship between these images and antisocial activities, all manner of social ills were linked to popular journalism. Such critiques ultimately gained credibility from their association with new "scientific" methods of social inquiry; a series of early social science studies "proved" that newspaper stories about sexual immorality and criminal activities encouraged imitation by impressionable newspaper readers.

Criticism of the daily press coincided with denunciations of a wide range of printed materials and political expression. And the attack on all kinds of "immoral publications," associated with Anthony Comstock for example, represented only one aspect of a broader effort to combat the apparent decay of the traditional bourgeois moral order, especially in American cities.[23]

Prominent legal writers joined the chorus. In his *Treatise on the Limitations of the Police Power*, Christopher Tiedeman charged that newspaper publishers printed "sensational, and oftener false, accounts of individual wrongs and immoralities, to such an extent that newspapers too often fall properly within the definition of obscene literature." Writing in the *Central Law Journal* in 1904, P. L. Edwards condemned sensational journalism for appealing to the worst instincts of the mass of "evil" people and for inflaming "their naturally bad dispositions to the point of the commission of crime. . . ."[24]

Addressing the New York State Bar Association in 1900, Justice Henry Billings Brown of the United States Supreme Court offered a bitter critique of American journalism. Justice Brown chided editors and publishers who used various "news making" techniques in order "to create a sensation, or to advertise a paper. . . ." He decried use of dramatic headlines to attract readers to stories about "domestic scandals, prize-fights, baseball games, ward politics, and the thousand and one things which a conscientious editor would wish to hide away in a corner, if he felt bound to notice them at all. . . ." Brown also complained that editors sent out political reporters "not to investigate facts, but to make a case, by hook or crook, against some prominent official." And when a dramatic story called for pictures, "an enterprising editor never allows the trivial fact that he has no photograph of a particular individual to prevent his publishing one. With hundreds of pictures in his collection, why should he not take his choice? . . ."[25]

Fears about the effects of unrestrained speech and publication gained particular force from social and economic tensions, especially from the upsurge of labor militancy during the late nineteenth century. Faith that the liberal marketplace would ultimately produce consensus and social harmony seemed increasingly difficult to sustain. As precipitous ups and downs, especially the great depressions of the 1870s and 1890s, buffeted the economic marketplace, radical ideas and movements shook the political spectrum. Groups such as the Molly Maguires, the Knights of Labor, the radical wing of the populist movement, and ultimately the Industrial Workers of the World (IWW) urged policies that would fundamentally change, not simply re-form, liberal institutions.

The short-term successes of these groups indicated the significant amount of "free space" that even social radicals enjoyed. In some cases, of course, radicals did meet stern resistance; both Emma Goldman and organizers of the IWW became nearly as famous for their "free speech" fights as for their social and economic ideas. On many other occasions, though, radical groups found that both local sentiment and local authorities respected their claims of free expression. Dissenting writers and speakers could draw large numbers of supporters, and many felt little need to temper their rhetoric. In the 1890s, the editor of the *Southern Mercury*, a populist journal published in Dallas, felt free to suggest that revolution appeared to be the only solution for the nation's problems and openly advised "every loyal American citizen, who is not a craven coward, [to] get his gun."[26]

To restrict the flow of information and to establish some sort of limits on the range and content of public discourse became important goals in the general reform efforts that climaxed in the "progressive" movement of the early twentieth century. It should be emphasized, though, that the crusade to bring greater order to the marketplace of ideas was every bit as diverse and fragmented as the political efforts that have been lumped under the rubric of progressivism. The general trend was unmistakably toward tighter control of dangerous public speech, but this restrictionist impulse lacked the unity and coherence of a concerted movement.

The issue of privacy, a legal question increasingly linked to defamation, provides an example. A wide range of press critics complained about newspaper invasions of privacy, but there was no consensus on the proper response. Writing in the *Forum*, Joseph Bishop still trusted in the self-regulating mechanisms of the marketplace to halt "newspaper espionage" into the lives of politicians and leading citizens. If newspaper editors continued to combine the functions of scandalmonger and moral guide, they would only lose influence, prestige, and eventually their readership. For it was "a libel on the American people," Bishop argued, to suppose that they would continue to patronize newspapers that had no other purpose "in the world than to amuse and entertain the thoughtless and vicious. . . ." Louis D. Brandeis and Samuel Warren, two Boston lawyers who were outraged by newspaper forays into the affairs of their hometown society, placed less faith in nonlegal solutions. In their famous *Harvard Law Review* article of 1890, they proposed recognition of a new right of privacy, a tort remedy that would allow people whose private lives had been discussed in nonlibelous stories to take newspapers to court.[27]

Similar differences emerged over the best way to handle anarchist agitation. When the Haymarket violence of 1886 provoked numerous calls for new laws restricting anarchist speeches and publications, Henry Adams, the prominent historian and grandson of the president whose reputation still bore the stigma of the Sedition Act, urged caution. Surveying the traditional liberal arguments for trusting in the free marketplace of ideas, Adams conceded that new social conditions raised doubts about these ancient faiths. "Milton did not write for a people of mixed education, nor did Mill contemplate a rapid increase of the foreign element." And the ready availability of dynamite placed a power "in the hands of a single man [that] far exceeds the just weight of that man's opinion in shaping public sentiment." These developments, he allowed, "lead us to be a little more severe in guarding public discussion than might otherwise be necessary."

But Adams ultimately rejected the argument for new controls on expression. In a prediction that has proven all too accurate, he warned that the reach of restrictive measures would constantly expand until perfectly legitimate and law-abiding organizations became ensnared by "police surveillance." Adams also believed that suppression of radical speech would likely boomerang, converting anarchists into martyrs in the cause of free expression. Finally, he maintained his liberal faith that even the propertied classes benefited by allowing excessive social tensions to vent in heated rhetoric. "It is never wise to sit for any considerable length of time on the safety valve." Adams was, however, ready for some action. He urged that authorities invoke existing criminal statutes, especially conspiracy laws, against anarchist "outlaws" and suggested that lawyers who defended anarchists might be indicted "as 'accessories to the crime after the facts.' "[28]

In his address to the New York State Bar Association, Justice Henry Brown also advised a cautious approach to new legislative restrictions. Legislatures could easily pass symbolic statutes, but would the measures prove enforceable? Brown feared not. A sensitive defender of the status quo, he warned that the "policy of enacting laws, which the legislature had no intention of enforcing, is even more deplorable than the evils they are designed to punish. The contempt of the press for the rights of individuals is bad enough," he fumed, but the successful flouting of a legislative command by the press seemed to strike "at the whole foundation of social order."[29]

Legislatures, however, did not necessarily heed the advice of people like Henry Adams and Justice Brown. Although proposals for licensing journalists never got beyond the talking stage (press associations lobbied extensively to halt legislation aimed at the large daily papers), some new restrictive legislation was enacted. A Kansas statute of 1891, upheld as constitutional by the state supreme court in 1895, proscribed the printing of papers "devoted largely to the publication of scandals, intrigues, and immoral conduct. . . ." California passed a law banning publication of pictures or caricatures of any living persons, except state officials or convicted criminals, unless the press obtained prior permission. Another California statute required the press to identify the author of every article that was libelous on its face. In addition, several states enacted new restrictions aimed at anarchist publications, especially in the wake of Leon Czoglosz's assassination of President William McKinley in 1901.[30]

McKinley's assassination by an avowed anarchist also prompted the re-prosecution of the nation's foremost radical editor, Johan Most. The editor of the *Freiheit* had already served a year in prison for an 1887 address condemning the execution of the Haymarket anarchists, and New York officials prosecuted him fourteen years later for an article advocating violence against governmental officials, which appeared the same day McKinley was shot. Johan Most tried to retrieve copies of the *Freiheit*, and the article was a reprint of a piece written nearly a half century earlier. But the supreme court of New York had no difficulty sustaining Most's conviction. By appending the phrase "this is true even to-day" to the article, Most "adopted the words of another to express his wishes" that revolution and murder be used to obtain political goals. Thus, the court ruled that the purpose of Most's publication "was not to criticize or discuss public officers, or public affairs," but to incite others to breaches of the peace. At points, the court opinion suggested that the criminality of Most's publication sprang merely from its "bad tendency," but Judge Vann also argued that Most's reprinted article created what Justice Holmes would later call a "clear and present danger." Whatever its standard of liability, the court agreed that Most's constitutional defense, sprinkled with appropriate citations to Thomas Cooley's *Constitutional Limitations*, carried no weight. Adopting a neo-Hamiltonian approach to the issue of free expression, the Court invoked Chancellor Kent's opinion in *People* v. *Croswell* and the liberty-licentious formula of Joseph Story's *Commentaries*.[31]

The New York Supreme Court's reliance upon *People* v. *Croswell*, the century-old criminal libel case, to deal with the anarchism of Johan Most represented more than a search for precedents. By 1902, the neo-Hamiltonianism of early nineteenth-century libel cases enjoyed a legal renaissance. Writing shortly after McKinley's death, Henry Wolf Biklé, a law professor at the University of Pennsylvania, urged revival of federal indictments for libelous criticism of the American constitutional system and national officials. The idea that "a nation pretending to an equality of rank with the greatest nations of the globe" lacked the power to prosecute seditious libel was nonsensical, Biklé argued. All governments possessed the inherent right of self-protection, even from criticism that carried only a bad tendency. "The fact that published attacks upon the government, whether verbal or written, do not so closely affect the welfare of society and the existence of the nation, does not affect the principle involved."

Rejecting Thomas Cooley's views about freedom of expression as too libertarian, Biklé embraced the old formulas of Alexander Addison and Alexander Hamilton. Biklé conceded that courts might find it difficult to distinguish liberty of speech from licentiousness, but he argued that courts already performed a similar task in political libel cases. Would it be more difficult to draw a line in criminal prosecutions, he asked, than to locate "the line which is constantly required to be drawn between fair comment and libelous writings?" The old Hamiltonian formula—truth plus good motives and justifiable ends—Biklé concluded, provided a reasonable standard for national libel prosecutions. William Gaynor, a prominent New York judge who played an important role in retaining his state's tough civil libel doctrines, joined Biklé in urging a return to the Hamiltonian view of criminal libel. Every libel should be presumed false until proven true; truth alone could be no defense; and defendants should bear the burden of showing good motives and justifiable ends.[32]

During the final days of Theodore Roosevelt's administration, federal officials did attempt to revive national criminal libel prosecutions. Shortly before leaving office in 1908, Roosevelt ordered his attorney general to seek grand jury indictments against the *Indianapolis News* and Joseph Pulitzer's *New York World*. An inveterate foe of muckraking journalism, Roosevelt objected to stories that criticized his machinations surrounding the acquisition of the Panama Canal zone and the building of the Isthmian waterway. Libelous attacks upon the nation's chief executive and his foreign policies, Roosevelt claimed, constituted crimes against the entire American people.[33]

The Rooseveltian theory of political criticism received immediate public support from *The Outlook*, one of the bastions of genteel culture and a journal often critical of popular newspapers. Quickly dismissing claims that these prosecutions violated freedom of press, *The Outlook* contended that publication of libelous falsehoods about public officials was no different than commission of more violent crimes like robbery: the real complainant in the "Panama Libel Cases" was not Theodore Roosevelt but the American people.

Any publisher who used his press "to rob an honorable man of a well-earned reputation, and to mystify and mislead the public on public questions," should be "put in the same prison alongside the . . . thief" who used "his cane to break in a jeweler's window. . . ."[34]

But just as there was no national statute against jewel heists in 1909, there was no federal criminal libel law. For want of a sturdy legal vehicle upon which to carry forward his cases, Roosevelt's charges against Pulitzer and the *Indianapolis News* ultimately broke down. In the Indiana prosecution, Judge Albert B. Anderson quashed the indictment against the *Indianapolis News* and curtly rejected the government's theory that it could prosecute every libelous word that circulated within a federally owned area.[35] The following month, January of 1909, a federal district judge in New York also quashed the indictment against Pulitzer, a ruling that the government appealed to the United States Supreme Court. In a unanimous decision, the Court held that the allegedly libelous publication, which had been printed in the state of New York and not on federal land, could not possibly be covered by the obscure federal statute upon which the government claimed jurisdiction. Although the Court did not totally close the door to national libel prosecutions under state libel laws, it did reject the government's contention that it could proceed here against Pulitzer's Gotham-based paper.[36]

The Supreme Court's dismissal of the Panama libel cases was a victory, though not a surprising one, for the institutional press. A ruling that an obscure federal statute could allow the national government to prosecute newspapers like the *New York World* would have been a striking departure from settled precedents. During the late nineteenth century—and particularly during the 1890s—the Supreme Court did radically reinterpret a number of settled precedents—particularly in the critical areas of labor law, economic regulation of business, and taxation authority—in order to reach socially conservative ends. After 1900, however, the Supreme Court followed a more cautious approach.[37]

In most cases, the Supreme Court had no need to depart from settled legal doctrines in order to rule in favor of legal controls over the press. Although the Court quashed the indictment against the *New York World*, most of the justices were neither enthusiastic readers of the popular press—Justice Holmes read no newspaper at all—nor critics of traditional legal restraints.

Several years before the Panama libel case, for example, a majority of the Court had reaffirmed its support of neo-Hamiltonian libel doctrines and its opposition to libertarian interpretation of the First Amendment. In 1897, Justice Brown had suggested that "the freedom of speech and of the press . . . does not permit the publication of libels, blasphemous or indecent articles, or other publications injurious to public morals or private reputation." In two later decisions, one in 1907 and another in 1909, Justice Oliver Wendell Holmes, Jr., adopted a similarly hard-line policy toward libelous publications and irresponsible political criticism.[38]

Reversing decisions by the District Court for the Northern District of Illinois and the Seventh Circuit Court of Appeals, Justice Holmes sent back the libel suit of *Peck v. Tribune Co.* for trial on its merits. Both the District and Circuit Courts had erred, he ruled, when they held that the plaintiff, a teetotaler whose picture had been included in an advertisement for a patent medicine liberally laced with alcohol, could not maintain a defamation action. The fact that publication of the plaintiff's picture might have been the result of an innocent mistake, he argued, could not allow the press to escape legal liability. Rejecting any notion of a qualified privilege here, Justice Holmes cited the eighteenth-century view of Lord Mansfield—"Whenever a man publishes, he publishes at his peril"—and held that "the usual principles of tort" subjected publishers to liability "if the statements are false, or are true only of someone else." In addition, he disputed the lower courts' theory that, as a practical matter, the drinking of an alcoholic patent medicine was the type of vice that would cause a successful plaintiff only nominal damages.

Although Justice Holmes did allow that experience showed that "the action for libel is of little use" in cases such as this, he still thought that the logic of the law demanded that the plaintiff be allowed to press on, if she wished. The case "should be governed by the general principles of tort. If the advertisement obviously would hurt the plaintiff in the estimation of an important and respectable part of the community, liability is not a question of a majority vote."[39]

In *Patterson v. Colorado*, a case involving a publisher who had been convicted of contempt of the supreme court of Colorado for printing critical editorials and cartoons, Holmes adopted a similar stance toward freedom of expression. The Colorado Supreme Court was perfectly justified, Holmes ruled, in denying the defendant any opportunity to plead the truth of his criticism. Although the issue of the First Amendment was not directly before the Court, Justice Holmes still opined that its guarantee of free expression prohibited only prior restraints. Citing late eighteenth- and early nineteenth-century libel decisions, he argued that the right of free speech and freedom of press did not "prevent the subsequent publishing of such as may be deemed contrary to the public welfare." This theory about the limited impact of the First Amendment was roughly consistent with the view that Justice Holmes and the Supreme Court followed a decade later when they decided the earliest sedition cases from World War I. Moreover, the decisions in *Patterson v. Colorado* and in the World War I prosecutions paralleled the approach followed by most state judges, including Justice Holmes while he was on the supreme court of Massachusetts, toward political libel suits.[40]

Reviving the Law of Libel

Restrictionists proposed a number of new types of legal restraints; but despite complaints about its ineffectiveness, the law of libel remained the most available remedy. During the last three decades of the nineteenth century, journalists often complained about a growing volume of libel cases, criminal prosecutions as well as civil suits. Although only painstaking studies of individual jurisdictions and trial courts can yield precise figures, evidence from appellate courts and literary sources conclusively shows that libel suits became more common in the late nineteenth century. The *New York Herald* first noted a sudden revival of libel suits, especially ones in which politicians and leading public figures sued for sizable sums. "For some years there was quite a lull . . . and libel suits were rather few and far between," the *Herald* accurately noted. But according to a survey compiled by the *Herald* in 1869, the press had faced more than 700 recent suits with damage claims totalling $47,500,000. James Fisk, the notorious railroad promoter, for example, sued the *Springfield Republican* and the *New York Tribune* for $100,000 apiece, and he hit Henry Raymond of the *New York Times* with a claim for $1,000,000. The number of reported criminal libel cases rose steadily after 1876, reaching an all-time high in the decade between 1896 and 1905.[41]

The impact of all these libel cases is difficult to determine. Initially, at least, some large publishers did not worry much. Wilbur Storey of the *Chicago Times* accumulated so many libel suits that a careful historian found it impossible to reconstruct the *Times*'s caseload during the spring of 1875, a period of frequent defamation suits against the paper. One of Storey's associates, Franc Wilkie, estimated that the *Times* was defending at least twenty-four suits at once, including six by different members of the Chicago City Council. During the 1884 presidential campaign, Joseph Pulitzer's *New York World* rolled up twenty-one libel cases, and Fremont Older of the *San Francisco Chronicle* once faced a string of eighteen libel cases.[42]

Libel plaintiffs discovered that large newspaper publishers could play even rougher after they had been sued. During the 1884 campaign, for example, presidential candidate James G. Blaine sued the *Indianapolis Sentinel* when the paper claimed that the Plumed Knight's wedding had been a shotgun affair. Defending this charge as true, the *Sentinel* later alleged that Blaine had obliterated the birth date on his deceased son's tombstone in order to conceal the time of conception. Legal resistance also stiffened because large publishers began to consider defending libel suits part of the cost of printing a paper. Franc Wilkie, of the *Chicago Times*, took pride in his paper's defense tactics: a "system of demurring and pleading, the deliberate absence of witnesses, the taking of action we knew would not be sustained—anything to delay so as to worry and wear out the plaintiff. . . ." The *Times*'s battle plan usually worked.

The largest defeat suffered by the *Times* was a verdict for $2,500, a small figure considering Storey's great wealth and the fact that this case involved a particularly vicious libel against a private citizen. Finally, as several of the suits against Storey in Chicago and James Scripps in Detroit suggest, plaintiffs could encounter difficulty even getting their cases to juries, because some trial judges willingly accepted the defense of qualified privilege as outlined by Thomas Cooley's treatises.[43] Thus, many prominent lawyers and public officials charged that the law of libel was too lax and courts too lenient with the press.

Writing in 1876, when Wilbur Storey was busy collecting his libel suits, the prominent attorney David Dudley Field catalogued the failures of American libel law. First, he agreed with most authorities that defamation law itself was a morass of contradictory doctrines and conflicting cases. But more important, Field believed that courts were too slow in hearing cases and judges too lax in trying them. He suggested a number of radical changes: allowance of two-thirds verdicts in civil libel suits in order to yield more judgments against the press; provisions to give defamation cases preference on crowded court dockets; fixing of minimum recovery schedules in order to eliminate juries' wrangling over precise money figures; and stricter evidentiary rules to prevent newspaper defendants from, in effect, relibeling plaintiffs during the ordeal of a public trial. It was no longer the rights of the press that were under attack, Field concluded, "but it was the right of reputation [that] should be declared one of the fundamental rights of men" and be protected more rigorously by courts and legislatures.[44]

Field's radical proposals, including moving defamation cases to the top of court dockets, went unheeded. A decade later, David Brewer, Field's nephew and a future Supreme Court justice, still complained that criminal prosecutions were ineffective, because of jurors "who, having little or no character [themselves] to lose, think an attack on character no crime." Similarly, Brewer condemned juries for awarding minimal damages in most civil suits, a practice that afforded a libeler the "pleasant privilege of asserting that the plaintiff's character is found to be worthless." Numerous studies of trial courts have confirmed contemporary impressions: suits for defamation never became more than a small fraction of American judicial business.[45]

In time, though, it does appear that tougher stands by appellate courts began to make newspaper publishers more cautious of defamation law. Certainly libel suits were always more of a problem for small papers than for large corporate publishers. The editor-publisher of the *Pennsylvania Telegram*, for instance, was forced to sell his paper after a series of small libel suits. Finally, even larger publishers began to complain about the time and money spent on libel suits, many of which they blamed on "shyster" lawyers who were allegedly using the new system of contingency fees to speculate in defamation claims. Those who spoke for newspaper interests continually complained that libel laws were too harsh or too confusing to be applied in any consistent manner.[46]

Press associations sought a number of revisions in the law of libel. In general, they wanted immunity, at least from imposition of punitive damages, in cases where innocent mistakes had crept into print. Newspaper interests offered several other proposals: requirement of security bonds in order to reduce the number of frivolous libel suits; provisions for change of venue in criminal libel cases; definition of malice according to its common meaning rather than intricate legal fictions; and procedures for substituting newspaper retractions for legal actions.[47]

Members of the legal establishment opposed most revisions suggested by the press. In 1894, for example, the Special Committee on Libel Law Revision of the New York Bar Association helped defeat a press-sponsored bill that would have virtually eliminated recovery of punitive damages. Two years later, members of the Pennsylvania Bar Association strongly opposed a bill, ultimately enacted in 1897 but repealed four years later, that restricted libel judgments to recovery of actual damages. Although lawyers did not constitute a solid phalanx against changes in defamation law, the best men of the bar generally did oppose measures that would have restricted the ability of plaintiffs to recover against newspaper publishers.[48]

In 1892, the *Journalist*, the first successful trade paper for the newspaper business, complained that legal restrictions, especially libel laws, were becoming a serious problem for the press. "A writer cannot be too careful, for it is an easy thing to involve a publication in trouble. . . ." By the early nineties, the *Journalist* noted, some papers were beginning to hire in-house lawyers who could provide prepublication advice on potential legal problems.[49]

Intrusion of libel lawyers into the newsroom raised an important issue—self-censorship. Overly restrictive libel laws, as Justice William Brennan argued in *New York Times* v. *Sullivan*, can exert a "chilling effect" on free speech; forced to operate under tough libel laws, "would-be critics may be deterred from voicing their criticism, even though it is believed to be true and even though it is in fact true, because of doubt whether it can be proved in court or fear of the expense of having to do so." As a result, critics "tend to make statements which 'steer far wider of the unlawful zone' " than they might otherwise express.[50]

The chilling effect of libel laws was not a discovery of twentieth-century judges and First Amendment scholars; nineteenth-century commentators recognized that tough defamation laws encouraged self-censorship, and greater self-censorship was precisely what most late nineteenth-century lawmakers wanted, especially in libels involving the reputations of the best men.

The attempt to discourage libelous falsehoods, rather than to encourage (in the 1964 words of Justice Brennan) "uninhibited, robust, and wide-open" public debate, became the stated policy goal of political re-formers from the upper and middle classes. Concerned about government's inefficiency and corruption as well as social radicalism, the re-formers sought to rationalize and to professionalize public affairs. In large part, this involved ousting working-class representatives from local office and replacing them with prominent middle-class professionals; it required removal of the old political bosses, and election or appointment of the "best men" at all levels of government; and this whole re-formation effort demanded that irresponsible newspaper stories not mislead voters into rejecting re-form candidates or losing confidence in capable public officials. Herbert Croly, author of *The Promise of American Life*, for example, denounced William Randolph Hearst for his "systematic vilification of the trust, the 'predatory' millionaires and their supporters. . . ." Condemning Hearst's "rowdy journalism" as a modern equivalent of abolitionist "fanaticism," Croly judged that "Hearst and Hearstism is [sic] a living menace to the orderly process of reform and to American national integrity."[51]

This search for greater order in political life led most members of the legal elite to reemphasize the libel doctrines of Hamilton, Story, and Kent. Although political critics could invoke the defense of fair comment for expression of pure opinion, the vast majority of state courts embraced the doctrine of strict liability for libelous statements of fact, even in cases involving criticism of public officials or discussions of public affairs.

A brief, but carefully considered, opinion by William Howard Taft heralded the dominant direction of late nineteenth- and early twentieth-century libel law. The case, *Post Publishing Co. v. Hallam*, was decided while Taft served as a justice on the Circuit Court of Appeals. The lawsuit grew out of a bitter fight for the Democratic nomination for the United States Congress from Kentucky; Hallam sued for libel after he was accused of accepting a payoff in return for dropping out of the contest and throwing his support to one of his former rivals. Taft's opinion acknowledged the force of arguments, such as those of Thomas Cooley and George Chase, in favor of a qualified-privilege rule in political libel cases and recognized the realities of self-censorship; but Taft placed greater importance on the need to frame defamation doctrines that would protect the public's interest in being represented by "honorable and worthy men." The danger of driving such honorable and worthy men out of public life "by allowing too great latitude in attacks upon their characters," Taft argued, "outweighs any benefit that might occasionally accrue to the public from charges of corruption that are true in fact, but are incapable of proof." He also took judicial notice of the fact that newspaper readers could not seriously believe that "statements of fact concerning public men, and charges against them, are unduly guarded or restricted." Both reason and experience, then, supported Taft's conviction that rejection of the old Cooley position did not endanger liberty of expression.[52]

Most other judges, including Oliver Wendell Holmes, Jr., supported this position, which soon became known as the "majority rule" for political and public libel cases. In the most celebrated libel opinion he wrote on the Supreme Judicial Court of Massachusetts—*Burt* v. *Newspaper Advertiser Co.*— Holmes invoked a free-speech test that he would later use on the United States Supreme Court. The *Burt* case involved a suit by a private citizen whom the paper had implicated in various activities of the scandal-ridden New York Customs Office. Reviewing a judgment in the plaintiff's favor, Holmes readily agreed that the story's topic—"the administration of the customs house"—was a proper "subject of public interest" and that the *Boston Advertiser* enjoyed a wider privilege than it would have possessed under strict Blackstonian libel doctrines. Holmes insisted, though, on a strict distinction "between the so-called privilege of fair criticism upon matters of public interest" and the publication of libelous "facts [that] are not true." The first type of expression was "criticism" and therefore privileged; but no kind of privilege, Holmes ruled, applied to libelous falsehoods. The traditional doctrine of strict liability still applied.

Holmes invoked a balancing test to justify rejection of the "minority rule" that the doctrine of qualified privilege would cover libelous misstatements of fact. In cases such as *Burt*, "as in many other instances, the law has to draw a line between conflicting interests, both intrinsically meritorious." Plaintiffs in libel cases such as *Burt* had their reputations at stake, while the general citizenry had a legitimate interest in broad-ranging debate of public issues. "But what the interest of private citizens in public matters requires is freedom of discussion rather than of statement," Holmes argued.[53] Thus, the manner in which courts classified public speech—discussion or statement—determined for Holmes the bounds of legal protection. Discussion fell inside the protected zone, while libelous falsehoods, even about important public issues, remained outside.

Holmes's critics—such as Judge Rousseau Burch of the supreme court of Kansas, author of the definitive justification of the minority view on qualified privilege—accused the Massachusetts jurist of adopting a thoroughly disingenuous approach to free speech in the *Burt* case. The general category, public speech, apparently merited special legal consideration in libel cases; yet, by injudicious choices in language, political writers could make false "statements" and find themselves stripped of any legal protection. Citing Cooley's *Constitutional Limitations* and *Atkinson* dissent, Judge Burch denounced the *Burt* opinion as too narrow and as hopelessly artificial. The "distinction between comment and statements of fact," Judge Burch argued, "cannot always be clear to the mind." What, for instance, was "a charge of intoxication—an inference from conduct and appearances and therefore fair comment or the statement of a fact?" By insisting upon "the distinction between comment and statements of fact," Holmes left "the law very much in the attitude of saying to the newspaper: 'you have full liberty of free discussion, provided, however, you say nothing that counts.' "[54] Judge Burch's view was, however, the "minority" one; the majority rule won endorsement from the vast majority of state and federal courts.[55]

Leading treatise writers also embraced this majority rule. Mason Newell, a Chicago attorney who compiled the leading early twentieth-century work on the law of libel and slander, concluded that there should be no penalty for "the publication of truths which it is in the interest of the people to know," but the circulation of "falsehood and calumny" against public officers and candidates was "an offense most dangerous to the people, because the people may be deceived and reject the best citizens to their great injury." Writers were liable for any libelous falsehoods, no matter how good their motives for publishing them. Although praising the demise of the Blackstonian construction of seditious libel, Van Vechten Veeder, a New York judge and expert on defamation law, fully supported the majority view on political defamation. He saw Taft's position as a necessary compromise among the voters' need for political information, the public interest in honorable officials, and an individual's right of reputation.[56]

The 1906 revision of Thomas Cooley's *Treatise on Torts* graphically illustrated the triumph of Taft's neo-Hamiltonian view of political libel. In editing the popular treatise, John Lewis changed Cooley's original view of freedom of press. Although he retained the author's statement that liberty of discussion required both freedom from prior restraints and exemption for nonmalicious falsehoods, Lewis added a significant qualification. "But a candidate for public office does not surrender his private character to the public and he has the same remedy for defamation as before. And the publication of false and defamatory statements concerning him, whether relating to his private character or public acts, are not privileged." Cooley's theory of a free press and political criticism had been overturned in his own work. The privilege to comment upon officers and candidates, according to the late judge's treatise, was no broader than the right to discuss private individuals and their actions.[57]

The revival of Hamiltonian libel doctrines accompanied a general reconceptualization of tort law. Between 1880 and 1920, a new generation of legal scientists proclaimed that they could dissect the vast body of precedents, extract meaningful substantive rules from appellate cases, and use the results to draw clear, objective legal boundaries. In theory, this meant that the law of torts no longer needed to be deprecated as a "potpourri of leftover civil, non-contractual wrongs"; instead, legal scientists championed torts as "that branch of private law that dealt with [the breach of] universally imposed duties."[58]

These conceptualizers came to dominate both the teaching of law and the newest forms of legal communication—law review articles, casebooks for students, and annotated reports. These works helped to support the trend against the old Cooley view of conditional privilege.

One of the first of the modern torts casebooks, *Selection of Cases on the Law of Torts* (1893) by James Barr Ames and Jeremiah Smith gave students an English case as the most instructive decision on the issue of conditional privilege. The key distinction, according to *Davis and Sons* v. *Shepstone*, involved factual allegations that were both defamatory and incorrect (and thus entitled to no conditional privilege) and fair comments (which did carry a conditional privilege). Although cases endorsing Cooley's minority position were listed for the careful student-scientist to consult, the longest additional quotations came from Holmes's *Burt* v. *Advertiser* opinion. The 1919 revision, undertaken by Harvard's Roscoe Pound, contained no new material on Cooley's views and still featured *Burt* as the leading American precedent.[59]

The real significance of this reconceptualization movement was not simply that the majority of pre-1920 literature rejected the old Cooley position; more important was the fact that the whole process of engaging in scientific legal debate over the rules of defamation gave additional force to the jurisprudence of doctrinal boundary drawing. Thus, the debate over competing positions generally took place in a highly rarified, abstract form. Both proponents and opponents of the Cooley-*Atkinson* position spoke the same language; they debated in the same objective, scholarly manner; they emphasized (which was not easy to do in a legal field so erratically plowed as defamation law) the conceptual coherence of their doctrinal positions; and they focused upon formalistic rules rather than upon the murky relationship between defamation suits and the realities of political life in a rapidly changing society. In an intricate discussion of the question of whether "charges against the moral character of a candidate for an elective office [are] conditionally privileged," for example, Jeremiah Smith praised both "the able and elaborate essay of Prof. George Chase" for the minority view and "an able essay by Judge Veeder" for the majority position. And Smith's analysis, like those of Veeder and Chase, dealt almost entirely with the realm of doctrine. Development of any realistic view of how the legal process actually operated in the case of defamation law would be postponed until the arrival of a new generation of legal scholars.[60]

The views of Henry Schofield, a law professor at Northwestern, epitomized the hegemony of the neo-Hamiltonian position and the faith in boundary-drawing jurisprudence. Although one later commentator hailed Schofield's

1914 paper before the American Sociological Society as a "sophisticated" and "relatively libertarian" analysis, his ideas about political libel actually represented a clear step backward from the early positions of Thomas Cooley and from the view adopted by the supreme court of Kansas in *Coleman* v. *MacLennon*.[61] In fact, Schofield condemned the "judge-made liberty of the press to publish defamatory falsehoods on matters of public concern" as "unauthorized judicial legislation destructive of men's reputations and property, inviting and encouraging the owners and editors of newspapers and periodicals to found their educational power on falsehood. . . ." As a remedy, Schofield called for Congress and state legislatures to enact new legislation, "at least for the better protection by the courts of personal reputation and property from defamatory falsehoods. . . . Indeed, constitutional liberty of the press in the United States is nothing more nor less than a fine popular attempt to employ the law and its machinery to realize the great saying: 'And ye shall know the truth, and the truth shall make you free.' " Thus, Schofield praised Holmes's *Burt* v. *Advertiser* decision as "the best American opinion I know of." And in a good example of his generation's unbounded faith in boundary drawing, he claimed that as "far as our constitutions are concerned, there can be no conflict between the right of liberty of the press and the right of personal reputation."[62]

Legal Science and Hamiltonian Principles: Libel Law, 1880–1920

Although the rise of popular journalism in the style of Joseph Pulitzer and the Scripps brothers exerted the most direct impact on the effort to shore up libel law, there were other developments that contributed to the attempt to re-form the process of political communication and, indirectly, to resurrect defamation law. A number of fundamental changes altered American political culture in the late nineteenth century and ultimately affected the ways in which prominent people viewed political debate.

First, as scholars such as Walter Dean Burnham and Robert Marcus have noted, political leaders began to lose their grip over the sources of information. The rise of wealthy independent urban publishers was only part of the process. By the 1880s, the old system of party newspapers, as historian Culver Smith has shown, crumbled; political chieftains could no longer rely upon a faithful string of party organs. Neither could they easily mobilize large numbers of loyal party voters. Beginning in the late 1880s, the post–Civil War party system began to come apart. Politicians from both major parties complained that too many voters lacked the old partisan loyalties and remained unmoved by banners, parades, stump speeches, and the other tried-and-true techniques of the battlefield style of politics. Party alignments suddenly fluctuated; old voting patterns came unraveled. Finally, at the same time, insurgent political movements tried to redefine, in an age of emerging corporate capitalism, the meaning of words like "social justice" and "democracy," and to sustain, in an era of increasingly large media institutions, older ideals of free and open political discussion. The late nineteenth-century populists, for example, created their own jerry-built newspaper network, their own National Reform Press Association, and their own answer (in the form of populist-produced inserts) to syndicated news services. Thus, insurgent movements like populism sought to wrest both the terms and the channels of political debate from the hands of a new political-corporate elite.[63]

The response of corporate-inspired political re-formers was to depoliticize a variety of public issues, especially those relating to the organization of the economic order. In large part, this meant changing the ground rules and framework for political debate. Just as new techniques of industrial management augmented earlier means of usurping workers' control of industrial information and of controlling their expression in the workplace, so did new methods of political management aim at subjecting the channels of popular political communication to new types of leverage from above. One need not be nostalgic about, or overstate, the degree of popular participation in the early and mid–nineteenth century to recognize the fundamental changes that were occurring around the turn of the twentieth century. Such diverse scholarly studies as those of Richard Jensen, Lawrence Goodwyn, and Christopher Lasch have all observed what Jensen called the switch from the battlefield to the marketplace approach to political debate. With the erosion of voter regularity and the disappearance of the party press, a new generation of political strategists—people such as Marcus Alonso Hanna—embraced the merchandising styles of progressive-minded business leaders. They approached political candidates and political ideas as products that had to be marketed aggressively and scientifically.[64]

Although a full examination of these efforts—which, by most scholarly accounts, succeeded in narrowing, without ever totally homogenizing, the whole process of political debate—obviously lies beyond the scope of this study of libel law, their general thrust clearly paralleled, and also complemented, attempts to revive neo-Blackstonian defamation doctrines. Thus, the transition from the battlefield to the marketplace put a new premium on a politician's good name and on truth in political advertising; and the general insistence on strict liability for libelous political falsehoods represented the legal analogue to these developments. When relations between the new political and the new informational institutions could not be managed successfully or smoothed over in other forms, the legal system, including suits for political defamation, offered another means of continuing the political battle over what kinds of information could be disseminated and over how certain issues and personalities were to be discussed.[65] The law, as the post-realist legal literature suggests, operates not simply (or, perhaps, not even primarily) as a set of instrumental tools. Law, like religion and media images, "is one of these clusters of belief" that try to convince people "that all the many hierarchical relations in which they live and work are natural and necessary."[66] During the late nineteenth and early twentieth centuries, the best legal science on the law of defamation offered a hierarchical vision of political discussion that proposed considerable deference on the part of political writers for the reputations of the best men. Although this view did not go unchallenged, it came to have dominant sway among judges and legal theorists.[67]

Chapter Nine | Libel Law from World War I to the Cold-War Era

Twentieth-Century Libel Law: Framing the Issues

Analyzing political libel law during the twentieth century presents a variety of problems. First, one confronts a tremendous bulk of legal materials. Although criminal prosecutions for libel have declined over the course of the twentieth century, and though civil defamation suits have never become a significant percentage of the caseload of any single state or federal jurisdiction, demographic and journalistic trends have expanded the absolute number of cases. Put most simply, more journalists have produced more column inches about more events of "public interest" which involved more "newsworthy" people than ever before. Inevitably, this has meant—as some late nineteenth-century jurists had already come to recognize—that the potential for libelous statements and comments has been immense. The number of civil libel cases collected in West Publishing Company's *Decennial Digests* became sizable.

But even a detailed analysis of these reported cases—a time-consuming though possibly manageable task—would only begin to explore the legal environment of twentieth-century libel law. Reported libel suits, as is the case with all types of reported litigation, represent only the tip of the legal iceberg. Cases collected in published reports, with some exceptions, capture only those lawsuits and prosecutions heard by appellate courts; cases adjudicated, but never appealed, would be underrepresented. Moreover, research in published legal materials cannot reveal the instances when important people threatened to file libel suits or to initiate actions that were later dropped. *Editor & Publisher*, the weekly trade publication for the American newspaper industry, for instance, has regularly reported numerous examples of libel actions that were never filed or never reached the trial stage. And even trade publications would not reveal the times when prominent political figures privately used the threat of libel actions in hopes of influencing future journalistic treatment of their activities.[1]

Similarly, the historian of twentieth-century libel law must deal with changes in both the quantity and quality of legal commentary. As already noted, the legal-science movement of the late nineteenth and early twentieth centuries brought new forms of legal literature, such as casebooks and law review articles, to the fore. While this literature was expanding in volume, it also reflected fundamental changes—such as the rise and fall of the "realist" movement—within the legal community. In the case of defamation law, one must deal not only with important changes in constitutional law (especially after 1960) but also with changes in the law of torts.[2]

More important, twentieth-century debates on the general issue of free expression have seldom directly involved the law of libel, the topic that had been at the heart of most nineteenth-century discussions. Even as committed a civil libertarian as Zechariah Chafee, the Harvard Law School professor who authored the first significant twentieth-century analysis of free expression, found no important First-Amendment issues lurking within the law of libel. Thus, any discussion of twentieth-century political libel law must proceed in light of the fact that until the early 1960s, defamation law was not a prominent free-expression issue. Perhaps the same discussion can explain why libel law assumed the secondary place it has occupied within First-Amendment theory.

Origins of a National Surveillance State

Issues surrounding the law of libel must be viewed against a background of growing debate about the meaning of the First Amendment in a variety of different social and political circumstances. Enactment of restrictions upon supposedly dangerous expression during World War I—the Espionage and Sedition Acts—produced the first significant set of United States Supreme Court decisions on how the First Amendment affected the national government's power over speech and press. The high court's halting movement toward "nationalization" of the Bill of Rights—through a series of cases holding that the due-process clause of the Fourteenth Amendment made certain provisions of the first nine amendments, including the entire First Amendment, binding upon state governments—also gave free-speech issues new visibility.

The flow of First-Amendment cases through the Supreme Court, as historian Paul Murphy has shown, sprang from political and social conflicts, especially ones growing out of the organization of labor and radical political activities. Efforts to tighten the legal clamps on political debate, evident in the revival of neo-Blackstonian libel doctrines, continued during the first decades of the twentieth century, reaching a high point in the nationally directed repression during World War I. Although wartime suppression of aliens and dissenters grew out of prewar roots, Woodrow Wilson's administration took unprecedented new steps. Emma Goldman, for example, had spent her public career fighting various efforts to muzzle her anarchist statements; until World War I, however, she and her supporters dealt fairly successfully with local censorship. As her biographer Richard Drinnon observed, Emma Goldman never lived "in a 'Golden Age of American Freedom,'" but she was almost always able to stand up to local pressures and eventually have her say. In contrast, the new nationally directed effort that ultimately led to her deportation "succeeded in making the entire United States forbidden territory." Thus, a sizable (and ever-growing) national police apparatus—the kind of surveillance establishment that Henry Adams had warned about in 1886—replaced localized, ad hoc suppression.

Creation of national surveillance institutions paralleled similar developments in other areas of American life. The early twentieth century was a time of reordering and rationalization, and the efficiency-minded gospel of Frederick Winslow Taylor affected more than the work routines of factory laborers. The way in which officials handled political dissent, for example, was also reordered and systematized; repression became, in effect, Taylorized. During the Spanish-American War, as Drinnon has noted, "Emma Goldman could safely be an anarchist and vehemently oppose" the war, "while for the same 'crimes' two decades later she was locked up and the full weight of [J. Edgar] Hoover's General Justice Division was thrown behind the effort to deport her once and for all."[3]

Revelations of police-state tactics during the 1970s helped to refocus historical attention upon the World War I origins of political repression. Thus, Paul Murphy sketched the beginnings of what he called the "surveillance state," what Drinnon earlier had labeled "bureaucratic authoritarianism." And on a more sweeping scale, Frank Donner surveyed the "Age of Intelligence," examining the full range of political monitoring and persecutorial activities undertaken by various levels of government and by private groups in the name of national and domestic "security."[4]

Development of an extensive internal police and surveillance system represented a sharp break with the nineteenth-century liberal tradition. To people like Frederick Grimke and Thomas Cooley, maintenance of an open system of free expression advanced national security. A vigorous system of free expression, for example, helped to ensure that the liberty of citizens would be secure from overbearing public officials. In addition, free expression helped to promote the larger security interests of the country by allowing new ideas to percolate up from below, by subjecting those in authority to constant (and sometimes unfair) criticism, and by permitting people alienated from mainstream ideas to vent their anger in words and paragraphs. The end product of this system, mid-century liberals argued, would be harmony and general stability.[5]

But when liberal faiths were confronted by growing social disorder, Thomas Cooley himself found it difficult to believe that the marketplace of ideas and the late nineteenth-century political machinery could produce harmony and consensus. By World War I, liberal political leaders like Woodrow Wilson were sponsoring their own updated versions of Federalist and moderate Jeffersonian restrictions on political debate.

America's entry into war provided the occasion for official oversight of American newspapers through George Creel's Committee on Public Information. The Committee on Public Information's "Preliminary Statement on the Press of the United States," issued in late May of 1917, reflected Creel's initial faith that voluntary censorship could succeed. As Creel, a former journalist, explained to other administration officials and to the president himself, the American press was too disorganized and too riddled by "the small but powerful lawless elements . . . who observe no rules" to operate under the official censorship system used in Britain. Creel hoped that the government could encourage leaders of the journalism profession to reexamine and change their ways of covering public issues. Yet he found himself approving and participating in efforts to proscribe, initially through an intergovernmental Censorship Board, publications that merely placed United States' policies in a bad light or that contained opinions officials considered too "dangerous" for sale in the marketplace of ideas. After considerable bureaucratic infighting, Creel eventually secured complete authority over newspaper censorship. The kind of "irresponsible" journalism that had not yielded to libel law and other judicial restraints could, at least during wartime, be subjected to bureaucratic direction.[6]

But the Committee on Public Information's role diminished after the Wilson administration announced plans for more thoroughgoing controls over political expression. Wilson himself urged passage of an Espionage Act that could be used against all domestic opponents of the war, whether or not they were actually pro-German. Although pressure from the American Society of Newspaper Editors and from Wilson's Republican foes in Congress helped to defeat a provision authorizing presidential censorship of the press, the Espionage Act did contain a broad, catchall section. It proscribed efforts "willfully [to] obstruct the recruiting or enlistment service of the United States, to injury of the service or of the United States." Under this section and later amendments, the government secured more than 1,000 convictions against various antiwar speakers and writers; leaders of the radical Industrial Workers of the World (IWW), Socialist chieftain Eugene Debs, and a Republican nominee for the United States Senate were among those convicted.

The nation's second Sedition Act, proposed by the Wilson administration in the spring of 1918, sought to extend the government's reach even further. Believing that the administration's proposed sedition bill cut too deeply into legitimate political criticism, senators Joseph France of Maryland and Hiram Johnson of California offered an amendment to guarantee that "nothing in this act shall be construed as limiting the liberty or impairing the right of any individual to publish or speak what is true, with good motives, and for justifiable ends." Attorney General Thomas Gregory strongly opposed the old Hamiltonian libel formula as too lax; "some of the most dangerous types of propaganda," he argued, "were either made from good motives, or else their traitorous motives were not provable" in court. The final version of the Sedition Act, enacted with strong bipartisan support, made it a crime to utter, print, write, or publish "any disloyal, profane, scurrilous or abusive language intended to cause contempt, scorn, contumely or disrepute as regards the form of government of the United States, or the Constitution, or the flag. . . ."[7]

Although there was some opposition from within the legal community to the Espionage and Sedition Acts, none of the justices on the United States Supreme Court dissented when the Court heard the first Espionage Act cases—*Schenck* v. *United States*, *Frowerk* v. *United States*, *Sugarman* v. *United States*, and *Debs* v. *United States*. In all of these appeals, especially the one involving Eugene Debs, defense attorneys condemned the government's reliance on the neo-Blackstonian bad-tendency test that had been used in early nineteenth-century political libel cases and urged acceptance of the more libertarian doctrines that had been sketched in the writings of people like Thomas Cooley. The government's brief in the *Debs* case did hedge its support of the neo-Blackstonian position that Justice Holmes had invoked in the 1906 *Patterson* case, but it steadfastly maintained that "all authorities" saw seditious speech, when judged by any prevailing standard, falling totally outside the bounds of protected expression.[8] All the justices of the Supreme Court accepted the way in which the prosecution drew the constitutional boundaries in these cases.

Oliver Wendell Holmes, Jr. wrote the opinions in the three major decisions—*Schenck*, *Frowerk*, and *Debs*. These opinions added further irony to Holmes's record on free-speech issues. Had the "great dissenter" left the Court in March of 1919, subsequent libertarian scholarship would have judged him very harshly. While serving on both the Massachusetts and the United States Supreme Courts, Holmes had embraced an essentially neo-Blackstonian view of free expression.

It is ahistorical and anachronistic, however, to charge that Holmes handled *Debs*, *Frowerk*, and *Schenck* as "routine" criminal appeals. In truth, Holmes candidly acknowledged that the conviction of the antiwar activists raised important free-speech issues, and he developed his own new rationale for why the antiwar speeches in these cases fell outside the bounds of protected free speech.[9] In the *Schenck* opinion, Holmes announced his "clear and present danger" test, one that he applied in all three cases.

Discarding the neo-Blackstonian position he had employed in *Patterson*, Holmes returned to a view analogous to the one in *Burt* v. *Advertiser Newspaper Co.*, the celebrated political libel decision he had written while on the Massachusetts Supreme Court. Taking note of Schenck's claims, Holmes

conceded—as had the government prosecutors—the narrowness of the orthodox Blackstonian position, even suggesting that his own reading of the First
Amendment in *Patterson* had been too restrictive. "It well may be that the
prohibition of laws abridging the freedom of speech is not confined to previous
restraints, although to prevent them may have been the main purpose, as
intimated in *Patterson* v. *Colorado*. . . ." He even "admit[ted] that in many
places and in ordinary times" Schenck's opinion (that military conscription
"was despotism in its worst form and a monstrous wrong against humanity in
the interest of Wall Street's chosen few") qualified as protected speech.[10] But
then Holmes confidently reverted to the same "inside/outside" boundary distinction that he had used in the *Burt* case. Just as certain types of libelous
political criticism fell outside the boundaries of fair comment in defamation
law, some political statements did not enter the protected zone of the First
Amendment. In *Schenck*, Holmes's distinction now turned not only upon the
nature of the utterance but also upon the "circumstances in which it was done."
In every case, he continued, the legal protection granted to political speech
ended when words "are used in such circumstances and are of such a nature as
to create a clear and present danger that they will bring about the substantive
evils that Congress has a right to prevent."[11]

Ironically, Holmes's clear-and-present-danger test, used to justify denial of
free-speech claims in these wartime cases, ultimately became the banner of
many twentieth-century defenders of liberty of expression. The evolution of
clear and present danger, beginning with the celebrated dissents of Holmes and
Brandeis in subsequent cases, is an oft-repeated—if still jumbled—tale and
need not be untangled in a study focusing upon libel law. It is significant,
though, that development of an extensive body of new First-Amendment
thought, and even the Supreme Court's application of these ideas to state
action through the Fourteenth Amendment, failed to halt the growth of a
surveillance state. In fact, as Frank Donner has suggested, development of
new courtroom remedies may only have helped to obscure the growth of the
surveillance state "by offering deceptive relief from its excesses without destroying its power."[12]

Libel Laws Are Not Enough:
The Search for New Restraints

Creation of this national surveillance state had a paradoxical relationship to the law of libel. On the one hand, the intellectual rationale for state
oversight of political communication rested, at least in part, on the revival of
early nineteenth-century libel doctrines. In theory, it will be remembered,
political libel cases—including civil suits for damages—did more than safe-

guard the individual right of reputation. Thus, the underlying premise of the new surveillance state and neo-Blackstonian libel rules was essentially the same: government and public officials needed firm legal controls in order to discourage dangerous political statements. And in the case of Oliver Wendell Holmes, Jr., the type of free-speech analysis that could be used to justify legal authority under the Espionage Act derived from his earlier handling of libel cases.

Yet, on the other hand, creation of the surveillance state meant that the law of libel itself would no longer be a major legal weapon against unorthodox public speech. In the nineteenth century, government possessed few legal tools, other than libel law, that restrained discussion. By the beginning of the twentieth century, though, enactment of various new state laws regulating expression began to alter this situation.

The availability of new restraints was noted by one perceptive analyst of libel law, Judge Rousseau Burch of Kansas. A bitter critic of the fact-opinion distinction and the champion of Thomas Cooley's *Atkinson* dissent, Burch wrote the leading early twentieth-century rationale for continued adherence to the old nineteenth-century libertarian faiths. In *Coleman v. MacLennon* (1908), Judge Burch argued for a broad conditional privilege that "must apply to all officers and agents of government, municipal, state, and national; to the management of all public institutions, educational, charitable, and penal; to the conduct of all corporate enterprises affected with a public interest, transportation, banking, insurance; and to innumerable other subjects involving the public welfare." In arguing for such a privilege, he recited the justification offered in Cooley's *Constitutional Limitations* and *Atkinson* dissent, and he argued that opponents of Cooley's doctrine could cite no evidence for their claim that departure from neo-Hamiltonian libel rules would drive the best men out of public life.[13]

But Judge Burch's opinion contained a line of argument that would not—and could not—have appeared in nineteenth-century libertarian analyses. One reason for accepting the doctrine of qualified privilege in all political and public libel suits, according to Burch, was the availability of a broad range of other, perfectly legitimate, means of restraining dangerous expression. He believed that the state police power extended to publications "devoted largely to the publication of scandals, lechery, assignations, intrigues of men and women, and other immoral conduct." His own state of Kansas had passed a statute against such newspapers in 1891, and the state supreme court upheld its constitutionality only thirteen years before hearing the *Coleman* case.[14] "Likewise, newspapers may be suppressed which are made up principally of criminal news, police reports, and pictures and stories of bloodshed, lust and crime." More important, Burch approved the constitutionality of laws, such as the New York statute that Johan Most had violated, that suppressed anarchist publications. Just as guarantees of free expression did not protect libelers who breached their qualified privilege, they did not prevent governments, under the police power, from proscribing publications "which imperil the public peace by advocating the murder of governmental officials and the destruction of organized society. Constitutional government may at least protect its own life. . . ."[15]

During the early twentieth century, similar proposals to augment the law of libel constantly bedeviled the press. "For some time past there has been a distinct trend towards regulation of the American press," observed *The Nation* in 1915. Sixteen years later, *Editor & Publisher* warned that at least seventeen state legislatures were considering new measures to regulate some aspect of press operations. *Editor & Publisher* also worried about the growing popularity of injunctions to halt publications considered dangerous to individuals or to the public welfare. These prepublication restraints, the trade paper feared, represented "censorship in a new guise, dangerous in the extreme, and to be fought to a finish."[16]

Support for new controls did not come solely from political "ins" who wanted to protect their own skins and from reactionaries who misunderstood the principles of free speech. Many of these attempts to exert greater control over the marketplace of ideas paralleled efforts to extend governmental authority into the economic, political, and moral marketplaces. In 1919, for example, Edward Paul proposed a variety of measures that were supposed to guarantee compulsory veracity in American newspapers. Defending his proposals against charges that they violated democratic principles and constitutional guarantees, Paul appealed to the example of pure food and drug laws. "Compulsory veracity in the newspapers is no more an infringement on our democratic rights than compulsory purity in foods. In maintaining that a pure news act would be interfering with the 'freedom' of the press, the press leads us to infer that Democracy is more interested in a healthy body than in a healthy mind."

Paul proposed a number of new measures. He suggested, for example, that newspapers be required to reserve space for a column written by a popularly elected "literary defender," a public servant who might highlight items that editors might otherwise bury in the back pages or might criticize positions taken by the paper itself. Paul also urged passage of statutes that harkened back to the colonial laws against "divulgers of false news." These would declare that "whoever shall publish in a newspaper or other periodical a statement wilfully misrepresenting the facts, or shall publish as facts statements known to them to be untrue or erroneous through gross carelessness, shall be guilty of a misdemeanor."[17]

Although such proposals seemed outlandish—as well as sinister—to members of the press, supporters of these measures saw them as filling gaps left by the law of libel. For example, a youthful Walter Lippmann emphasized in his classic study, *Public Opinion* (1922), that "the general reader of a newspaper has no standing in law if he thinks he is being misled by the news." The law of libel, of course, only applied to falsehoods that were also libelous, and was invariably invoked by citizens who felt themselves personally aggrieved. Paul's false-news statute was intended to provide legal controls that extended beyond the rather limited role assigned to defamation actions. A similar rationale applied to "right of reply" laws that were proposed in several states and actually passed in Florida and Ohio. The Ohio reply law, enacted as part of a revision of the state's electoral code in 1930, slipped through without the notice of newspaper interests. It required papers to provide, free of charge, opportunities for political candidates to reply to stories about them in previous issues. (Due to an apparent error in the drafting process, the final measure covered every story, though the initial proposal was designed to apply only to false discussions.) These reply laws were not simply an alternative to suits for libel—a course that numerous twentieth-century tort law experts have suggested—but a legal means of trying to provide greater outside access to the pages of privately owned papers. These measures, then, sought to go beyond the legal remedies that had been traditionally offered by defamation law.[18]

There were also efforts to augment the censorial powers that lurked within the law of libel itself. In a *Harvard Law Review* article of 1916, Roscoe Pound defended the constitutionality of injunctions against defamatory publications. A celebrated theorist of "sociological jurisprudence," Pound sought to show that prepublication restraints on libelous material were consistent with modern theories of social relations as well as with traditional understandings of free-speech guarantees.

Pound outlined three established "doctrines as to the scope of liberty of publication." First, he argued, there was the old Blackstonian view that freedom of press meant merely exemption from prepublication restraints; then, there was the Hamiltonian argument that liberty of expression guaranteed only the freedom to publish the truth, with good motives and for justifiable ends; finally, there was Thomas Cooley's view, which Pound interpreted to provide "immunity from legal censure and punishment for the publication so long as it is not harmful in its character when judged by such standards as the law affords." (Needless to say, Pound's reading of Cooley's views was highly selective and skewed toward the end that Pound wanted to reach.) In Pound's analysis, only the old Blackstonian position, the one formula that specifically mentioned prepublication restraints, clearly proscribed "preventive judicial justice as against defamation; that as to writing and speaking, all legal action must necessarily come after the act."

In Pound's view, this orthodox Blackstonian position needlessly prevented lawmakers from dealing with obvious social problems, including the spread of defamatory publications that injured individual reputations and disrupted general social relations. Thus, Pound leveled a unique criticism at the Blackstonian view of free expression. "Blackstone's doctrine has usually been criticized as not going far enough in securing against imposition of liability after publication upon arbitrary or unreasonable grounds. Equally it goes too far in denying to law all power of restraint before publication."[19]

Fifteen years later, Pound's *Harvard Law Review* article became part of the scholarly apparatus used to support the constitutionality of the famous Minnesota "gag law" of 1925. This prior-restraint statute, which was ultimately struck down by the United States Supreme Court (*Near v. Minnesota*, 1931), demonstrated the relationship between the supposed infirmities of traditional libel doctrines and the push for new speech-and-press regulations.

Enacted after a series of criminal libel prosecutions had failed to halt the political crusading of a small weekly newspaper in Duluth, the Minnesota statute authorized a procedure by which courts could permanently enjoin "nuisance" publications. This law gained the support of some of the state's leading newspapers. The *Minneapolis Tribune* and *Minneapolis Journal*, for instance, believed enforcement of the measure would help to distance their papers from the type of "scandal-mongering" carried on by small weekly papers in many American communities during the 1920s. Although the law was never used against the paper in Duluth—it went out of business without any legal encouragement—Minnesota officials soon used it against a Minneapolis weekly that was crusading against an alleged conspiracy involving city leaders and a ring of "Jewish gangsters." Officials obtained an injunction against Jay Near's *Saturday Press*, and a permanent restraining order barred further publication of the weekly "scandal sheet."

The case of the *Saturday Press* attracted the attention of Colonel Robert McCormick, the swashbuckling publisher of the *Chicago Tribune*. The colonel recognized that Minnesota's new statute offered a much more serious threat to the press than ordinary libel laws, and he bankrolled Jay Near's appeals to the Minnesota and United States supreme courts.[20]

Much of the legal debate surrounding Minnesota's gag law involved the viability of traditional libel rules and the power of government to adopt measures that augmented defamation laws. In upholding the restraining order against the *Saturday Press*, the supreme court of Minnesota argued that the paper was really in the business of blackmailing citizens who, if they did not buy off the *Press*, would find their lives unveiled in forthcoming editions. The gag law, then, was not directed at threatened libel but "at an existing business which, generally speaking, involves more than libel." It concluded that defamation laws simply offered too limited a remedy for operations like those of the *Saturday Press*. The Minnesota Supreme Court agreed with Edward Paul about the dangerous impact of sensationalized journalism: even when statements were true and nonlibelous, there should be no legal right to print them. "There is no constitutional right to publish a fact," the Minnesota court argued, "merely because it is true. It is a matter of common knowledge that prosecutions under the criminal libel statutes do not result in efficient repression or suppression of the evils of scandal." The Minnesota gag law, the court emphasized, was "not for the protection of the person attacked nor to punish the wrongdoer. It is for the protection of the public welfare."[21]

Four members of the United States Supreme Court, led by Pierce Butler, a Minnesotan personally familiar with the *Saturday Press*, endorsed this argument. Jay Near conceded that a previous owner had used the *Press* to blackmail prominent residents of the Twin Cities, and Butler's opinion recounted several violent episodes (including the gangland slaying of Near's former partner) in the paper's checkered history. Butler argued that Minnesota's police power permitted, under proper legal procedures, control of public nuisances like the *Saturday Press*, especially when "existing libel laws are inadequate effectively to suppress evils resulting from the kind of business and publications that are shown in this case." Thus, Butler agreed with the Minnesota Supreme Court: even criminal libel prosecutions could not provide "efficient repression or suppression of the evils of scandal." The Minnesota gag law, Butler concluded, provided a necessary addition to the law of libel.[22]

But a five-judge majority, led by Chief Justice Charles Evans Hughes, rejected Butler's reasoning and declared the Minnesota statute an unconstitutional prior restraint. Once he cut through the details of the Minnesota procedures, Hughes found that the requirement of satisfying a judge not only of the truth, but also of the good motives and justifiable ends of soon-to-be political charges constituted "the essence of censorship."

In reaching this decision, Hughes closely tied the issues in *Near* to the law of political libel. But the chief justice drew conclusions very different from those of Pierce Butler. The *Saturday Press* stories so offensive to Butler, Hughes argued, dealt with "charges against public officers," with allegations of "official dereliction" of public duties. Although Hughes suggested that courts of equity might legitimately restrain libelous publication that involved purely private issues, he believed that this case raised the kind of issues that should be handled within the confines of libel law. The state of Minnesota, Hughes concluded, "appropriately affords both public and private redress by its libel laws" for "whatever wrong the appellant has committed or may commit, by his publications. . . ."[23]

During oral arguments on the *Near* case, Justice Louis Brandeis suggested that he also saw the Minnesota controversy in terms of libel law. "Of course, there was defamation," Brandeis mused, but the matters discussed in the *Saturday Press*'s stories needed to be aired. Author of "The Right to Privacy" and a long-time foe of scandalmongering, Brandeis nonetheless believed that the justices were not dealing "with a sort of scandal too often appearing in the press, and which ought not to appear to the interest of anyone, but with a matter of prime interest to every American citizen"—corruption in a large American city. "What sort of matter could be more privileged?" he asked.[24]

There was also the hint—in Hughes's opinion as well as in Brandeis's oral examination—that at least some members of the Court believed, as had Thomas Cooley, that constitutional guarantees of free speech demanded some protection for libelous political falsehoods. Emphasizing again and again the political nature of the stories Minnesota was trying to suppress, Hughes painted a gloomy picture of political conditions in large cities. During the century and a half since the First Amendment had been framed, "the administration of government has become more complex, the opportunities for malfeasance and corruption have multiplied, crime has grown to most serious proportions, and the danger of its protection by unfaithful officials and of the impairment of the fundamental security of life and property by criminal alliances and official neglect, emphasizes the primary need of a vigilant and courageous press, especially in great cities." If, in exposing scandals, a "vigilant and courageous press" overstepped the bounds of propriety, "subsequent punishment for such abuses as may exist is the appropriate remedy, *consistent with constitutional privilege.*" Thus, Hughes appeared to believe that some libel suits could raise constitutional issues, ones that the court need not discuss in *Near.*[25]

The Supreme Court did not confront, in a direct manner, the issues of libel law for another thirty-three years, until it handed down *New York Times* v. *Sullivan* in 1964. Although the Court greatly expanded, between *Near* and *Sullivan*, the corpus of its rulings on the First Amendment, it discussed libel only in offhand *dicta*, some of which contradicted the hints of Chief Justice Hughes in the *Near* case.

In *Chaplinsky* v. *New Hampshire* (1942), for example, Justice Frank Murphy seemed to read libelous publications as outside the bounds of First-Amendment protection. Libelous utterances were apparently among those "well-defined and narrowly limited" types of expression that "have never been thought to raise any Constitutional problem," Justice Murphy wrote. Here, Murphy joined many other pre-*Sullivan* liberals in worrying about the impact of defamatory attacks by "right-wing zealots" against those people and groups they viewed as "progressives" and "democrats." Libel law, even members of the American Civil Liberties Union (ACLU) urged, could be used to protect democratic values.[26]

The Law of Libel: Familiar Debates and New Approaches

Although the Supreme Court issued no rulings on the constitutional status of libel laws, political defamation suits did not disappear. Libel suits continued to hold great fascination for both lawyers and the general public. When in 1919, two industrial giants, Henry Ford and Colonel McCormick of the *Chicago Tribune*, met in a dramatic libel case, both of the disputants formed their own publicity teams and regularly issued bulletins on their respective views of the lengthy trial's progress. When celebrated trial lawyer Louis Nizer published his memoirs, he devoted two chapters to his excursions into libel law, including his involvement in the headline-grabbing clash between Quentin Reynolds and the Hearst columnist Westbrook Pegler.[27]

Libel law also remained an issue of some importance and controversy among members of the legal profession. Law review commentators regularly churned out articles on various aspects of defamation law, and law-school casebooks kept the issues in front of future attorneys. The first college texts designed for journalism students included chapters on the law of libel, and discussion of defamation law became an important part of new courses in "the law of the mass media." In addition to watching out for novel regulations that might interfere with their traditional prerogatives, such as right-of-reply statutes, leaders of the newspaper industry closely monitored court and legislative actions that might alter defamation doctrines.[28]

Some members of the legal profession refought doctrinal battles similar to those Thomas Cooley had waged in the late nineteenth and early twentieth centuries. During the 1930s, for example, members of the American Law Institute (ALI), a group of lawyers who hoped to clarify the law by reducing it to a series of logical and orderly principles and rules, clashed over a proposal that their *Restatement of the Law of Torts* endorse a qualified privilege for libelous statements about public officials and candidates. Under the direction of Professor Fowler Harper of Yale, the Institute initially approved the following section:

> (2) An occasion is conditionally privileged when the circumstances are such as to induce a correct or reasonable belief that
> > (a) the public interest in the qualifications of a public officer or a candidate for office is affected, and
> > (b) the recipients are persons who, as members of the public have an interest in the qualifications of the officer or candidate.[29]

Such a rule had support from a number of prominent professors of tort law, including Harper and John Hallen of the University of Texas, but it angered other prominent lawyers who served on the committee that ultimately approved the *Restatement of Torts*. The formal debate over the issue, which took place in May of 1937, included some of the leading American lawyers of the time: Judges Learned and Augustus Hand, two of the most prominent federal judges in the country; Laurence Eldredge, who was just beginning a fabled career as libel lawyer; Rousseau Burch, the former associate justice of the supreme court of Kansas and author of the most widely cited judicial justification of the Cooley position; and (posthumously through a memorandum prepared in response to the initial proposal), the prominent torts theorist, Van Vechten Veeder.

Augustus Hand immediately attacked Fowler Harper's draft proposal and his claim that the "authority is just about equally divided" on the issue of conditional privilege. Hand recalled that, in a preliminary vote, ALI members had rejected the position ultimately reported by Harper, and he announced that Judge Veeder "utterly disagrees" with Harper's analyses of the leading cases. Hand attacked Harper's proposal as "a dangerous and unwarranted departure from the whole doctrine of libel. . . . It seems to me revolutionary and would be warranted by no public policy." Newspapers would be able to defame candidates and public officials "even where the facts are all the other way." With the dinner hour fast approaching, Hand successfully urged delegates to postpone discussion. "This is an important matter . . . the most important we have had so far this year. . . ."

The debate on the following day replayed thoroughly familiar themes. Acceptance of the minority rule, urged Veeder's memorandum, would mean that "public officers and candidates for office, minor as well as major, would be exposed to almost unlimited defamation without practical means of self-defense or redress." The "public's interest" in defamation law, Veeder argued, was "served only by (a) the statement of the truth with respect to facts, and (b) the right to draw inferences therefrom by way of [fair] comment and discussion." In response, Rousseau Burch insisted that the minority rule gave "no license whatever to newspapers to defame," and he accurately noted that the majority position represented little more than a restatement of the neo-Blackstonian fears of Chancellor Walworth in *Root* v. *King*. The so-called liberal rule was still "hedged about" by enough limitations that it simply did not, in fact, permit complete "freedom of statement" or license scurrility by the press. Veeder's kind of "speculation," Burch crustily concluded, "ought not to go ahead filling up the law books and the law magazines."

But Judge Learned Hand and the ALI held firm. Although Hand admitted that he had "no delusions" about the overall effectiveness of libel law, the strict rule still offered something to politicians who had been defamed and also laid down sound public policy. The minority rule simply gave the press "unbridled license" to defame political figures. The Hand brothers, with help from the late Judge Veeder, carried the day: delegates voted 98–22 to reject the rule and enshrined the principle of strict liability for libelous political falsehoods in the first *Restatement of Torts*.[30]

The ALI, of course, followed in the tradition of the late nineteenth-century legal scientists. Its labors rested upon the conviction that one could best understand defamation law as a set of universal, objective rules, doctrines that enabled judges to draw clear and precise boundaries in individual disputes. By the time the ALI had completed its section on defamation, however, this conceptualist-boundary view of legal analysis was meeting considerable opposition from "legal realists."

In critically appraising the work of the "Restaters," for instance, the realist Leon Green challenged their whole conceptual approach. As Green understood torts, analysis should focus not upon a set of supposedly objective and universal black-letter principles but upon "all the everyday, informal conflicts"—including those over reputation—"which take place in a busy world between human beings." If one really wanted to analyze this "conglomerate mass of hurts," the basic question was "How does government deal with them?" And before beginning to formulate answers, legal scholars had to recognize that "government has set up machinery in the form of judges and juries with certain comprehensive and flexible processes which may be utilized to *individualize* each case as it arises." Thus Green and most realists tried to understand the functions of tort law and to unmask workings of the judicial process itself.[31]

Although legal realism, as recent historical scholarship has emphasized, hardly comprised a coherent intellectual movement, most realists did share certain insights relevant to the issue of political defamation. Realists who considered defamation law, for example, generally tried to look at how the law operated in practice rather than to debate the doctrinal nuances that had so divided the ALI. And though the conceptual boundary drawers had never neglected policy issues entirely, realists tended to be much more interested in the public policy implications of defamation, generally lining up against the neo-Hamiltonian predilections of the prevailing conceptualist view of political libel.

Even before the Restaters had finished their work, Leon Green's controversial torts casebook, *The Judicial Process in Torts Cases* (1931), offered a rival, "functional" approach to defamation law. Rather than organizing his treatment of defamation into a chapter (or chapters) introducing supposedly clear-cut doctrinal positions—as did, for example, the classic casebooks of Francis Bohlen—Green encouraged students to think about how the judicial process dealt with defamatory attacks upon various tangible interests. Thus, Green's numerous cases on defamation fell under the broad, general category of "Interests in Relation to Others" and under subsections entitled "Social Relations,"

"Professional Relations," and "Political Relations." And as befitted his own reformist political sentiments, Green gave more prominence than earlier conceptual casebooks to decisions, such as *Coleman* v. *MacLennon*, that rejected a neo-Hamiltonian view of public discussion.[32]

In their anecdotal, but very perceptive, popular work, *Hold Your Tongue!* (1932), Morris Ernst and Alexander Lindey also showed how a dose of legal realism changed the way in which defamation law might be analyzed. After looking at how courts and juries disposed of defamation claims, Ernst and Lindey concluded that Americans generally operated on the principle that most politicians were scoundrels and the "more prominent the man, the wider the scope for free-for-all libel." Citing several well-known cases of technically libelous political pieces that had escaped legal liability, Ernst and Lindey claimed that political figures were now unlikely even to threaten libel actions. They believed, for example, that Herbert Hoover had "established new frontiers for attack on public officials" by his refusal to sue, especially for material that had appeared in Drew Pearson and Robert Allen's *Washington Merry-Go-Round* column. Pearson's numerous libel problems eventually showed that *Hold Your Tongue!* exaggerated the death of political libel suits, but the book, which was heavily influenced by the legal realism of the 1930s, accurately captured an important (if somewhat obvious) truth that the ALI's *Restatement of Torts* ignored: there was a considerable gap between tough-looking libel laws and the ability of plaintiffs to invoke them successfully.[33]

The Realities of Libel Litigation

The series of libel suits brought by Ohio Representative Martin Sweeney against Drew Pearson helped to highlight some of the insights of the realist scholars. In a 1938 column, Drew Pearson had claimed that Democratic members of Congress were engaged in a "hot behind-the-scenes fight" over the efforts of Father Charles Coughlin to block appointment of a Jewish judge and that Congressman Sweeney, identified as "the chief congressional spokesman of Father Coughlin" was offering "violent opposition" to appointment of a Jewish judge. Denouncing Pearson's story as a "deliberate falsehood," Sweeney began a series of libel suits against scores of papers, all of whom had carried Pearson's syndicated column. In one of the lawsuits, *Sweeney* v. *Schenectady Union Publishing Co.*, Learned Hand joined Judge Harrie Chase in reversing a federal district court ruling that had dismissed Sweeney's complaint. The appellate court held that Sweeney was entitled to bring his lawsuit before a jury. Judge Chase's opinion argued that constitutional guarantees of free speech provided liberty to present the truth and to comment fairly upon established fact; it offered no one "a license to spread damaging falsehoods in the guise of news gathering and its dissemination."[34]

Sweeney v. *Schenectady Union Publishing Co.* represented only the tip of a huge legal iceberg, for no plaintiff since James Fenimore Cooper had invested so much time and money in libel suits as Martin Sweeney. Conversely, no journalist since late nineteenth-century muckrakers like Wilbur Storey and James Scripps had pursued libel cases with the enthusiasm of Drew Pearson.

Pearson's approach to libel, like his vigorous reporting style, was distinctive. Although Pearson carefully screened his columns for libelous language, oftentimes with the assistance of an attorney, he willingly took greater risks than other Washington columnists. Reluctant to alert the targets of his exposés, Pearson rarely verified tips with the subjects themselves; if Pearson felt that information was genuine, he did not elaborately cross-check facts. And fearing the heavy hand of prepublication censorship, Pearson refused to carry libel insurance. Finally, as the *Sweeney* cases indicated, Pearson had very little fear of libel suits. According to the most reliable tally, Pearson accumulated a grand total of 108 suits, with damage claims totaling more than $100,000,000. He also appeared in fifteen other libel suits as a plaintiff. Clearly, Pearson was willing to devote both considerable time and money to fighting through the complexities of defamation law.

In Martin Sweeney, Pearson found a determined adversary. The precise number of lawsuits he filed is not known exactly, but Drew Pearson's private files indicated sixty-eight separate suits. Most of Sweeney's suits were dismissed on the grounds that Pearson's statements did not meet the basic criterion for libelous charges: courts simply held that saying that a public official opposed a judicial candidate who was Jewish was not libelous per se. Six papers, including the *Reading* (Pennsylvania) *Eagle*, which was trying to clear its books before an upcoming sale, did settle out of court, but only the *Eagle* paid Sweeney more than $200. And only the *Schenectady Union* case resulted in a judicial determination that Sweeney had a cause of action. Still, even in that case, Sweeney was eventually thwarted; he received no damages on his return trip to the district court.[35]

The complexity and multiplicity of libel law doctrines generally worked to the advantage of libel defendants, especially large newspapers, and to the disadvantage of plaintiffs. Preparation and trial of a libel case required considerable experience. Laurence Eldredge, one of the small group of specialists in defamation law, warned that libel cases required "special skill and knowledge" and that being "a good general trial counsel is not sufficient to do the most effective job" in a libel trial. Other attorneys, for instance, marveled at the skill with which Drew Pearson's libel lawyer, John Donovan, moved his client's cases through complex technicalities.[36]

The celebrated libel battle between Henry Ford and Colonel Robert McCormick's *Chicago Tribune* graphically illustrated one of Eldredge's caveats: the ease with which inexperienced libel lawyers could unintentionally turn their plaintiff-clients into the *de facto* defendants. The *Tribune* had denounced Ford as an "anarchist," a supporter of "anarchistic" ideas, and an "ignorant idealist." Rather than limiting their complaint to the terms "anarchist" and "anarchistic," words that were likely to be held libelous per se, Ford's attorneys, experts in corporate work but novices in defamation law, cited the *Tribune's* entire attack as libelous. This mistake gave Colonel McCormick's veteran libel lawyers the opening they wanted. Aided by very generous rulings on admissibility of evidence, the defense, in effect, put Ford on trial, and they convinced jurors that the famed auto maker was woefully ignorant about American politics, government, and history. (The Ford trial underscored Roscoe Pound's observation that the witness stand could be "the slaughterhouse of reputation.") Ford ultimately prevailed, after a trial lasting more than three months, but the jury awarded him a judgment of six cents, a figure that gave his already abused reputation yet another bruise. McCormick, meanwhile, boldly proclaimed the meager value of Ford's good name.[37]

Newspaper defendants had other ways to go on the offensive. In several of his libel suits, for example, Drew Pearson filed various types of countersuits, including some for defamation. And when threatened by a libel suit from Douglas MacArthur, Pearson's investigative apparatus unearthed several extremely embarrassing facts about the vain general's personal life. Pearson then used the new information to pressure MacArthur into dropping any ideas about a courtroom showdown.[38]

When newspaper libel defendants could not take the offensive, as in the *Ford* and *MacArthur* cases, they could adopt variations of the delaying tactics pioneered by Wilbur Storey and other late nineteenth-century publishers. For his work on behalf of Drew Pearson, John Donovan became known as the "master of the technique of delay." The normal Pearson libel suit would take four or five years to come to trial, with Donovan using motion after motion in order to drag out the proceedings. As a result, a number of Pearson's adversaries finally decided to drop their claims against the columnist.[39]

In this regard, the basic structure of the American legal system, as well as the complexities of libel law, worked in favor of the press. In the twentieth-century United States, the very nature of the "litigation game" tends to favor those who play fairly often—people and institutions whom law professor Marc Galanter calls "repeat players"—especially when they square off against "one-shot players," those who rarely enter the legal arena. One-shotters face formidable obstacles when they seek to recover damages or to assert a legal right against repeat players who can both outspend and "out-lawyer" them.[40]

A lawsuit involving a libel plaintiff and the mass media represents a perfect example of the one-shotter versus the repeat player, and the whole structure of the game tends to favor the media defendant. A study done in 1942 by David Riesman, for example, supported Galanter's later suggestion that repeat players generally enjoy access to more experienced legal talent than one-shot players. Riesman concluded that "a review of reported American cases demonstrates that diverse and unknown counsel appear for the plaintiff in most suits, even in New York City where a large proportion of the cases originate." In addition, the passivity of the court system—the fact that plaintiffs must constantly push their cases forward—favors newspaper defendants and hinders plaintiffs seeking to recover damages. Similarly, chronically overcrowded courts inevitably aid defendants who want to pursue a general strategy of delay. As early as 1876, David Dudley Field recognized this structural reality when he suggested that libel cases be given priority on crowded court dockets. Such changes, of course, were never enacted, and libel plaintiffs continued to confront the problems outlined by Field. Nearly a century later, a prominent Chicago trial lawyer advised his fellow attorneys against accepting libel cases against a newspaper, advice that some of Martin Sweeney's attorneys might have wished they had taken.[41]

As repeat players who were represented by experienced attorneys, newspaper libel defendants also enjoyed considerable tactical and strategic flexibility. When especially outrageous libels indicated the likelihood of defeat or when lawsuits threatened judicial rulings that might tighten libel doctrines, newspaper defendants possessed the financial resources to settle out of court and to avoid both litigation costs and potentially damaging changes in the law of libel. Conversely, when a decision seemed likely to go in their favor and when adjudication promised to produce desirable precedents, large publishers could cooperate in order to speed the litigation process. In cases where Drew Pearson could rely upon conditional privilege doctrines similar to those favored by Thomas Cooley and Rousseau Burch, for example, his attorneys abandoned their usual delaying tactics and pressed for rapid resolution.[42]

Large newspapers could also take preventive action. Beginning in the 1920s, use of in-house libel censors increased. *Editor & Publisher* reported that one New York newspaper shelled out $108,000 in 1924 to settle all of its pending suits and then instituted a system of prepublication censorship. During the next seven years, the paper never paid out more than $5,500 per annum, and most years its expenses totaled less than $1,500. As a result of rigorous prepublication libel checks, two newspapers in Boston and two more in Washington, D.C. all but eliminated defamation suits in the early 1930s. In addition, some papers purchased libel insurance as a means of protecting them against unexpected claims. But representatives for the *Chicago Sun* and the *Washington Post* considered the threat of truly damaging claims too remote even to justify the expense and the complications of buying libel insurance.[43]

Media executives were, of course, concerned about legal issues that could affect their business, and even the briefest perusal of *Editor & Publisher* suggests the energy with which prominent journalists surveyed the legal thicket in search of possible snares. But between about 1920 and 1960, the era during which the operations of larger publishers assumed many of the same characteristics of other large capitalist firms, the law of libel seemed only one of the many legal problems that media managers might confront. Libel law, though fairly restrictive in its doctrine, rarely loomed as a major threat to most publishers.

Living with the Law of Libel

Zechariah Chafee's comprehensive 1947 study on the legal status of the twentieth-century American media, a work financed by Henry Luce of Time, Inc., found prominent newspaper lawyers and executives basically satisfied with American defamation law. According to Chafee, the managing editor of a New York City paper advised that the Empire State's seemingly tough position on libel "works well although it looks bad on paper. No newspaper editor has just cause for complaint."[44]

The notion that editors had no just cause against libel doctrines reflected, among other things, the triumph of a new sense of "professional responsibility" among leading members of what would come to be called the "Fourth Estate." Throughout the nineteenth century, leading journalists had constantly expounded on the necessity for the newspaper people to elevate their calling to the level of a profession, to accept the responsibilities of professionalism. By 1904, Joseph Pulitzer, whose bombastic "oldspapers" had ironically helped to spark much of the criticism about journalism's ethics, was championing the elevation of journalism into one of the learned professions and helping to underwrite college training for newspaper people. "We need a class feeling among journalists," he wrote, "one based not upon money, but upon morals, education and character."[45]

Casper Yost, an editor for the *St. Louis Globe Democrat*, a president of the American Society of Newspaper Editors, and author of one of the first college textbooks on journalism, epitomized the links between professionalism, editorial responsibility, and the law of libel. Yost's text discussed libel under the general heading, "The Rejection of News." Libel suits, he argued, were "unprofitable even when the newspaper is vindicated. . . ." Thus, "unless some distinctive public purpose" justifies the risk, editors should censor libelous comments from stories. By the same token, a sense of professionalism required that editors display a healthy regard for the rights of those who might be defamed and exercise self-censorship over their columns. Adopting an analogy that recalled the "dangerous weapon" formula of nineteenth-century judges, Yost suggested that the same rule applied to both newspaper editors and railroaders: "Stay on the safe side. . . . 'you never get a libel suit for what you don't print.' " In fact, he specifically recommended Hamilton's truth-plus-good-motives-and-justifiable-ends formula as still the best definition of freedom of press.[46]

Nancy Barr Mavity of the *Oakland Tribune* endorsed Yost's general view of libel law in her text, *The Modern Newspaper* (1930). Defending the "modern press" against charges that it lacked principles, Mavity argued that most newspapers were now "precisely as fair-minded and tolerant as the public will allow them to be." Claiming that "any far-reaching and drastic criticism of the press is a criticism of the nation at large," Mavity credited leaders of the media with working to uplift popular tastes. In the case of potentially defamatory publication, this meant keeping in mind the clear line between freedom of press and libel.[47]

Although critical media analysts became increasingly wary, especially after the experience of World War I, of simplistic theories of "factual" reporting, even skeptical observers like Walter Lippmann believed that journalists must retain the ideal of objectivity, especially in the writing of everyday affairs. Journalists of the 1920s and 1930s, according to sociologist-historian Michael Schudson, felt they "needed" the ideal of objectivity as "a framework within which they could take their own work seriously and persuade their readers and critics to take it seriously, too." As Nancy Barr Mavity argued, the "true subject matter of the newspapers . . . is the world of what is rather than what ought to be."

One result of the emphasis, in the 1920s and 1930s, upon careful, factual reporting was a renewed respect for the supposed value of libel law. "The beneficent effect of the law of libel upon journalism is generally recognized," argued Leon Nelson Flint, a professor of journalism at the University of Kansas. Quoting an unnamed publisher, Flint maintained that libel laws insured " 'the freedom of the press with the same certainty that it protects the citizen from the abuse of the press's power.' " Moreover, libel law encouraged good, factual reporting because " 'it fixes the responsibility for errors, thereby tending to prevent their repetition, and puts on record writers who are habitually careless or untruthful.' "

At the same time, proponents of responsible journalism also saw value in the law of libel. The business of criticizing journalism continued to flourish during the 1920s and 1930s, and popular works like Silas Bent's *Ballyhoo* proclaimed that journalism was getting worse instead of better. Similarly, the notoriety of "scandal sheets" such as the various publications of Bernarr McFadden—the targets of several well-publicized libel suits—lent credence to such critical commentaries. As a result, some of the profession's guardians embraced libel law as a necessary antidote to irresponsible and unfair reporting. Going one step beyond the views of Leon Flint, a fellow professor of journalism, Nelson Crawford, advised that fair, responsible, and accurate journalists would not even venture near the limits of libel law. "Be Fair. Don't let the libel laws be your measure as the printing of a story. . . . If you are fair, you need not worry about libel laws." Another journalism professor totally rejected the view of press responsibility advanced by nineteenth-century libertarians like Thomas Cooley. The press, claimed Albert F. Henning, lacked either a duty or any legal privilege to unmask crime and immorality in public life. "Society has done no more than provide by statute that in certain cases the newspaper may print the truth without liability for damages, if it can prove that it is the truth."[48]

Thus, journalists could take two general approaches to libelous material. One path, suggested by the practices of nineteenth-century journalists from P. T. Barnum to James Scripps, was to see libelous commentary as an inevitable part of publishing. A popular manual, first published in the 1960s, summarized the revised version of this doctrine: "Libel is not a dirty word." The other path, suggested by the early texts of Yost, Mavity, and Flint, viewed libel as a symbol of the type of "irresponsible" and "unprofessional" journalism practiced by McFadden and satirized in Ben Hecht and Charles MacArthur's *The Front Page*. Two popular libel handbooks of the 1940s—*Dangerous Words* and *Say It Safely*—reflected the general triumph of the Yost-Mavity-Flint view. Although *Say It Safely* stated that its "basic purpose and theme . . . is not to deter the publishing and broadcasting of material that should be communicated to the public," it contained lists of words that journalists were to avoid when discussing political figures. The title of *Dangerous Words* highlighted its message: certain words were "prohibited by law," and writers must proceed cautiously, even when dealing with political matters.[49]

Zechariah Chafee's 1947 study of the legal status of the American media epitomized this trend. One of the legal community's most renowned civil libertarians, Chafee had long crusaded against neo-Hamilton free-speech doctrines. To this New England patrician, a nonrestrictive, relatively open system of political expression helped to bolster basic American values such as toleration, fair play, and moderation. Court-enforced guarantees of civil liberties helped to prevent the growth of extremism from both the political left and the right.[50] As his interviews with newspaper executives suggested, Chafee's approach to legal matters had been affected by realist scholarship; yet, as his elaborate discussions of First-Amendment rules demonstrated, he still believed that doctrinal analysis could provide the kind of sober rationality and continuity that the law must embody. In contrast to *Hold Your Tongue!*, for example, Chafee's discussion did not dismiss common law defamation rules as relatively unimportant to the understanding of libel law issues. Chafee's analysis followed the basic pattern of much of the twentieth-century's mainstream legal scholarship: it identified certain minor problems in major doctrines, suggested certain modifications, but pronounced the law, as a whole, in good health. Thus, Chafee argued that the "outline of the main rules of libel . . . does not look to me like a museum of antiquities. On the contrary, those rules seem intelligent attempts to adjust conflicts between the need for an unblemished reputation and the need for frank discussion of important topics."[51]

Chafee drew, in part, from the earlier study of David Riesman. Published as three separate essays in *Columbia Law Review*, Riesman's work, much more deeply than Chafee's, bore the imprint of legal realism. Although he still worked with appellate case law doctrines, Riesman displayed a great interest in the functions of defamation law, a preoccupation with the policy implications of judicial decisions, an appreciation of how defamation law really worked, and a zeal for adapting social science research to the cause of legal reform. In addition to these concerns—all staples of realist scholarship—Riesman also compared the operation of defamation law in the United States and Europe.

Riesman saw global, instrumentalist implications in defamation law. He credited England's relatively tough libel laws, for example, with helping to prevent the triumph of "demagogic fascism" in the British Isles. Conversely, he cited the Nazis' campaigns of calculated libels against opposition politicians and their use of defamation suits as reasons for their ultimate success. He argued, for example, that Weimar Germany's political wars had often gone into the courtrooms and that libel litigation augmented a large campaign of antidemocratic propaganda. "Indeed, during these turbulent years," Riesman concluded, "hardly an important [German] political issue existed which did not turn up in the guise of a libel litigation." And when the Nazis took power, libel law was one of the first weapons that they turned against their political opposition.[52]

Although Riesman ultimately accepted the basic foundations of American libel law, the European experiences led him to urge changes in order to erect stronger barriers, as supposedly existed in England, against "anti-democratic" propaganda. Riesman called for "realistic" changes, ones that would cut through the formalistic rules and recognize how defamation operated in the fourth decade of the twentieth century. The greatest threats to free discussion, he claimed, no longer "spring from 'the state,' but from 'private' fascist groups in the community" who used defamatory attacks against labor unions, racial minorities, and insurgent political forces.[53] Anxious to use law as a tool for social engineering, Riesman urged courts to "guide the direction of social change by deciding what groups are to be free to criticize and what groups are to be curbed." Libel doctrines, he complained, showed little awareness of "the reactionary significance of the typical patterns of anti-union defamation." Similarly, judges had not recognized the need to use libel law "to protect those weaker groups and weaker critics who cannot rely on wealth or power over public opinion as their safeguard."[54]

Riesman proposed a number of new departures. He urged, for example, greater flexibility in assessing damages; more conscious "manipulation of privileges and defenses," especially in cases of political libel; wider use of retraction as an alternative to money judgments; and adoption of right-of-reply statutes, laws patterned after European measures. Generally, these proposals aimed at reducing the impact of libel suits, particularly upon smaller newspapers, journals of political opinion, and various individual writers. But Riesman also called for strengthening libel laws, especially in cases where "systematic falsehood" had become part of antidemocratic political movements. Thus, he suggested use of heavy punitive damages and even injunction proceedings in cases of the "wilful repetition" of libels. And he also joined a number of liberal opponents of fascism in urging greater consideration of group libel prosecutions as a means of combating antidemocratic propaganda.[55]

Riesman's most popular proposal involved the use of libel laws and similar measures against the "far right." In 1938, for example, Karl Loewenstein contributed two often-cited law review essays, upon which Riesman relied, that praised European governments for "legislative control of political extremism." That same year, Franklin Roosevelt became so angry by attacks from William Dudley Pelley, the American Nazi sympathizer, that the president himself considered a libel suit. Several years later, during World War II, his administration successfully prosecuted Pelley for sedition, and the celebrated analyst of propaganda, Harold Lasswell, offered lengthy and apparently persuasive testimony about the similarities between Pelley's publications and those of the European Nazis.[56]

But controversy over the efficacy and constitutionality of group libel laws slowed their full-scale adoption and implementation. Even some of the most determined foes of racism and antisemitism, for example, worried that convictions for group libel would only produce right-wing martyrs, while acquittals might imply vindication. And when the politics of the cold war shifted the antidemocratic focus from the fascism of Hitler to the "red fascism" of Stalin, the architects of the post–World War II national security state considered group libel laws too tame and too visible a set of weapons. They preferred to expand upon the array of legal and extralegal techniques first unveiled during World War I.[57] Moreover, the constitutionality of group libel remained debatable. By 1952, when a bitterly divided Supreme Court upheld Illinois's group libel statute, enthusiasm for this use of criminal defamation law had largely faded.[58]

Riesman's suggestions for rearranging the common law of defamation were pushed aside even more quickly. First, leaders of the American media, people who would (as the *Near* case had shown) push for significant legal changes in other circumstances, saw no real reason to tilt against existing libel laws. Because lawsuits could generally be contained through prepublication self-censorship, courtroom stratagems, and private insurance plans, the mandarins of the media could dismiss defamation law as a minor problem. Proclaiming that "professional" journalists had little reason to complain, industry leaders saw libel as a potential danger only to their irresponsible brethren. Moreover, the few legal experts who expressed real discontent with the existing law of defamation often suggested alternatives, such as retraction and right-of-reply statutes, measures that most members of the press considered infringements upon their journalistic domain. The media's best course, it seemed, was to let well enough alone.[59]

Prominent liberals, many of whom would support substantial modifications in libel law during the pre- and post-*Sullivan* days of the 1960s, were also content before then to drift along on the libel issue. Although zeal for using group criminal libel laws to shoot down defamatory missiles from antidemocratic firebrands subsided rather quickly, many liberals seemed to believe that the civil law of defamation, though a bit rusty with age, remained a weapon to keep in the attic. During the cold-war era, for instance, liberals equated attacks from the radical right with political defamation. Owen Lattimore, one of Joseph McCarthy's most abused targets, justifiably entitled the account of his travails *Ordeal by Slander*, and friends of Don Hollenbeck, a CBS journalist who committed suicide while under siege by right-wing publicists, concluded that defamatory mudslinging could have serious personal, as well as political consequences.[60]

Some beleaguered liberals did attempt, with mixed results, to use libel law against their anticommunist accusers. When the swearing match between Alger Hiss and Whittaker Chambers first hit the media, for example, prominent liberals urged Hiss to challenge Chambers's veracity with a slander suit; when Chambers embellished his charges, Hiss quickly filed a second suit. All the while, several of the liberal establishment's highest powered law firms participated in the elaborate pretrial maneuvers. In the end, ironically, Hiss's legal counterattack contributed to his undoing, for it helped lead to discovery of some of the famous (and still controversial) materials that tipped the evidentiary scales over to Chambers's side.[61] John Henry Faulk, a journalist at CBS, fared somewhat better. His libel suit against the right-wing media watchdog organization, Aware, Inc., brought him ultimate legal vindication, though it did relatively little to revive his blacklisted media career. Still, Faulk and his lawyer, Louis Nizer, both drew reassuring messages from the experience; the law of libel and the legal system could be used, even by "one lone man," to vindicate "our sacred rights." The best people and the best causes could prevail.[62]

At the same time, few members of the legal profession crusaded for changes in defamation law. The organized group with the largest direct self-interest, the coterie of lawyers who specialized in defending libel suits, were satisfied. To traditionalists, many of David Riesman's ideas for integrating social science data and techniques into the litigation process smacked too much of interfering with settled common law practice. Moreover, most academic specialists in torts and defamation could find no need for significant changes.[63]

Libel Law from World War I to the Cold-War Era

Between about 1920 and 1960, questions involving defamation law seemed to recede into the shadows of free-speech consciousness. Attempts to define the legal limits on speech and press no longer began with the rules of defamation law; twentieth-century legal controversies took in an ever-wider range of state and federal issues. With the "nationalization" of the First Amendment in 1925, its application to state regulation of expression via the due-process clause of the Fourteenth Amendment, the United States Supreme Court steadily formulated, refined, and re-refined rules and doctrines that, at least in theory, safeguarded the constitutional rights of free speech and freedom of the press.

Resulting debates over where constitutional boundaries should be drawn, and over what kinds of juridical measures were to be employed, rarely touched the law of libel directly. Put simply, the free-speech issues of the twentieth century, as framed by the day-to-day historical struggles, could no longer be comprehended solely within the classical, liberal, citizen-versus-governmental official context of political libel. The labor fights of the early twentieth century, for example, encompassed a whole range of free-speech issues—such as union organizers' access to various public forums and to corporate power centers—that fell outside the view of political communication that dominated libel law analysis.[64] By 1920, a set of "corporate liberal" political structures and a corporate liberal worldview—both of which were global in scope and very different from the classical liberalism out of which political libel had grown—dominated American life.[65]

Although individualistic, marketplace models retained a tenacious hold—and were still used often in free-speech analysis—the real centers of power shifted inexorably to organized groups, especially business corporations, which were constituted on a large scale. Indeed, the organization and history of the ACLU offers testimony to the fact that even the struggle for individual civil liberties became linked to a national, organizational effort. The ACLU played an important role in pushing a final test of the Minnesota gag law toward the Supreme Court, bowing out only after Colonel Robert McCormick put the organizational power of his publishing empire behind Jay Near's potentially lonely cause. In contrast, the ACLU itself, until the 1960s, took the position that libel law lacked the kind of broader, collective consequences that would call forth its efforts. Similarly, David Riesman's greatest concerns about the issue of libel came in the area of group libel and in the use of what he considered systematic defamation by political groups on the far right.[66]

For the most part, post-1920 discussions of the law of libel assigned questions involving defamation to the vast domain of "private law," outside the purview of the new body of the "public law," constitutional doctrines being developed by the Supreme Court. Criminal prosecutions, whether for group or individual libels, remained rare, and civil defamation suits never achieved the kind of attention that nineteenth-century writers such as Thomas Cooley had given them.

When post-1920 libel suits by political figures clearly raised public issues, state courts and doctrinal writers generally concluded that the "evolving" common law of defamation could adjust any serious concerns. In terms of legal doctrine, most states formally embraced the neo-Hamiltonian position of William Howard Taft's *Hallam* opinion, but a handful of states adopted some version of the old Cooley-Kansas rule on qualified privilege.[67] In all jurisdictions, whatever the officially prevailing doctrines, the careful scholar could unearth "odd" cases, ones that seemed "exceptional" or "anomalous." To students of doctrine, such cases were simply that—unusual deviations from the prevailing evolutionary pattern. But to students who worked in the realist mode of analysis, these "odd" cases showed that in defamation law, as in other areas of law, legal rules could be adjusted to fit the needs of the particular cause at hand. Thus, where the more orthodox legal scientists found relatively clear lines of common law development, the more "deviant" ones discovered fragmentation and contingency.[68]

From either of the major jurisprudential paradigms of the early twentieth century, however, the law of libel seemed safely removed from the center of free-speech action. To doctrinalists, such as those who debated libel before the American Law Institute, properly trained legal minds could still identify and apply defamation rules without great difficulty; to those realists who looked at defamation, the facts of political and social life revealed no immediate need to adopt new policies in the area of libel. Blending both perspectives, Zechariah Chafee concluded that the rules of defamation appeared fundamentally sound and that the actual process of dispute settlement over reputation operated essentially smoothly and fairly. Although Chafee, like all re-formers, offered the Luce Commission several ideas to make a basically good system even better, he concluded that neither plaintiffs nor defendants had serious cause for complaint in the area of libel law.[69]

Chafee's confident judgments about defamation law, as we shall see, proved far too sanguine; neither doctrinalists nor the march of American "progress" solved the fundamental tensions embedded in the law of slander and libel. True, few ordinary citizens—though they continued in their everyday lives to struggle, both individually and collectively, to define and defend their images in the eyes of others—ever became involved in formal defamation litigation. And even though some of the nation's more prominent citizens—including the Presidents Roosevelt, Henry Ford, Dr. Hiram Evans of the KKK, Ely Culbertson of contract bridge fame, General Douglas MacArthur, and Benjamin Davis of the American Communist Party—possessed the resources to file libel suits, such actions, for the reasons suggested earlier, raised only minor legal problems. Yet, the underlying tensions of the politics of reputation, especially where the names of the best men were involved, remained.

Chapter Ten | The Law of Libel
in Troubled Times

During the decades that followed World War II, First-Amendment freedoms became a subject of intense legal debate. Free-speech claims, especially those made by people who had run afoul of legislative investigations or who had been charged under the sedition law of 1940 (the Smith Act), initially provoked the most controversy; but eventually the law of political libel also came under scrutiny. Had Zechariah Chafee issued his generally upbeat conclusions about the state of libel law in 1964, rather than a decade and a half earlier, his views would have been challenged. By the early 1960s, defamation law became, as it had been in the nineteenth century, a subject for extensive and serious legal debates. The case of *New York Times* v. *Sullivan* (1964), in which the United States Supreme Court mandated a whole new national approach to defamation law, encapsulated most of the issues surrounding the law of libel; it also reflected many of the social-political-legal dilemmas of mid–twentieth-century liberalism. As always, the law of libel could not be understood apart from the larger history of the time.

The Supreme Court Confronts Libel Law

Times v. *Sullivan* grew out of the civil rights battles of the 1950s and 1960s, struggles in which activists first converted the streets of the Deep South into free-speech forums and then enlisted the mass media as an ally for attracting new political supporters, especially ones from outside the South. In their challenge to the white southern legal structure, the civil rights movement soon ran headlong into the law of libel.

The most prominent defamation suit resulted from a paid political advertisement entitled "Heed Their Rising Voices," which appeared in the 29 March 1960 issue of the *New York Times*. A plea for funds to finance new campaigns of nonviolent civil disobedience, the advertisement charged officials in Montgomery, Alabama, with repression of civil rights activists and condemned a "reign of terror" by private vigilantes. L. B. Sullivan—a Montgomery police commissioner who claimed that the ad falsely accused him of ordering repressive measures and of inciting violence—sued the *Times* and four prominent black civil rights leaders, including Ralph David Abernathy. "Heed Their

Rising Voices" did, in fact, contain substantial inaccuracies, and a trial judge charged an all-white jury that the ad included libelous falsehoods that, under Alabama's conventional defamation laws, were unprotected by any qualified privilege. The jury returned an award of $500,000, and the Alabama Supreme Court sustained the judgment.[1]

Times v. *Sullivan* brought together—in legal form—many of the domestic challenges that liberalism faced in the mid-1960s. Certainly the legal issues raised by the libel judgment against the *Times* could not be separated easily from broader questions about the future of civil rights activities. The *Sullivan* suit, as Justice William Brennan noted, was only one of many libel cases involving the civil rights movement. The total value of claims reached more than $6,000,000, and the specter of protracted litigation threatened to pressure even the largest media corporations to self-censor their coverage from the Deep South.[2]

In fact, southern libel laws seemed about to inhibit political discussion even more seriously than had the infamous Sedition Act of 1798. Between 1798 and 1800, it will be recalled, Federalist partisans had failed to stifle political dissent through libel prosecutions; political divisions had run too deep. Thus, when Justice Brennan drew an analogy between the *Sullivan* suit and the Sedition Act prosecutions, he probably understated—rather than exaggerated—the potential for a serious "chill" in the discussion of civil rights issues. The controversy over the mailing of antislavery materials into the South during the 1830s offered a more appropriate historical comparison. Just as nineteenth-century white slaveholders had tried to prevent northern antislavery materials from being mailed into the slave states, so twentieth-century segregationists sought to employ state libel laws to cut off outside criticism of "massive resistance" to racial integration.[3]

Comparison between the 1830s and the 1960s can also help to explain why a sweeping assault on libel law seemed to be the most appropriate response in the *Sullivan* case. During the 1830s, the Democratic party of Andrew Jackson rested upon a proslavery, southern base, and party leaders quickly accepted southern demands that antislavery writers be denied free access to the nation's mails. Conversely, in the 1960s, the civil rights movement found powerful northern support for its claims that traditional libel doctrines unconstitutionally infringed upon freedom of expression.

The *Sullivan* case highlighted the persistence of local resistance not only to the civil rights movement but to the desires of national, agenda-setting elites. As Richard Cloward and Frances Fox Piven have suggested, priority-setting elites were determined to channel the civil rights crusade toward issues that could be handled by liberal institutions. The Kennedy administration, for example, hoped to convince civil rights leaders that voter registration drives offered greater opportunities, especially for their Democratic party, than broadly focused demonstrations against a variety of different forms of racial discrimination. The political process, prominent liberals repeatedly told young militants, could be made to yield results. But if the technicalities of libel law could be used to mute criticism—or even discussion—of segregationist policies, claims about the openness of the political process were hardly credible. If local power brokers within the South could halt coverage of civil rights by the national media, how could liberal political leaders realistically promise progress toward a more just society? An obvious answer to such questions was to eliminate state libel laws that interfered with discussion of civil rights issues.[4]

Here, the fundamental issue at stake, from the standpoint of black and white activists, was the legitimacy of the larger political process. The brief submitted on behalf of Reverend Abernathy and the other civil rights leaders emphasized this dimension. It characterized the *Sullivan* libel suit as a "further refinement" on "a distinct pattern of resistance" to the "century-long struggle of the Negro people for complete emancipation and full citizenship. . . ." The "flood" of libel suits in Alabama, the Abernathy brief suggested, was "part of a concerted, calculated program to carry out a policy of punishing, intimidating and silencing all who criticize and seek to change Alabama's notorious political system of enforced segregation." Alluding to what civil rights leaders considered the likelihood of similar cases, including slander suits against speakers, the brief claimed that it required "little imagination to picture the destructiveness of such weapons in the hands of those who, only yesterday, used dogs and fire hoses in Birmingham, Alabama, against Negro petitioners leading non-violent protests against segregation practices."[5] Therefore, the Abernathy brief directly challenged liberals to justify claims that the system really did work and that the guardians of the rule of law could redraw the boundaries of liberty so as to safeguard the rights of blacks and those who preached their cause.

During the 1940s and 1950s, libertarians had begun to argue for new approaches to unblock the political process and to safeguard the free speech rights of those who urged social change. In beating back the use of libel law by segregationist forces, lawyers for the media and civil rights activists could draw upon this broad body of legal thought, one that might be called "cold-war libertarianism." In approaching the issues raised by *Sullivan*, both free-speech advocates and sympathetic judges saw the legal questions as intimately related to this corpus of First-Amendment theory.

Cold-War Libertarianism

The years between about 1940 and 1964 constitute an important and distinct era in the history of First-Amendment controversies. The first date

238 | Protecting the Best Men

marks, among other things, the passage of the Smith Act and the climax of a divisive battle within the American Civil Liberties Union (ACLU) that ended with the expulsion of a founding member, Elizabeth Gurley Flynn, because she had joined the Communist Party and had published several articles critical of the ACLU itself. The implications of these events—enactment of a national law criminalizing political speech and association, and bitter conflict among old libertarian allies—became apparent during the 1940s and 1950s. In response to what they considered unprecedented threats to First-Amendment freedoms, the cold-war libertarians broke with the free-speech theories associated with Holmes, Brandeis, and Chafee and tried to devise new constitutional guarantees. These people, who came almost exclusively from the academic world, believed that the freedoms covered by the First Amendment truly ranked first in any scheme of democratic constitutionalism. In contrast to analysts of the late 1930s and 1940s, who worried about the impact of anti-democratic propaganda and group libels, the cold-war libertarians argued that attempts to obstruct the flow of even dangerous political ideas struck at the very foundations of a free society. While remaining firmly within the traditions of liberal constitutionalism, cold-war libertarians sought to expand the boundaries of free expression beyond those staked out by earlier First-Amendment theorists and to convince a majority of the Supreme Court of the soundness of their approach.[6]

In 1948, for example, the philosopher Alexander Meiklejohn published his seminal *Free Speech and Its Relation to Self-Government*. Articulating a theme that he would expound for the next fifteen years, Meiklejohn helped to lead much of First-Amendment analysis away from earlier approaches. Associated with an "absolutist" interpretation of the First Amendment, Meiklejohn always struggled against what he considered "caricatures" of his position. In his final essay, written when he was nearly ninety, Meiklejohn ridiculed the idea that any "competent" person would even argue that the First Amendment guaranteed "an unlimited license to talk." Speech, like any form of human action, was "subject to regulation in exactly the same sense as is walking, or lighting a fire, or shooting a gun." But what was "absolute," in Meiklejohn's view, was the system of democratic self-government to which the First Amendment was inextricably tied. The First Amendment protected "the freedom of those activities of thought and communication by which we 'govern.' " Meiklejohn's prose recalled the rhetoric of nineteenth-century democrats such as Theophilus Fisk and the early Thomas Cooley. Self-government and free expression were more than rights; they were sacred responsibilities of free people. According to Meiklejohn, democratic citizens must constantly attempt to understand public issues; to judge how public officials, their agents, were dealing with these issues; and to "share in devising methods by which those decisions can be made wise and effective or, if need be, supplanted by others which promise greater wisdom and effectiveness." In order to carry out these weighty duties, citizens needed the widest possible access to information and opinions about public issues. "Public discussions of public issues, together with the spreading of information and opinion bearing on these issues, must have a freedom unabridged by our 'agents.' " Even stupid ideas and misguided assertions could not be proscribed because they, too, could help people clarify their own ideas and reconsider their previous views.[7]

One of the implications of Meiklejohn's theory—that freedom of expression was indivisible and that no one could enjoy its full benefits unless the First Amendment protected its use by everyone—formed the cornerstone of the First-Amendment views of another cold-war libertarian, Hugo L. Black. "I believe," Justice Black wrote in a 1952 Supreme Court dissent, that "we must have freedom of speech . . . for all or we may eventually have it for none." Untrammeled political debate, though a cause for periodic disruption and a continual bother for politicians, was necessary if the United States were to remain true to what Black considered its democratic heritage. The framers of the First Amendment, he argued, had weighed the dangers of free expression "against the dangers of censorship and had deliberately chosen the First Amendment's unequivocal command" that free expression "shall not be abridged." Such liberty might be "too dangerous for bad, tyrannical governments to permit," but free governments could have no less. Thus, Black concluded that "the First Amendment grants an absolute right to believe in any governmental system, discuss all government affairs, and argue for desired changes in the existing order."[8]

Edmund Cahn of New York University Law School, a close friend of Hugo Black, reiterated many of the justice's ideas in his own influential writings on the First Amendment. Cahn's views balanced a deep skepticism about the political acuity of ordinary citizens and even about the efficacy of discussion, with a faith that unrestrained communication still offered the last best hope for saving free governments. Writing in the aftermath of World War II and concerned about the spread of "totalitarianism," Cahn and others believed that the main threats to democratic government came not simply from corrupt officials but from a corrupted citizenry. Liberty's greatest enemies were "mental sloth, conformity, bigotry, superstition, credulity, monopoly in the marketplace of ideas, and utter, benighted ignorance." Thus, the success of popular government depended upon citizens receiving "enough information to grasp public issues and make sensible decisions"; First-Amendment law should prevent the channels of public information from becoming blocked, especially by governmental restraints.

Cahn expanded upon Black's idea of the indivisibility of the First Amendment. Although First-Amendment cases superficially involved the rights of newspapers and individuals, the real parties to any free-speech controversy were "the whole conglomerate mass of the community audiences . . . including those who are almost sure they will never wish to speak and those who are completely sure they do not wish to listen." The modern libertarian view of free speech, Cahn acknowledged, would "never provide a courteous, deferential, or dainty society"; in fact, it recognized that "a political life consonant with the demands of conscience" would produce political criticism that was sometimes unfair and untrue. But he concluded that a free people owed themselves "emancipation from the fear of printed words and from trembling before epithets. A certain small dose of error and malice . . . can gradually immunize us against the disease of credulity."[9]

Most of the cold-war libertarians eventually confronted the law of libel. Indeed, defamation helped to clarify Alexander Meiklejohn's ideas about just how "absolute" the First Amendment really should be. In cases of purely private defamation, where libelous comments had "no relation to the business of governing," the First Amendment provided no protection, he argued. But where libelous publications involved issues such as "the unfitness of a candidate for governmental office," the "disapproval and condemnation" of governmental policies, or "even the structure of the Constitution," defamatory statements were absolutely privileged because of their relationship to the whole process of self-government.[10]

Justice Black also found orthodox libel law in conflict with First-Amendment requirements, but here his views were more "absolutist" than Meiklejohn's. The entire law of libel, Black believed, violated the central meaning of free speech. In a 1962 "public interview" with Cahn, Black argued that the First Amendment, as written and adopted, "intended that there should be no libel or defamation law in the United States, under the United States Government. . . ." In Black's view, there was "time enough for government to step in to regulate people when they *do* something, not when they *say* something. . . ." Returning once again to his conviction about the indivisibility of free expression, he bluntly stated that he did not believe "that there is *any* halfway ground if you enforce the protections of the First Amendment."[11]

Similarly, Edmund Cahn took direct aim on traditional libel law, advocating a kind of rugged individualist approach to defamatory political speech. In a 1962 address at the Hebrew University of Jerusalem, Cahn proclaimed that "libertarians are not content with the defense of truth" in defamation cases. "We need to hear all voices, even those that sound the worst, so that we find our own way and judge for ourselves." Citing Jewish as well as American texts, Cahn observed that one could not find "sharper, more critical, more caustic statements" about the Hebrew people than in the Old Testament and in the Talmud. "Far from hiding invidious facts," Jewish literature recorded any dispute, "no matter how charged with defamation. Our classical sages," he noted, "seem to have understood perfectly that if men can listen to good statements, good commandments, and good exhortations without automatically becoming good, they can be exposed to bad ones without automatically becoming bad." Thus, Cahn expressed some doubts about the real consequences of free communication—"For good or ill, words simply do not have the magical efficacy that fearsome people attribute to them"—but he ultimately embraced the cold-war libertarian standard "as the best and highest that political man has ever produced."[12]

Although he acknowledged that the "tough-minded" might judge the cold-war libertarians as "sentimental and soft-headed," Harry Kalven, Jr., of the University of Chicago Law School, did not back away from the derogatory labels of potential critics. Writing and speaking in 1952, the height of the hard-nosed, cold-war consensus, Kalven elected to "take my stand with the soft-headed" on the issue of libel. Viewing defamation through a historical lens, he sought to reintroduce lawyers to the legacy of Thomas Cooley and Rousseau Burch's opinion in *Coleman v. MacLennon*. In the late nineteenth and early twentieth centuries, Kalven accurately noted, discussions of free expression almost always revolved around the law of defamation; in contrast, mid–twentieth-century analyses, even those of libertarians such as Zechariah Chafee, Jr., downplayed the broader significance of defamation. In contrast, Kalven chose "to exercise the prerogative of a teacher of law by elaborating on the question"—"What are the implications of the tort law of defamation for a theory of speech?"—without ever really answering it.[13]

In the course of an admittedly rambling discussion, Kalven dissented from the mainstream view of defamation and raised some of the basic issues that Justice William Brennan would confront twelve years later in *Sullivan*. Kalven proposed to shift the focus of debate away from "clear and present danger" and back to the issue of libel. Introducing the formulation that Justice Brennan's majority opinion would ultimately adopt, Kalven suggested that "the most exciting free speech question of our day is, oddly enough, whether the Sedition Act of 1798 was and would be constitutional. For it is on this issue that the real stakes in free speech turn." And though he did not use the term, Kalven also speculated that defamation laws might actually have a more "chilling" effect on free discussion than more orthodox analysts, such as Chafee, might allow. Similarly, drawing upon late nineteenth-century libertarianism, Kalven argued—as would Justice Brennan in 1964—that any libel doctrine that dealt with the motives of a defendant is "a slender reed on which to rest the right to speech. . . ." A "vital theory" of free expression "must contemplate not restricting discussion to those our side would regard as men of good will."[14]

Although this cold-war libertarianism rejected the old boundary-theory approach to free expression as overly simplistic, it retreated from some of the more useful insights of legal realism. Thus, Alexander Meiklejohn's basic distinction between public and private speech rejected one of realism's key insights. "What a wonderful faith Meiklejohn must have had," later wrote Dean Harry Wellington of Yale Law School, "if he believed that any person could draw the public-private line sharply and clearly." Cold-war libertarianism also abandoned realism's skepticism about the centrality of doctrines in legal analysis. Thomas Emerson of Yale Law School, for instance, obviously recognized that the reality of free speech in any society "hinges upon many different considerations," but he emphasized that "in the United States today we have come to depend upon legal institutions and legal doctrines as a major technique for maintaining our system of free expression." The "role of law," according to Emerson, was "to mark and guard the line between the sphere of social power, organized in the form of the state, and the area of private right. The legal problems involved in maintaining a system of free expression fall largely into this realm." Most of Emerson's analysis of this system, then, focused on purely doctrinal issues.[15] Thus, in contrast to the more radical realists of the 1920s and 1930s, and to the critical legal studies movement of the 1970s and 1980s, cold-war libertarianism did not view the liberal approach to rights as "internally inconsistent, vacuous, or circular" or believe that lawyers "can generate equally plausible rights justifications for almost any result." Trusting in the viability of "reasoned elaboration," cold-war libertarians tried to construct convincing policy arguments on behalf of their view of free-speech rights.[16]

Most important, then, many of the tenets of cold-war libertarianism did not depart all that much—at least from the perspective of realism or of the critical legal studies approach—from the process-oriented jurisprudence that dominated post–World War II legal thought. Although cold-war libertarians were skeptical that existing judicial and political institutions and practices would consistently offer fair and open processes, they still expressed confidence that liberal jurisprudence, when formed along the lines they themselves suggested, represented the best that any society could achieve. Even when Edmund Cahn expressed clear doubts about the viability of traditional ideas of free discussion in an age of mass, monopolistic institutions, he could still offer no alternative to time-honored faiths. Thus, most of the cold-war libertarians still often invoked the language and images of the marketplace of ideas, and restoration of this mythical marketplace constituted one of the main goals of post–World War II libertarian thought. This approach to civil liberties issues, as lawyer Frank Donner has argued, tended to ignore the realities of what was going on within the ever-expanding surveillance state. Of what value were liberal-constitutional values and procedures in a political culture where crisis government was becoming institutionalized? In contrast to the legal skeptics of the 1930s, postwar legal thinkers tended to use the labels and language of liberal constitutionalism.[17]

Although the cold war libertarians totally conquered neither academia nor the legal profession—let alone public opinion—their views increasingly set the terms of debate for the legal elite's First-Amendment discussions in the late 1950s and 1960s. Within the academic community, for example, the writings of Thomas Emerson—which culminated in his magnum opus, *The System of Freedom of Expression*—became the starting point for most analyses of First-Amendment issues. And with two of their number, Justices Black and William O. Douglas, on the Supreme Court, this new group of libertarians could also command attention from the legal establishment's most prestigious forum.

Cold-war libertarianism ultimately helped to shape the legal argument against traditional libel law in *Sullivan*. In 1952, when the Court had upheld the constitutionality of an Illinois group-libel law, debate had swirled around the old clear-and-present-danger test of Holmes and Brandeis; but twelve years later, the *Sullivan* discussions assumed a Kalvenesque-Meiklejohnian tone.[18]

The *Sullivan* Case

The Court's opinion in *New York Times* v. *Sullivan*, authored by Justice William Brennan, aimed at three general goals: (1) to eliminate yet another weapon in the arsenal of segregationists in the South; (2) to reformulate the law of libel and thereby to eliminate what Justice Brennan called "the chilling" effect of traditional defamation laws; (3) most ambitiously, to link the changes in libel law to a new constitutional approach to free-speech issues, one that supposedly broke away from old legal formulas.

1. The justices, as most court watchers of the 1960s had predicted, overturned the libel judgment in favor of L. B. Sullivan; and they did so in a way that underscored the Court's full support for the liberal civil rights coalition. Justice Brennan's majority opinion, for example, alluded to the fact that Sullivan's suit seemed only the first in a series of new segregationist attacks against both the civil rights movement and the liberal northern media.

Most important, after a good deal of complex wrangling and maneuvering, the Court ultimately went beyond a simple reversal of Sullivan's $500,000 award. In a crucial portion of his opinion, Justice Brennan reexamined the evidence that had originally been brought before the Alabama trial court and found that it could never "constitutionally sustain the judgment" for Sullivan "under the proper rule of law." Over the initial objections of Justices John Marshall Harlan and Tom Clark, Brennan and Chief Justice Earl Warren insisted that the Supreme Court take this unusual, almost radical stance toward the authority of state judicial systems. If the Court did not forthrightly quash Sullivan's suit, Warren feared, it would "merely be going through a meaningless exercise." Segregationists in Alabama would quickly devise "another improvisation" in their campaign of harassment, and the problem of political libel "would be back to us in a more difficult posture." Justice Clark accepted this approach, provided that the Supreme Court's evidentiary review were justified as necessary to provide guidance for the state court judges who would have to administer Justice Brennan's new constitutional guidelines. After incorporating Clark's view into the language of his majority opinion, Brennan finally won over Justice Harlan, who capitulated the night before the Court rendered its opinion. Neither the *Times* nor the civil rights leaders who were codefendants would have to worry about L. B. Sullivan or about southern courts applying traditional common law libel rules in political cases.[19]

2. In announcing the new constitutional standard, Justice Brennan aligned the Court's majority with those legal writers who had rejected the old common law rule of strict liability in political libel cases. Dressed up in fresh constitutional language and introduced as the "actual malice" test, the court's new rule bore at least some resemblance to the old minority rule of qualified privilege that had been urged by Thomas Cooley in the 1870s, accepted by the supreme court of Kansas in 1908, and endorsed by a number of prominent twentieth-century legal scholars.[20]

By adopting their own version of a qualified-privilege test, the Court's majority stopped short of eliminating all political libel suits; under certain conditions, Justice Brennan allowed, political officials could still maintain libel suits. At this point, Brennan's opinion lost the Court's cold-war libertarians, when Justices Black and Douglas joined in a concurring opinion. Justice Black argued that the First Amendment did more than limit governmental power over political libel laws; it "completely prohibit[ed]" governments "from exercising such a power." Justice Brennan's actual malice standard was "an elusive, abstract concept, hard to prove and hard to disprove." It offered "at best an evanescent protection for the right critically to discuss public affairs. . . ." Justice Arthur Goldberg issued his own concurring opinion that, though more restrictive than Justice Black's on issues relating to the private conduct of public officials, also criticized Justice Brennan's opinion for pulling up short of the cold-war libertarians' goal.[21]

Although unsatisfactory to those cold-war libertarians who had wanted the Court to end political libel suits altogether, the new constitutional test did, as post-*Sullivan* decisions would underscore, go beyond old common law protections, especially in its stiff requirement of what type of evidence was necessary to defeat the qualified privilege granted to critics of public officials. As Justice Brennan first stated the rule, any public-official plaintiff would now have to show—with "convincing clarity"—that his or her critics had published a libelous falsehood with actual knowledge that the slander was untrue or "with reckless disregard" of whether or not it was true. This new First-Amendment test applied, of course, to all state jurisdictions through the due-process clause of the Fourteenth Amendment.[22]

3. Finally, Justice Brennan justified this new national standard by invoking

a general constitutional theory of free speech that, at first glance at least, owed more to the libertarianism of Justices Black and Douglas than to that of Justices Holmes and Brandeis. Justice Brennan not only ignored the clear-and-present-danger rationale followed in *Beauharnais* v. *Illinois*, but all other traditional First-Amendment tests, such as those the Court had recently used in obscenity cases.

Instead, Brennan's opinion picked up the earlier suggestion of Harry Kalven and tried to take a fresh look at First-Amendment issues by going back to the old Sedition Act of 1798. Justice Brennan argued that the tangled history of this long-expired measure offered the Court a new, clear view of the First Amendment. Niftily sidestepping the historical minefields surrounding the validity of the Sedition Act as tested by the constitutional ideals of the late eighteenth century, Justice Brennan adopted an "ongoing approach" to legal history. The issue, he asserted, was not how the Sedition Law would have been judged in 1798 but how it should be viewed in 1964, in light of the history of the intervening years.

Justice Brennan confidently concluded that the Jeffersonian attacks on the constitutionality of the Sedition Act had "carried the day in the court of history." The idea that the state or public officials could not be harmed merely by libelous words, "which first crystalized" in the 1790s, soon grew into "a national awareness of the central meaning of the First Amendment," he claimed. And this central meaning seemed obvious. Citizens should not have to fear, as they did under the old law of seditious libel (and under the traditional common law), that they might be prosecuted or sued for damages because they authored political statements later adjudged to be both false and libelous.[23]

This central meaning of the First Amendment, Justice Brennan continued, rested on a fundamental principle. The ongoing history of the First Amendment demanded that the Court judge the common law of libel "against the background of a profound national commitment to the principle that debate on public issues should be uninhibited, robust, and wide open, and that it may well include vehement, caustic, and sometimes unpleasantly sharp attacks on government and public officials." Libel rules that caused political critics undue concern about subsequent legal difficulties exerted a "chilling effect" on free speech; such doctrines, even if they did not result in a trip to the law courts or a letter from a libel lawyer, forced political writers and the mass media's editors to censor themselves. Even when they believed charges to be true, "would-be critics of official conduct may be deterred from voicing their criticism" and "tend to make only statements which 'steer far wider of the unlawful zone.'" Thus, traditional libel laws, including ones that allowed some type of qualified privilege, dampened "the vigor," limited "the variety of public debate," and clashed with the new actual-malice test for political libel suits.[24]

Harry Kalven, who became *Sullivan*'s most prominent interpreter, quickly lauded Justice Brennan for apparently jettisoning older First-Amendment formulas, and he accurately predicted that the justices would soon expand the rationale of *Sullivan* to other kinds of libel suits. In an essay published only months after the *Sullivan* decision was announced, Kalven urged the Court to push on and to "work out for itself the theory of free speech that Alexander Meiklejohn has been offering us for some fifteen years now." Meiklejohn himself told Kalven that the *Sullivan* decision was "an occasion for dancing in the streets."[25]

Although few, if any, Americans took to the streets as a direct result of *Sullivan*, the decision did bring smiles to the faces of the nation's journalists. For at the same time that the cold-war libertarians were expounding their views during the late 1950s and early 1960s, the interests of the mass media began to change.

As journalist-historian Godfrey Hodgson has noted, national television executives became more aggressive in seeking out stories not to be found in governmental and corporate handouts. In 1961, NBC's news department, for example, hired seventeen additional news producers, more than quintupling their staff. This new energy, Hodgson explained, grew largely out of the networks' self-interest. The TV industry's reputation had been badly damaged by the quiz show scandals of the late 1950s, and emphasis on television's informational potential offered one means of recouping lost prestige and of neutralizing the FCC's anti-TV chair, Newton Minow. Moreover, competition between the news departments at CBS and NBC (ABC then ran an insignificant third) helped to sharpen the critical edges of at least some television news coverage. Although programs such as Edward R. Murrow's "Harvest of Shame," a searching examination of corporate-controlled agriculture, were not the norm—as early coverage of American involvement in Vietnam proved—the electronic media's coverage did become more pointed than it had been during the days of John Cameron Swayze's "Camel Caravan."

Hodgson's thesis also suggested that this expanded television news coverage helped to create a milieu in which fundamental social problems became subjects of more intensive media—and ultimately public—concern. In Hodgson's image, the electronic media acted as "a lens," concentrating "all the rays of heat from a world on fire, until they burned into the viewers' minds with an almost unbearable intensity." This climate, Hodgson argued, inevitably affected the print as well as the electronic media; print publications also became more sensitive to the seamier sides of American life. In such an atmosphere, quite obviously, the chance of writers and publishers stepping on important people's reputations increased, and problems with the law of libel assumed considerable importance.[26]

Libel suits did become more of a concern, even for the largest publishers, in the late 1950s and early 1960s. Francis Murnaghan, an experienced trial lawyer, has written that "after a relatively long period of desuetude," libel suits enjoyed a renaissance in the late 1950s and early 1960s. Similarly, Arthur Hanson, the long-time counsel for the American Newspaper Publishers Association, also observed a sudden surge of troublesome libel suits; he claimed that the number of suits had increased in the late 1950s by "several hundred percent."[27]

The revitalization of libel law did not, as Francis Murnaghan noted, grow simply out of an increased sensitivity of plaintiffs or greater muckraking by the media. Although "one-shot" plaintiffs still played at a considerable handicap against "repeat players" from the mass media, a remarkable inflation in the size of defamation judgments undoubtedly made the gamble of victory more tempting. The reasons for the sudden inflation in jury awards deserve further study, but Murnaghan's hypothesis, while incomplete, is suggestive. He argued that the key to the increase in libel awards may be found in the gambler psychology of many modern jurors. Jurors, whose own "unequal struggle with the Micawber equation has led [them] on occasion to seek escape in the big hit in the numbers game or the successful long-shot at the racetrack," may feel "vicarious satisfaction in helping a libel case plaintiff to the pot of gold at the end of the rainbow, especially when the defendant often symbolizes the forces which press on the average urban citizen and to which he [or she] ascribes many of his [or her] misfortunes."[28]

In any event, the steady escalation in the size of libel awards, and the equally steady increase in the price of legal fees, prompted leaders of the media to take another look at defamation laws and to press more forcefully for changes in traditional doctrines. The *Sullivan* briefs presented to the Supreme Court by the *New York Times* and *Washington Post* reflected this new approach: although willing to settle simply for reversal, media lawyers also pushed, from the outset of the appeals process, for a "landmark ruling."[29]

Finally, it might be noted, the Court's decision to nationalize the law of libel and announce a First-Amendment standard for political suits fell into the pattern of other Warren Court decisions and faithfully mirrored the theories of liberal jurisprudence. *Sullivan* presented a textbook example of illiberal "blockages" in the political and intellectual marketplaces. Through use of libel suits, a minority of segregationists threatened to disrupt the flow of information through the marketplace of ideas and to delay the march of civil rights programs through the political marketplace. In removing such blockages, the Supreme Court was pursuing a familiar theory of constitutional decision making. Once freed to operate properly, the process of unblocked discussion would help people of good will discover the best solution to the racial problems besetting the nation.[30]

Thus, the Supreme Court's ruling in *Sullivan* expressed several fundamental, new libertarian theories that only needed a case to which they could be applied: a liberal legal consciousness that emphasized the ability of judicial officials to restore marketplace mechanisms; changes in the interests and needs of the mass media that led industry strategists to endorse a bold assault on state libel laws; and social ferment that threatened some of the basic assumptions about the openness and flexibility of liberal politics. Any Supreme Court decision that did not forthrightly remove the threat of politically motivated libel suits, and not simply the single action of L. B. Sullivan, would only postpone the day of reckoning. As repeat players, the mass media would have soon returned to the Supreme Court—civil rights activists had already shown that they would not passively accept legal decisions that threatened the progress of their movement—and the contradictions of liberal politics, which had given rise to the *Sullivan* case, might only have grown more severe.[31]

Sullivan's Travels

Despite rhetoric about central meanings, robust debate, and uninhibited discussion, the *Sullivan* could still be dismissed as nothing but an expanded version of the old liberty-licentious formula. Justice Brennan, of course, avoided old labels like "licentious" and "scurrilous" and drew the boundaries of prohibited speech more generously than had previous liberal constitutionalists; but he still ruled that some types of libelous political comments fell out of bounds. To the more absolutist cold-war libertarians like Justice Black, the *Sullivan* test simply extended "licentious" to mean the knowing publication of libelous political falsehoods; similarly, *Sullivan* redefined "scurrilous" political critics as those who published in reckless disregard of the truth.

Ralph Ginzburg, the publisher of numerous magazines outside the liberal mainstream and the twentieth-century successor to "scandalmongers" like William Cobbett, seemed to personify the terms "reckless disregard" and "knowing falsehood." Not surprisingly, Ginzburg became the first celebrated libel defendant to incur liability under the *Sullivan* rule. In his short-lived *FACT* magazine, Ginzburg claimed that the 1964 Republican presidential candidate, Barry Goldwater, lacked the mental stability to hold high office. Bolstered by questionnaires sent to more than 10,000 psychiatrists, Ginzburg's evidence drew fire from the head of the American Psychiatric Association and from professional pollsters. When Goldwater sued Ginzburg for libel, testimony from such professionals helped convince jurors that the Arizona senator had met the constitutional burden required under *Sullivan*. After jurors awarded Goldwater $1 actual and $75,000 punitive damages, Ginzburg appealed to the United States Supreme Court.

Over the bitter dissents of Justices Black and Douglas, the Court refused even to grant *certoriari* in the *Ginzburg* case. Justice Black fumed: "The public has an unqualified right to have the character and fitness of anyone who aspires to the Presidency held up for the closest scrutiny. Extravagant, reckless statements and even claims which may not be true seem to be inevitable and perhaps [an] essential part of the process by which [the] voting public informs itself of the qualities of a man who would be president." Black denounced Goldwater's successful action as "repressive" and "ominous" for the future of free expression, and he singled out the disparity between the amounts awarded for actual and for punitive damages as "incomprehensible."[32]

At least in the area of political defamation, Black and Douglas joined those other cold-war libertarians who were willing to trust in the free marketplace of ideas. Franklyn Haiman, author of a leading free-speech treatise in the tradition of cold-war libertarianism, later argued that the whole central-meaning rationale of *Sullivan* fell apart once judges began to devise formulas to define certain types of irresponsible speech out of the marketplace. "If it is acknowledged that the law of defamation serves as a deterrent to some willfully irresponsible communication, it follows that it must also have a chilling effect on the expression of those who are not sure whether charges they felt impelled to voice could be proved to the satisfaction of a court if suit were brought."[33]

The arguments of cold-war libertarians notwithstanding, the Supreme Court, even in the days of the Warren majority, stuck with the actual-malice approach. As a result, the justices confronted dilemmas very similar to those faced a century earlier by Thomas Cooley when he adopted an analogous (though slightly narrower) approach to political libel cases. As long as judges saw libel law—no matter how liberalized—as a means of curbing irresponsible political dialogue, they inevitably became editors of last resort for the American media. Just as Thomas Cooley had assumed a quasi-editorial role on the Michigan Supreme Court during the 1880s, so the members of the United States Supreme Court shouldered a similar responsibility in the 1960s and 1970s.[34]

In the case of Wallace Butts, for example, even though the Court extended the *Sullivan* rule to libel cases brought by public figures, a majority of the justices found that the *Saturday Evening Post* had exceeded its qualified privilege. Here, an article in the once-staid weekly charged Butts, athletic director at the University of Georgia, with passing his football team's game plan to the coach of a rival school. Butts sued and ultimately recovered damages of $460,000. In upholding the award, Justice John Marshall Harlan stressed that the *Post* was not pursuing a "hot news" item and that their investigatory procedures ignored "elementary precautions." "In short," he concluded, "the evidence is ample to support a finding of highly unreasonable conduct constituting an extreme departure from the standards of investigation and reporting ordinarily adhered to by *responsible* publishers." Moreover,

Harlan (and presumably the three other justices who joined his opinion) singled out the *Post*'s motives. By instituting a policy of "sophisticated muckraking," the *Post* seemed (according to Harlan) to have caved in to "the pressure to produce a successful exposé" and had printed a story that lacked sufficient supporting evidence.[35]

Sprouse v. Clay Communication, Inc., a West Virginia case that the United States Supreme Court refused to hear on appeal, offered another example of judges acting as postpublication censors of both journalistic techniques and motives. This libel suit stemmed from a series of investigative reports, by the *Charleston Daily Mail*, on the personal finances of a candidate for governor of West Virginia. The state's highest appeals court upheld a damage award of $250,000, primarily on the grounds that the *Mail*'s editors had used words such as "land grab," "dummy firms," and "bonanza" in headlines. According to the West Virginia justices, these terms implied illegal conduct, although they found that the candidate's activities merely involved violations of business ethics. Therefore, the court concluded that the paper's headline charges, since they insinuated criminal actions, were false. Moreover, it held that use of misleading words in headlines—when the editors phrased the articles themselves in more temperate language—provided the necessary proof of actual malice. In effect, the *Daily Mail* ran afoul of a libel judgment because the court disliked the way its editors had constructed headlines and disapproved of the words used to characterize certain business dealings. Such judicial scrutiny of political reporting, critics of the *Sprouse* decision charged, seemed to reintroduce the kind of chilling effect that *Sullivan* was supposed to have warmed out of libel law.[36]

In other appeals to the Supreme Court, however, the media fared much better. Although the Court never embraced the Douglas-Black approach, post-*Sullivan* cases emphasized that public officials and public figures could not show actual malice by evidence of ill will or bad motives. These strict holdings on the burden of proof gained additional value when they allowed political critics to win libel suits on the basis of summary judgments; in a number of lawsuits, once public-figure plaintiffs failed to offer clear and convincing proof that their detractors had falsely libeled them with actual malice, defendants could receive dismissals without having to undergo the further expense of jury trials.[37]

Sullivan's travels ultimately led to a series of cases in which lawyers for the media claimed that the *Sullivan* standard should apply to all defamation cases involving "newsworthy" stories. In *Rosenbloom v. Metromedia* (1971) Justice Brennan, along with the unlikely duo of Chief Justice Warren Burger and Justice Harry Blackmun, did endorse extension of the actual-malice privilege to all stories involving matters of "public or general interest." In real terms, the *Rosenbloom* test meant that private citizens who had been falsely defamed by the media, in stories that touched newsworthy matters, could not collect libel damages unless they could produce evidence to satisfy the *Sullivan* test.[38] But the post-*Sullivan* cases had increasingly divided the Court, and the splits already evident by the time of *Butts* had widened significantly by the time of *Rosenbloom*. In retrospect, of course, such divisions were inevitable.

Events of the late 1960s, 1970s, and 1980s underscored Alvin Gouldner's judgment that the "problem of dealing with the media [had become] a central and special problem for all social institutions."[39] The history of this period was, in many ways, the story of how major institutions, as well as their opponents, sought to influence the ways in which the media covered their activities and presented their versions of realities. Richard Nixon, for example, openly lobbied for overturning the *Sullivan* case. In a radio address on 8 March 1974, Nixon claimed that changes in political libel doctrines would encourage "more good people to run for public office." A political candidate should know "that he has recourse in the case of an attack which is totally untrue and would otherwise give him a right to sue for libel." Deeply ensnarled in clumsy efforts to cover up innumerable crimes, Nixon charged that "some libel lawyers" were viewing the *Sullivan* decision "as being virtually a license to lie where a political candidate, a member of his family, or one of his supporters or friends is involved." And even before the unraveling of the Watergate tapes made the situation desperate, the Nixon administration made Herculean efforts—including use of a variety of carrot-and-stick techniques—to shape the media's image of its activities.[40]

Similarly, powerful "private governments" joined other institutions in mounting unprecedented efforts to influence media coverage. The large oil companies, for instance, launched experiments with expensive "editorial advertising," and business corporations became increasingly attentive to how educational institutions and the news media presented questions of political economy. Even organized crime worked on its media image. Joseph Columbo formed an organization to protect the reputations of Italian-Americans; Joey Gallo became a prominent media celebrity; and other organized-crime figures filed a number of libel suits against the media. The *Rosenbloom* test was, in fact, applied more frequently in lawsuits involving allegations of organized crime than in any other single area.[41] Despite the fact that the implications of the *Sullivan* test reduced the likelihood of ultimate recovery, libel plaintiffs—and not simply people linked by the media to organized crime—continually presented courts with opportunities to rethink the ways in which the judiciary might honor Justice Brennan's view that public discussion should be "uninhibited, robust, and wide-open."

Several things helped to produce a constant supply of libel suits in the late 1960s and early 1970s. Despite its creation of new privileges for the press, the Warren Court itself contributed to the number of libel suits by helping to make people more sensitive to the issue of individual rights. Why should the right of reputation, attorneys for libel plaintiffs could logically argue, receive any less recognition than the other liberties that the Supreme Court was seeking to protect? In a narcissistic age in which upwardly mobile people were coming—as social historian Christopher Lasch has argued—to invest a great deal of financial and psychological capital in winning images, one's stake in reputation, defined increasingly broadly, could be considerable. And even if potential plaintiffs might be discouraged by the new constitutional defenses, they could take heart from the whopping judgments that successful litigants were beginning to receive. The prevalence of libel suits in the face of increasing obstacles to successful litigation also highlighted the fact that something other than a careful cost-benefit calculation motivated many libel plaintiffs. The decision to plunge head-on against the legal tide could demonstrate just how seriously a plaintiff viewed an allegedly libelous charge and underscore just how valid he or she considered the claim to be. Similarly, the fact that defamation law now apparently favored defendants erased some of the stigma traditionally associated with filing a libel suit; when powerful political or public figures sued for libel, they could no longer be accused of exploiting old libel doctrines. And with the growing wealth of the modern media-giants—corporations armed with high-priced legal talent and with law books filled with new, pro-press precedents—few plaintiffs would have to bear taunts, as Teddy Roosevelt once had, that they were picking on the "little guys."[42]

Finally, any analysis of recent developments in libel law must consider changes within the American print and electronic media. Although critical publications, such as *[MORE]* and the *Columbia Journalism Review*, documented numerous cases of journalistic deference to established institutions, important countertrends did emerge in the 1960s and 1970s. The internecine battles for the attention of readers and viewers, which began in the early 1960s, continued. Meanwhile, the radical challenges associated with left-of-center political groups and the counterculture placed the "straight" media on the defensive. Publications as diverse as *I. F. Stone's Weekly* and *Ramparts* showed how easily journalists could poke holes in official explanations. The bureaucratic wishful thinking and outright lying associated with the war in Vietnam seemed to confirm the need for more vigorous investigative reporting and for shedding the guise of objectivity in favor of advocacy journalism.[43]

The new emphasis on muckraking investigations and upon advocacy journalism had a considerable impact upon the ways in which journalists approached prominent people and important institutions. Even though Edward J. Epstein's research has helped to deflate some of the extravagant claims for the original contributions of investigative reporters, some journalists increasingly exploited leaks from within giant governmental and private bureaucracies.[44] In seeking leaks, the press benefited from the political polarization of the era.

Although public relations experts still produced endless supplies of prepackaged puffs, dissidents like Daniel Ellsberg and whistleblowers like Ernest Fitzgerald offered their own prepackaged alternatives to official views of reality. When linked to advocacy reporting, investigative journalists dropped the late nineteenth- and early twentieth-century canons of objectivity and argued for particular positions, often ones that conflicted with the views presented by leading politicians and public figures.

Although these new journalistic styles did not dominate the media, they did embroil the press in some bitter political and legal disputes. The "Pentagon Papers" prior-restraint case, pitting the Nixon administration against two of the nation's most prestigious papers, the *New York Times* and the *Washington Post*, was only the most spectacular legal showdown.[45] Libel suits growing out of the trend toward investigative reporting repeatedly raised the threat and sometimes the reality of lawsuits. The fallout could be serious, if not deadly. The *Texas Observer*, a well-respected muckraking journal, almost succumbed to the legal costs of simply defending a $5 million libel suit; the price of Wallace Butts's successful libel suit hastened the demise of the old *Saturday Evening Post*; and the *Alton* (Illinois) *Telegraph* was forced into bankruptcy court because of defamation suits.[46]

Another journalistic trend of the 1970s, the much discussed "celebrification" of the news, also touched the libel question. Celebrity journalism was nothing new; it had been a staple of the papers of Scripps and Pulitzer, and it had matured in the gossip columns of the 1930s. Coverage of the Kennedy family, especially after John F. Kennedy's assassination, helped to reinvigorate this style of journalism, until the manner in which the media covered political figures such as Jerry Brown and Henry Kissinger merged with the ways in which it approached celebrities from the entertainment world. The celebrity journalism of the 1960s and 1970s dovetailed with changes in libel law. As media critic Edwin Diamond has suggested, celebrity journalism, like advocacy and investigative reporting, suspended "the normal rules of journalism. In a sense, that is what the word *gossip* implies: the story doesn't have to be true." And in Diamond's view, *Sullivan* and succeeding libel cases encouraged this type of reporting: the press could "say just about anything . . . about public persons as long as what it says isn't recklessly untrue or malicious."[47]

Even as Diamond was writing, however, a realigned Supreme Court was in the process of retreating from Justice Brennan's *Rosenbloom* opinion. *Gertz* v. *Robert Welch, Inc.* (1974) highlighted the judicial misgivings expressed in earlier cases such as *Butts*, *Sprouse*, and *Ginzburg*. Ever since *Butts*, Justice John Marshall Harlan had been urging the Court to reject application of the *Sullivan* standard to an ever-widening group of cases; *Gertz* finally gave Harlan his triumph.

In *Gertz*, a case brought by a prominent Chicago attorney whose involvement in a much-discussed incident of alleged police brutality earned him several fierce attacks from the John Birch Society, a majority of the Court abandoned the public-or-general-interest approach as the single national standard. *Gertz* held state libel laws to the *Sullivan* test only in those cases brought by public officials, candidates, or public figures; private citizens, even those connected to newsworthy stories, no longer automatically had to show actual malice in order to collect libel damages from the mass media. State courts could, under *Gertz*, still adopt Brennan's *Rosenbloom* test on their own, but they were no longer required to do so as a matter of constitutional law.[48]

At the same time, the *Gertz* opinion narrowed the legal definition of a public figure. According to Justice Lewis Powell, one of the new Nixon appointees, the revised constitutional law of libel now recognized at least two kinds of public figures. First, there were those relatively few people who had achieved "general fame or notoriety in the community" or who had demonstrated "pervasive involvement in the affairs of society." Such people were public figures "for all aspects of their lives" and, therefore, would have to meet the *Sullivan* test in any libel suit they might file against the mass media. A second, and larger, category of public persons included those who "voluntarily inject[ed] themselves" or were "drawn into a particular public controversy" and thus became public figures "for a limited range of issues" and for a particular defamation action.[49]

In contrast to Justice Brennan's *Sullivan* opinion, Powell's *Gertz* opinion did not even attempt to find any principled First-Amendment anchor; the new ruling was, unabashedly, an example of ad hoc balancing. Thus, Powell argued that the rollback of *Rosenbloom* would be balanced by several new concessions to the media.

First, he argued that the law of libel could reach only false statements of fact and not allegedly erroneous opinions. "Under the First Amendment," Powell held, "there is no such thing as a false idea." Presumably, then, *Gertz* provided absolute protection for the expression of "pure opinion." Second, and more important, *Gertz* threw out one of the most sacrosanct common law libel rules and held that all libel plaintiffs, even purely private ones, would have to show some degree of negligence in order to prevail against media defendants. *Gertz*, therefore, finally abandoned all applications of the traditional common law principle of strict liability for libelous falsehoods. Finally, and most important, Powell's *Gertz* ruling limited its modification of the *Rosenbloom* test to the recovery of actual damages. Thus, even though private defamation plaintiffs could recover compensation for actual injuries under standards less stringent than the *Sullivan* rule, they still had to clear the actual-malice hurdle if they wished to enter the more lucrative realm of punitive damages. This concession, it was claimed, would make it less likely that media defendants would be hit with huge liability claims. In theory, only the most egregious examples of journalistic irresponsibility would raise the specter of high damage claims.[50]

After *Gertz*, two things (and perhaps only two) were clear. First, defamation law had become more complex and confusing than ever. The confusion that reigned in pressrooms, trial courts, law review articles, and appellate court opinions soon confirmed the judgment that *Gertz*, rather than offering any new solutions, only compounded old problems. Second, despite this general shroud of uncertainty, *Gertz* did signal a new toughness on the part of the Supreme Court, one that seemed likely to produce even more libel problems for the media.[51]

The next important Supreme Court defamation case, *Time v. Firestone* (1976), confirmed some of the worst fears of media lawyers. Here, the Court did send back, for retrial under the principles of *Gertz*, a $100,000 judgment in favor of a prominent socialite from Palm Beach, Florida. But at the same time, the Court reemphasized *Gertz*'s approach to the public figure issue by holding that the plaintiff, who had hired a press clipping service in order to keep abreast of her notoriety, was a private person for the purposes of this defamation suit against *Time* magazine. On the question of damages, the Court adopted a broad rather than a narrow reading of *Gertz*. It held that, in defamation cases, state courts could award damages for other than purely reputational injuries—for things such as personal humiliation and mental anguish. In *Firestone*, for example, the plaintiff did not even allege that there had been an injury to her reputation but rested her case upon nonreputational damages.[52]

The Law of Libel in Troubled Times

In response to the moral fervor of the civil rights crusade, the political pressures of the early sixties, and the prompting of the mass media, the Supreme Court, in 1964, inaugurated a series of decisions designed to liberalize traditional defamation laws. Invoking either directly (in the opinions of Justices Black and Douglas) or indirectly (in the case of Justice Brennan's actual-malice test) the ideas of cold-war libertarians such as Alexander Meiklejohn and Harry Kalven, the justices proposed to reinvigorate the American marketplace of ideas by reducing the censorial power that ultimately rested in the law of libel. The *Sullivan* formula, its supporters hoped, would remove the law of libel as a serious impediment to public debate. Clear, simple, national standards would replace old, incoherent, state libel doctrines. And when linked to other First-Amendment decisions of the 1960s, *Sullivan* was supposed to remove the chill from public debate.

This trend lasted only a decade. Ten years after *Sullivan* a new set of justices—who were responding to a quite different social and political climate, and to a significantly changed media environment—abruptly halted *Sullivan*'s somewhat confused travels. In the decade following the *Gertz* decision of 1974, defamation law enjoyed a new burst of energy. Critics of the new line of decisions claimed that a good deal of chill returned to the law of libel and to the hearts of many journalists.[53]

Libel awards steadily escalated. A former Miss Wyoming recovered $26,-500,000 (a sum later reduced and ultimately overturned on appeal) against *Penthouse* magazine. Similarly, the costs of defending libel suits climbed, sometimes reaching six figures and running ahead of amounts paid out in damages. Judicial attempts to deal with the confusion resulting from *Gertz*—and older issues stemming back to *Sullivan*—created additional problems. For example, elimination of the *Rosenbloom* general-or-public-interest test in favor of one focusing upon the public or private status of the plaintiff created considerable difficulty for editors who had to make rapid prepublication decisions as well as for judges in their own more leisurely postpublication deliberations. One decision held a belly dancer to be a public figure, but another found that a vice president of Gulf and Western was a purely private-person plaintiff.[54] Finally, post-1974 cases extended the reach of defamation law into new areas. *Herbert* v. *Lando*, which grew out of a controversial CBS documentary about one aspect of the United States' role in Indochina, gave libel plaintiffs wide latitude, during the pretrial discovery process, to seek evidence that publishers had exceeded the actual-malice privilege of *Sullivan*. In the case of *General William Westmoreland* versus *CBS*, another lawsuit that resulted from the painful process of debating what happened in Vietnam, pretrial discovery and the aborted trial resulted in a lengthy historical investigation of events surrounding the Tet offensive of 1968.[55] And in *Bindrim* v. *Mitchell and Doubleday*, the Supreme Court gave the general literary community the kind of jolt that journalists had received earlier: it held that the new defamation laws applied to works of fiction.[56] Faced with what they considered ominous trends, those interested in defending defamation suits, including journalists and insurance companies, formed the Libel Defense Resource Center as a clearinghouse for research and practical advice.[57]

Abandoning any attempt to justify libel decisions by invoking fundamental principles or central First-Amendment meanings, the Supreme Court tried to balance, on an ad hoc basis, the conflicting issues raised by the libel cases of the 1970s and early 1980s. Meanwhile, under the freedom granted them by *Gertz*, state courts tried to devise their own standards. The results were seldom satisfactory either to those who hoped that the American media could operate without any great concern about the law of defamation or to those concerned about the alleged decline of "responsible" journalism.[58] As at other times when defamation law became a topic of intense debate, the search for bugs in this ancient tort involved considerations of legal doctrine, public policy, constitutional principles, and social values served by laws protecting personal reputations, especially those of the best people. As before, the supposedly timeless, apparently fundamental, legal formulations of one era—in this case, those general theories of free expression and defamation embraced by the liberal center of the Warren Court—had proved as time bound and historically contingent as the earlier ones of Alexander Hamilton, Thomas Cooley, William Howard Taft, and Rousseau Burch.[59]

Conclusion | An Interpretation of
the History of Political Libel Law

Although this study has insisted that the history of political libel reveals no clear line of development and no natural evolutionary pattern, certain themes have recurred. At its simplest, political libel has always addressed a basic legal-constitutional question: how much critical speech can a supposedly open, liberal society safely permit? And since at least the early nineteenth century, American legal discussions of this problem have repeatedly revolved around two other central issues: the efficacy of the concept of a free marketplace of ideas, and the judicial enterprise of drawing precise legal boundaries between protected and unprotected speech. It seems useful to recapitulate, and then to comment critically, upon these themes.

The Basic Themes of Political Libel Law

Historically, Anglo-American law had always proscribed some kinds of political speech. The elites who dominated Britain's old authoritarian state, of course, assumed that mere words could be so corrosive to both social order and political authority that strict legal controls were needed to restrict dangerous discussions. The Star Chamber law of seditious libel, which extended to all political criticism, epitomized this approach. In theory, Britain's liberal revolutions of the seventeenth century overthrew the authoritarian state and its view of political expression. Yet even though the new liberal order traced ultimate authority back to an act of popular will (the Lockean contract), both theory and practice placed substantial limits on political insurgency in general and critical speech in particular.

The basic boundaries, as English historian Christopher Hill argues, were drawn in the seventeenth century. The victorious political coalitions "established the sacred rights of property (abolition of feudal tenures, no arbitrary taxation), gave political power to the propertied (sovereignty of Parliament and the common law, abolition of prerogative courts), and removed all impediments to the triumph of the ideology of the men of property—the protestant ethic." The revolution that according to Hill "might have established communal property, and a far wider democracy in political and legal institutions" only threatened to happen. Similarly, in North America, where radical republican ideas seeped more deeply into the general political culture than in England, the ideal of blended, constitutional government still dominated political imaginations. This meant that constitutionally sanctioned government tempered the desires of the populace, including the desire to criticize governmental and public officials, by the reason of the common law and statutory restrictions.[1]

Drawing the precise legal lines between legitimate and illegitimate political criticism proved a difficult task. Some Anglo-American constitutionalists, such as Sir William Blackstone, argued that common law reason dictated that all libelous criticism of governmental and public officials—regardless of accuracy, motives, and intentions—should be subject to postpublication criminal penalties. But this restatement of Star Chamber law always faced challenges. As Andrew Hamilton's argument in the *Zenger* case suggested, belief in a real, though ill-defined, liberty to "complain" about a "bad" administration described the eighteenth-century realities of libel and free speech more accurately than any generalization derived from the views of political and legal elites. Certainly the British officials trying to deal with the "seditious" speeches and writings of their colonial opponents understood this to be the case. So did Thomas McKean when he tried to prosecute Eleazer Oswald in the 1780s, and so did most officials in George Washington's administration when they considered Alexander Hamilton's request for indictments against the Whiskey Tax protestors in the early 1790s.

By the mid-1790s, however, Federalists like Hamilton and Alexander Addison came to fear the impact of popular political criticism, and the rise of the Jeffersonian opposition intensified their misgivings. The Sedition Act of 1798 represented their legal response. It marked not only the first attempt in post-Revolutionary America to use systematic criminal libel prosecutions as a part of political conflict, but also one of the first legislative efforts to respond to criticism of Blackstonian libel doctrines by accepting the Zengerian principles—truth as a defense and jury determination of the "law of the case"—as formal additions to defamation doctrines.

The Sedition Act was part of more than a decade of debate over how a republican society should determine the legitimate limits upon free speech, and libel law provided the focus. Differences generally centered upon the proper forums for legal adjudication (state or federal courts), the appropriate kind of legal action (criminal or civil), and the precise legal-constitutional standards (the Zengerian or the more restrictive Hamiltonian position). Prominent Jeffersonians rejected, with a few notable exceptions, the elitist notion that libel law should protect public leaders from all defamatory criticism; nevertheless, they joined Federalists in agreeing that the law should proscribe certain libelous attacks and in fearing that defamatory criticism could drive the best men from public life and corrupt the whole process of political discussion.

In fact, Jeffersonians like George Hay and Thomas McKean urged augmenting libel law through prepublication good-behavior bonds. Most important, even the Jeffersonian libertarians agreed that the law of libel, when bounded by certain legal-constitutional safeguards, did not clash with the basic liberal idea of what constituted liberty of political expression. Although a full-blown justification for constitutional boundary drawing and for judicial protection of free-speech rights would not emerge until later in the century, debates of the early nineteenth century did enshrine the proposition that trained legal minds could separate legitimate political speech, the kind that bolstered a republican society's basic goals, from expression that undermined its fundamental values and essential political mechanisms. To most members of the early nineteenth century's legal and political establishments, the Hamiltonian emphasis upon truth, good motives, and justifiable ends seemed a wise and legitimate accommodation between the need for protecting political criticism and the necessity for protecting the reputations of the best men and for safeguarding the integrity of public debate.

In addition to sparking the first extensive American debates over judicially drawn boundaries for expression, events of the late eighteenth and early nineteenth centuries also prompted the first serious discussions in North America of the dominant liberal image of free expression: the marketplace of ideas. The basic metaphor could be traced back to the seventeenth century, especially to John Milton, but the Jeffersonian opponents of the Sedition Act first gave it an important place in American legal discussions. During the Jacksonian era, especially in justifications for tolerating the party and popular presses, and for accepting their *de facto* immunity from most libel suits, marketplace imagery dominated both legal and popular discussions.

The model of a free marketplace for expression and the task of common law boundary drawing came together in the writings of Thomas Cooley. Cooley's theory of political libel clearly bore the imprint of mid–nineteenth-century political realities. Reared in the political culture of the antebellum North, Cooley rejected the antipress policy arguments of earlier libel law theorists and incorporated a positive view of the party and popular presses into his overall approach to libel and free expression. He praised the press for giving citizens useful information on a wide variety of public issues, and he criticized outdated defamation laws for blocking the free flow of knowledge and opinion. Mindful of popular opposition to political libel suits, confident of the progressive impact of market mechanisms, and fearful of overbearing governmental authority, Cooley insisted that the state should not unnecessarily interfere with political discussion, even if governmental involvement were limited to applying Hamiltonian libel doctrines in civil cases like *Root* v. *King*. Although it stopped short of protecting all libelous political falsehoods, Cooley's view of conditional privilege built a new libertarian legal theory by linking common law doctrines and marketplace imagery to constitutional guarantees of free expression.

By the 1880s, however, even Cooley began to back away from a faith in an essentially self-regulating intellectual marketplace. Mr. Justice Cooley's final opinions on the Michigan Supreme Court showed that the actual process of boundary drawing could prove far more malleable and far less precise than Thomas Cooley, law professor and treatise writer, had claimed. Although Cooley's own judicial opinions never openly repudiated his libertarian principles, the vast majority of state and federal court decisions and the bulk of legal writing ultimately did. Cooley's earlier writings were still cited fairly often; but for mainstream legal theorists, they came to represent doctrinal and policy positions that were to be rejected in favor of more restrictive ones.

In the late nineteenth century, discussions about defamation law returned to an essentially Hamiltonian framework. Reviving older policy arguments, most members of the legal and political establishments proposed that libel law should draw the boundaries of free speech at libelous falsehoods, even when statements related to the conduct and character of political figures or to issues of general public concern. Although a dissenting minority position persisted—expressed most completely and forcefully in the neo-Cooley opinion of *Coleman* v. *MacLennon* (1908)—on the eve of World War I, a neo-Hamiltonian view of libel and free expression generally prevailed.

Meanwhile, by the early twentieth century, libel law was ceasing to be the central focus for legal discussions of free expression. World War I, which brought the beginnings of a national surveillance state, roughly marks the time in which libel law receded into the background of what was now becoming known as First-Amendment constitutional theory. Yet this new constitutional thought actually grew, in large part, out of assumptions about the nature of political communication and the role of law that had been shaped in earlier debates over the law of libel.[2]

For about the next fifty years, discussions over libel law took place at the periphery of First-Amendment debates, and libel law became the primary concern of those interested in the mass media and of specialists in tort law. The 1934 debates of the American Law Institute and the black-letter law in most jurisdictions suggested that libel rules should reach most defamatory falsehoods, even ones that involved public affairs. But, as the realist scholars of the twenties and thirties stressed, there was a considerable gap between neo-Hamiltonian doctrines and the actual process of public discussion. Countless judicial precedents and statutory changes threw up counterdoctrines and offered libel defendants, especially those in the media, alternative legal courses. Moreover, the realities of the tort litigation process raised numerous practical obstacles for plaintiffs, although they generally allowed defendants to take advantage of the well-known inertia of the legal system. And politicians who filed libel suits always had to overcome popular suspicions about the virtue of those public officials who took their detractors to court. Libel suits, including ones involving political figures and public issues, did not disappear; but for those who had to fight them, especially members of the mass media, and for those who had to explain them, prominent members of the legal community, the law of libel seemed to pose few problems that could not be managed within the confines of traditional common law battlegrounds.

When a changing social and political milieu ultimately forced the United States Supreme Court to constitutionalize defamation law in 1964, it adopted a set of policy arguments about political dissent and free markets and an approach to boundary drawing that resembled those advanced a century earlier by Thomas Cooley. At first glance, it seemed that the libertarian legacy—one that brought together the marketplace vision of Anglo-American liberalism, the common law traditions of liberal legalism, and the newer currents of cold-war liberal thought—had reached its mature development. According to supporters of *New York Times* v. *Sullivan* and its progeny, the law of libel had been transformed into the law of free speech.

A Critical Analysis of Political Libel

Instead of institutionalizing any evolutionary, libertarian theory, the *Sullivan* decision only highlighted the ambiguous nature of this ambiguous heritage. On a number of different levels, the *Sullivan* approach revealed contradictions within the liberal approach to free speech in general, and defamation in particular.

Sullivan and its travels showed the problems with liberal boundary theory. This theory, applied to libel law, rested upon the proposition that judges could objectively find the line, somewhere within the common law tradition, that separated protected from unprotected speech, the speaker/publisher's right of expression from the public official/plaintiff's right to reputation, the freedom to speak from the security for another's good name. As long as political critics remained safely within their bounded zone, they could aim libelous darts pretty much where they desired; only when they stepped over the judicially drawn line would they risk retaliation in the form of libel law.

Even under the best of circumstances, as legal realism taught, judicial boundary drawing is a dubious concept. To take one of the most obvious difficulties, the general theory tends to ignore the fact that in almost any legal dispute, the interests and desires of both litigants could be framed in terms of conflicting rights. As we have seen, this has always been the case in political libel suits. At the individual level, one encounters the critic's right to complain versus the libel defendant's right to a good name. The claim, sometimes used by advocates of a broad conditional privilege, that the individual politician's interest in reputation should give way to the larger public's right to know, ultimately collapses into the same dilemma. Raised to the level of conflicting public interests and policies, a dimension almost always emphasized in political libel cases, one confronts the public's interest in receiving critical information and having a robust marketplace of ideas versus its interest in not having the channels of public communication debased and in not having honorable people slandered out of public life. Upon what grounds of fundamental principle are courts to choose one right over the other? One set of policy arguments rather than the other set? And how can boundary theorists answer the realist critique that what courts cite as the *reason* for their decision—the superiority of one right over another—"is, in fact, only the *result?*"[3]

Justice William Brennan's actual-malice test, which represented a compromise between the traditional, majority principle of strict liability for defamatory falsehoods and the Black-Douglas principle of absolute immunity for all political libels, only compounded the problems with boundary drawing.[4] Much like Thomas Cooley's earlier version of qualified privilege, Brennan's test soon required postpublication scrutiny of the motives, the choice of language, the editorial judgment, and even the intellectual significance of publishers' products. Judges inevitably became editors of last resort, and any survey of their blue-penciling belies the claim that they could draw the clear, objective, and rational lines that strict boundary theory demanded of them.[5]

Although libertarians of different eras have located the boundaries of free speech at varying spots, they have invariably agreed that the stakes are to be placed within a relatively open battlefield of ideas. A faith in the free exchange of ideas, which grew up alongside the belief in the free trade of goods, exemplifies one of the main differences between a liberal and authoritarian society. First, and most obviously, marketplace theory removes the visible hand of government from the forefront of intellectual life. (In practice, this often means—as in the case of England's most successful eighteenth-century prime minister, Robert Walpole, or in the contemporary American surveillance state—that public officials connive to conceal the heavy hand of government.)[6] Second, as in the theory of the economic marketplace, the idea of an intellectual marketplace posits an initial equality of opportunity for all buyers and sellers. Thus, in contrast to the preliberal system of communication, which was obviously weighted toward the words of traditional authorities like clergymen and aristocratic elites, the marketplace vision supposedly separates speakers from their traditional positions of authority. Certain people and their ideas, it is claimed, are not automatically "credited" because of their social, economic, or political status. The best men cannot automatically claim any broad immunity from criticism by their "inferiors."[7] And, as in the economic marketplace, the preference of the sovereign consumer supposedly provides the most reliable and efficient tests for determining the worth of products.

The theory of the free marketplace of ideas, like the notion of freedom of contract, has been criticized from a number of different perspectives. As a model of how communication takes place in liberal society, for example, it ultimately rests upon its own logic—and upon faith. Jeffersonians could never really answer Federalist complaints that actual writers and publishers, and certainly not ones linked to the Democratic-Republican political machinery, would ever reply to—let alone counteract—the libelous attacks raining down upon the virtuous rulers of the 1790s. Jerome Barron's important critiques of the *Sullivan* decision updated this basic point. Whatever might have been the case in 1800, Barron argued, by the mid–twentieth century the notion of an open marketplace of ideas had become a romantic myth. In light of the obvious inequalities in access to the mass media, how could anyone possibly believe that libelous falsehoods would be answered through any self-correcting mechanism?[8]

The marketplace model has proved a generally shaky foundation for a consequentionalist approach to libel law. As the experience of Thomas Cooley showed, for instance, defamation rules designed to operate in some idealized marketplace, in which journalists merely supply their consumers' demand for useful information, seriously distorted the ways in which private media corporations manufactured a commodity called news and helped to create a public appetite for media products that, in the view of media watchers like Cooley himself, entertained as well as informed.[9]

Thus, attempts to change libel law doctrines, although certainly not irrelevant to either publishers or readers, have never exerted a significant, independent impact on the actual process of public communication. The Supreme Court's attempt in the 1960s to eliminate libel law as a reason (or an excuse) for self-censorship could not automatically turn the dominant media institutions into forums for critical examination of the basic direction of the United States' foreign and domestic policies.

The stated policy goal of *Times v. Sullivan*—to encourage robust and vigorous debate by removing the chilling effect of formal, governmentally enforced restrictions—missed many of the basic issues in the relationship between the channels of mass communication and movements for social change. As the very different studies of Alvin Gouldner, Godfrey Hodgson, Todd Gitlin, and Edward J. Epstein have all suggested, the media's attention to social problems in the 1950s and 1960s primarily ebbed and flowed in relationship to nonlegal pressures from within the communications industry itself and to the complex links between the Fourth Estate and other powerful institutions, especially those of the cold-war security state. Despite Justice William Brennan's attempt to announce the central meaning of free-speech questions, his defamation-oriented focus ultimately proved too narrow, even for a primarily legal analysis. The central free-speech issues of the post–World War II era involved the expansion of a vast surveillance apparatus, the growing power of an increasingly monopolistic communications industry, and the problems of its ties to other private and public centers of power. Although the question of seditious libel was not irrelevant, it was neither as central, nor did it always operate in the precise way, as those who embraced the *Sullivan* decision assumed.[10]

An Interpretation of the History of Political Libel Law

How, then, should legal historians ultimately approach defamation law? Libel suits have provided one way of dealing with the dangers that some people's words pose to others. But we should not become so concerned with the outcomes of particular cases, with the means used by legal writers to justify these outcomes, or even with the general historical shape of libel law that we lose sight of the most fundamental issues at stake.

First, libel law, like law of any kind, has never operated independently of historical forces. Legal materials and phenomena, once they are examined critically, can always be seen as historically contingent.[11] At certain times and in certain places—such as in the political frenzy of the 1790s or in the Deep South of the early 1960s—defamation law could become a prominent instrument in social-political struggles. Even in those cases, though, things distinctly legal, such as defamation laws, could not be separated from the larger social and cultural context of the era.[12] In light of the fierce political, ideological, and social struggles over the meaning of republicanism, for example, the Sedition Act gave Federalists a relatively flimsy legal tool. Similarly, in the political culture of the antebellum North, James Fenimore Cooper's effort to use civil libel actions only helped to discredit the legal and political principles he hoped to vindicate. In this sense, legal history can provide a useful corrective to one-dimensional, developmental views of legal, as well as general historical, change.

Second, libel law should be seen as a legal manifestation of fundamental battles over the nature of social and political power relationships in United States history. The history of defamation has involved one important aspect of what Duncan Kennedy has identified as "the fundamental contradiction—that relations with others are both necessary to and incompatible with our freedom. . . ."[13] Defamatory statements—most narrowly defined as injuries to one's image in the eyes of others, more accurately also including damage to one's image of oneself—have affected, and have limited, the freedom to form meaningful social relationships.[14] Political libel has reflected this same basic contradiction, albeit reduced to a smaller stage on which the principal actors have been less numerous, but one where their roles have been defined as more demanding than those in the larger society. Indeed, political libel law, with its emphasis upon protecting the reputations of the best men, has helped to legitimate this view of how the world should operate: since the early colonial era, defamation law has primarily protected the good names of the few while reducing the reputational conflicts of the mass of people to the realm of petty disputes. A history of changing approaches to defamation highlights this reality and shows how law has been one means by which ruling elites have sent powerful ideological messages about the nature and division of power.

And, then, there are two very basic, and very difficult, questions that, in recent years, have increasingly confronted legal analysts: the real value of legal guarantees for rights such as free speech, and the efficacy of the whole idea of the rule of law. Once the disturbing messages of legal realism are at least acknowledged, faith in traditional ideas of boundary drawing and of framing meaningful, neutral rules must be shaken.[15] Even writers who ultimately embrace the rule of law readily acknowledge that the doubts of critical writers should not be dismissed with rhetoric about "our tradition of a government of laws" and with warnings about the perils of abandoning this heritage in a dangerous age.[16]

When legal history is removed from traditional frameworks, it can be as disquieting as legal realism once was. The historical record shows no natural, evolutionary story of defamation law and no clear view of what the Founding Fathers—even assuming that their intentions should still be relevant—meant by the language of the First Amendment. The search for neat, developmental patterns or for pat answers about original understandings of legal-constitutional doctrines are both "misconceived quests."[17]

More fundamentally, the history of libel law casts some doubt upon the positivist, instrumentalist approach as the sole way to think about law. As a practical matter, legal protection for the right of reputation has really been available only to the best people, primarily wealthy and powerful men in the forefront of civic life. And this right, even for the people with the resources to play the legal game, has been more efficacious on paper than in the realities of the litigation process. Thus, to take a concrete example, the evidence belies any claim that tougher libel laws were functionally necessary to shore up elite power in the late nineteenth century. In some cases, of course, political libel suits have punished critical publications and may have even "chilled" some potential writers into silence or obfuscation. But those involved in the late nineteenth-century libel game, especially members of the political and legal elite, were playing for much higher stakes; most fundamental, they were struggling to define the categories, terms, and tone of political discourse. On the other hand, of course, legal protection for speech, including expression that calls forth the law of defamation, has always been contingent upon a variety of social and historical forces rather than solely upon the workings of an independent, autonomous legal order. And these same protections have represented something more than a set of instrumental tools for safeguarding individual, or even social, rights and needs; they have also comprised part of the general ideology of free speech, and part of the way in which people are supposed to think about the possibilities and limits of political life.

Thus, in some ways, political libel law has served at least as much as a means of disseminating messages about the general nature of American society as it has served as a discrete set of self-contained legal mechanisms. Defamation doctrines, for example, have always expressed one of the central tenets of liberal society: the supposedly clear separation between the public and private spheres. In the heyday of boundary-drawing theory, jurists argued that trained legal minds could, in the area of defamation law, use legal doctrines to demarcate subjects that were open to at least fair comment and those that were totally closed to defamatory public discussion. More recently, courts have announced ever more elaborate divisions, proposing that they can determine the difference between all-purpose and limited-purpose public figures and can separate communications that are of legitimate public interest from ones that merely titillate the interest of individual readers in the privacy of their homes.[18] Other messages have varied more with place and time. In the early and again in the late nineteenth century, defamation law provided a medium for underscoring the ideas that the reputations of political figures needed special love and care and that the whole marketplace for political speech required reordering. In a different historical time, decisions such as *Times* v. *Sullivan* proudly announced broad libertarian ideas of free communication, though nothing in the legal doctrines themselves or in the process by which courts applied them addressed the fundamental issues of how minority opinions really gained access to the dominant means of communication or how dissidents could effect legal guarantees of expression once they become the targets of the surveillance mechanisms of private and governmental bureaucracies.[19]

An understanding of the deeper implications of legal realism and of the historical contingency of legal phenomena provides no simple way out of contemporary dilemmas. The questioning of old faiths can, as it did for some legal realists, produce cynicism and resignation.[20] It can also, as it did for many legal scholars in the post–World War II era, lead back to traditional modes of denial and accommodation, to the assertion that the liberal mode of law ultimately will solve the fundamental contradiction. (Such a view, of course, represents simply another version of marketplace liberalism or what law professor Arthur Selwyn Miller has called "Micawberism," the idea that *something*, in this case legal protections, will *eventually* turn up.)[21]

There may, however, be still other paths besides those that lead off into despair or back to where we have already traveled. If law is not an autonomous, suprahistorical entity, neither is it simply a mass of conflicting prejudices or the clever trick of some amorphous ruling class.[22] History, as always, provides no clear road maps out of the present; but the questioning of old faiths and certainties may be able to offer clearer avenues for thought and action. By giving us a view of the past that is complex, challenging, and sometimes puzzling, it can warn against understanding both the perils and possibilities of the present—and of the future—in simplistic terms.

Abbreviations

AASP	*American Antiquarian Society Proceedings*
ABFRJ	*American Bar Foundation Research Journal*
AHR	*American Historical Review*
AJLH	*American Journal of Legal History*
AL	*American Lawyer*
ALIP	*American Law Institute Proceedings*
ALM	*American Law Magazine*
ALRec	*American Law Record*
AmLR	*American Law Review*
AmLReg	*American Law Register*
APSR	*American Political Science Review*
AQ	*American Quarterly*
AQR	*American Quarterly Review*
AR	*American Review*
Arena	*The Arena Magazine*
AzLR	*Arizona Law Review*
B&B	*Bench and Bar*
BrkLR	*Brooklyn Law Review*
BufLR	*Buffalo Law Review*
BULR	*Boston University Law Review*
CatULR	*Catholic University Law Review*
CBR	*Canadian Bar Review*
ChiLJ	*Chicago Law Journal*
CLJ	*Central Law Journal*
CLQ	*Cornell Law Quarterly*
CLR	*Cornell Law Review*
ColJR	*Columbia Journalism Review*
ColLR	*Columbia Law Review*
DLJ	*Duke Law Journal*
DR	*Democratic Review*
E&P	*Editor & Publisher*
Forum	*The Forum Magazine*
FRD	*Federal Rules and Decisions*
GeoLJ	*Georgetown Law Journal*
GeoWLR	*George Washington Law Review*
HCRCLLR	*Harvard Civil-Rights Civil-Liberties Law Review*
HLJ	*Hastings Law Journal*
HLR	*Harvard Law Review*
HofLR	*Hofstra Law Review*

IaLB	*Iowa Law Bulletin*
IlLR	*Illinois Law Review*
IR	*Independent Review*
JAH	*Journal of American History*
JH	*Journalism History*
JQ	*Journalism Quarterly*
JSH	*Journal of Social History*
KyLJ	*Kentucky Law Journal*
LAI	*Law and Inequality*
LCP	*Law and Contemporary Problems*
LQR	*Law Quarterly Review*
LRA	*Lawyers Reports Annotated*
LSR	*Law and Society Review*
MdLR	*Maryland Law Review*
MichH	*Michigan History*
MinnLR	*Minnesota Law Review*
MissLJ	*Mississippi Law Journal*
MLQ	*Massachusetts Law Quarterly*
MLR	*Michigan Law Review*
NAR	*North American Review*
NCLR	*North Carolina Law Review*
NEQ	*New England Quarterly*
NWULR	*Northwestern University Law Review*
NYH	*New York History*
NYHSQ	*New York Historical Society Quarterly*
NYULR	*New York University Law Review*
NYURLSC	*New York University Review of Law and Social Change*
OSLJ	*Ohio State Law Journal*
PAH	*Perspectives in American History*
PASS	*Proceedings of American Sociological Society*
PMHB	*Pennsylvania Magazine of History and Biography*
RIAH	*Reviews in American History*
RILS	*Research in Law and Sociology*
RLR	*Rutgers Law Review*
SCLR	*Southern California Law Review*
SCR	*Supreme Court Review*
Soc	*Sociology*
SQR	*Southern Quarterly Review*
SR	*Socialist Review*
StanLR	*Stanford Law Review*
StJLR	*St. Johns Law Review*
SWULR	*Southwestern University Law Review*
TLR	*Texas Law Review*
UChiLR	*University of Chicago Law Review*
UCLALR	*University of California, Los Angeles Law Review*

UPaLR	*University of Pennsylvania Law Review*
UPSLR	*University of Puget Sound Law Review*
USFLR	*University of San Francisco Law Review*
VaLR	*Virginia Law Review*
VaLReg	*Virginia Law Register*
VaMHB	*Virginia Magazine of History and Biography*
VLR	*Vanderbilt Law Review*
VV	*Village Voice*
W&LLR	*Washington and Lee Law Review*
WiscLR	*Wisconsin Law Review*
WLJ	*Western Law Journal*
WMLR	*William and Mary Law Review*
WMQ	*William and Mary Quarterly*
YLJ	*Yale Law Journal*

Notes

INTRODUCTION

1. Alfred H. Kelly, "Constitutional Liberty and the Law of Libel: A Historian's View," *AHR* 74 (1968): 429–49, provided the original impetus.

2. William L. Prosser, *Handbook of the Law of Torts*, 4th ed. (St. Paul, Minn., 1971), p. 737. This has been the prevailing view since at least the late nineteenth century. See, for example, "Slander and Libel," *AmLR* 6 (1871–72): 593–613.

3. Leon Green, "Political Freedom of the Press and the Libel Problem," *TLR* 56 (1978): 341–77, 352.

4. This commonly cited definition is from Kimmerle v. New York Evening Journal, 262 N.Y. 99, 186 N.E. 217, 218 (1933). Such definitions, of course, simply offer a rough guide to the problem of defamation law. In addition to other books and articles cited in the introduction, see "Developments in the Law—Defamation," *HLR* 69 (1956): 875–960.

5. Roy Robert Ray, "Truth: A Defense to Libel," *MLR* 16 (1949): 43–69, and 44–46, offers a brief, straightforward discussion.

6. Theodore F. T. Plucknett, *A Concise History of the Common Law*, 4th ed. (Boston, 1956), pp. 485–86; Colin Rhys Lovell, "The 'Reception' of Defamation by the Common Law," *VLR* 15 (1962): 1051–71, 1059–60; William T. Mayton, "Seditious Libel and the Lost Guarantee of a Freedom of Expression," *ColLR* 84 (1984): 91–142, esp. 98–106.

7. Plucknett, *Concise History of Common Law*, pp. 485–89. Frederick Seaton Siebert, *Freedom of the Press in England, 1476–1776: The Rise and Decline of Government Control* (Urbana, Ill., 1952; reprint, Urbana, 1965), pp. 21–63 contains an extensive discussion of the Tudor system of controls. Pat O'Malley, "From Feudal Honour to Bourgeois Reputation," *Soc* 15 (1981): 79–93 is highly suggestive.

8. De Libellis Famosis, 5 Coke 125a, 77 English Reporter 250 (1606).

9. Sir William Holdsworth, *A History of English Law*, 16 vols. (London, 1956–66), 5:208–12; Plucknett, *Concise History of Common Law*, pp. 489–90; Lovell, " 'Reception' of Defamation," pp. 1060–63.

10. Plucknett, *Concise History of Common Law*, pp. 496–501. In addition, common law courts heard cases involving blasphemy, defamation of religion. See Leonard W. Levy, *Emergence of a Free Press* (New York, 1985), pp. 7–8, and Levy, *Treason Against God: A History of the Offense of Blasphemy* (New York, 1981). Levy classifies prosecutions for obscenity as subsets of the general category of criminal libel. *Emergence of a Free Press*, p. 7.

11. Initially, what would be now considered civil suits for defamation were heard not by common law courts, but by local and church tribunals. See Chapter 1. In addition, see Van Vechter Veeder, "The History and Theory of the Law of Defamation,"

ColLR 3 (1903): 546–73, *ColLR* 4 (1904): 33–56; Richard C. Donnelly, "History of Defamation," *WiscLR* (1949): 99–126; and R. H. Helmholz, "Canonical Defamation in Medieval England," *AJLH* 15 (1971): 255–68. After abolition of Star Chamber, of course, common law courts heard all types of defamation suits—oral, written, criminal, and civil. The early common law history of civil defamation, including the growing distinction between slander and libel, is discussed in Holdsworth, *History of English Law*, 6:361–78 and Lovell, " 'Reception' of Defamation," pp. 1067–71. Today, slander suits are extremely rare, and the bulk of defamation cases involve civil libel suits. See also Chapter 1, and O'Malley, "Feudal Honour to Bourgeois Reputation," pp. 84–87.

12. Under English common law, a defendant could maintain an action for libel (written defamation) by putting the publication in evidence and proving that the defendant was the author or publisher. There was no need to prove that the statement was false or that the plaintiff had suffered any harm measurable in pounds or in shillings. (Although malice, in the sense of ill will, was supposedly an essential element in the lawsuit, the pleading of malice was, in fact, a mere formality at the outset of a suit.) On the other hand, an action for slander required that the statement fall within certain specific boundaries (e.g., commission of a serious crime or unchastity in a woman), comprising the category of "slander per se," or that the plaintiff prove he or she had suffered specific pecuniary damages because of the injury to reputation. In practice, the requirement of proof of "special" pecuniary damages was a real barrier (as common law judges intended it to be) against most slander suits. See Joel D. Eaton, "The American Law of Defamation through *Gertz v. Robert Welch, Inc.* and Beyond: An Analytical Primer," *VaLR* 61 (1975): 1349–1451, esp. 1352–57 and Holdsworth, *History of English Law*, 6:361–78. In time, the requirement of special damages crept into libel law. The result? Doctrines so complex and convoluted that most courts and even many specialists threw up their hands over the origin of the difference between and the implications of "libel per se" and "libel per quod." See Francis D. Murnaghan, "From Figment to Fiction to Philosophy—The Requirement of Proof of Damages in Libel Actions," 22 *CatULR* (1972): 1–22 for a summary and evaluation of the famous debate between William L. Prosser and Laurence H. Eldredge, two of the twentieth century's leading experts on defamation law, on the differences between "libel per se" and "libel per quod." Since 1964, the United States Supreme Court has altered, as a matter of constitutional law, traditional common law doctrines relating to falsity, responsibility of publishers, and actual damages. See Eaton, "The American Law of Defamation," pp. 1364–1439.

13. Green, "Political Freedom and Libel," p. 348. In Gertz v. Robert Welch, Inc., 418 U.S. 323, 349 (1974) the United States Supreme Court acknowledged as a matter of constitutional law what was happening in fact: that libel plaintiffs were collecting damages for injuries to their personal feelings, for mental anguish, and for a sense of personal humiliation, as well as for injuries to their standing in the eyes of others. To Leon Green, one of the country's most influential theorists on libel law, the focus upon personal injury to the plaintiff, rather than upon his relations with others, meant that *Gertz* was not really a libel case at all but a personal injury case masquerading as a suit for libel. Green, "Political Freedom and Libel," 559 n. 67, 370. Green was even more insistent that the Supreme Court's celebrated reemphasis of *Gertz*—Time, Inc. v.

Firestone, 424 U.S. 448 (1976)—could not be a libel case; here the plaintiff made no claim at all about any injury to her reputation but sued *only* for personal injuries to her feelings (p. 460). See also the earlier analysis in Walter Probert, "Defamation, A Camouflage of Psychic Interests: The Beginnings of a Behavioral Analysis," *VLR* 15 (1962): 1173–1201.

14. Harvey L. Zuckman and Martin J. Gaynes, *Mass Communications Law in a Nutshell* (St. Paul, Minn., 1977), pp. 34–36.

15. See Chapter 1, and P. R. Handford, "Tort Liability for Threatening or Insulting Words," *CBR* 54 (1976): 563–89.

16. See Chapter 1. In addition, see the suggestive analysis in Probert, "Defamation, A Camouflage of Psychic Interests," pp. 1176–78.

17. For a detailed account of a modern libel trial, from the perspective of a plaintiff, see Marc A. Franklin, *The Biography of a Legal Dispute* (Mineola, New York, 1968); for the "biography of an eighteenth-century case," see John Adams, *The Legal Papers of John Adams*, ed. L. Kinvin Wroth and Hiller Zobel, 3 vols. (Cambridge, Mass., 1965), 2:20–31.

18. As a popular handbook for journalists explains, to label a story as "libelous merely means that the person has been defamed. He will recover damages only if there is no defense in the libel law for publishing the article. . . . Libel is not a defenseless publication; it is a publication requiring a defense." Robert H. Phelps and E. Douglas Hamilton, *Libel: Rights, Risks, Responsibilities*, rev. ed. (New York, 1978), pp. 9–10. English lawyers have disagreed on why truth constituted a complete defense to an action for civil libel. Sir William Blackstone argued that courts sought to protect defendants who performed the public service of truthfully exposing the misdeeds of plaintiffs. *Commentaries on the Laws of England*, Book IV, p. 125. Most authorities, however, claim that courts did not want to reward plaintiffs for something they never possessed: an unblemished reputation. Holdsworth, *History of English Law*, 5:207.

19. John W. Wade, "The Communicative Torts of the First Amendment," *MissLJ* 48 (1977): 671–711, 673.

20. For discussions of qualified or conditional privileges see Prosser, *Handbook of Torts*, section 115 and "Developments in the Law—Defamation," pp. 924–31. As we shall see (Chapters 7–10), in the nineteenth century, American lawyers began to argue that libel suits involving public officials and candidates for office fell within the bounds of qualified privilege. This meant, in effect, that in jurisdictions that granted a qualified privilege, defendants would not have to prove the truth of libelous political charges in order to escape liability; they would "only" have to show the absence of legal malice. This was ultimately the view adopted by the United States Supreme Court when it laid down its own actual-malice standard in 1964 in New York Times v. Sullivan, 376 U.S. 254 (1964).

21. See, for example, Robert Gordon, "Introduction: J. Willard Hurst and the Common Law Tradition in American Legal Historiography," *LSR* 10 (1975): 9–55; Wythe Holt, "Morton Horwitz and the Transformation of American Legal History," *WMLR* 23 (1982): 663–723; William E. Nelson, "Standards of Criticism," *TLR* 60 (1982): 447–93.

22. John T. Noonan, Jr., *Persons and Masks of the Law* (New York, 1976), p. x.

23. Daniel J. Boorstin, "Tradition and Method in Legal History," *HLR* 54 (1951): 424–36.

24. The distinction between internal and external legal history is developed in Gordon, "Hurst and the Common Law Tradition," esp. p. 11. For constitutional history, see Paul L. Murphy, "Time to Reclaim: The Current Challenge of American Constitutional History," *AHR* 69 (1963): 64–79. The phrase "distinctly legal" is from Gordon, "Hurst and the Common Law Tradition," p. 10.

25. See Morton J. Horwitz, "The Conservative Tradition and the Writing of American Legal History," *AJLH* 17 (1973): 275–94.

26. See, for example, Donald M. Gillmor and Jerome A. Barron, *Mass Communications Law: Cases and Comment*, 3rd ed. (St. Paul, 1979), pp. 195–310. Leon Green, in contrast, entirely avoids the term "public libel" and argues that "political matters" should not be controlled by the law of libel at all. Green, "Political Freedom and Libel," at pp. 351 n. 45, 352, 353 n. 47. Green's definition of political seems too narrow; moreover, because courts *do* hear libel cases involving political publications, it serves no useful purpose (at least for a historian) to classify political cases as something else. See for example, Green's view that Goldwater v. Ginzburg, 414 F.2d 324 (2 Cir. 1969), cert. denied 396 U.S. 1049 (1970) was not a political libel case. Green, "Political Freedom and Libel," pp. 375–76. See Norman L. Rosenberg, "The New Law of Political Libel: A Historical Perspective," *RLR* 28 (1975): 1141–83.

27. Gordon, "Hurst and the Common Law Tradition," p. 11.

28. These were the strategies used in two of the most impressive examples of the new legal history—William E. Nelson, *The Americanization of the Common Law: The Impact of Legal Change on Massachusetts Society* (Cambridge, Mass., 1975), and Morton J. Horwitz, *The Transformation of American Law, 1780–1860* (Cambridge, Mass., 1977).

29. David Kairys, "Freedom of Speech," in *The Politics of Law*, ed. Kairys (New York, 1982), pp. 140–71, esp. 163–67. See also Mark Tushnet, "An Essay on Rights," *TLR* 62 (1984): 1363–1403, esp. 1370–71; Robert F. Nagel, "How Useful Is Judicial Review in Free Speech Cases?" *CLR* (1984): 302–40; and Stanley Ingber, "The Marketplace of Ideas: A Legitimizing Myth," *DLJ* (1984): 1–91.

30. Two works, breaking sharply with the traditional studies on the history of journalism, are Michael Schudson, *Inventing the News: A Social History of American Newspapers* (New York, 1978); and Dan Schiller, *Objectivity and the News: The Public and the Rise of Commercial Journalism* (Philadelphia, 1981).

On the value of history, see William Appleman Williams, *Contours of American History* (Chicago, 1966), pp. 17–23, and Noonan, *Persons and Masks of the Law*, p. 167. In contrast to Professor Noonan's views, however, one might note those of another law professor who has read eighteenth-century legal history. Peter Teachout gloomily concludes that legal history sheds "only an intermittent or flickering light. . . . In the end, after all, it may be mistaken to think that history can provide us with much more than this. Perhaps in the modern world we must all proceed in 'darkness,' and the light we can expect from history can at most be only 'light in ashes.' " "Light in Ashes: The Problem of 'Respect for the Rule of Law' in American Legal History," *NYULR* 53 (1978): 241–88.

31. Leon Green, "The Right to Communicate," *NYULR* 35 (1960): 903–24, esp.

907. The fact that, as a historian, I have difficulties with Green's history (see, for example his nineteenth-century Whiggish view of early American settlements in "Political Freedom and Libel," at 353) does nothing to diminish my enormous regard for his path-breaking work on tort law in general and defamation law in particular. See Chapter 9.

32. See Robert Gordon, "Historicism in Legal Scholarship," *YLJ* 90 (1981): 1017–56.

33. Christopher Hill, *Milton and the English Revolution* (New York, 1975), pp. 93–107, 149–62.

34. Norman L. Rosenberg, "Thomas M. Cooley, Liberal Jurisprudence, and the Law of Libel, 1868–1884," *UPSLR* 4 (1980): 49–98; Laurence Tribe, "Toward a Metatheory of Free Speech," *SWULR* 10 (1978): 237–45. See also, C. Edwin Baker, "The Process of Change and the Liberty Theory of the First Amendment," *SCLR* 55 (1978): 293–344.

35. Alvin Gouldner, *The Dialectic of Ideology and Technology* (New York, 1976).

36. See, e.g., Tushnet, "Essay on Rights," pp. 1390–91, "Symposium: National Security and Civil Liberties," *CLR* 69 (1984): 685–894, and Frank J. Donner, *The Age of Surveillance* (New York, 1980). For an exception, see Stanley I. Kutler, *The American Inquisition* (New York, 1982), pp. 215–42.

37. See, e.g., Tavoulareas v. Washington Post Co., 567 F.Supp. 651 (DDC, 1983). My view of the relationship between the media and other large corporations draws heavily upon the theoretical structure in Gouldner, *The Dialectic of Ideology and Technology*. For two interpretations of twentieth-century politics supportive of the view outlined in this paragraph, see R. Jeffrey Lustig, *Corporate Liberalism* (Berkeley, Cal., 1982) and Ira Katznelson, *City Trenches* (New York, 1981).

CHAPTER ONE

1. See, e.g., Holmes's dissent in Abrams v. U.S., 250 U.S. 616, 630 (1919), Thomas F. Carroll, "The Evolution of the Theory of Freedom of Speech and of the Press," *GeoLJ* 11 (1922): 27–45, and Zechariah Chafee, Jr., *Free Speech in the United States* (Cambridge, Mass., 1948), pp. 16–22. The United States Supreme Court employed an expansionist history of the First Amendment in New York Times v. Sullivan, 376 U.S. 254 (1964). For an example of the libertarianism of the cold-war era, see Thomas I. Emerson, *The System of Freedom of Expression* (New York, 1970). See also, Nat Hentoff, *The First Freedom* (New York, 1980).

2. Rex v. Tuchin, 14 Howell's State Trials 1095, 1128 (1704); William Hawkins, *Pleas of the Crown*, 2 vols. (London, 1716, 1721; reprint, 1973), 1:194.

3. Sir William Blackstone, *Commentaries on the Laws of England*, 4 vols., ed. Thomas M. Cooley (London, 1765–69; reprint, Chicago, 1873), 2:150–52.

4. Leonard W. Levy, *Freedom of Speech and Press in Early American History: Legacy of Suppression* (Cambridge, Mass., 1960; reprint, New York, 1963), p. xxiii.

5. See, e.g., Lawrence H. Leder, *Liberty and Authority: Early American Political Ideology, 1689–1763* (Chicago, 1968), pp. 19–36 (a broad libertarianism did exist); Mary Ann Yodelis, "Boston's First Major Newspaper War: A 'Great Awakening' of

Freedom," *JQ* 51 (1974): 207–12 (black letter law ineffective); and Stephen Botein, "'Meer Mechanics' and an Open Press: The Business and Political Strategies of American Colonial Printers," in Donald Fleming and Bernard Bailyn, eds., *Perspectives in American History* 9 (1975): 127–228.

6. Levy, *Emergence of a Free Press* (New York, 1985), pp. vii, xi, xii. Levy's book appeared while this volume was at press, but Levy had indicated in an earlier piece that a revised edition of *Legacy of Suppression* would modify some of his earlier judgments. See Terry Hynes, "A Conversation with Leonard Levy," *JH* 7 (1980): 96–103.

7. The generalizations in this paragraph are discussed at greater length in Chapter 10.

8. The concept of making a balance is developed in Laura Nader, "Styles of Court Procedure: To Make the Balance," in *Law and Culture in Society*, ed. Nader (Chicago, 1969), pp. 69–91.

9. John Russell Bartlett, ed., *Records of the Colony of Rhode Island and Providence Plantations in New England*, 10 vols. (Providence, 1856–65), 1:156, 184; Staughton George et al., eds., *Charter to William Penn, and the Laws of the Province of Pennsylvania, Passed between the Years 1682 and 1700* (Harrisburg, 1879), pp. 114–15, 198; J. Hammond Trumbell, ed., *The Public Records of the Colony of Connecticut*, 15 vols. (Hartford, 1850–90), 1:537–38.

10. George et al., *Laws of Pennsylvania*, p. 198.

11. Douglas Greenberg, *Crime and Law Enforcement in the Colony of New York, 1691–1776* (Ithaca, N.Y., 1976), pp. 59, 64–67, 93–95, 111–12; Kai Erikson, *Wayward Puritans: A Study in the Sociology of Deviance* (New York, 1966), pp. 171–81.

12. One of the dominant trends in recent colonial historiography, I fully recognize, is the production of detailed local studies. Although I applaud such work, I also find myself in agreement with Douglas Greenberg, author of one of the best of these local studies, that "an acknowledgement of the differences" among various locales need not obscure "their functional similarities" and common realities. "Our Town," *RIAH* 9 (1981): 454–58, at 456. Thus, although I concede that not every area or legal jurisdiction followed *precisely* the same pattern, I am confident of the validity of my *general* characterization of early American defamation law. For the sources for this paragraph, see, e.g., *Records and Files of the Quarterly Courts of Essex County, Massachusetts, 1656–1683*, 8 vols. (Salem, Mass., 1912–21), 1:57–60 ("lascivious speeches"); *Records of the Court of Assistants of the Colony of Massachusetts Bay, 1630–1692*, 3 vols. (Boston, Mass., 1901–28), 1:355 ("reproachful words"); *Records of the Court of Chester County [Pennsylvania]* (Philadelphia, 1910), p. 161 ("speaking and uttering scandalous and Dishonourable words"), p. 104 ("false news"); *Records of the General and Particular Courts [of Connecticut] from April, 1636 to December, 1649* in Trumbell, ed., *Public Records of Connecticut*, ("pernicious" speeches against the Commonwealth); Zechariah Chafee, Jr., ed., *Records of the Suffolk County Court, 1671–1680* in *Publications of the Colonial Society of Massachusetts* 29–30 (1933), p. 234 ("pernicious lying"); ibid., p. 674 ("contempt of authority"); *Courts of Essex County*, 5:413 ("pernicious lie"); William Hening, ed., *The Statutes at Large, Being a Collection of All the Laws of Virginia (1619–1792)*, 13 vols. (Richmond, Va., 1809–1823), 1:434–35, 2:109 ("false news" statutes); *Particular Courts of Connecticut*, p. 50 ("divulging misreports").

In researching a work of this scope, I have only been able to examine selected, published colonial court records. In addition to the collections cited in notes 12, 36, 37, and 41, I have used the following: Susie Ames, ed., *County Court Records of Accomack-Northampton, Virginia, 1632–1640* (Washington, D.C., 1954), and Ames, ed. *County Court Records of Accomack-Northampton, Virginia, 1640–1660* (Charlottesville, Va., 1973); Edwin Bronner, ed., "Philadelphia's Court of Quarter Sessions and Common Pleas, 1695," *AJLH* 1 (1957): 79–95, 175–90, 236–50; Leon deValinger, Jr., ed., *Court Records of Kent County, Delaware, 1680–1705* (Washington, D.C., 1959); and *Records of the Courts of Chester County [Pennsylvania]* (Danboro, Pa., 1972). In addition to the secondary works cited in other notes to this chapter, the following have been most helpful: George L. Haskins, *Law and Authority in Early Massachusetts* (New York, 1960); George Billias, ed., *Law and Authority in Colonial America* (Barre, Mass., 1965); Herbert Johnson, *Essays in New York Colonial Legal History* (Westport, Conn., 1981); Herbert Fitzroy, "Punishment of Crime in Provincial Pennsylvania," *PMHB* 60 (1936): 242–69; Fitzroy, "Richard Crosby Goes to Court, 1683–97," *PMHB* 62 (1938): 12–19; Note, "More Light on an Old Court: The Kent County Court, 1647–1655," *NWULR* 68 (1973): 110–28; and Richard L. Abel, "The Rise of Capitalism and the Transformation of Disputing: From Confrontation over Honor to Competition for Property," *UCLALR* 27 (1979): 223–55.

13. See John Winthrop, *Winthrop's Journal: History of New England*, ed. James Kendell Hosmer, 2 vols. (New York, 1908), 2:229–40; Robert Emmet Wall, Jr., *Massachusetts Bay: The Crucial Decade, 1640–1650* (New Haven, Conn., 1972), pp. 93–120.

14. *Records of Massachusetts Bay*, 2:16; Arthur P. Scott, *Criminal Law in Colonial Virginia* (Chicago, 1930), pp. 181–82.

15. *Suffolk County Court*, p. 231.

16. Ibid.; Michael Dalton, *Country Justice 1619* (London, 1619; reprint, London, 1973), pp. 169, 173; see also William Simpson, *The Practical Justice of the Peace and Parish-Officer of His Majesty's Province of South-Carolina* (Charleston, S.C., 1761; reprint, New York, 1972), pp. 67–249.

17. H. R. McIlwaine and W. L. Hall, eds., *Executive Journals of the Council of Virginia*, 5 vols. (Richmond, 1925–45), 2:11–12; see, e.g., *Suffolk County Court*, p. 43 ("three pounds Damages & costs or that Sarah the wife of John Machee make an acknowledgement in Open Court to the Satisfaction of said Court . . .").

18. Bradley Chapin, *Criminal Justice in Colonial America, 1606–1660* (Athens, Ga., 1983), p. 132.

19. Frank Carr, "The English Law of Defamation," *LQR* 71 (1902): 266.

20. See, e.g., Gilbert v. Gould, in *Courts of Essex County*, 4:419; Parker v. Weller, ibid., p. 242; Edwards v. Fellowes, ibid., pp. 199, 206–7; Lewis v. Dement and Dement v. Lewis. *Particular Courts of Connecticut*, pp. 159–60, 168–69. On the use of defamation laws in incidents involving alleged witchcraft, see John Demos, *Entertaining Satan: Witchcraft and the Culture of Early New England* (New York, 1982), p. 249.

21. For a suggestive discussion of the legal game, viewed from the perspective of litigant-players, see Marc A. Galanter, "Why the 'Haves' Come Out Ahead: Speculation on the Limits of Legal Change," *LSR* 9 (1974): 95–160. Galanter suggests that the

legal system may be viewed as an "iceberg" in which formal adjudication and litigation are only the most visible portions. In his model, the legal system looks something like this: Adjudication; Litigation; Appended Settlement Systems; Private Settlement Systems; Self-Help; Inaction ("lumping it").

22. See Kenneth Lockridge, *A New England Town: The First Hundred Years* (New York, 1970), p. 13; and Emil Oberholzer, Jr., *Delinquent Saints: Disciplinary Action in the Early Congregational Church of Massachusetts* (New York, 1956).

23. The concepts of self-help and lumping it are borrowed from Marc Galanter, "Why the 'Haves' Come Out Ahead," p. 134.

24. Michael Zuckerman, *Peaceable Kingdoms: New England Towns in the Eighteenth Century* (New York, 1970) emphasizes the concern among political leaders that disputes not be polarized unnecessarily, thereby escalating social conflict. See also, Jessica Kross, *The Evolution of an American Town: Newton, New York, 1642–1775* (Philadelphia, 1983), pp. 119–20.

25. Lawrence Friedman, "Legal Culture and Social Development," *LSR* 4 (1969): 29–44. In gaining a clearer perspective on the role of gossip, slanderous attacks on reputation, and dispute settlement in early America, it is helpful to compare seventeenth-century communities with heterogenous neighborhoods in the contemporary United States. In the latter, verbal backbiting and threats to reputation are ultimately resolved very differently from seventeenth-century North America; the twentieth-century legal system offers ordinary citizens little hope of settling disputes over reputation. As a result, self-help (such as violence and avoidance of social contacts) and lumping it (simply enduring verbal assaults) become necessary alternatives to playing the legal game. See Sally Engle Merry, "Going to Court: Strategies of Dispute Management in an American Urban Neighborhood," *LSR* 13 (1979): 891–925. On the capacity for lumping it, even in the case of serious physical injuries, in a rural Illinois county during the 1970s, see David M. Engel, "Cases, Conflict, and Accommodation: Patterns of Legal Interaction in an American Community," *ABFRJ* (1983): 803–74, esp. 822–23.

26. Friedman, "Legal Culture and Social Development," p. 34. Legal doctrines themselves, of course, also function as cultural and ideological messages, ones that can help to shape popular values and attitudes toward law. See, e.g., Betty Mensch, "Freedom of Contract as Ideology," *StanLR* 33 (1981): 753–72.

27. This was not the case in the mid–nineteenth century, for example, when public officials who sued for libel risked considerable popular opprobrium. See Chapter 6.

28. See Erikson, *Wayward Puritans*.

29. F. G. Bailey, ed., *Gifts and Poison: The Politics of Reputation* (New York, 1971), pp. 1–24, 281–99. The distinction between small and large politics is developed from Bailey's analysis.

30. Ibid., p. 3.

31. Ibid., pp. 19–20, 284–89.

32. Ibid., p. 283.

33. The most famous example of a neighborhood dispute becoming a major legal issue involved Goodwife Sherman's claim, in 1637, that Robert Keayne had killed her sow. This soon escalated into a war of words, a successful defamation suit by Keayne, and finally a direct challenge to the authority of John Winthrop, the governor of Mas-

sachusetts Bay. See Wall, *Massachusetts Bay*, pp. 48–64. On the relationship between defamation suits and deeper social conflict, see also Demos, *Entertaining Satan*, pp. 250–56, 288–90.

34. Sir William Holdsworth, *A History of the Common Law*, 16 vols., 7th ed. (London, 1956–66), 8:353–56. 21 James I., c. 16 (1624) provided that in slander actions in which the jury awarded less than forty shillings in damages, successful plaintiffs could recover no more in legal costs. John March, *Actions for Slander* (London, 1647), pp. 2–3, quoted in Holdsworth, *History of the Common Law*, 8:353, n. 1.

35. Michael Stephen Hindus, "The Contours of Crime and Justice in Massachusetts and South Carolina, 1767–1878," *AJLH* 21 (1977): 212–37, at 220–21.

36. The generalizations in this paragraph derive from the published court records listed in note 12 and here, from scattered court reports from the eighteenth century, and from the major secondary works in colonial legal history. See, e.g., Clara Ann Bowler, "Carted Whores and White Shrouded Apologies," *VaMHB* 85 (1977): 411–26, at 422–26; Scott, *Criminal Law in Virginia*, p. 185; William E. Nelson, *Dispute and Conflict Resolution in Plymouth County, Massachusetts, 1725–1825* (Chapel Hill, N.C., 1981), p. 24, 159 n. Thus, despite the fact that at least in Massachusetts court dockets became crowded in the eighteenth century—see, e.g., David Allen, *In English Ways* (Chapel Hill, N.C., 1981), pp. 236–37—only a fraction of this legal activity involved defamation. See, e.g., Nelson, *Dispute and Conflict Resolution*, p. 159 n., and Joseph Smith, ed., *Colonial Justice in Western Massachusetts (1639–1702): The Pynchon Court Record* (Cambridge, Mass., 1961), p. 170. The Connecticut Statute of 1708 may be found in Trumbell, ed., *Public Records of Connecticut*, 5:54–55. There is no evidence, however, that this law produced any upsurge in formal litigation involving defamation. The major increase in legal business in eighteenth-century Connecticut came in the area of litigation over debts. See Richard L. Bushman, *From Puritan to Yankee: Character and the Social Order in Connecticut, 1690–1765* (Cambridge, Mass., 1967), Appendix III; and Bruce H. Mann, "Rationality, Legal Change, and Community in Connecticut, 1690–1760," *LSR* 14 (1980): 187–221. See also Laura Becker, "The People and the System: Legal Activities in a Colonial Pennsylvania Town," *PMHB* 105 (1981): 135–49, at 138, 146.

The fact, however, that litigation did not formally center on defamation action did not mean that the politics of reputation could not still be present. By suing a neighbor for debt or by instigating a criminal prosecution, for instance, one party could try to damage the reputation of a rival, using the legal process as the instrument of defamation. See Hendrik Hartog, "The Public Law of a County Court: Judicial Government in Eighteenth Century Massachusetts," *AJLH* 20 (1976): 282–329, at 319; and Mann, "Rationality, Legal Change, and Community," pp. 198–200.

37. *Colonial Laws of New York from the Year 1664 to the Revolution*, 5 vols. (Albany, 1894–96), 1:154–56. For similar statutes in other colonies, see, e.g., Joseph H. Smith and Philip A. Crowl, eds., *Court Records of Prince Georges County, Maryland, 1696–1699*, 3 vols. (Washington, D.C., 1964), I:lix; and George, *Laws of Pennsylvania*, pp. 345–46.

38. Hening, ed., *Laws of Virginia* (1662), 2:166–67.

39. Ibid., (1661) 2:72–73. For English developments, see Holdsworth, *History of Common Law*, 8:353–56. The Virginia legislature made clear it was not suggesting by

this statute that "any scurrilous person" could "abuse others at his pleasure," and they empowered local justices of the peace to bind defamers to good behavior. For a fuller discussion, see Bowler, "Carted Whores," pp. 412–13.

40. John Adams, *The Legal Papers of John Adams*, ed. L. Kinin Wroth and Hiller B. Zobel, 3 vols. (Cambridge, Mass., 1965), 1:141–49; 2:20–31.

41. Richard B. Morris, ed., *Select Cases of the Mayor's Court of New York City, 1674–1784* (Washington, D.C., 1945), pp. 333–36 (Drury v. Husk); pp. 340–43 (Ruston v. Salisbury).

42. Francis W. Laurent, *The Business of a Trial Court: 100 Years of Cases* (Madison, Wis., 1959), pp. 49, 163–64 (table); see also, Charles Clark and Harry Shulman, *A Study of Law Administration in Connecticut* (New Haven, 1937), pp. 12–13, 30–31, 44.

43. According to a careful study of criminal prosecutions in Essex County, Massachusetts, for example, defamation constituted the second leading form of crime for men and the third for women in the mid–seventeenth century. C. Dallet Hemphill, "Women in Court: Sex-Role Differentiation in Salem, Massachusetts, 1636–1683," *WMQ* 39 (1982): 164–75, at 171, n. 36.

44. Leon Green, "The Right to Communicate," *NYULR* 35 (1960): 903–24, at 905, n. 8, citing an unpublished study by George A. Canon. Two decades later, however, specialists in tort law were beginning to note the rejuvenation of libel law. See, e.g., Rodney A. Smolla, "Let the Author Beware: The Rejuvenation of the American Law of Libel," *UPaLR* 132 (1983): 1–94. Although libel suits apparently did become more prevalent in the late 1970s than they had been in, for example, the late 1940s, suits still rarely involved ordinary citizens as had the slander actions of the colonial era. Instead, most cases in the late 1970s involved political leaders, prominent media personalities, and affluent members of the business world. On the absence of slander suits, see Chapter 1, n. 25.

45. Green, "Right to Communicate," p. 907.

CHAPTER TWO

1. H. R. McIlwaine and W. L. Hall, eds., *Executive Journals of the Council of Virginia*, 5 vols. (Richmond, 1925–45), 1:75; Staughton George et al., eds., *Charter to William Penn, and the Laws of the Province of Pennsylvania, Passed between the Years 1682 and 1700* (Harrisburg, 1879), p. 198; Douglas Greenberg, *Crime and Law Enforcement in the Colony of New York, 1691–1776* (Ithaca, N.Y., 1976), p. 111.

2. See Timothy Breen, *The Character of a Good Ruler* (New Haven, 1970), pp. 240, 245–47.

3. Quoted in Edmund S. Morgan, *American Slavery, American Freedom: The Ordeal of Colonial Virginia* (New York, 1975), p. 187.

4. In general, Stephen Botein's analysis of the trade strategies of colonial printers seems more persuasive than Lawrence Leder's thesis that members of the colonial press articulated a broadly principled defense of freedom of press. See Stephen Botein, " 'Meer Mechanics': Strategies of Colonial Printers," in Donald Fleming and Bernard Bailyn, eds., *PAH* 9 (1975): 131–225, and Lawrence Leder, *Liberty and Au-*

thority: Early American Political Ideology (New York, 1968), pp. 19–36.

5. The quotations from Franklin's "Apology for Printers" may easily be found in the brief essay. See Benjamin Franklin, *The Papers of Benjamin Franklin*, ed. Leonard Labaree et al., 21 vols. to date. (New Haven, 1959–), 1:194–99.

6. See Botein, " 'Meer Mechanics.' "

7. *New-York Weekly Journal*, 19 Nov. 1733, reprinted in *Freedom of the Press from Zenger to Jefferson*, ed. Leonard Levy (Indianapolis, Ind., 1966), p. 31 (emphasis added).

8. Benjamin Franklin, *The Autobiography of Benjamin Franklin*, ed. J. A. Leo Lemay and P. M. Zall (Knoxville, Tenn., 1981), pp. 94–95.

9. Ibid., pp. 123–24; see also Botein, " 'Meer Mechanics,' " p. 189.

10. Quoted in David Hawke, *Franklin* (New York, 1976), p. 34.

11. Franklin, *Papers of Franklin*, ed. Labaree et al., 1:249–50.

12. Leonard Levy, *Emergence of a Free Press* (New York, 1985), pp. 30–32.

13. Herbert Fitzroy, "Punishment of Crime in Provincial Pennsylvania," *PMHB* 60 (1936): 242–69, at 265 n; Greenberg, *Crime and Law Enforcement*, pp. 140, 142.

14. Clyde Duniway, *The Development of Freedom of the Press in Massachusetts* (Boston, 1906), p. 93.

15. Levy, *Emergence of a Free Press*, pp. 14, 17–18.

16. See *New England's Spirit of Persecution Transmitted to Pennsilvania . . . in the Tryal of Peter Boss, George Keith, Thomas Budd, and William Bradford . . .* (Philadelphia, 1693); see also Levy, *Emergence of a Free Press*, pp. 22, 26; and Gary Nash, *Quakers and Politics: Pennsylvania, 1681–1726* (Princeton, N.J., 1968), pp. 126–61.

17. I have used Stanley N. Katz's edition of James Alexander, *A Brief Narrative of the Case and Trial of John Peter Zenger, of the New York Weekly Journal* (Cambridge, Mass., 1963).

18. *Brief Narrative of Trial of Zenger*, pp. 74–75.

19. *Cato's Letters*, No. 15. "Of Freedom of Speech: That the Same is inseperable from Publick Liberty," reprinted in *The English Libertarian Heritage*, ed. David Jacobson (Indianapolis, Ind., 1965), pp. 38–44, at 42.

In using the term "country" to characterize eighteenth-century ideology, I follow Lance Banning, *The Jeffersonian Persuasion* (Ithaca, N.Y., 1980), esp. pp. 130–40, and, to a lesser extent, Forrest McDonald, *The Presidency of Thomas Jefferson* (Lawrence, Kan., 1976). The literature on eighteenth-century political ideology is extensive; I have found the following most useful: Bernard Bailyn, *The Origins of American Politics* (New York, 1968); Issac Kramnick, *Bolingbroke and his Circle* (Cambridge, Mass., 1968); J. G. A. Pocock, *The Machiavellian Moment* (Princeton, N.J., 1975); Peter Shaw, *The Character of John Adams* (Chapel Hill, N.C., 1976); Henry F. May, *The Enlightenment in America* (New York, 1976); and John Murrin, "The Great Inversion, or Court versus Country: A Comparison of the Revolution Settlements in England," in *Three British Revolutions: 1641, 1688, 1776*, ed. J. G. A. Pocock (Princeton, N.J., 1980). Also, in *The Lost Soul of American Politics: Virtue, Self-Interest, and the Foundations of Liberalism* (New York, 1984), p. 31, John P. Diggins emphasizes how eighteenth-century political ideology offered critics of authority a full-blown "rhetoric of accusation."

20. *Brief Narrative of Trial of Zenger*, Appendix A, pp. 109–38.

21. See No. 15, "Of Freedom of Speech," in *Libertarian Heritage*, ed. Jacobson, pp. 38–44; No. 32, "Reflections upon Libelling," ibid., pp. 73–80; No. 100, "Discourse upon Libels," ibid., pp. 230–36; and No. 101, "Second Discourse upon Libels," ibid., pp. 236–42. For Alexander's use of *Cato*'s ideas, see *New-York Weekly Journal*, 19 Nov. 1733; ibid., 11 Feb. 1734, and 18 Feb. 1734, reprinted in *Zenger to Jefferson*, ed. Levy, pp. 31, 32–33, 33–35.

22. Levy, ed., *Zenger to Jefferson*, p. 31.

23. Ibid., p. 33.

24. Ibid., p. 34.

25. *Brief Narrative of Trial of Zenger*, p. 65.

26. Ibid., p. 79. A prosecution by information did not require a grand jury indictment and had been a highly controversial practice in colonial New York, for all types of criminal cases, for a number of years. See Paul Finkleman, "The Zenger Case: Prototype of a Political Trial," in *American Political Trials*, ed. Michal Belknap (Westport, Conn., 1981), pp. 21–42, at 28–29.

27. The concept of the "indivisibility of freedom" is developed in William Spinrad, *Civil Liberties* (Chicago, 1970), p. 30.

28. *Brief Narrative of Trial of Zenger*, p. 75 (emphasis in original).

29. Ibid., p. 95.

30. Ibid., p. 81. Hamilton consistently talked about the "right to complain" (p. 81), the "right of complaining" (p. 94), or the "liberty of complaining" (p. 87), rather than about "freedom of the press." Similarly, as historian Edward Countryman suggests, he also tried to shift "the terms of the debate from freedom of the press to the power and legitimacy of the [anti-Cosby] assemblymen." Edward Countryman, *A People in Revolution* (Baltimore, 1981), p. 87.

31. For the distinction between small and large politics, which I also use in Chapter 1, see F. G. Bailey, ed., *Gifts and Poison: The Politics of Reputation* (New York, 1971), pp. 1–24. In his lengthy study, *The Constitutionalist*, for example, George Anastaplo insists that the First Amendment "elevated freedom of speech to the status theretofore held only by 'liberty of the press.'" George Anastaplo, *The Constitutionalist: Notes on the First Amendment* (Dallas, Tex., 1971), p. 125. Similarly, David Anderson concludes that freedom of speech "was a late addition to the pantheon of rights" and that "freedom of the press occupied a central position from the beginning." David Anderson, "The Origins of the Press Clause," *UCLALR* 30 (1983): 455–541, at 533. The structure of Andrew Hamilton's argument and his overall strategy in the *Zenger* trial casts doubt upon this view, as do the various studies on nonprinted communication during the Revolutionary era. See, e.g., Harry S. Stout, "Religion, Communications, and the Ideological Origins of the American Revolution," *WMQ* 34 (1977): 519–41. As the First-Amendment scholar Kent Greenawalt notes, throughout most of human history, conversations with neighbors, friends, and family were the main sources for political consciousness. Kent Greenawalt, "Speech and Crime," *ABFRJ* (1980): 645–785, at 677. See also, Alvin Gouldner, *The Dialectic of Ideology and Technology* (New York, 1976), pp. 105–8.

32. Elaine G. Breslau, "Wit, Whimsy, and Politics: The Uses of the Tuesday Club of Annapolis, 1744 to 1756," *WMQ* 32 (1975): 295–306; see also, Robert Micklus,

" 'The History of the Tuesday Club': A Mock-Jeremiad of the Colonial South," *WMQ* 40 (1983): 42-61.

33. See, generally, Stout, "Religion, Communications, and Ideological Origins," pp. 532-33. The quotation about the writings of the Revolutionaries is by Gordon Wood, quoted in Stout's essay, p. 533, n. 49.

34. Quoted in Robert J. Dinkin, *Voting in Provincial America* (Westport, Conn., 1979), p. 110.

35. Despite my respect for the important work by Gary Nash on the urban colonial press and politics, his evidence shows, I believe, the intermittent, rather than regular, nature of the type of highly organized political conflict that included newspaper and pamphlet wars. This type of political activity did, however, become more frequent over the course of the eighteenth century. Gary Nash, *The Urban Crucible*, (Cambridge, Mass., 1979), pp. 83-84, 90, 99-100, 131, 139-40, 142, 224, 226-27, 268-69. Also compare Botein, " 'Meer Mechanics,' " with Nash, *Urban Crucible*, p. 440, n. 46.

36. In Milton Klein, ed., *The Independent Reflector* (Cambridge, Mass., 1963), p. 40.

37. All of the above quotations in ibid., at pp. 341-42.

38. This point is suggested in Gordon S. Wood, *Creation of the American Republic* (Chapel Hill, N.C., 1969), p. 63 and developed more fully in Richard Buel, Jr., "Freedom of the Press in Revolutionary America: The Evolution of Libertarianism, 1760-1820," in *The Press & the American Revolution*, ed. Bernard Bailyn and John B. Hench (Worcester, Mass., 1980), pp. 59-97.

39. *American Weekly Mercury*, 25 April 1734, reprinted in *Zenger to Jefferson*, ed. Levy, pp. 41-42; see also Anna J. DeArmond, *Andrew Bradford: Colonial Journalist* (Newark, Del., 1948; reprint, New York, 1969), pp. 84-118.

40. Levy, ed., *Zenger to Jefferson*, p. 40.

41. John Webbe, quoted in Leder, *Liberty and Authority*, p. 30.

42. If one uses Stephen Botein's categories, at least four of his "neutral" printers—Thomas Fleet, William Parks, Hugh Gaine, and James Parker—faced libel prosecutions at one time or another.

43. See Nash, *Urban Crucible*. Stout, "Religion, Communications, and Ideological Origins" contains a good discussion of the historical debate over the relative contributions of oral versus printed forms of communication to the general "popularization" of political discussion. But any hard-and-fast distinction between printed and oral communication can distort the nature of eighteenth-century political communication. Even if people did not, or could not, read printed materials themselves, they could still have become acquainted with them through the simple process that historians of political communication call bridging—the transmission of printed materials through public readings and discussions in taverns and coffee houses. See John Brewer, *Party Ideology and Popular Politics at the Accession of George III* (London, 1976), pp. 155-57.

44. Quoted in Larry R. Gerlach, *Prologue to Independence: New Jersey in the Coming of the American Revolution* (New Brunswick, N.J., 1976), p. 117. Smith is quoted in William Allen Benton, *Whig-Loyalism* (Rutherford, N.J., 1969), p. 99.

There are a number of analyses of the McDougall case; see, e.g., Roger J. Champagne, *Alexander McDougall and the American Revolution in New York* (Schenectady, N.Y., 1975), pp. 27–36.

45. Josiah Quincy, ed., *Reports of Cases Argued and Adjudged in the Superior Court of the Judicature of the Province of Massachusetts Bay, Between 1761 and 1772* (Boston, 1865), p. 309. For an interesting, and instructive, comparison between the impotence of Thomas Hutchinson and the power of colonial authorities in Ireland over libels, see John Phillip Reid, *In a Defiant Stance: The Conditions of Law in Massachusetts Bay, the Irish Comparison, and the Coming of the American Revolution* (University Park, Pa., 1977), pp. 46–48, 52, 156. Local juries possessed considerable clout in pre-Revolutionary Massachusetts. Even when courts ruled on what view of the law should apply, defense lawyers were still free to argue a contrary position to the jury. Thus, the attempt of Orthodox Whigs to reject this practice in the case of seditious libels would have seemed a big step toward the type of arbitrary judicial power that juries were supposed to check. See William E. Nelson, *Americanization of the Common Law: The Impact of Legal Change on Massachusetts Society, 1760–1830* (Cambridge, Mass., 1975), pp. 3–4; Reid, *In a Defiant Stance*, pp. 27–40. Fragmentary evidence also suggests that prosecutions for contempt of authority, not simply prosecutions for seditious libel, became more difficult to obtain by the middle of the eighteenth century than they had been in the seventeenth. Data from Middlesex County, for example, show a considerable decline; although such raw figures must be used cautiously, they are still suggestive. See Michael Stephen Hindus, "The Contours of Crime and Justice in Massachusetts and South Carolina, 1767–1878," *AJLH* 21 (1977): 217–37, at 217.

46. See, e.g., *An Answer to the Pamphlet Entitled the Conduct of the Paxton Men* (Philadelphia, 1764).

47. *An Answer to the Plot* (Philadelphia, 1764); see, generally, Nash, *Urban Crucible*, pp. 262–90.

48. In 1770, for example, some residents of Annapolis tried to revive the old style of elite debate by forming a "Harmony Club." This effort quickly fell victim to the passions swirling through Maryland politics. Breslau, "Wit, Whimsy, and Politics," pp. 305–6. For New York examples, see Countryman, *A People in Revolution*, pp. 1–98, and for urban politics in a number of different areas see Nash, *Urban Crucible*.

49. See, generally, Bernard Bailyn, *The Ordeal of Thomas Hutchinson* (Cambridge, Mass., 1974), pp. 60–61, 198–99.

50. Quoted in Hiller B. Zobel, *The Boston Massacre* (New York, 1970), pp. 109–10.

51. Quoted in Quincy, ed., *Reports*, pp. 266–67.

52. Quoted in "Additions to Thomas Hutchinson's *History of Massachusetts*," ed. Catherine Barton Mayo, *AASP* 59 (n.s., 1949): 47.

53. *Boston Evening Post*, 1 Dec. 1766, by "Philanthrops." See also, ibid., 19 May 1766, by "A Merchant."

54. Ibid., 1 Dec. 1766.

55. Ibid., 15 Dec. 1767.

56. Ibid., 5 Jan. 1767.

57. *Boston Gazette*, 29 Dec. 1766.

58. *Boston Evening Post*, 14 Oct. 1765.

59. See, e.g., *Boston Gazette*, 29 Dec. 1766.

60. *Boston Evening Post*, 14 Oct. 1765.

61. *Boston Gazette*, 11 Sept. 1769.

62. *Boston Evening Post*, 14 Oct. 1765.

63. See Thomas C. Leonard, "News for a Revolution: The Exposé in America, 1768–1773," *JAH* 67 (1980): 26–40.

64. Here, the line of argument follows the suggestive comments of Alvin Gouldner, *The Dialectic of Ideology and Technology*, pp. 96–99.

65. *New York Gazette*, 19 March 1770, reprinted in *Zenger to Jefferson*, ed. Levy, p. 113.

66. *Boston Evening Post*, 30 March 1767.

67. The literature is large. The preceding paragraphs draw upon Levy, *Legacy of Suppression*, pp. 176–88; Wallace Brown, *The King's Friends* (Providence, R.I., 1965); Robert M. Calhoon, *The Loyalists in Revolutionary America, 1760–1781* (New York, 1973); Richard Buel, *Dear Liberty: Connecticut's Mobilization for the Revolutionary War* (Middletown, Conn., 1980); Stephen Botein, "Printers and the American Revolution," in *The Press & the American Revolution*, ed. Bernard Bailyn and John B. Hench (Worcester, Mass., 1980), pp. 11–57; Janice Potter and Robert M. Calhoon, "The Character and Coherence of the Loyalist Press," in ibid., pp. 229–72; and Richard Buel, Jr., "Freedom of the Press in Revolutionary America: The Evolution of Libertarianism, 1760–1820," in ibid., pp. 59–98, at 59–82. See also Greenawalt, "Speech and Crime," pp. 689–90.

68. Quoted in Sidney Pomerantz, "The Patriot Newspaper and the American Revolution," in *The Era of the American Revolution*, ed. Richard B. Morris (New York, 1939), p. 331.

69. Quoted in Pomerantz, ibid.

70. Quoted in Lyman Butterfield, ed., *The Letters of Benjamin Rush*, 2 vols. (Philadelphia, 1951), 1:236 n. 2.

71. John Adams, *The Works of John Adams*, ed. Charles Francis Adams, 10 vols. (Boston, 1850–56), 7:182.

72. For a suggestive analysis, see Brewer, *Party Ideology and Popular Politics*, pp. 139–200, 219–39 and Brewer's "The Wilkites and the Law, 1763–74: A Study of Radical Notions of Governance," in *An Ungovernable People: The English and Their Law in the Seventeenth and Eighteenth Centuries*, ed. John Brewer and John Styles (New Brunswick, N.J., 1980), pp. 128–71; and Countryman, *A People in Revolution*.

73. See Robert Cover, "The Supreme Court 1982 Term, Foreward: *Nomos* and Narrative," *HLR* 97 (1983): 4–68, at 43; and Robert W. Gordon, "Historicism in Legal Scholarship," *YLJ* 90 (1981): 1017–56, esp. 1022–23.

74. Levy, *Emergence of a Free Press*, p. xii.

CHAPTER THREE

1. See, e.g., the newspaper complaints collected in Merrill Jensen and Robert A. Bender, eds., *The Documentary History of the First Federal Elections, 1788–1790*, 1 vol. to date (Madison, Wis., 1976–), 1:459, 539, 685, 720.

2. The most energetic theorist of the access issue has been law professor Jerome

288 | Notes to Pages 57–61

Barron. See, *Freedom of the Press for Whom?* (Bloomington, Ind., 1973). There is no adequate historical treatment of the issue. The general discussion in Bruce Owen, *Economics and Freedom of Expression* (Cambridge, Mass., 1975), pp. 33–44 displays too much nostalgia for the days of easy access to the public media. The quote is from Owen's book, p. 44. For a refutation of this view, see both the primary documents and editorial commentary on the access question in late eighteenth-century Boston and Philadelphia in John P. Kaminski and Gaspare J. Saladino, eds., *Commentaries on the Constitution: Public and Private, Volume I, 21 February to 7 November 1787* (Madison, Wis., 1981), pp. 312–23, 573–81. See also the views of a Massachusetts farmer, William Manning, quoted in Samuel Eliot Morison, ed., "William Manning's Key of Liberty," *WMQ* 13 (1956): 202–54, at 232, 249–50.

3. William F. Steirer, Jr., "A Study in Prudence: Philadelphia's 'Revolutionary' Journalists," *JH* 3 (1976): 16–19; Van Beck Hall, *Politics Without Parties: Massachusetts, 1780–1792* (Pittsburgh, 1972), pp. 81–83; Benjamin Rush, *The Letters of Benjamin Rush*, ed. Lyman Butterfield, 2 vols. (Philadelphia, 1951), 1:460 (Rush to Jeremy Belknap, 6 May 1788); Jensen and Bender, eds., *Documentary History*, 1:102 (William Bingham to Tench Coxe, 25 Aug. 1788).

4. Herbert J. Storing, ed., *The Complete Anti-Federalist*, 7 vols. (Chicago, 1981), 3:132.

5. Chandler Robbins, *A Sermon Preached before His Excellency John Hancock* . . . (Boston, 1791), pp. 35–36; see also, Timothy Dwight, *Virtuous Rulers a National Blessing* (Hartford, 1791), pp. 28–29, and *Candid Considerations on Libels* . . . *With Some Observations on the Liberty of the Press* (Boston, 1791).

6. Jensen and Bender, eds., *Documentary History*, 1:180.

7. Ibid., 1:467.

8. Benjamin Franklin, "An Account of the Supremest Court of Judicature of the State of Pennsylvania, VIZ. The Court of the Press," reprinted in *Freedom of the Press from Zenger to Jefferson*, ed. Leonard W. Levy (Indianapolis, Ind., 1966), pp. 154–58, at 155.

9. Jensen and Bender, eds., *Documentary History*, 1:354.

10. Ibid., p. 359.

11. Hall, *Politics Without Parties*, pp. 83–85. For an analysis of the issues at stake in the political battles of the 1780s, see Jackson Turner Main, *Political Parties Before the Constitution* (Chapel Hill, N.C., 1973). On the importance of character and virtue in the political discourse of the late eighteenth century, see Garry Wills, *Cincinnatus: George Washington and the American Enlightenment* (Garden City, N.Y., 1984), pp. 99–132, and Andrew Fraser, "Legal Amnesia: Modernism Versus the Republican Tradition in American Legal Thought," *Telos* 60 (1983): 15–52, at 22–23.

12. This account of Oswald's troubles relies upon Dwight L. Teeter, "The Printer and the Chief Justice: Seditious Libel in 1782–83," *JQ* 45 (1968): 235–42, 260, and G. S. Rowe, *Thomas McKean: The Shaping of an American Republicanism* (Boulder, Colo., 1978), pp. 184–87.

13. "Hitherto Unpublished Correspondence Between Chief Justice Cushing and John Adams in 1789," *MLQ* 27 (1922): 12–16, reprinted in *Zenger to Jefferson*, ed. Levy, pp. 147–53; Hamilton quoted in Jacob Cooke, ed., *The Federalist* (Middletown, Conn., 1961), p. 580.

14. The clauses in the Pennsylvania Constitution of 1776 on freedom of press are discussed in David A. Anderson, "The Origins of the Press Clause," *UCLALR* 30 (1980): 455–541, 465–66.

15. Franklin, "An Account," in *Zenger to Jefferson*, ed. Levy, pp. 157–58.

16. Respublica v. Oswald, 1 Dall. 319, 319–23 (Pa., 1788).

17. Ibid., pp. 324–25.

18. Ibid., p. 325.

19. Ibid., pp. 326, 329.

20. Ibid., pp. 330–32 n.

21. Ibid., pp. 335–36 n. The resolution for impeachment failed. See ibid., pp. 336–37 n. See also Rowe, *Thomas McKean*, pp. 254–56.

22. *The Proceedings Relative to Calling the [Pennsylvania Constitutional] Conventions of 1776 and 1790* (Harrisburg, Pa., 1825), pp. 277–79. (Hereafter cited as *Proceedings*.)

23. Pennsylvania Constitution of 1790, Art. IX, Sec. 7, 11.

24. See McKean's interpretation of the clause in Respublica v. Cobbett, Nov. 1797, in Francis Wharton, ed., *State Trials of the United States During the Administrations of Washington and Adams* (Philadelphia, 1849; reprint, New York, 1970), pp. 322–32. The clause protecting reputation was in Art. IX, Sec. 11.

25. James Wilson, *The Works of James Wilson*, ed. Robert G. McCloskey, 2 vols. (Cambridge, Mass., 1966), 2:650.

26. Ibid., pp. 593–94.

27. Ibid., pp. 651–52.

28. Ibid., p. 650.

29. Ibid., p. 593.

30. "Hitherto Unpublished Correspondence," in *Zenger to Jefferson*, ed. Levy, p. 151.

31. Ibid., p. 153.

32. Several publications in Boston carried reports of the Freeman trial. The judges' charges appear in *Massachusetts Magazine* (March–May 1791), but the most complete report is in the *Independent Chronicle* (24 Feb.–27 March 1791).

33. James Wilson's defense of the absence of any free-speech or free-press guarantee came in a public speech on 6 October 1787, reprinted on 9 October in the *Pennsylvania Herald*. See Merrill Jensen, ed., *Documentary History of the Ratification of the Constitution*, 2 vols. to date (Madison, Wis., 1976–), 2:167–72, at 168. The fears of "An Old Whig" are reprinted in Storing, ed., *Complete Anti-Federalist*, 3:21.

34. William Findley, *Address from an Officer in the Late Continental Army* (Philadelphia, 1787), p. 2, reprinted in Storing, ed., *Complete Anti-Federalist*, 3:92ff.

35. Storing, ed., *Complete Anti-Federalist*, 3:59.

36. Bernard Schwartz, ed., *The Bill of Rights: A Documentary History*, 2 vols. (New York, 1971), p. 734; Storing, ed., *Complete Anti-Federalist*, 4:121; ibid., 2:330. See also "Cincinnatus I: To James Wilson, Esquire," in *Commentaries on the Constitution*, ed. Kaminski and Saladino, pp. 529–34, at 531–33. Most attribute this Cincinnatus essay to Richard Henry Lee, and the views on libel law in this piece do parallel very closely those contained in Lee's letter to Samuel Adams in October of 1787. See ibid., pp. 323–24, at 324.

37. See Chapter 4, at pp. 72–74.

38. Emphasis added. Linda Grant DePauw, ed., *Documentary History of the First Federal Congress of the United States: Senate Legislative Journal*, 3 vols. (Baltimore, 1972–77), 1:152 (3 September 1789). Anderson, "The Press Clause," pp. 475–85 discusses the legislative history of what would become the First Amendment. (In truth, the "first" amendment was submitted to the states for ratification as the third of twelve proposed amendments.)

39. On the absolutist views of Black and Douglas, see Chapter 10, at pp. 248–50.

40. See Kent Greenawalt, "Speech and Crime," *ABFRJ* (1980): 645–785.

41. *Proceedings*, p. 383.

42. These two paragraphs, of course, hardly begin to survey all of the various theories of the original understanding of the First Amendment. See, e.g., Leonard Levy's hypothesis in "Liberty and the First Amendment: 1790–1800," *AHR* 68 (1962): 22–37. Here, Levy argues, as did southerners like John C. Calhoun in the nineteenth century, that the First Amendment prohibited all legislation by Congress and left statutory regulation of expression to the states. See Calhoun's views in "Report from the Select Committee on the Circulation of Incendiary Publications" (1836), in *The Papers of John C. Calhoun*, ed. W. Edwin Hemphill et al., 15 vols. to date (Columbia, S.C., 1959–), 13:53–66, esp. 55. But, in contrast to state-rights theorists like Calhoun, Levy also argues that the First Amendment was unclear about the validity of common law prosecutions for libel in federal courts. Levy, *Emergence of a Free Press* (New York, 1985), pp. 274–79. (See, e.g., the 1797 common law libel prosecution against Samuel J. Cabell, discussed in Levy, *Emergence of a Free Press*, pp. 276–77, 300.)

In a fascinatingly original article, William Mayton argues that the founding fathers wanted to deny the national government any power to prosecute critics of government. William T. Mayton, "Seditious Libel and the Lost Guarantee of a Freedom of Expression," *ColLR* 84 (1984): 91–142. But Mayton argues that the place to find their original understanding is not in the First Amendment, but in the structure of the Constitution itself—in its "uniquely American components, federalism and a central government of limited powers" (ibid., p. 97). He asserts that a broad "understanding was reached at the convention and during the ratification process that the national government had no power over speech" (ibid., p. 118). The Blackstonian view of the First Amendment, Mayton contends, was nothing more than "a piece of post hoc grafting," used by Federalists to justify the Sedition Act of 1798 (ibid., p. 126). Although offering some new insights, Mayton overstates his case, one bolstered by fairly insubstantial evidence. He cites, for example, Madison's 1800 "Report" against the Sedition Act as authoritative evidence of the original understanding of 1787–89, even though other founding fathers, such as Hamilton and Washington, drew very different conclusions. More important, I think, ideas about law and free speech and press changed during the 1790s, a point that interpreters who easily link the Sedition Act debates with earlier events tend to ignore. See, e.g., Michael Perry, *The Constitution, the Courts and Human Rights* (New Haven, Conn., 1982), pp. 63–64, 196 n. 32.

The most fundamental flaw, I believe, in the arguments of writers such as Mayton is their desire to find one clear, one unmistakable original understanding from the founding fathers. Even as perceptive an analyst as David Anderson can fall into this trap. Thus, one can agree with Anderson that "the generation that wrote the Declaration of

Independence, the Constitution, and the Bill of Rights" considered freedom of the press as "a necessary restraint on what the patriots viewed as government's natural tendency toward tyranny and despotism." Anderson, "The Press Clause," p. 533. But the evidence also shows that members of this same generation, including those who would have agreed with Anderson's statement, *also* feared the harmful impact of a licentious press upon good rulers; even though many rejected Blackstonian orthodoxy, they also accepted the necessity for some types of legal controls over publications that corrupted the wellsprings of republicanism. In short, eighteenth-century Americans who thought deeply about the place of the press were mindful of *both* its virtues and its vices, and believed that legal doctrines needed to deal with both.

Finally, the controversy over the original understanding of the First Amendment (or the Constitution itself) inevitably merges with the broader debate over interpretivist versus noninterpretivist approaches to constitutional adjudication. See generally, Perry, *The Constitution, The Courts*. My own views on all these issues have been informed by anti-interpretivists like Paul Brest and Mark Tushnet. See Paul Brest, "The Misconceived Quest for Original Understanding," *BULR* 60 (1980): 204–38, and Mark Tushnet, "Following the Rules Laid Down: A Critique of Interpretivism and Neutral Principles," *HLR* 96 (1983): 781–823. Leonard Levy's position now seems more ambivalent toward one clear, original meaning for the First Amendment. *Emergence of a Free Press*, pp. 266–81, esp. pp. 268, 281.

43. William Cobbett, *The Democratic Judge* (Philadelphia, 1798), p. 51; *Baltimore American* quoted in Donald Stewart, *The Opposition Press of the Federalist Period* (Albany, N.Y., 1969), p. 30; *Aurora*, 4 Oct. 1790.

44. Harold Syrett et al., eds., *The Papers of Alexander Hamilton*, 26 vols. (New York, 1961–79), 12:308 n. 5.

45. Hamilton to George Washington, 1 Sept. 1792, in ibid., 12:312 ("indictable offense"); and Hamilton to John Jay, 3 Sept. 1792, in ibid., 12:316 ("contradiction in terms").

46. Randolph to Hamilton, 8 Sept. 1792, in ibid., 12:337.

47. Ibid.

48. A copy of the remonstrance is reprinted in ibid., 16:259–60 n. 1.

49. Randolph to Alexander Hamilton, Henry Knox, and William Bradford, 14 April 1794, ibid., 16:259.

50. Ibid., 16:259, 260 n. 2.

51. Ibid., 16:260 n. 2.

52. See 4 *Annals of Congress* 901–2 (1794) (William Smith); ibid., pp. 935–37 (Samuel Dexter); ibid., pp. 923–27 (Fisher Ames).

53. Philip Foner, ed., *The Democratic-Republican Societies: 1790–1800: A Documentary Source Book* (Westport, Conn., 1976), pp. 96, 99–100, 194. The role of these societies in developing and spreading free-speech arguments needs more study, as does their role in creating new channels for popular political expression and participation.

54. 4 *Annals of Congress* 937 (1794) (Murray and Dexter); ibid., pp. 926–27 (Ames).

55. E. F. Hall et al., eds., *Official Opinions of the Attorneys-General of the United States*, 40 vols. (Washington, D.C., 1752–1949), 1:52–53. This case, of course, was

precisely the kind that "A Democratic Federalist" had predicted in 1787. See also, Daniel Hoffman, "Contempt of the United States: the Political Crime That Wasn't," *AJLH* 25 (1981): 343–60, at 346–48.

56. Julius Goebel, Jr., *History of the Supreme Court of the United States: Antecedents and Beginnings to 1801* (New York, 1971), p. 629. In 1797, however, national authorities again prosecuted Greenleaf for allegedly libeling a British official, Sir John Temple. This time, they carried the indictment through to a successful prosecution. Ibid.

57. See James Lloyd, *Address of General James Lloyd to the Citizens of Kent and Queen-Anne's Counties in Answer to the late Calumnious Charge Made Against Him by Robert Wright* (Annapolis, Md., 1794). Although Lloyd considered the charges against him libelous and "an attempt to subvert the laws of our country" (ibid., p. 37), he used this pamphlet, rather than the law courts, to redress the injuries to his reputation and the larger public interest. Four years later, he would take another tack and introduce the Sedition Act. See Chapter 4, p. 81. For a similar example of using a pamphlet to reply to calumnies, see Matthew Carey, *Address of Matthew Carey to the Public* (Philadelphia, 1794).

58. Addison's charges were printed in Alexander Addison, *Reports of Cases in the County Courts of the Fifth Circuit, and in the High Court of Errors and Appeals of the State of Pennsylvania, and Charges to Grand Juries of those County Courts* (Washington, Pa., 1800; reprint, Philadelphia, 1883), pp. 373 ff. (Hereafter cited as *Addison Reports*.) See also, Norman L. Rosenberg, "Alexander Addison and the Origins of Federalist First-Amendment Thought," *PMHB* 108 (1984): 399–417.

59. *Addison Reports*, pp. 401, 469, 493, 533.

60. Addison's defense of the Sedition Act, originally a grand jury charge, was published in many pamphlet editions. See, e.g., Alexander Addison, *Liberty of Speech and of the Press* (Washington, Pa., 1798). See also, John Jay, *Charge of Chief Justice Jay to the Grand Jury on the Eastern Circuit* (Portsmouth, N.H., 1790), pp. 73–74.

61. G. J. McRee, *Life and Correspondence of James Iredell*, 2 vols. (New York, 1857–58), 2:485; ibid., 2:510; ibid., 2:505; ibid., 2:511–13.

62. Ibid., 2:507, 509.

63. Ibid., pp. 511–13, 560–61.

64. Cobbett, *Democratic Judge*, pp. 44–45; 84–86.

65. Ibid., p. 86.

66. Ibid., pp. 81–82.

67 Ibid., p. 87. The vote went along party lines: nine Jeffersonians voted for indictment and ten Federalists against. See George Spater, *William Cobbett: The Poor Man's Friend*, 2 vols. (New York, 1982), 1:99.

68. In *Securing the Revolution* (Ithaca N.Y., 1972), Richard Buel devotes considerable attention to debates during the 1790s over free speech, and he restates his praise for Jeffersonian libertarianism in an essay entitled "Freedom of the Press in Revolutionary America: The Evolution of Libertarianism, 1760–1820," in *The Press & the American Revolution*, ed. Bernard Bailyn and John B. Hench (Worcester, Mass., 1980), pp. 59–97. His work is invaluable in linking the Sedition Act and the libel prosecutions of 1798 to 1800 to something other than a sudden Federalist decision. But Buel's argument that Federalists feared public opinion (because they had lost

touch with it), while Jeffersonians embraced it, simplifies the issues too much. See, e.g., Richard Ellis's critique in "The Impact of the Revolution on Politics in the 1790s," *RIAH* 1 (1973): 504–7, at 506–7. As I argue in Chapters 4 and 5, leaders of both parties expressed doubts that republicanism could flourish in a political culture where partisans tried to corrupt political debate. Though Jeffersonian leaders identified different sources of corruption than Federalists, and though most proposed different means of redress, a majority of those who espoused the Jeffersonian position did not advocate an unregulated marketplace for political ideas.

CHAPTER FOUR

1. Alexander Hamilton, *The Papers of Alexander Hamilton*, ed. Harold Syrett et al., 26 vols. (New York, 1961–79), 21:238–39.

2. Syrett, ed., *Hamilton Papers*, 24:5–6 (Hamilton to Josiah Hoffman, 6 Nov. 1799). For an account of the trial, see Francis Wharton, ed., *State Trials of the United States During the Administrations of Washington and Adams* (Philadelphia 1849; reprint, New York, 1970), pp. 649–51. Although Hamilton was a witness for the prosecution and urged the court to permit the defendant, David Frothingham, a journeyman printer in the shop of the *Advertiser*, to introduce evidence of the truth, the trial proceeded to a conviction under traditional, Orthodox Whig doctrines. The court imposed a stiff sentence, including four months in jail, on the unlucky printer.

3. Abraham Bishop, *Connecticut Republicanism: An Oration on the Extent and Power of Political Delusion* (New Haven, 1800), pp. iv, 30, 33, 35, 51, 54, 58. See also Samuel Eliot Morison, ed., "William Manning's Key of Liberty," *WMQ* 13 (1956): 202–54, at 232.

4. See Chapter 3, pp. 76–77.

5. James Morton Smith, *Freedom's Fetters: The Alien and Sedition Laws and American Civil Liberties* (Ithaca, N.Y., 1956; reprint, Ithaca, N.Y., 1966), pp. 94–155 contains an extensive discussion of the framing of the act.

6. Leonard Levy, "Liberty and the First Amendment: 1790–1800," *AHR* 68 (1962): 22–37 and Levy, *Emergence of a Free Press* (New York, 1985), pp. 298–301 explain why the Federalist majority decided to pass a statute rather than to rely upon prosecutions under common law. As Levy notes, British authorities followed a similar course during the 1790s. Fox's Libel Act of 1792, which allowed juries to return general verdicts but did not authorize defendants to plead truth as a defense, was followed by a rash of prosecutions.

When the Sedition Act first passed the United States Senate, it included no provision for admitting truth as a defense; this section of the law was added in the House. 8 *Annals of Congress*, 2133–34 (1798). The section authorizing juries to determine both the law and the facts originated with a Jeffersonian congressman but was ultimately accepted by the Federalist majority. Ibid., pp. 2135–38. In its final version, the Sedition Act, on its face at least, included the Zengerian guarantees only for prosecutions involving published defamation, even though the act supposedly covered spoken as well as written statements. See 1 *U.S. Statutes at Large*, Chap. 75, pp. 596–97.

7. [Charles Lee], *Defence of the Alien and Sedition Laws* (Philadelphia, 1798),

294 | Notes to Pages 82–87

p. 21; [Thomas Evans], *An Address to the People of Virginia, respecting the Alien and Sedition Laws* (Richmond, 1798), p. 49. For a modern assessment that makes essentially the same argument, see Richard Kohn, *Eagle and Sword* (New York, 1975), esp. p. 212. See also William Winslow Crosskey, *Politics and the Constitution*, 3 vols. (Chicago, 1953–80), 2:767–78.

8. 10 *Annals of Congress* 410 (1800). Bayard added "that upon any prosecution it shall be lawful for the defendant to give in his defence the truth of the matters charged as a libel." Ibid. Bayard's proviso, of course, forced Jeffersonians to go on record as opposing the Zengerian principles, if they voted down his motion. Bayard's move, a clever response to a motion by Nathaniel Macon to repeal the Sedition Act before its natural expiration date, actually won approval by a 50–48 margin. But then many Jeffersonians turned around and got themselves out of an embarrassing bind by voting down Macon's amended motion. Ibid., at pp. 409, 410, 419, 423–25. Had they repealed the Sedition Act, Jeffersonians would have been forced, because of Bayard's ploy, to validate common law prosecutions and in effect to accept the Federalist position that the Sedition Act was simply a measure declaratory of the common law. On this last point, see, e.g., Robert Goodloe Harper's justification in *Circular Letters of Congressmen to their Constituents, 1789–1829*, ed. Noble Cunningham, 3 vols. (Chapel Hill, N.C., 1978), 1:168, 238.

9. See, e.g., Henry Lee to James Iredell (21 Jan. 1795), in G. J. McRee, *Life and Correspondence of James Iredell*, 2 vols. (New York, 1857–58), 2:435–36; Governor Samuel Johnston of North Carolina to Iredell (10 May 1792), in ibid., 2:356; and Paul Allen, *Oration* (1796), pp. 6, 13.

10. [Henry Lee], "A Citizen of Westmoreland County," *Plain Truth* (Richmond, Va., 1799), p. 24; *Address to the Federal Republicans of the State of New-Jersey . . .* (Trenton, 1800), p. 11.

11. *Virginia Report of 1799–1800 . . .* (Richmond, 1850), pp. 132, 134.

12. "Grand Jury Charge at Philadelphia, April 1799," in McRee, ed., *Life and Correspondence of Iredell*, 2:565. 10 *Annals of Congress* 410 (1800).

13. See Norman L. Rosenberg, "Alexander Addison and the Pennsylvania Origins of Federalist First-Amendment Thought," *PMHB* 108 (1984):399–417, and Gordon S. Wood, "Conspiracy and the Paranoid Style: Causality and Deceit in the Eighteenth Century," *WMQ* 39 (1982):401–41.

14. Addison, "The Constitution as a Security of Liberty," in *Addison Reports*, p. 526; McRee, ed., *Life and Correspondence of Iredell*, 2:524.

15. McRee, ed., *Life and Correspondence of Iredell*, 2:564.

16. *Addison Reports*, p. 589.

17. *Virginia Report*, p. 135.

18. 10 *Annals of Congress* 955–56 (1801).

19. Ibid., pp. 924–26 (Dana); ibid., pp. 407–9 (Bayard); ibid., p. 947 (Bayard).

20. Addison, *Liberty of Speech and of the Press* (Washington, Pa., 1798), p. 20.

21. 1 *U.S. Statutes at Large*, Chap. 75, p. 596.

22. 8 *Annals of Congress* 2168 (1798).

23. Addison, *Liberty of Speech and Press*, p. 25; Iredell, "Charge to the Grand Jury," in *State Trials*, ed. Wharton, p. 479; Chase, ibid., pp. 712–13. In the trial of Thomas Cooper, Chase offered a different standard, charging the jury that Cooper

should be acquitted if he proved the truth *or* if he could show that he had published libelous falsehoods without any malicious intent. Chase quickly negated any value of this interpretation for Cooper by further charging jurors that the burden of proof was on the defendant and that he had failed to satisfy it. Ibid., pp. 670–77.

24. Quoted in James Morton Smith, "The Grass Roots Origins of the Kentucky Resolutions," *WMQ* 27 (1970): 221–45, at 231. Federalists, in turn, argued that popular opinion supported the Sedition Act. The law "has received the highest and most repeated proofs of approbation on the part of the American nation," claimed Robert Goodloe Harper in January of 1801. 10 *Annals of Congress* 939 (1801).

25. Smith, *Freedom's Fetters*, pp. 159–217 contains the best account of the act's enforcement.

26. On the Adams prosecution, see ibid., pp. 247–57; on the Frothingham trial, ibid., pp. 398–415 and Wharton, ed., *State Trials*, pp. 649–51.

27. On Adams's alleged eating habits, see ibid., p. 335; on Callender, see ibid., pp. 688–718. As a contemporary First-Amendment scholar, Frederick F. Schauer, has observed, nearly every political communication includes "some element of opinion, belief or interpretation." Viewed on a continuum, with reports of "direct observation of physical objects" at the "factual" end and purely "normative" judgments at the other, in between "these extremes lie statements reflecting varying degrees of inference, synthesis, and value judgment, the presence of each making the process of verification somewhat less certain." Frederick F. Schauer, "Language, Truth, and the First Amendment: An Essay in Memory of Harry Cantor," *VaLR* 64 (1978): 263–302, at 279. Professor Schauer argues, therefore, that the distinction between beliefs and facts can unduly limit the free and creative use of language and of human communication. One person's false fact—"Barry Goldwater talks like a Fascist" or "John Adams eats like George III"—is another's creative use of words and imagery. Ibid., pp. 300–301. Between 1798 and 1800, some Jeffersonians made the similar point. See, e.g., Albert Gallatin in 8 *Annals of Congress* 2162 (1798). Not every student of language and political rhetoric—including people as diverse as Alexander Addison and Harold Lasswell—would agree. See, e.g., Addison's views in *Addison Reports*, pp. 588–89 and Lasswell's testimony in the trial of the American Nazi, William Dudley Pelley in U.S. v. Pelley 132 F.2d 170, 176 (7 Circ., 1942), cert. denied 318 U.S. 764 (1943).

28. Wharton, ed., *State Trials*, pp. 670–77. Justice Chase's view of the rules of evidence and pleading are considered correct by Julius Goebel, Jr., *The Supreme Court: Antecedents and Beginnings to 1801* (New York, 1971), pp. 640–45 and criticized in Stephen B. Presser, "A Tale of Two Judges: Richard Peters, Samuel Chase, and the Broken Promise of Federalist Jurisprudence," *NWULR* 73 (1978): 26–111, at 97, 97 n. 311.

29. For Chambers's definition, see "Politics in the Early American Republic," *RIAH* 1 (1973): 499–503. Most accounts portray the Callender trial, during which the defendant's attorneys walked out in exasperation, as a classic example of judicial bias against a defendant and in favor of the state. Although Chase's conduct was hardly exemplary, George Hay and his fellow Jeffersonian defense attorneys found themselves in an uncomfortable position when they agreed to represent the unreliable and unpredictable Callender. See, e.g., Hay's testimony at the subsequent impeachment trial of Chase. *Trial of Samuel Chase, An Associate Justice of the Supreme Court of the*

United States, 2 vols. (Washington, D.C., 1805; reprint, New York, 1970), 1:168–79. As Hay conceded, the defense team intended to "render a service, not to the man, but to the cause. . . ." Ibid., p. 169. John P. Kennedy, the nineteenth-century biographer of another member of Callender's defense contingent, strongly hints that the attorneys deliberately baited the easily irascible Chase; anticipated his explosive response; and planned from the outset to walk out of the courtroom and leave Callender to his fate. See John P. Kennedy, *Memoirs of the Life of William Wirt*, 2 vols. (New York, 1849; reprint, New York, 1973), 1:81–84.

30. See, generally, Lance Banning, *The Jeffersonian Persuasion: Evolution of a Party Ideology* (Ithaca, N.Y., 1978).

31. "Minority Report on Repeal of the Sedition Act," 9 *Annals of Congress* 3005 (1799).

32. The relevant works include George Hay's two tracts. The first was published in Philadelphia in 1799 under the title *An Essay on the Liberty of the Press* (Philadelphia, 1799). It was republished in Richmond, four years later, along with a second essay entitled *An Essay on the Liberty of the Press, Shewing that the Requisition of Security for Good Behavior from Libellers is Perfectly Compatible with the Constitution and Laws of Virginia* (Richmond, 1803). Both tracts have been published in a modern reprint, *Two Essays on the Liberty of the Press* (New York, 1970). The other tracts of the Jeffersonian libertarians include Tunis Wortman, *A Treatise Concerning Political Inquiry and the Liberty of the Press* (New York, 1800; reprint, New York, 1970); John Thomson, *An Enquiry Concerning the Liberty and Licentiousness of the Press, and the Uncontroulable Nature of the Human Mind* (New York, 1800; reprint, New York, 1970); James Madison, "Report on the Virginia Resolutions," *The Debates in Several State Conventions on the Adoption of the Federal Constitution . . . and Other Illustrations of the Constitution*, ed. Jonathan Eliot, 5 vols. 2nd ed. (Philadelphia, 1941), 4:547–80; St. George Tucker, *Blackstone's Commentaries: With Notes of Reference, to the Constitution and Laws, of the Federal Government of the United States; and of the Commonwealth of Virginia*, 5 vols. (Philadelphia, 1803). For Leonard Levy's evaluation of these writings, which differs from mine in several respects, see *Emergence of a Free Press*, pp. 303–37.

33. 8 *Annals of Congress* 2140 (1798) (Nicholas); Thomson, *An Enquiry*, p. 7; Hay, *An Essay* (1799), pp. 27–28; Madison, "Report," p. 575; 8 *Annals of Congress* 2162 (1799) (Gallatin).

34. The characterization of Wortman's book is from Leonard Levy, *Freedom of Speech and Press in Early American History: Legacy of Suppression* (Cambridge, Mass., 1960; reprint, New York, 1963), p. 283. The quoted portions are from Wortman, *A Treatise*, p. 253 ("coercion of violence is sufficient"); pp. 172–73 ("imprisoned for credulity"); p. 257 ("more formidable than the evil").

35. Hay, *An Essay* (1799), p. 25.

36. See, e.g., the claims of C. C. Claiborne, 8 *Annals of Congress* 2135 (1798); and John Nicholas, 9 *Annals of Congress* 3009 (1799).

37. James Alexander, *A Brief Narrative of the Case and Trial of John Peter Zenger, Printer of the New York Weekly Journal*, ed. Stanley Nider Katz (Cambridge, Mass., 1963), p. 84.

38. See Chapter 3, pp. 60–64. Oswald is quoted by Robert Allen Rutland, *The*

Ordeal of the Constitution (Norman, Okla., 1966), p. 267; and see Smith, "Grass Roots Origins," pp. 226–27, 230–31.

39. Wortman, *A Treatise*, p. 156.

40. Ibid., pp. 245–47; quote at 261.

41. Ibid., p. 176.

42. Ibid., p. 260. See also, Hay, *An Essay* (1799), p. 23; and Madison, "Report," p. 573.

43. Tucker, ed., *Blackstone*, 1: Note G, "Of the Right of Conscience, and of the Freedom of Speech and of the Press,'' p. 30.

44. Ibid.; Hay, *An Essay* (1799), p. 23; Madison, "Report," p. 573. Hay applied the same doctrine to the press, *An Essay* (1799), p. 23. For the case law in Virginia, see Commonwealth v. Morris, 1 Va. Cas. 176 (1811).

45. Wortman, *A Treatise*, pp. 259–60; see also, ibid., pp. 150–51, 169, 257. Wortman's book was reviewed critically by the young Daniel Webster in 1806; see Daniel Webster, *The Writings and Speeches of Daniel Webster*, ed. J. W. McIntyre, 18 vols. (Boston, 1903), 15:548–51. On the *Croswell* case, see Chapter 5, pp. 109–14.

46. Wortman, *A Treatise*, p. 259. "The character of every man should be deemed equally sacred," he argued, "and of consequence entitled to equal remedy." Ibid. The proposition that legal remedies should be the same for public and private persons was rejected by nineteenth-century libertarians such as Thomas Cooley. See Chapter 7, pp. 161–73.

47. William Cobbett, *The Democratic Judge* (Philadelphia, 1798); and *A Report for An Action for Libel, Brought by Dr. Benjamin Rush, against William Cobbett* (Philadelphia, 1800).

48. See Respublica v. Cobbett, 2 Yeates 352 (Pa. Sup. Ct., 1798); Respublica v. Davis, 3 Yeates 128 (Pa. Sup. Ct., 1801); Respublica v. Cobbett, 3 Yeates 93 (Pa. Sup. Ct., 1800). For the arguments of the prosecutor and defense counsel, see 3 Yeates 93, 97–100.

49. Respublica v. Cobbett, 3 Yeates 93, 100–101 (Pa. Sup. Ct., 1800). As early as 1792, the Pennsylvania Supreme Court, per Chief Justice McKean, had upheld the use of good behavior bonds in libel cases. See Respublica v. Agnew, 1 Yeates 186 (Pa. Sup. Ct., 1792).

50. [James Sullivan], *A Dissertation upon the Constitutional Freedom of the Press in the United States of America* (Boston, 1801), pp. 13, 18–19, 21, 47 (emphasis added). Sullivan was both a moderate, centrist Jeffersonian and a strong critic of partisan politics. See Ronald P. Formisano, *The Transformation of Political Culture: Massachusetts Parties, 1790s–1840s* (New York, 1983), pp. 68–72.

51. John Page, *An Address to the Citizens . . .* (Richmond, 1798), pp. 17–18, 37.

52. See Chapter 6, pp. 145–52.

53. Tucker, ed., *Blackstone*, 1: Note G, p. 30.

54. Thomson, *An Enquiry*, pp. 12, 15, 76–77, 82.

55. Ibid., pp. 83, 84.

56. Ibid.

57. Ibid., pp. 80–81, 82.

58. Ibid., p. 84.

59. [Charles Lee], *Defence of the Alien and Sedition Laws* (Philadelphia, 1798),

pp. 14, 21, 23. See also, David Daggett, *Sunbeams May be Extracted from Cucumbers, but the Process is Tedious* (New Haven, Conn., 1799), pp. 24–25, 27; [Henry Lee], *Plain Truth*, p. 29.

60. Richard Ellis, *The Jeffersonian Crisis: Courts and Politics in the Young Republic* (New York, 1971).

61. Potter Stewart, "Or of the Press," *HLJ* 26 (1975): 631–37, and Melville B. Nimmer, "Is Freedom of the Press a Redundancy: What Does It Add to Freedom of Speech?" ibid., pp. 639–58.

CHAPTER FIVE

1. *Trial of Samuel Chase, An Associate Justice of the Supreme Court of the United States*, 2 vols. (Washington, D.C., 1805; reprint, New York, 1970). See also, Richard Ellis, "The Impeachment of Samuel Chase," in *American Political Trials*, ed. Michal Belknap (Westport, Conn., 1981), pp. 57–78 and Peter Charles Hoffer and N. E. H. Hull, *Impeachment in America, 1635–1805* (New Haven, 1984), pp. 228–55.

2. George Griffen as quoted in James Cheetham, *The Trial of the Hon. Maturin Livingston against James Cheetham for a Libel* (New York, 1807), pp. 31–32. See also, T. H. Emmett as quoted in William Coleman, *A Faithful Report of the Trial of the Cause of Philip I. Arcularius* (New York, 1807), p. 44. The following political studies have proved the most helpful in placing the question of libel law in a larger context: Sanford Higgenbotham, *The Keystone in the Democratic Arch* (Harrisburg, Pa., 1952); David Hackett Fischer, *The Revolution of American Conservatism* (New York, 1965); Richard Hofstadter, *The Idea of a Party System* (Berkeley, Cal., 1969); Donald Stewart, *The Opposition Press of the Federalist Period* (Albany, N.Y., 1969); Gerald Stourzh, *Alexander Hamilton and the Idea of Republican Government* (Stanford, Cal., 1970); Linda K. Kerber, *Federalists in Dissent* (Ithaca, N.Y., 1970); James M. Banner, Jr., *To the Hartford Convention* (New York, 1970); Dumas Malone, *Jefferson the President: First Term, 1801–1805* (New York, 1970), and *Jefferson the President: Second Term, 1805–1809* (New York, 1974); Forrest McDonald, *The Presidency of Thomas Jefferson* (Lawrence, Kan., 1976); John Zvesper, *Political Philosophy and Rhetoric: A Case Study of the Origins of the American Party Politics* (New York, 1977); Robert M. Johnstone, Jr., *Jefferson and the Presidency* (Ithaca, N.Y., 1978); Douglass Adair and John Schutz, eds., *The Spur of Fame* (San Marino, Cal., 1980); and Ronald P. Formisano, *The Transformation of Political Culture: Massachusetts Parties, 1790s–1840s* (New York, 1983).

3. 10 *Annals of Congress* 940 (1801).

4. Jefferson to Levi Lincoln, 24 March 1802, in *The Writings of Thomas Jefferson*, ed. Paul Leicester Ford, 10 vols. (New York, 1892–99), 8:139. Significantly, Jefferson also fully endorsed libel actions, both criminal and civil, by private individuals. According to the president, "a full range is proper for actions by individuals, either public or private, for slanders affecting them. . . ." He repeated, and reemphasized, this in his second inaugural address. See Saul Padover, ed., *The Complete Jefferson* (New York, 1943), pp. 413–14.

5. *Complete Jefferson*, pp. 341–48.

6. The Kentucky prosecution is discussed in Mary Bonsteel Tachau, *Federal Courts in the Early Republic: Kentucky, 1789–1816* (Princeton, N.J., 1978), pp. 135–36; Jefferson to Thomas Seymour, 11 Feb. 1807, in *Writings of Jefferson*, ed. Ford, 9:28–31.

7. On the Connecticut prosecutions, see the discussion from a perspective generally sympathetic to Jefferson's plight (if not his methods for remedying it) in Dumas Malone, *Jefferson the President: Second Term, 1805–1809* (Boston, 1974), pp. 371–91. See also the contemporary Federalist view in "Hampden," *A Letter to the President of the United States Touching the Prosecutions, under his Patronage* (New Haven, Conn., 1807) and the essentially anti-Jeffersonian account in Leonard W. Levy, *Jefferson and Civil Liberties: The Darker Side* (Cambridge, Mass., 1963; reprint, New York, 1973), pp. 42–69, esp. 61–66.

8. U.S. v. Hudson and Goodwin, 7 Cranch 32 (U.S., 1812).

9. See Jefferson to McKean, 19 Feb. 1803, in *Writings of Jefferson*, ed. Ford, 8:218–19. The editor ultimately indicted on this advice was undoubtedly Joseph Dennie. See Respublica v. Dennie, 4 Yeates 267 (Pa., 1805) and "Sketch of the Editor's Trial," *Portfolio* 5 (1805): 410–14. Dennie was acquitted. See also, Levy, *Jefferson and Civil Liberties*, p. 59.

10. See, e.g., Commonwealth v. Duane, 1 Bin. 601 (Pa., 1809); *Message from His Excellency the Governor . . .* (Boston, 1812). For complaints by Federalists about other Jeffersonian prosecutions, see, e.g., *Hudson Balance*, 22 Feb. 1803, 8 May 1804; *New York Spectator*, 27 April 1803; *Gazette of the United States*, 10 March 1803, 15 April 1803; *New York Evening Post*, 16 March 1803; *Albany Balance*, 10 Feb. 1807.

11. Tillotson v. Cheetham, 2 Johns. Rep. 64 (N.Y., 1806), and Tillotson v. Cheetham, 3 Johns. Rep. 56 (N.Y., 1808). The relative frequency of political libel actions may be seen, for example, by an examination of the first ten years of New York's appellate court reports and from Joel Munsell, *The Typographical Miscellany* (Albany, N.Y., 1850), pp. 14–20. See also the list compiled in Milton W. Hamilton, *The Country Printer: New York State, 1785–1830* (New York, 1936), Appendix III, Table II.

12. George Hay, *An Essay on the Liberty of the Press, Shewing that the Requisition of Security for Good Behavior from Libellers is Perfectly Compatible with the Constitution and Laws of Virginia* (Richmond, 1803), p. 43 (emphasis added).

13. Ibid., pp. 4, 41.

14. Ibid., pp. 41–45. Hay's ideas quickly drew Federalist fire. See, e.g., "Marcellus," *Essay on the Liberty of the Press* (Richmond, 1803), pp. 3, 6–7; *Charleston Courier*, 28, 29, 31 Jan., 1 Feb. 1803. See also Steven H. Hochman, "On the Liberty of the Press in Virginia: From Essay to Bludgeon, 1798–1803," *VaMHB* 84 (1976): 431–45, at 436–45.

15. *Journal of the Senate of the Commonwealth of Pennsylvania* (Philadelphia, 1807), pp. 13–14. In New York, Jeffersonians also sought good behavior bonds in advance of libel trials. See, e.g., *Hudson Balance*, 1, 8, 15 Feb. 1803.

16. On Virginia, see Hochman, "On the Liberty of the Press," pp. 439–41; on John Taylor's opposition, see *Charleston Courier*, 27 Jan. 1803. On Pennsylvania, see *Aurora*, 12, 13, 14 Aug. 1806; and Higgenbotham, *The Keystone in the Democratic Arch*, pp. 114, 123–25.

17. *New York Evening Post*, 31 May 1803; *A Report of the Trial of Andrew Wright* (Northampton, Mass., 1806). See also *Exeter* (N.H.) *Constitutional*, 21 May 1810 ("licentiousness of the press").

18. On Cheetham, see Frank Luther Mott, *American Journalism: A History, 1690–1960*, 3d. ed. (New York, 1962), p. 183; on Duane, see *Portsmouth* (N.H.) *Oracle*, 10 Dec. 1808. Duane himself admitted to having gathered by 1806 about sixty defamation suits. *Aurora*, 12 Aug. 1806.

19. State v. Lehre, 2 Rev. Reps. 447 (S.C., 1811); Territory v. Nugent, 1 Martin 108 (La., 1810); and *H. P. Nugent's Reply to the Calumnies of the Honorable F. X. Martin* (Natchez, Miss., 1811). See also the dictum in Harris v. Huntington, 2 Tyler 129 (Vt., 1802); People v. Croswell, 3 Johns. Cas. 337 (N.Y., 1804); and Isaac 'Espinasee, *A Digest of the Laws of Actions and Trials . . .*, 2 vols. (Walpole, N.H., 1808), 2:507; and James Sullivan, *A Dissertation upon the Constitutional Freedom of the Press in the United States of America* (Boston, 1801), pp. 19–20.

20. St. George Tucker, *Blackstone's Commentaries: With Notes of Reference, to the Constitution and Laws, of the Federal Government of the United States; and of the Commonwealth of Virginia*, 5 vols. (Philadelphia, 1803), 1: Appendix, Note G, pp. 20–21; People v. Tracy, 2 Wheeler Crim. Cas. 358 (N.Y., 1804). See also Commonwealth v. Morris, 1 Va. Cas. 176, 179–80 (1811); argument of counsel in People v. Croswell, reprinted in *Hudson Balance*, 25 Jan. 1803; and argument of H. D. Wells in Coleman, *A Faithful Report*, p. 33.

21. *Aurora*, 19 Dec. 1808; see also, ibid., 28, 29 Nov. 1808. The law of libel could be used, as was done by Dr. Michael Lieb, as a prime example of the danger of American courts adopting English common law doctrines. See, e.g., Harry Croswell in the *Hudson Balance*, 27 Sept. 1803; William Sampson, "Postscript," in Coleman, *A Faithful Report*, pp. 60–62; "Marcellus," *Essay on Liberty of the Press*, p. 8; and Erastus Root in *Reports of the Proceedings and Debates of the [New York Constitutional] Convention of 1821* (Albany, 1821), pp. 489–90.

22. *Journal of the Nineteenth House of Representatives of the Commonwealth of Pennsylvania . . . 1808–09* (Lancaster, Pa., 1809), pp. 320–22; *Journal of the Senate of the Commonwealth of Pennsylvania . . . 1808–09* (Lancaster, Pa., 1809), pp. 288–90; Commonwealth v. Duane, 1 Bin. 601 (Pa., 1809).

23. Ingersoll, "Report of Jared Ingersoll, Attorney General of Pennsylvania, Jan 21, 1813," in *American Jurisprudence* 1 (1821): 325–45, 341. For an analysis of the broader, legal-political struggle, in which Pennsylvania's libel laws became symbols, see Richard R. Ellis, *The Jeffersonian Crisis: Court and Politics in the Young Republic* (New York, 1971).

24. People v. Croswell, 3 Johns. Cas. 337 (N.Y., 1804).

25. Hamilton's view of libel law has been reconstructed from several sources: *The Speeches at Full Length . . . in the Great Cause of the People Against Harry Croswell* (New York, 1804); James Kent's "Notes on Hamilton's Argument"; and Hamilton's own "15 Propositions on the Law of Libel." All are reprinted in Julius Goebel, ed., *The Law Practice of Alexander Hamilton*, 2 vols. (New York, 1964, 1969), 1:808–42. The quotes in this paragraph are from ibid., pp. 809–10, 833.

26. Ibid., pp. 832, 839.

27. Ibid., pp. 809, 812–13.

28. Ibid., pp. 810–13, 823–24, 839.

29. Ibid., pp. 819–20.

30. Ibid., pp. 830, 838.

31. Ibid., pp. 830–31, 838, 839 (emphasis in original).

32. Ibid., pp. 831, 840.

33. Chief Justice Lewis and fellow Republican Brockholst Livingston supported Lewis's original position on the law and Croswell's conviction. Federalist James Kent and another Jeffersonian judge, Smith Thompson (Kent's former law clerk), supported Hamilton's view and a new trial under non-Blackstonian doctrines. The final member of the court, Ambrose Spencer, had to disqualify himself because of his role as prosecutor in the trial court. People v. Croswell, 3 Johns. Cas. 337, 394–411 (Lewis's opinion); ibid., pp. 363–93 (Kent's opinion). The state never moved for final judgment against Croswell; as a result, the supreme court awarded him a new trial, which was never held. Ibid., p. 413. As late as 1833, Ambrose Spencer still received taunts for his role in the Croswell prosecution. See Arthur Stansbury, *Report of the Trial of James H. Peck* (Boston, 1833), p. 333.

34. Spencer secured indictments against Samuel Freer of the *Ulster Gazette* for criminal libel. See *Hudson Balance*, 30 Aug. 1803. See also People v. Tracy, 2 Wheeler Crim. Cas. 358 (N.Y., 1804). Spencer and his deputy attorney general also filed several criminal actions against Croswell and his partner. See, e.g., Foot v. Croswell, 1 Caines 498 (N.Y., 1804).

35. Thomas Green Fessendon, *Democracy Unveiled* (Boston, 1805), p. 8.

36. People v. Croswell, 3 Johns. Cas. 337, 393 (N.Y. Sup. Ct., 1804).

37. *Journal of the Senate of the State of New York [1804]* (Albany, 1805), p. 10. A vote to override the Council of Revision's veto failed. Ibid., p. 12; *Laws of the State of New York [1804–05]* (Albany, 1805), pp. 451–53; *Hudson Balance*, 27 March 1804. Prior to the *Croswell* case, several other states had modified, by statute, Blackstonian doctrines. In 1803 the North Carolina legislature made truth a justification to all indictments for libel. Several other states—including New Jersey, Connecticut, Maryland, and Vermont—adopted statutes that provided libel defendants could introduce evidence of truth, without specifying whether or not proof of truth would constitute a "sufficient defense." See Paul G. Willis, "Political Libel in the United States, 1607–1949" (Ph.D. diss., Indiana University, 1949), pp. 201–2.

38. In the unreported cases of Commonwealth v. Carleton (1803) and Commonwealth v. Wright (1806), the state allowed defendants to introduce evidence of truth. In the latter case, however, Chief Justice Theophilus Parsons barred the defendant from offering oral evidence. See *Report of the Trial of Andrew Wright* (Northampton, Mass., 1806), pp. 12, 16–22, and Joseph T. Buckingham, *Personal Memoirs and Recollections of Editorial Life*, 2 vols. (Boston, 1852), 1:534–35.

39. Commonwealth v. Clap, 4 Mass. 163, 165 (1808).

40. Ibid., pp. 168–69.

41. Ibid., pp. 169–70. Clap's sentence of two months' imprisonment was upheld.

42. "Charge of Judge Isaac Parker to Grand Jury of Supreme Judicial Court," in *Boston Patriot*, 28 Dec. 1811; *Message from His Excellency*, pp. 5–6. The Massachusetts Senate debates are reprinted in the *Boston Weekly Messenger*, 24 Jan. 1812; Boston *Scourge*, 30 Nov. 1812. For accounts of the bitter political battles that produced

the libel controversies, see Ronald P. Formisano, *The Transformation of Political Culture: Massachusetts Parties, 1790s to 1840s* (New York, 1983), pp. 72–76, and George Athan Billias, *Elbridge Gerry: Founding Father and Republican Statesman* (New York, 1976), pp. 315–23.

43. Indiana (1816), Illinois (1818), and Maine (1820) all adopted the "Pennsylvania rule" (or some variation), which allowed defendants to introduce evidence of truth in cases involving public people. Mississippi (1817), Connecticut (1818), and Missouri (1820) recognized the right of defendants to plead truth in all prosecutions. The constitutions of Alabama (1819) and Massachusetts (1820) contained no provisions on libel. See Carol Rochat, "Analysis of the Freedom of Press Clauses in the American Constitution" (M.A. thesis, University of Illinois, 1948), pp. 115–16.

44. *Reports of the Proceedings and Debates of the Convention of 1821* (Albany, 1821), pp. 167–68, 487, 488, 492. Several supporters of Kent's position conceded that the issue of truth should be a consideration in libel cases involving public officials and candidates; but judges, in their view, should be able to exclude evidence designed to show truth in prosecutions involving private individuals. Ibid., pp. 489, 494 (William Irving Dodge); ibid., pp. 492–93 (N. Williams). Kent never made this distinction.

45. Ibid., pp. 483–95. The libel suit in question was Van Ness v. Hamilton, 19 Johns. Rep. 349 (N.Y., 1822). The final vote in favor of the Hamiltonian rule was 97 to 8.

46. *Journal of Debates and Proceedings in the Convention of Delegates, Chosen to Revise the Constitution of Massachusetts, Nov. 15, 1820–Jan. 9, 1821* (Boston, 1853), pp. 471, 538–42, 551.

47. Joseph T. Buckingham, *Trial for a Libel on Reverend John T. Maffett* (Boston, 1822). Buckingham claimed that this pamphlet account of his trial sold more than 12,000 copies. Buckingham, *Memoirs*, 1:105–10.

48. [Harrison Gray Otis], *A Letter to the Hon. Josiah Quincy . . . By a Member of the Suffolk Bar* (Boston, 1823).

49. Ibid., pp. 11–15, 31–35, 38–39. Otis's position received important support in Massachusetts. See, e.g., the two separate prosecutions against Joseph Buckingham in Peter Thacher, ed., *Reports of Criminal Cases Tried in the Municipal Court of the City of Boston* (Boston, 1845), pp. 29, 36, 51, 53–54; Buckingham, *Memoirs*, 1:115–20. See also the influential opinion of Isaac Parker, Chief Justice of Massachusetts, in Commonwealth v. Blanding, 20 Mass. 304 (1825). Oliver Wendell Holmes, Jr., among others, continued to cite Commonwealth v. Blanding as good law as late as 1907. Patterson v. Colorado, 205 U.S. 454, 462 (1907).

50. [Edmund Kimbull], *Reflections upon the Law of Libel . . . .* (Boston, 1823), pp. 38–48, 52–54; *Laws of Massachusetts . . . 1826* (Boston, 1826), Chap. 107, Sec. 1. The act also guaranteed the right to plead truth in all civil defamation suits as well.

51. See Douglass T. Adair, "Fame and the Founding Fathers," *Fame & the Founding Fathers: Essays by Douglass Adair*, ed. Trevour Colbourn (New York, 1974), pp. 3–26; Julian P. Boyd, ed., *The Papers of Thomas Jefferson*, 21 vols. to date (Princeton, N.J., 1950–), 9:215 (Jefferson to Jay, 25 Jan. 1786); ibid., 9:86–87 (replying to Jay to Jefferson, 9 Dec. 1785); ibid., 9:450 (Jay to Jefferson, 5 May 1786).

52. See Spencer v. Sampson, 1 Caines 497 (N.Y., 1804); Foot v. Croswell, 1

Caines 498 (N.Y., 1804); Livingston v. Cheetham, 1 Johns. Rep. 61 (N.Y., 1806); Van Vechten v. Hopkins, 2 Johns. Rep. 373 (N.Y., 1807). Under procedures in New York, both sides struck twelve jurors from the original panel of forty-eight; then the trial jury was chosen, in the ordinary manner, from the remaining twenty-four. Struck juries were also used for a time in complicated commercial disputes. See Morton J. Horwitz, *The Transformation of American Law, 1780–1860* (Cambridge, Mass., 1977), pp. 155–59.

53. Gray v. Pentland, 4 Serg. & Rawle 419, 422 (Pa. 1819); see also Reid v. De-lorme, 2 Brev. 76 (S.C., 1806); Harris v. Huntington, 2 Tyler 129 (Vt., 1802); Thorn v. Blanchard, 5 Johns. Rep. 508 (N.Y., 1809).

54. Mayrant v. Richardson, 1 Nott & McCord 347, 450 (S.C., 1818).

55. Ibid., pp. 351–53.

56. Ibid., p. 348. See Herbert W. Titus, "Statement of Fact Versus Statement of Opinion—A Spurious Dispute in Fair Comment," *VLR* 15 (1962): 1203–46.

57. Mayrant v. Richardson at pp. 349, 353–54. In a common law action for libel, harm to the defendant, according to accepted theory, constituted the essential element of the case, and courts often followed the procedure used here by Justice Nott: adopt the plain meaning of the allegedly defamatory statement. See William Odgers, *A Digest of the Law of Libel and Slander*, 2nd ed. (London, 1896), pp. 14–19, 144. For critiques of this approach, which is still used in libel cases, see Frederick F. Schauer, "Language, Truth, and the First Amendment: An Essay in Memory of Harry Cantor," *VaLR* 64 (1978): 263–302, esp. 281–94, and Paul G. Chevigny, "Philosophy of Language and Free Expression," *NYULR* 55 (1980): 157–94.

58. Lewis v. Few, 5 Johns. Rep. 1, 13–15 (N.Y., 1809).

59. Ibid., pp. 35–37.

60. On the rise of instrumental reasoning, see Horwitz, *Transformation of American Law*, pp. 1–30.

61. Stow v. Converse, 4 Conn. 8, 33 (1822).

62. Foot v. Tracy, 1 Johns. Rep. 46, 51 (N.Y., 1806). The court divided equally, 2 to 2, and the judgment in favor of Foot was upheld. As in the *Croswell* case, Ambrose Spencer disqualified himself. The real surprise was James Kent, who voted against his own circuit court ruling. Kent's reasoning and motives are difficult to discern. See the two excellent articles by Donald Roper: "Justice Smith Thompson: Politics and the New York Supreme Court in the Early Nineteenth Century," *NYHSQ* 51 (1967): 128–39, and "James Kent and the Emergence of New York's Libel Law," *AJLH* 17 (1973): 223–31.

63. Dole v. Lyon, 10 Johns. Rep. 447, 450 (N.Y., 1812)

64. Tillotson v. Cheetham, 3 Johns. Rep. 56, 56–59 (N.Y., 1808); the previous suit was Tillotson v. Cheetham, 2 Johns. Rep. 64 (N.Y., 1806).

65. Tillotson v. Cheetham, 3 Johns. Rep. 56, 63. (N.Y., 1808).

66. Ibid., pp. 58, 64–65.

67. Spencer v. Southwick, 11 Johns. Rep. 573, 394 (N.Y., 1814).

68. A complete copy of the trial judge's charge is contained in the report of the New York Court of Errors. Root v. King, 4 Wend. 113, 119–34 (N.Y., 1829). The supreme court's decision is reported in 7 Cowen 613 (N.Y., 1827).

69. Root v. King, 4 Wend. 113, 133–34, 138. Four members of the court dissented

on the grounds that the defendant should have been permitted to offer evidence on Root's general character in order to mitigate the amount of damages awarded.

70. See Ronald P. Formisano, "Deferential-Participant Politics: The Early Republic's Political Culture, 1789–1840," *APSR* 68 (1974): 473–87, and Formisano, *Transformation of Political Culture*, passim, but esp. 3–23, 128–48.

71. Hollingsworth v. Duane, 12 Fed. Cas. at 366 (Case No. 6, 617).

72. The law of libel was not the only area in which legal doctrines were used to underscore the idea that the best men should play an important role in civic life. See, e.g., the similar emphasis in various areas of early nineteenth-century corporate law. Andrew Fraser, "The Corporation as a Body Politic," *Telos* 57 (1983): 5–40, esp. pp. 16–20. One might compare, for example, the opinions of Isaac Parker, chief justice of Massachusetts, in Baker v. Fales, 16 Mass. Rep. 487 (1820) (case involving church governance) and in Commonwealth v. Blanding, 20 Mass. Rep. 304 (1825) (criminal libel prosecution). See also, Fraser, "Corporation as Public Body," pp. 17–19.

CHAPTER SIX

1. "To the American People," *Aurora*, 4 July 1834.

2. For an earlier version of this argument, see Norman L. Rosenberg, "The Law of Political Libel and Freedom of Press in Nineteenth Century America: An Interpretation," *AJLH* 17 (1973): 336–52.

3. See, e.g., *Proceedings and Debates of the Convention of the Commonwealth of Pennsylvania to Propose Amendments to the Constitution*, 14 vols. (Harrisburg, 1839), 12:7–9; *Debates and Proceedings of the Minnesota Constitutional Convention*, reported officially by Francis H. Smith (Minneapolis, 1857), pp. 284–88; Benjamin F. Shambaugh, ed., *Fragments of the Debates of the Iowa Constitutional Conventions of 1844 and 1846* (Iowa City, 1900), p. 41; Harold M. Dorr, ed., *The Michigan Constitutional Conventions of 1835–36: Debates and Proceedings* (Ann Arbor, 1940), pp. 290–92; *Report of the Proceedings and Debates in the Convention to Revise the Constitution of the State of Michigan* (Lansing, 1850), p. 43.

4. State v. Burnham, 9 N.H. 34, 41–45 (1837).

5. Thomas Cooper, *A Treatise on the Law of Libel and the Liberty of the Press* (New York, 1830; reprint, New York, 1970), pp. 109–13, at 112, 113. The Hamiltonian view dominated antebellum treatises. See, e.g., Joseph Story, *Commentaries on the Constitution of the United States*, 4 vols. (Boston, 1833), 3:597–98; James Kent, *Commentaries on American Law*, 8th ed., 4 vols. (Boston, 1858), 1:631–34; Nathaniel Chipman, *Principles of Government: A Treatise on Free Institutions* (Burlington, Vt., 1833), pp. 103–6; David Hoffman, *A Source of Legal Study, Addressed to Students and the Profession Generally*, 2nd ed. (Baltimore, 1836); Anon., "The Law of Libel," *AQR* 5 (1829): 71–84, and Anon., "The Law of Libel," *SQR* 12 (1847): 246–68; see also, Marc A. Franklin, "The Origins and Constitutionality of Limitations on Truth as a Defense in Tort Law," *StanLR* 16 (1964): 789–848, at 790–805.

6. Hunt v. Bennett, 19 N.Y. 173, 175–76 (1859).

7. Hotchkiss v. Oliphant, 2 Hill 510, 513–14, 514–15 (N.Y., 1842). See also, Dole v. Lyon, 10 Johns. Rep. 447 (N.Y., 1812).

8. Lansing v. Carpenter, 9 Wisc. 493, 494–95 (1859).

9. Usher v. Severance, 20 Me. 9, 15 (1841). See also, Root v. King, 4 Wend. 113 (N.Y., 1829).

10. Aldrich v. Press Printing Co., 9 Minn. 133, 138 (1864).

11. Among the general works in legal history that have helped to shape my approach to libel law, the following deserve special mention: J. Willard Hurst, *Law and the Conditions of Freedom in the Nineteenth-Century United States* (Madison, Wis., 1956); Leonard W. Levy, *The Law of the Commonwealth and Chief Justice Shaw* (Cambridge, Mass., 1957); Perry Miller, *The Life of the Mind in America* (New York, 1965); Maxwell Bloomfield, *American Lawyers in a Changing Society, 1776–1876* (Cambridge, Mass., 1976); Philip Paludan, *A Covenant with Death: The Constitution, Law, and Equality in the Civil War Era* (Urbana, Ill., 1975); Morton J. Horwitz, *The Transformation of American Law* (Cambridge, Mass., 1977); Harold Hyman and William Wiecek, *Equal Justice Under Law: Constitutional Development, 1835–1875* (New York, 1982); Alan Jones, "Thomas M. Cooley and 'Laissez Faire' Constitutionalism: A Reconsideration," *JAH* 50 (1967): 751–71; Duncan Kennedy, "Toward an Historical Understanding of Legal Consciousness: The Case of Classical Legal Thought in America, 1850–1940," *Research in Law and Sociology* 3 (1980): 3–24; Elizabeth Mensch, "The History of Mainstream Legal Thought," in *The Politics of Law*, ed. David Kairys (New York, 1982), pp. 18–39; and Patrick O. Gudridge, "The Persistence of Classical Style," *UPaLR* 131 (1983): 663–792.

12. For a brief, contemporary analysis of libel decisions arising out of business dealings, see Thomas M. Cooley, *Treatise on the Law of Torts* (Chicago, 1879), pp. 216–17.

13. The trial involved William P. Darnes, and the arguments of the defendant's attorneys provide interesting insights into what these lawyers thought about—and what they thought they could convince a jury to believe about—nineteenth century libel law. See John Davison Lawson, ed., *American State Trials*, 17 vols. (St. Louis, 1914–36), 16:100–105, 126–35, 180–91, 234–49.

14. See P. T. Barnum, *Struggles and Triumphs: Or, Forty Years' Recollections* (Hartford, Conn., 1870), pp. 63–65; John Niven, *Gideon Welles* (New York, 1973), p. 33; and Theophilus Fisk, *The Nation's Bulwark: An Oration on the Freedom of the Press* (New Haven, Conn., 1832), pp. 12–16.

15. Fisk, *The Nation's Bulwark*, pp. 1–5. See, Major L. Wilson, *Space, Time, and Freedom* (Westport, Conn., 1974), pp. 6–7.

16. Fisk, *The Nation's Bulwark*, pp. 5–12; *Letter to . . . Jurors Empaneled to Try the Indictment Against Joseph Whitmarsh* (Boston, 1838), p. 11; Lawson, ed., *American State Trials*, 16:182.

17. See *Report of a Trial in the Supreme Judicial Court . . . of Theodore Lyman, Jr., for an Alleged Libel on Daniel Webster* (Boston, 1828); *Report of the Trial of Timothy Upham vs. Hill & Barton for an Alleged Libel in the Court of Common Pleas, Rockingham County, October Term, 1830* (Concord, N.H., 1831); *Trial of the Case of the Commonwealth v. David Lee Child, for Publishing . . . a Libel of the Hon. John*

Keyes (Boston, 1829); and *The Great Libel Case: Opdyke v. Weed. A Full Report* (New York, 1865). See also the analysis in Rosenberg, "The Law of Political Libel," pp. 348–50.

Among the works on political culture that I have consulted, I have found the following most useful for the themes related to libel law: Robert Remini, *The Election of 1828* (Philadelphia, 1963); Richard P. McCormick, *The Second American Party System* (Chapel Hill, N.C., 1966); Richard Hofstadter, *The Idea of a Party System* (Berkeley, Cal., 1969); Eric Foner, *Free Soil, Free Labor, Free Men* (New York, 1970); Rush Welter, *The Mind of America: 1820–1860* (New York, 1975); Daniel Walker Howe, *The Political Culture of the American Whigs* (Chicago, 1979); Jean Baker, *The Political Culture of the Northern Democrats in the Mid-19th Century* (Ithaca, N.Y., 1983); Ronald P. Formisano, *The Transformation of Political Culture: Massachusetts Parties, 1790s–1840s* (New York, 1983); Michael Wallace, "Changing Concepts of Party in the United States: New York, 1815–25," *AHR* 74 (1968): 453–61, and Ronald P. Formisano, "Political Character, Antipartyism and the Second Party System," *AQ* 21 (1969): 683–709.

18. For analyses of Cooper's general political and legal outlooks, see John P. Mc-Williams, Jr., *Political Justice in a Republic* (Berkeley, Cal., 1972), and Brook Thomas, "*The Pioneers*, or the Sources of American Legal History: A Critical Tale," *AQ* 36 (1984): 86–111. In discussing Cooper's libel battles, I have relied upon the mass of correspondence in *Letters and Journals of James Fenimore Cooper*, ed. James F. Beard. 6 vols. (Cambridge, Mass., 1960–68), vols. 3 and 4, and Ethel R. Outland, *The "Effingham" Libels on Cooper* (Madison, Wis., 1929).

19. James Fenimore Cooper, *The American Democrat* (New York, 1838; reprint, New York, 1956), p. 127.

20. James Fenimore Cooper to Cornelius Matthews and Evert Augustus Ducycknick, 6 Dec. 1841, in Beard, ed., *Letters and Journals*, 4:202; "James Fenimore Cooper to William Fry," *National Gazette & Literary Register*, 21 Aug. 1840, reprinted in ibid., p. 580.

21. For the Stone proposal, see Outland, *Libels on Cooper*, pp. 52–53; *New-Yorker*, 23 Feb. 1839, reprinted in ibid., pp. 81–82. Another prominent nineteenth-century author, Edgar Allan Poe, had an even unhappier, though briefer, experience with libel law. In 1847 he sued the editors of the *New York Evening Mirror* for republishing a piece critical of his character. (A year earlier, Poe had enraged New York's literary circles by writing a gossip column, entitled "The Literati of New York City: Some Honest Opinions at Random Respecting their Authorial Merits, with Occasional Words of Personality." Quickly engulfed in a war of insults, Poe tried to solve his problems with a libel suit.) Eventually, Poe did win a judgment for $225.06, but the legal action only increased the torrent of criticism swirling around him. See Sidney P. Moss, *Poe's Literary Battles: The Critic in the Context of His Literary Milieu* (Durham, N.C., 1963), pp. 190–248, and Moss, ed., *Poe's Major Crisis: His Libel Suit and New York's Literary World* (Durham, N.C., 1970). (The second volume is a collection of documents.)

22. Thurlow Weed, "The Law of Libel," *Albany Evening Journal*, 20 May 1845, reprinted in Outland, *Libels on Cooper*, pp. 127–29, at 128.

23. See, e.g., William Seward, "Law of Libel," *WLJ* 2 (1845): 465–72. On

Greeley's role, see Outland, *Libels on Cooper*, pp. 130–66 and Daniel Walker Howe, *The Political Culture of the American Whigs* (Chicago, 1979), p. 186.

24. Beard, ed., *Letters and Journals*, 3: 284.

25. Michael Schudson, *Discovering the News: A Social History of American Newspapers* (New York, 1978), p. 27. See also, Allan R. Pred, *Urban Growth and the Circulation of Information* (Cambridge, Mass., 1973).

26. William Seward, *The Works of William Seward*, ed. G. E. Baker, 5 vols. (New York, 1853–54), 2: 37–38.

27. Ibid., p. 38.

28. Daniel Webster, *Writings and Speeches of Daniel Webster*, ed. J. W. McIntyre, 18 vols. (Boston, 1903), 2: 116. In addition to Schudson, *Discovering the News*, I have relied upon the following discussions of nineteenth-century journalism: Edwin and Michael Emery, *The Press and America: An Interpretive History of the Mass Media*, 4th ed. (Englewood Cliffs, N.J., 1978); James Crouthamel, *James Watson Webb* (Middletown, Conn., 1969); Alfred M. Lee, *The Daily Newspaper in America* (New York, 1937); Frank Luther Mott, *American Journalism: A History, 1690–1950*, 3rd ed. (New York, 1962); Dan Schiller, *Objectivity and the News* (Philadelphia, 1981); Culver Smith, *The Press, Politics, and Patronage* (Athens, Ga., 1977); Gerald Baldasty, "The Boston Press and Politics in Jacksonian America," *JH* 7 (1980):104–8; James Crouthamel, "The Newspaper Revolution in New York, 1830–1860," *NYH* 45 (1964): 91–113; and Alexander Saxton, "Problems of Class and Race in the Origins of the Mass Circulation Press," *AQ* 36 (1984): 211–34.

29. Editorial of the *New York Times*, 22 Dec. 1834, enclosed in George Strong to Martin Van Buren, 23 Dec. 1834, *Martin Van Buren Papers* (Microfilm Edition, Series 2, Reel 14); Thomas Hart Benton, *Thirty Years View*, 2 vols. (New York, 1845), 1:128–30.

30. *Memphis Daily Appeal*, 15 July 1855, quoted in Thomas Harrison Baker, *The Memphis Commercial Appeal: The History of a Southern Newspaper* (Baton Rouge, La., 1971), p. 42.

31. Ibid., pp. 37–38; *Chambersburg Valley Spirit*, 24 Aug. 1849, quoted in Richard H. McDonnell, "The Chambersburg Valley Spirit," *PMHB* 104 (1980): 200–220, at 201.

32. "The Newspaper Press," *AR* 2 (n.s. 1848): 584–99, at 597.

33. See George Forgie, *Patricide in the House Divided* (New York, 1979), pp. 7–8, 63, 69, 75. Baker ed., *Works of Seward*, 1:407.

34. A thorough new study of political communication in nineteenth-century America is long overdue.

35. Frederick Grimke, *The Nature and Tendency of Free Institutions*, ed. John William Ward (Cambridge, Mass., 1968), p. 397.

36. Ibid., p. 398.

37. Ibid., p. 400.

38. Ibid., pp. 400–401.

39. Ibid., p. 401.

40. Ibid., pp. 400–401.

41. Ibid., pp. 401–2; the distinction between small and large politics is developed in F. G. Bailey, ed., *Gifts and Poison: The Politics of Reputation* (New York, 1971).

For a critique of the tendency in nineteenth- and twentieth-century liberal political culture to delegitimate anger, see Peter Lyman, "The Politics of Anger: On Silence, Resentment, and Political Speech," *SR* 57 (1981): 55–74. In contrast, eighteenth-century political culture took popular anger more seriously. See, e.g., Dirk Hoerder, *Crowd Action in Revolutionary Massachusetts, 1765–1780* (New York, 1977), and Paul A. Gilje, "The Baltimore Riots of 1812 and the Breakdown of the Anglo-American Mob Tradition," *JSH* 13 (1980): 547–64.

42. Grimke, *Nature and Tendency*, p. 403. In his critique of stiff libel laws, William Seward made the same point: "the press has the antidote to its own poisons. If it sometimes wounds, it can effectually heal." Baker, ed., *Works of Seward*, 1:401.

43. Grimke, *Nature and Tendency*, p. 401.

44. Ibid., p. 398. At another point in his book, when discussing political toleration, Grimke reiterated his faith in the homogenizing effects of political debates. "I believe if we were to take any considerable series of years, it would be found that the leading measures which have been adopted in the United States have been the fruit of the joint exertions of all parties; that they have been ultimately so arranged as to reflect in part the opinions of the majority and in part those of the majority." Ibid., p. 256.

45. Ibid., p. 398.

46. John L. O'Sullivan, "The Democratic Principle," *DR* 1 (1837): 5.

47. "Freedom of Opinion," *DR* 22 (1848): 310; *AR* 2 (n.s. 1848): 597.

48. Quoted in Russel B. Nye, *Fettered Freedom: Civil Liberties and the Slavery Controversy, 1830–1860* (East Lansing, Mich., 1963; reprint, Urbana, Ill., 1972), p. 123. Those who sought to discuss the slavery issue were not the only people to find something less than a perfect "marketplace of ideas." See Chapter 7, pp. 153–56.

49. Quoted in Samuel Eliot Morison, *Harrison Gray Otis, 1765–1848*, rev. ed. (Boston, 1969), p. 469. On Garrison's libel troubles, see *A Brief Sketch of the Trial of William Lloyd Garrison, for an Alleged Libel on Francis Todd, of Massachusetts* (Boston, 1834), and "To the Editor of the Newburyport Herald," 1 June 1830, in *I Will Be Heard! The Letters of William Lloyd Garrison, 1822–35*, ed. Walter Merrill (Cambridge, Mass., 1971), pp. 97–103.

50. The South Carolina committee is quoted in Nye, *Fettered Freedom*, p. 139; see also ibid., pp. 138–40; J. H. Hammond, *Remarks . . . on the Question of Receiving Petition for the Abolition of Slavery. . .* (Washington, D.C., 1836), p. 16 (using defamation law as an analogy); Calvin Colton, *Abolition A Sedition* (Philadelphia, 1839), passim; and Paul Finkleman, "The Treason Trial of Castner Hanway," in *American Political Trials*, ed. Michal Belknap (Westport, Conn., 1981), pp. 79–100.

51. See, e.g., Curtis v. Mussey, 72 Mass. 261 (1856). This was a suit for a libel on a U.S. slave commissioner.

52. Quoted in Nye, *Fettered Freedom*, p. 126 (Theophilus Fisk), p. 125 (E. P. Barrows). See also the excellent discussion in Nye, pp. 117–73.

53. Weld quoted in Robert Abzug, *Passionate Liberator: Theodore Dwight Weld and the Dilemma of Reform* (New York, 1980), p. 136.

54. William Leggett, *Political Writings* (New York, 1839), pp. 33–39.

55. Grimke, *Nature and Tendency*, pp. 397–98.

CHAPTER SEVEN

1. Culver G. Smith, *The Press, Politics, and Patronage: The Government's Use of Newspapers, 1789–1875* (Athens, Ga., 1977), p. 72. Such a role—to "bring a manufactured public world into private space"—is inseparable from the operation of modern media institutions. See Todd Gitlin, *The Whole World is Watching* (Berkeley, Cal., 1980), pp. 1–13, at 1.

2. Dan Schiller, *Objectivity and the News: The Public and the Rise of Commercial Journalism* (Philadelphia, 1981), pp. 71–72. See also, Alexander Saxton, "Problems of Class and Race in the Origins of the Mass Circulation Press," *AQ* 36 (1984): 211–34.

3. The concept of distorted communication is developed in Claus Mueller, *The Politics of Communication* (New York, 1973).

4. Quoted in Robert Abzug, *Passionate Liberator: Theodore Dwight Weld and the Dilemma of Reform* (New York, 1980), p. 136. On the importance of gender distortions, see Alvin Gouldner, *The Dialectic of Ideology and Technology* (New York, 1976), p. 99. For a detailed critique of how expression by women was distorted in a more subtle way, see Ann Douglas, *The Feminization of American Culture* (New York, 1978), esp. pp. 50–93, 273–309.

5. Quote in Anthony F. C. Wallace, *Rockdale: The Growth of an American Village in the Early Industrial Revolution* (New York, 1978), p. 331. See also Paul Johnson, *A Shopkeeper's Millennium: Society and Revivals in Rochester, New York, 1815–1837* (New York, 1978), and Edward Pessen, "Who Has the Power in the Democratic Capitalistic Community: Reflections on Antebellum New York City," *NYH* 52 (1977): 129–53, at 145.

6. See Paul L. Murphy, *The Meaning of Free Speech* (Westport, Conn., 1972), pp. 14–16.

7. See, e.g., Mueller, *Politics of Communication*; and the works of Herbert Schiller, especially *Mass Communications and American Empire* (Boston, 1971), and *Communication and Cultural Domination* (New York, 1976).

8. See Chapter 8, pp. 190–206. We badly need a thorough, general history of free expression in the nineteenth-century United States, one that is sensitive to the larger political and legal cultures and one that uses, as does Dan Schiller's study of the penny presses, insights from the new social histories. Although Sean Wilentz's "On Class and Politics in Jacksonian America," *RIAH* 10 (1982): 45–63 does not touch directly upon the issues of political communication and free expression, some of his general suggestions for future research would apply to the study of speech and press in antebellum America. I have found the following to be the most helpful: Harold L. Nelson, ed., *Freedom of the Press from Hamilton to the Warren Court* (Indianapolis, Ind., 1966), an excellent document collection with a superb introductory essay; Clement Eaton, *The Freedom of Thought Struggle in the Old South*, 2nd ed. (New York, 1964); William Freehling, *Prelude to Civil War* (New York, 1966); Clifton O. Lawhorne, *Defamation and Public Officials: The Evolving Law of Libel* (Carbondale, Ill., 1971); Marc Franklin, "The Origins and Constitutionality of Truth as a Defense in Tort Law," *StanLR* 16 (1954): 789–840; and Margaret Blanchard, "Filling the Void: Speech and Press in State Courts Prior to Gitlow," in *The First Amendment Reconsidered*, ed. Bill

Chamberlin and Charlene J. Brown (New York, 1982), pp. 14–59. As my footnotes suggest, I have also relied heavily upon Russel B. Nye, *Fettered Freedom* for the relationship between the antislavery movement and free-speech issues.

9. Schiller, *Objectivity and the News*, pp. 12–75; Christopher Lasch, "Democracy and the 'Crisis of Confidence,'" *democracy* 1 (1981): 25–40, at 31; Wilentz, "Class and Politics," p. 56.

10. See Thomas Starkie, *A Treatise on the Law of Slander and Libel, and Incidently of Malicious Prosecution*, ed. John Wendell, 2 vols. (Albany, N.Y., 1843), 1:59; "Recorder's Charge to a Grand Jury of the Court of General Session," *New York Times*, 6 Oct. 1858; John Stevens et al., "Criminal Libel as Seditious Libel, 1916–65," *JQ* 43 (1966): 110–13. Stevens's study tabulated libel prosecutions reported in West's *American Digest* after 1865; my own search for pre-1865 cases similarly found a relatively small number of criminal libel prosecutions.

11. See, e.g., David Bogen, "The Free Speech Metamorphosis of Mr. Justice Holmes," *HofLR* 11 (1982): 97–189, at 107–31, and the works cited and critiqued in David Rabban, "The First Amendment in Its Forgotten Years," *YLJ* 90 (1981): 516–95.

12. William Seward, "Law of Libel," *WLJ* 2 (1845): 465–72. On twentieth-century legal communication, see generally, John W. Johnson, *American Legal Culture, 1908–1940* (Westport, Conn., 1981), pp. 52–72.

13. See, e.g., James Kent, *Commentaries on American Law*, 4 vols., 9th ed. (Boston, 1858), 1:631–34; Joseph Story, *Commentaries on the Constitution of the United States*, 4 vols. (Boston, 1833), 3:597–98, and David Hoffman, *A Source of Legal Study, Addressed to Students and the Profession Generally*, 2nd. ed. (Baltimore, 1836), p. 346.

14. The full title of Cooley's work was *A Treatise on the Constitutional Limitations which Rest Upon the Legislative Powers of the States of the American Union* (Boston, 1868).

15. Daniel Walker Howe, *The Political Culture of the American Whigs* (Chicago, 1979), pp. 7, 23–25, 148.

16. *The Case of Dewitt C. Littlejohn against Horace Greeley. . .* (New York, 1861), p. 12; Commonwealth v. Wright, 55 Mass. 46, 50 (1848); G. E. Baker, ed., *The Works of William Seward*, 5 vols. (New York, 1853–54), 1:408.

17. "Critical Notice: A Treatise on the Law of Slander and Libel," *ALM* 2 (1843–44): 247–56, at 255; *Trial of the Case of the Commonwealth v. David Lee Child, for Publishing . . . A Libel on the Hon. John Keyes* (Boston, 1829), p. 13; Baker, ed., *Seward Works*, 1:407–8.

18. *Public Acts, Passed by the General Assembly of the State of Connecticut, May Session 1855* (Hartford, 1855), p. 99; Hotchkiss v. Porter, 30 Conn. 414 (1862).

19. See Wendell's argument in Skinner v. Powers, 1 Wend. 451, 453–54 (N.Y., 1828); Starkie, *Treatise on Law of Slander and Libel*, ed. Wendell, 1:23, 25, 172–76 n.

20. See Chapter 5.

21. "Critical Notice," pp. 247, 254–55.

22. I have discussed Thomas Cooley's views at greater length in "Thomas Cooley, Liberal Jurisprudence, and the Law of Libel, 1868–1884," *UPSLR* 4 (1980): 49–98.

Interested readers may find fuller documentation on Thomas Cooley's writings and judicial work in this article.

23. Cooley, *Constitutional Limitations*, p. 421.

24. Ibid., p. 428.

25. Ibid., p. 427.

26. Ibid., p. 429.

27. Ibid., pp. 451–52, 356 n. 4.

28. Thomas Cooley, *The General Principles of Constitutional Law in the United States of America* (Boston, 1880), p. 274.

29. See Rosenberg, "Cooley, and the Law of Libel," pp. 58–59, n. 45.

30. Cooley, *Constitutional Limitations*, p. 452. Thomas M. Cooley's interest in the role and importance of communications was replicated in the work of his son, the prominent sociologist, Charles H. Cooley. See Daniel Czitrom, *Media and the American Mind* (Chapel Hill, N.C., 1982), pp. 91–102.

31. Ibid., p. 452.

32. Ibid., pp. 438–39; for a discussion of Root v. King, see Chapter 5, pp. 127–28.

33. David Potter, *Freedom and Its Limitations in American Life* (Stanford, Cal., 1976), p. 14.

34. Cooley, *Constitutional Limitations*, p. 429.

35. Ibid., p. 422.

36. Thomas Cooley, *Treatise on the Law of Torts* (Chicago, 1879), p. 217.

37. Cooley, *Constitutional Limitations*, p. 425; Cooley, *Torts*, p. 218 (emphasis added). See also, Rosenberg, "Cooley, and the Law of Libel," p. 64, n. 71.

38. Cooley, *Constitutional Limitations*, pp. 425, 431–35; Cooley, *Torts*, p. 215.

39. Cooley, *Constitutional Limitations*, p. 440; Cooley, *Torts*, p. 209, n. 3.

40. Cooley, *Constitutional Limitations*, p. 440. There has been disagreement among torts scholars over the differences between the defense of fair comment and that of qualified privilege for libelous falsehoods. On the defense of fair comment, see Fowler Harper and Fleming James, *The Law of Torts*, 2 vols. (New York, 1956), 1:456–63, and John Hallen, "Fair Comment," *TLR* 8 (1929): 41–100. The majority view holds that because Cooley called for protection of some libelous falsehoods, his position should not be called fair comment. Another view, however, asserts that the general privilege of fair comment has a minority position that protects both fact and opinion. See Joel Eaton, "The American Law of Defamation through *Gertz v. Robert Welch, Inc.* and Beyond: An Analytical Primer," *VaLR* 61 (1975): 1349–1451, at 1363 n. 52. Most authorities hold that the Supreme Court decisions since 1964 have, in effect, subsumed the old defense of fair comment within the new constitutional law of defamation. See, e.g., W. Page Keeton, "Defamation and Freedom of the Press," *TLR* 54 (1976): 1221–59, at 1240–59. In practice, however, traditional common law defenses such as fair comment have not entirely lost their relevance. See, e.g., the careful discussion in Donald M. Gillmor and Jerome Barron, *Mass Communication Law: Cases and Comment*, 4th ed. (St. Paul, Minn., 1984), pp. 259–72, esp. 266–70.

41. Cooley, *Constitutional Limitations*, pp. 455–56, n. 4.

42. G. Edward White, *The American Judicial Tradition: Profiles of Leading American Judges* (New York, 1975), pp. 119–21, at 121 for speech before Georgia Bar As-

sociation. See also White's study of *Tort Law in America: An Intellectual History* (New York, 1980), pp. 26–62, 115.

43. See Patrick O. Gudridge, "The Persistence of Classical Style," *UPaLR* 131 (1983): 663–792, esp. 671–73, 697–702; Elizabeth Mensch, "The History of Mainstream Legal Thought," in *The Politics of Law: A Progressive Critique*, ed. David Kairys (New York, 1982), pp. 18–39, at 19–26; Duncan Kennedy, "Toward an Historical Understanding of Legal Consciousness: The Case of Classical Legal Thought in America, 1850–1940," *RILS* 3 (1980): 3–24; and Robert Gordon, "Review of *Tort Law in America*," *HLR* 94 (1982): 903–18.

44. This characterization of late nineteenth-century opinions is from David Rabban, "The First Amendment in Its Forgotten Years," *YLJ* 90 (1981): 514–95, 523.

45. Clifton O. Lawhorne, *Defamation and Public Officials: The Evolving Law of Libel* (Carbondale and Edwardsville, Ill., 1971), pp. 87–110. See also the much briefer discussion in Lawhorne, *The Supreme Court and Libel* (Carbondale and Edwardsville, Ill., 1981), pp. 7–8, and Rabban, "The First Amendment," pp. 550–51. Alexis J. Anderson's "The Formative Period of First Amendment Theory, 1870–1915," *AJLH* 24 (1980): 56–75 does not deal with libel law. New York Times v. Sullivan, 376 U.S. 254 (1964) represented the culmination of what its supporters considered to be an expanding history of free expression in the United States. See Chapter 10, pp. 235–37.

46. Negley v. Farrow, 60 Md. 158, 170, 176–77 (1882).

47. Ibid., pp. 183–84.

48. George Chase, "Criticism of Public Officers and Candidates for Office," *AmLR* 23 (1889): 346–71, at 353.

49. Ibid., p. 368. Chase specifically praised "the able dissenting opinion of Judge Cooley" in Atkinson v. Detroit Free Press. Ibid., p. 363, n. 1.

50. Ibid., pp. 368–69.

51. Ibid., p. 370. Chase added: "The maxim, *salus populi, suprema lex*, can have no more vital application than in cases like these, in countries where the right to public office depends upon the suffrages of the citizens."

52. Atkinson v. Detroit Free Press Co., 46 Mich. 341, 349, 367–68, 9 N.W. 501, 505, 515 (1881).

53. All the quotations that follow are taken from Cooley's dissent: 46 Mich. 341, at 3ff, 9 N.W. 501, 508ff. (1881).

54. Miner v. Detroit Post & Tribune Co., 49 Mich. 358, 13 N.W. 773 (1882).

55. Ibid., pp. 361–62, 13 N.W., pp. 773–74.

56. Ibid., pp. 363–65, 13 N.W., pp. 775–76.

57. Ibid., pp. 364–65, 13 N.W., p. 776.

CHAPTER EIGHT

1. The more important of the cases was Detroit Daily Post v. McArthur, 16 Mich. 447 (1868). Cooley incorporated the case into the first edition of his treatise. Thomas Cooley, *A Treatise on the Constitutional Limitations Which Rest Upon the Legislative Powers of the States of the American Union* (Boston, 1868), p. 457.

2. Detroit Daily Post v. McArthur, 16 Mich. 447, 452, 454–55. At least one commentator on libel law saw this holding as a significant victory for the press. See John Proffat, "The Law of Newspaper Libel," *NAR* 131 (1880): 109–27, at p. 114 n. 11. See also Norman L. Rosenberg, "Thomas M. Cooley, Liberal Jurisprudence, and the Law of Libel, 1868–1884," *UPSLR* 4 (1980): 49–98.

3. See William Lutz, *The News of Detroit* (Boston, 1973), p. 9.

4. Foster v. Scripps, 39 Mich. 376, 383 (1878).

5. Ibid., pp. 383–84.

6. See Chapter 7, pp. 173–77.

7. Miner v. Detroit Post & Tribune Co., 49 Mich. 358, 364–65, 13 N.W. 773, 776 (1882).

8. Bathrick v. Detroit Post & Tribune Co., 50 Mich. 629, 644, 16 N.W. 172, 179 (1883).

9. Cooley, *Constitutional Limitations*, 5th ed. (Boston, 1883), pp. 562–63; the *Atkinson* dissent is printed at pp. 563–66 n. 1.

10. Ibid., p. 562. Cooley's effort here to distinguish between public and private persons resembles the labors of the United States Supreme Court, in the wake of Gertz v. Robert Welch, 418 U.S. 323 (1974), to accomplish the same task. See Rosenberg, "Cooley and the Law of Libel," pp. 81–82 at nn. 152–53, pp. 93–97, and Donald M. Gillmor and Jerome Barron, *Mass Communication Law: Cases and Comment*, 4th ed. (St. Paul, Minn., 1984), pp. 248–58.

11. MacLean v. Scripps, 52 Mich. 214, at 220, 211, 17 N.W. 815, at 817 (1883).

12. Ibid., pp. 223–50, at 241–42, 244, 17 N.W. 818–33, at 827, 828, 829 (J. Sherwood dissenting).

13. Scripps's petition for a rehearing was denied. MacLean v. Scripps, 52 Mich. 214, at 253, 18 N.W. 209, at 210 (1884).

14. Ibid. See also Rosenberg, "Cooley and the Law of Libel," p. 84 n. 166.

15. The "pioneer" historian of journalism was Robert Park. The quoted passage is from "The Natural History of the Newspaper," in *Robert E. Park on Social Control and Collective Behavior*, ed. Ralph H. Turner (Chicago, 1967), pp. 97–113, quote at 105. James Scripps is quoted in Lutz, *News of Detroit*, p. 9. The idea of a "use-paper," discussed below, is suggested in Garry Wills, "What's Wrong with this Magazine," [*MORE*] (June 1975), pp. 6–8.

16. Theodore Dreiser, *Sister Carrie*, ed. Claude Simpson (Boston, 1959), pp. 29, 30, 288, 291, 297, 325, 356, 408, extract at 288.

17. See Rosenberg, "Cooley and the Law of Libel," pp. 81–82 n. 152–53, pp. 93–97.

18. Alvin Gouldner, *The Dialectic of Ideology and Technology* (New York, 1976), p. 109 (emphasis in original). On journalism in the 1890s, see Michael Schudson, *Discovering the News: A Social History of American Newspapers* (New York, 1978), pp. 88–120 and George Juergons, *Joseph Pulitzer and the New York World* (Princeton, N.J., 1966). On the nature of the "graphic revolution," see Daniel Boorstin, *The Image* (New York, 1961; reprint, New York, 1971), esp. 12–17. The general theme of the reordering of late nineteeth-century society was first developed in Robert H. Wiebe, *The Search for Order* (New York, 1967). For a recent refinement of the Wiebe view, applied specifically to the legal profession, see Robert W. Gordon, "Legal

Thought and Legal Practice in the Age of American Enterprise, 1870–1920," in *Professions and Professional Ideologies in America*, ed. Gerald L. Geison (Chapel Hill, N.C., 1983), pp. 70–110.

19. Cooley, *Constitutional Limitations*, p. 440; Cooley, *Constitutional Limitations*, 4th ed. (Boston, 1878), pp. 514–15.

20. Atkinson v. Detroit Free Press Co., 46 Mich. 341, 381, 9 N.W. 501, 522–23 (1881) (Justice Cooley dissenting); Miner v. Detroit Post & Tribune Co., 49 Mich. 358, at 363–64, 13 N.W. 773, at 775, 776 (1882). Thomas Cooley seemed especially troubled when libels touched the reputations of physicians. The cases in which he took the hardest line against the press—*Foster, Bathrick,* and *MacLean*—all involved defamation suits by physicians.

21. MacLean v. Scripps, 52 Mich. 251, 253, 18 N.W. 209, 210 (1884) (motion for rehearing).

22. Burton Bledstein, *The Culture of Professionalism* (New York, 1976), pp. 65–79. See also E. L. Godkin, "The Rights of Citizens," *SM* 8 (1890): 58–67. The field of law, of course, was itself affected by the growing sense of professionalism. See, e.g., G. Edward White, *Tort Law in America: An Intellectual History* (New York, 1980), pp. xiii–xiv, 20–26; Jerold Auerbach, *Unequal Justice: Lawyers and Social Change in Modern America* (New York, 1976), pp. 14–73; and Gerald W. Gawalt, ed., *The New High Priests* (Westport, Conn., 1984).

23. Linda Hausman, "Criticism of the Press in U.S. Periodicals, 1900–1939: An Annotated Bibliography," *Journalism Monographs*, No. 4 (1967). Hausman catalogues turn-of-the-century critiques. For a good example of late nineteenth-century criticism, see Charles Dudley Warner, *The American Newspaper: An Essay Read before the Social Science Association . . . Sept. 6, 1881* (Boston, 1881); for an example of the use of modern social science methodologies, see F. Fenton, *The Influence of Newspaper Presentations upon the Growth of Crime and Other Anti-Social Activity* (Chicago, 1911). The impulse to restrict allegedly dangerous expression was a broad one. See, for example, Paul Boyer, *Urban Masses and Moral Order in America, 1820–1920* (Cambridge, Mass., 1920); David Pivar, *Purity Crusade* (Westport, Conn. 1973); and Lary May, *Screening Out the Past* (New York, 1980), pp. 43–59. Although advocates of stricter libel laws did not always endorse regulation of other forms of expression, the subject deserves more attention. William J. Gaynor, for example, a prominent judge and political figure from New York, championed efforts at tightening up the Empire State's defamation laws and measures to control the new medium of motion pictures. See, e.g., May, *Screening Out the Past*, pp. 56–57. William J. Gaynor, "Libel in England and America," *Century* 82 (1911), pp. 824–31, and Glenn W. Woodin, "Contributions of Mr. Justice Gaynor to the Law of Libel and Slander," *B&B* 12 (1917–18): 102–15.

24. Christopher G. Tiedeman, *A Treatise on the Limitations of the Police Power in the United States* (St. Louis, 1886), p. 190; P. L. Edwards, "Free Speech and Free Press in Relation to the Police Power of the State," *CLJ* 58 (1904): 383–86, 384.

25. Henry Billings Brown, "The Liberty of the Press," *AmLR* 24 (1900): 21–44 quotes at 326–27.

26. *Southern Mercury*, quoted in Bruce Palmer, "The Rhetoric of Southern Populists: Metaphor and Image in the Language of Reform" (Ph.D. dissertation, Yale Uni-

versity, 1972), p. 322. My view of late nineteenth- and early twentieth-century political culture owes a great deal to the following studies: Robert H. Wiebe, *The Search for Order* (New York, 1967); John G. Sproat, *The Best Men: Liberal Reformers in the Gilded Age* (New York, 1968); Walter Dean Burnham, *Critical Elections and the Mainsprings of American Politics* (New York, 1970); Robert D. Marcus, *Grand Old Party: Political Structure in the Gilded Age, 1880–1896* (New York, 1971); Richard Jensen, *The Winning of the Midwest* (Chicago, 1971); Morton Keller, *Affairs of State* (Cambridge, Mass., 1977); David Paul Nord, *Newspapers and New Politics: Midwestern Municipal Reform, 1890–1900* (Ann Arbor, Mich., 1981); Samuel P. Hays, "Political Parties and the Community-Society Continuum," in *The American Party Systems*, ed. William Nisbet Chambers and Walter Dean Burnham (New York, 1975), pp. 152–81; Walter Dean Burnham, "Party Systems and the Political Process," in ibid., pp. 277–307; and Robert B. Westbrook, "Politics as Consumption," in *The Culture of Consumption*, ed. Richard Wightman Fox and T. J. Jackson Lears (New York, 1983), pp. 145–73. And of extraspecial importance were Lawrence Goodwyn, *Democratic Promise: The Populist Moment in America* (New York, 1976) and R. Jeffrey Lustig, *Corporate Liberalism* (Berkeley, Cal., 1982). For overviews of legal-constitutional values, I have used, in addition to works cited in other notes, Arnold Paul, *Conservative Crisis and the Rule of Law* (Ithaca, N.Y., 1960); Loren P. Beth, *The Development of the American Constitution, 1877–1917* (New York, 1971); and Lawrence M. Friedman and Robert M. Percival, *The Roots of Justice* (Chapel Hill, N.C., 1981).

27. Joseph Bishop, "Newspaper Espionage," *Forum* 1 (1886): 529–38, at 537; Louis D. Brandeis and Samuel Warren, "The Right to Privacy," *HLR* 4 (1890): 193–200. See also Elbridge L. Adams, "The Right to Privacy and Its Relation to the Law of Libel," *AmLR* 39 (1905): 37–58. Brandeis and Warren's important article is criticized in Harry Kalven, "The Right to Privacy in Tort Law—Were Warren and Brandeis Wrong?" *LCP* 31 (1966): 326–41, and praised in Ruth Colker, "Pornography and Privacy: Towards the Development of a Group Based Theory for Intrusions of Privacy," *LAI* 1 (1983): 191–237, at 201–5. See also the valuable discussions in Dorothy J. Glancy, "The Invention of the Right to Privacy," 21 *AzLR* (1979): 1–39 and Dianne L. Zimmerman, "Requiem for a Heavyweight: A Farewell to Warren and Brandeis' Privacy Tort," *CLR* 68 (1983): 291–368.

28. Henry Adams, "Shall We Muzzle the Anarchists?" *Forum* 1 (1886): 445–64, at 449, 450–54.

29. Brown, "Liberty of Press," pp. 329–30. Brown later added that it "is exceedingly doubtful if any legislation be practicable which shall tend to restrict the excessive license indulged in by newspapers. . . . The law of libel affords [only] a nominal remedy, and if its administration be ineffectual, the same difficulties would probably attend the enforcement of a more rigorous statute. Such a statute, too, could hardly fail to operate as an infringement upon the liberty of the press." Ibid., p. 337.

30. For the Kansas statute, see In re Banks, 56 Kan. 242, 42 P. 693 (1895); the California legislation is noted in Brown, "Liberty of Press," p. 329; on antianarchist legislation, see Sidney Fine, "Anarchism and the Assassination of McKinley," *AHR* 56 (1955): 777–99. See also, Margaret A. Blanchard, "Filling in the Void: Speech and Press in State Courts Prior to *Gitlow*," in *The First Amendment Reconsidered*, ed. Bill F. Chamberlin and Charlene J. Brown (New York, 1982), pp. 14–59, at 26–30.

31. People v. Most, 171 N.Y. 423, 430, 431 (1902). Morris Hillquit's argument on behalf of Most drew heavily from Cooley. Ibid., p. 424.

32. Henry Wolf Biklé, "The Jurisdiction of the United States Over Seditious Libel," *AmLReg* 50 (1902): 1–26, at 3, 24, 25; William Gaynor, "Libel in England and America," *Century* 82 (1911): 824–31. See also Glenn Woodin, "Contributions of Mr. Justice Gaynor to the Law of Libel and Slander," *B&B* 12 (1917–18): 102–15. And Van Vechten Veeder, a prominent jurist who specialized in defamation law, argued that criminal libel laws should be used against those who would destroy the reputations of others. "Why deny to reputation a protection so largely afforded to every other possession?" "The History and Theory of the Law of Defamation," *ColLR* 4 (1904): 33–56, at 45.

33. See Clyde Pierce, *The Roosevelt Panama Libel Cases* (New York, 1959) and John Lofton, *The Press as Guardian of the First Amendment* (Columbia, S.C., 1980), pp. 146–68. Later, in 1912, hoping to stop libelous rumors about excessive drinking, Roosevelt sued the publisher of a small Michigan weekly for libel. See Melvin G. Holli and C. David Tompkins, "Roosevelt v. Newett, The Politics of Libel," *MichH* 47 (1963): 338–56.

34. "Stop Thief," *Outlook* 90 (1909): 841.

35. U.S. v. Smith, 171 F. 227, 232 (1909).

36. U.S. v. Press Publishing Co., 219 U.S. 1 (1911). See also *The Panama Libel Cases: The United States Plaintiff in Error vs. Press Publishing Company . . . Argument of DeLancey Nicoll . . . Before the Supreme Court, Washington, Oct. 24, 1910* (Washington, 1910), esp. pp. 5–10; Alexander H. Robbins, "The Action of the Government Against the New York *World* as a Revival of the Offense of Scandalum Magnatum," *CLJ* 68 (1909): 135–36; and *Panama Libel Case* (Indianapolis, Ind., 1909).

37. See Paul, *Conservative Crisis and the Rule of Law*; see, e.g., "Panama Libel Case," *B&B* 24 (1911): 43–48.

38. Robertson v. Baldwin, 165 U.S. 275, 281 (1897).

39. Peck v. Tribune Company, 214 U.S. 185, 189–90 (1909). Holmes's statement about the "general principles of tort" was slightly ironic. In the early twentieth century, tort law was becoming closely associated with the principle of negligence; defamation, which generally imposed liability without fault, represented an obvious exception to this general principle. See White, *Tort Law*, p. 38. But Holmes, who viewed the press much as Chancellor Kent had (as a dangerous force that needed to be contained by strict rules), saw defamation law as exemplifying another of his main principles of tort law: that "the general purpose of the law of torts is to secure a man indemnity against certain forms of harm to person, reputation, or estate, at the hands of his neighbors, not because they are [morally] wrong, but because they are harms." Oliver Wendell Holmes, *The Common Law*, ed. Mark DeWolfe Howe (Boston, 1963), p. 115. See also ibid., pp. 105, 110, where Holmes discusses his general approach to defamation.

40. Patterson v. Colorado ex rel. The Attorney General of the State of Colorado, 205 U.S. 454, 461–62 (1906). Holmes would have ducked the free-speech issues in *Patterson*, but a sharp dissent by John Marshall Harlan forced the question. See David Bogen, "The Free Speech Metamorphosis of Mr. Justice Holmes," *HofLR* 11 (1982):

97–189, at 125–31. See also David M. Rabban, "The First Amendment in Its Forgotten Years," *YLJ* 90 (1981): 514–95, at 533–34.

41. *New York Herald*, reprinted in Frederic Hudson, *Journalism in the United States, from 1690 to 1872* (New York, 1873), pp. 742–47, quote at 747. The *Tribune*, under Horace Greeley, had taken an active interest in libel law since the days of James Fenimore Cooper. See Chapter 6, pp. 139–40. On the figures for criminal libel prosecutions, see John D. Stevens et al., "Criminal Libel as Seditious Libel, 1916–65," *JQ* 43 (1966): 110–13. See also Samuel Merrill, *Newspaper Libel: A Handbook for the Press* (Boston, 1888), pp. 31–32.

42. Juergons, *Joseph Pulitzer and the New York World*, pp. 81–82; Franc B. Wilkie, *Personal Reminiscences of Thirty-Five Years of Journalism* (Chicago, 1891), pp. 231–35; Justin Walsh, *To Print the News and Raise Hell!* (Chapel Hill, N.C., 1968), p. 239; Evelyn Wells, *Fremont Older* (New York, 1936), p. 128.

43. *Journalist*, 6 Aug. 1884, p. 4; ibid., 6 Sept. 1884, pp. 5–6; ibid., 25 Oct. 1884, p. 2; Walsh, *To Print the News*, pp. 246–47.

44. David Dudley Field, "The Newspaper Press and the Law of Libel," *IR* 5 (1876): 479–91.

45. See, e.g., Charles Clark and Harry Shulman, *A Study of Law Administration in Connecticut* (New Haven, 1937), pp. 12–13, 30–31; Francis W. Laurent, *The Business of a Trial Court: 100 Years of Cases* (Madison, Wis., 1959), pp. 49, 163–64 (table); Robert A. Silverman, *Law and Urban Growth: Civil Litigation in the Boston Trial Court, 1880–1900* (Princeton, N.J., 1981), pp. 122, 130; and Leon Green, "The Right to Communicate," *NYULR* 35 (1960): 903–24, at 905.

46. David Brewer, "Libel," *CLJ* 22 (1886): 363–65, quote at 364; *Journalist*, 20 May 1891; ibid., 26 June 1891; *New York Herald*, 9 Feb. 1894; *New York Times*, 24 March 1894, p. 4; *New York Tribune*, 14 May 1903; Merrill, *Newspaper Libel*, pp. 31–32. Beginning in the 1870s, newspapers apparently did begin to suffer increasingly large libel judgments. See, e.g., Sweeney v. Baker, 13 W. Va. (1878) ($10,000); Wilson v. Fitch, 41 Cal. 363 (1871) ($7500); and Barr v. Moore, 87 Pa. St. 385 (1878) ($10,000; new trial granted because of "excessive" award). At the same time, members of the journalism profession raised a complaint familiar to media watchers of the 1970s and 1980s: the high costs of simply defending libel suits. See, e.g., Hudson, *Journalism in the U.S.*, p. 741, and Edwin Emery, *History of the American Newspaper Publishers Association* (Minneapolis, Minn., 1950), p. 49. Introduction of contingency fees, which became an almost universal custom by about 1880, may have helped to accelerate the expansion of newspaper libel suits and to fuel charges of defamation litigation being instigated by shyster lawyers. See Lawrence M. Friedman, *A History of American Law* (New York, 1973), pp. 422–23.

47. For examples of proposals for changes, see, e.g., *Journal of the House of Representatives of the Commonwealth of Massachusetts, 1896* (Boston, 1896), p. 208; *Journal of the House of Representatives of the Commonwealth of Massachusetts, 1897* (Boston, 1897), pp. 140, 148, 179, 196; *New York Herald*, 9 Feb. 1894, p. 8; William G. Rodgers, "The Proposed Libel Law," *Report of the Second Annual Meeting of the Pennsylvania Bar Association* (Philadelphia, 1896), pp. 175–81; *Journalist*, 28 April 1906, p. 15; *E&P*, 21 June 1902, p. 5.

48. For just a sampling of the proposals, see Rodgers, "The Proposed Libel Law," pp. 184–89; *New York Times*, 24 March 1894, p. 3. See also [Untitled Note], *HLR* 3 (1889): 89; E. J. Hamel, "Libel—Civil Liability in Illinois," *ChiLJ* 5 (n.s. 1894): 259–72; D. M. Mickey, "Reforms in the Law of Newspaper Libel," *CLJ* 42 (1896): 475–80; Moorfield Storey, "Address of the President," *American Bar Association, Reports, 1896*, pp. 179–252, at 216–17; W. A. Purrington, *An Examination of the Doctrine of Malice as an Essential Element of Responsibility for Defamation Uttered on a Privileged Occasion* (Albany, N.Y., 1898); Thomas R. White, "Constitutionality of the Pennsylvania Libel Law," *AmLReg* 51 (1903): 556–60; "A Warning to Newspapers," *ValReg* 19 (1913–14): 631–33; and "Privileged Publications, Misstatements of Facts Regarding Candidates for Public Office," *IaLB* 2 (1916): 154.

49. *Journalist*, 4 Aug. 1892, p. 8.

50. New York Times v. Sullivan, 376 U.S. 254, 279 (1964).

51. Herbert Croly, *The Promise of American Life* (New York, 1909; reprint, Indianapolis, Ind., 1965), p. 164. Croly was hardly the only progressive intellectual who viewed the American press with some alarm. See, e.g., Edward Alsworth Ross, *Social Psychology: An Outline and Source Book* (New York, 1925), pp. 85–86. Ross, however, was also a firm believer in an essentially consequentionalist, marketplace view of free expression. See ibid., pp. 308–14. A full-scale study of free-speech thought during the progressive era is badly needed.

52. Post Publishing Co. v. Hallam, 59 F. 530, 540, 541 (1893).

53. Burt v. Advertiser Newspaper Co., 154 Mass. 238, 242–43 (1891).

54. Coleman v. MacLennon, 78 Kan. 711, 737–38, 98 P. 281, 290–91 (1908).

55. For an exhaustive summary of the appellate case law, see George H. Parmele, "Annotation—Libel and Slander—Public Officer or Candidate," *LRA* (1918E): 271–87, esp. pp. 274–77 for scattered cases on the minority position. See also Clifton O. Lawhorne, *Defamation and Public Officials: The Evolving Law of Libel* (Carbondale and Edwardsville, Ill., 1971), pp. 87–110; Rabban, "First Amendment," pp. 550–51; and Norman L. Rosenberg, "The New Law of Political Libel: A Historical Perspective," *RLR* 28 (1975): 1141–83, at 1159.

56. Mason H. Newell, *The Law of Slander and Libel in Civil and Criminal Cases*, 3d. ed. (Chicago, 1914), pp. 93–94; Van Vechten Veeder, "The History and Theory of the Law of Defamation," *ColLR* 3 (1903): 546–73, and ibid. 4 (1904): 33–56, esp. 33–34, 44–45.

57. Thomas Cooley, *A Treatise on the Law of Torts*, 2d ed., ed. John Lewis, 2 vols. (Chicago, 1906), 1:442–43. See also the changed emphasis in Henry Campbell Black, *Handbook of American Constitutional Law* (St. Paul, Minn., 1895), pp. 472–76, and ibid., 4th ed. (St. Paul, Minn., 1927), p. 656.

58. White, *Tort Law*, p. 19. One of the earliest conceptualizers, Nicholas St. John Green, had once condemned defamation law for seeming "to have no general principle for its foundation" and had praised a nineteenth-century treatise writer for vainly trying "to classify under general principles a branch of the law which . . . does not admit of such classification." Green, "Slander and Libel," *AmLR* 6 (1872): 593–613, at 593, 612–13 (review of John Townshend, *A Treatise on the Wrongs Called Slander and Libel, and on the Remedy by Civil Action*, 2d ed., [1872]).

59. James Barr Ames and Jeremiah Smith, *A Selection of Cases on the Law of*

Torts, 2d ed., 2 vols. (Cambridge, Mass., 1909), 1:453, 455–56 n.; James Barr Ames and Jeremiah Smith, *A Selection of Cases on the Law of Torts*, new ed., ed. Roscoe Pound (Cambridge, Mass., 1919), p. 795 n. See also Francis H. Bohlen, *Cases on Torts* (Indianapolis, Ind., 1915). But, as Harry Kalven has noted, these early casebooks (even though they highlighted the majority view) still included some mention of the fact that the law of defamation could raise free-speech issues; in contrast, casebooks of the 1940s and early 1950s rarely dealt with such questions. Harry Kalven, Jr., "The Law of Defamation and the First Amendment," in *Conference on the Arts, Publishing, and the Law* (Chicago, 1952), p. 7.

60. Jeremiah Smith, "Are Charges Against the Moral Character of a Candidate for an Elective Office Conditionally Privileged?" *MLR* 18 (1919): 1–15, 104–25, at 105. To bring any sense of order, even highly artificial order, to defamation law was no small task; indeed, the law of slander and libel produced a cottage industry devoted to exposing its "absurdities." See, e.g., R. S. Guernsey, "When is a Libel, Not a Libel," *YLJ* 20 (1910–11): 36–43, and James C. Courtney, "Absurdities of the Law of Slander and Libel," *AmLR* 36 (1902): 552–58.

61. The characterization of Schofield's essay is in Rabban, "The First Amendment," pp. 559, 562, 564–65. Although Rabban's analysis is very valuable, he telescopes some developments incorrectly, especially when he lumps together Cooley's *Constitutional Limitations* and Schofield's essay as part of a new libertarian scholarship. As I have sought to demonstrate, Schofield's analysis represented a substantial modification of the old Cooley position. Schofield, in fact, pointed out that text writers on the law of libel rejected the minority rule announced in Coleman v. MacLennon, 78 Kan. 711, 98 Pac., 281 (1908) (and based on Cooley's *Atkinson* dissent and *Constitutional Limitations*) as "extreme or exceptional." See Henry Schofield, *Essays on Constitutional Law and Equity and Other Subjects*, 2 vols. (Boston, 1921), II:553–54. The essay was first published in PASS 9 (1914): 67–122.

62. Schofield, *Essays*, II: 554 n. 56, 569–70, 570–71.

63. See Burnham, "Party Systems and the Political Process," pp. 277–306, at 277, 279; Marcus, *Grand Old Party*, pp. 14–19; Culver G. Smith, *The Press, Politics, and Patronage: The American Government's Use of Newspapers, 1789–1875* (Athens, Ga., 1977); Goodwyn, *The Populist Moment*, pp. 206–12, 288–90.

64. Jensen, *Winning of the Midwest*, pp. 166–75; Christopher Lasch, *The Culture of Narcissism* (New York, 1979), pp. 135–51, 271–75; and Westbrook, "Politics as Consumption," pp. 145–73.

65. See the broad perspectives offered in Goodwyn, *Populist Moment*; Alvin Gouldner, *The Dialectic of Ideology and Technology* (New York, 1976); Todd Gitlin, *The Whole World is Watching* (Berkeley, Cal., 1980); and Charles Lindbloom, *Politics and Markets* (New York, 1977), pp. 201–16.

66. See Robert W. Gordon, "New Developments in Legal Theory," in *The Politics of Law*, ed. David Kairys (New York, 1982), pp. 281–93, quote at 287, and Peter Gabel and Jay M. Feinman, "Contract Law as Ideology," in ibid., pp. 172–84.

67. See, e.g., Melvin Dubofsky, *We Shall Be All: A History of the IWW* (New York, 1969), pp. 173–97; Alexis J. Anderson, "The Formative Period of First Amendment Theory, 1870–1915," *AJLH* 24 (1980): 56–75; Rabban, "The First Amendment," pp. 516–95; David M. Rabban, "The Emergence of Modern First Amendment

Doctrine," 50 *UChiLR* (1983): 1205–1355; and Blanchard, "Filling in the Void, pp. 14–59.

CHAPTER NINE

1. See, e.g., *E&P*, 18 Dec. 1920, p. 40 (former U.S. Senator dropped $600,000 suit); ibid., 12 April 1930, p. 54 (suspended sentence in criminal libel case in exchange for retraction); ibid., 1 Jan. 1938, p. 33 ($40,000 suit by Mystery Chef dropped); ibid., 7 May 1938, p. 10 (governor of Rhode Island dropped $500,000 suit in exchange for apology). For more recent examples of the threat of libel actions by highly-placed political and corporate officials, see Nat Hentoff, *The First Freedom* (New York, 1980), pp. 269–70 (by aircraft manufacturers), and Robert I. Friedman and Dan Moldea, "Networks Knuckle Under to Laxalt," *VV* (5 March 1985), pp. 10–14 (by U.S. Senator). West Publishing Company's *Decennial Digests* compile all of the cases, primarily from appellate courts, that were reported during the previous decade in West's own National Reporter System.

2. For a brief interpretation of changes in mainstream legal thought, see Elizabeth Mensch, "The History of Mainstream Legal Thought," in *The Politics of Law: A Progressive Critique*, ed. David Kairys (New York, 1982), pp. 18–39, at 23–37. On changes in tort law, see G. Edward White, *Tort Law in America: An Intellectual History* (New York, 1980), pp. 63ff, and Richard Abel, "Torts," in *Politics of Law*, ed. Kairys, pp. 185–200.

3. Richard Drinnon, *Rebel in Paradise: A Biography of Emma Goldman* (Chicago, 1961; reprint, New York, 1976), p. 226. See also, Paul Murphy, *The Meaning of Free Speech: First Amendment Freedoms from Wilson to Roosevelt* (Westport, Conn., 1972), and David Kairys, "Freedom of Speech," in *Politics of Law*, ed. Kairys, pp. 140–71, at 142–53.

4. Paul Murphy, *World War I and the Origin of Civil Liberties in the United States* (New York, 1979), pp. 71–132; Drinnon, *Rebel in Paradise*, pp. 224–27; and Frank J. Donner, *The Age of Surveillance* (New York, 1980).

5. See Chapter 6.

6. This discussion relies upon Stephen Vaughn, "First Amendment Liberties and the Committee on Public Information," *AJLH* 23 (1979): 95–119. See also Vaughn's book, *Holding Fast the Inner Lines: Democracy, Nationalism and the Committee on Public Information* (Chapel Hill, N.C., 1980), and David Kennedy, *Over Here: The First World War and American Society* (New York, 1980), pp. 45–92.

7. See Murphy, *World War I and Civil Liberties*, pp. 74–84 and 40 *Stat. at Large*, Chap. 75, 553–54, at 553.

8. See the careful analysis of the briefs in David Rabban, "The First Amendment in Its Forgotten Years," *YLJ* 90 (1981): 516–95, at 582–84. For the cases themselves, see Schenck v. U.S., 249 U.S. 47 (1919); Frowerk v. U.S., 249 U.S. 204 (1919); Sugarman v. U.S., 249 U.S. 182 (1919); and Debs v. U.S., 249 U.S. 211 (1919).

9. The characterization is Harry Kalven's. See "Professor Ernst Freund and Debs. v. United States," *UChiLR* 40 (1973): 235–39, at 238.

10. Schenck v. United States, 249 U.S. 47, 51–52 (1919).

11. Ibid., at p. 52.

12. Donner, *The Age of Surveillance*, p. xix. On the origins and modifications of
the free-speech consciousness articulated during the World War I era, see the follow-
ing: Rabban, "The First Amendment," pp. 578–95; David Rabban, "The Emergence
of Modern First Amendment Doctrine," *UChiLR* 50 (1983): 1205–1355; Fred Ragan,
"Justice Oliver Wendell Holmes, Jr., Zechariah Chafee, Jr., and the Clear and Present
Danger Test for Free Speech: The First Year, 1919," *JAH* 58 (1971): 24–45; Gerald
Gunther, "Learned Hand and the Origins of Modern First Amendment Doctrine: Some
Fragments of History," *StanLR* 27 (1975): 719–73; Robert M. Cover, "The Left, the
Right, and the First Amendment: 1918–1928," *MdLR* 40 (1981): 349–88; Murphy,
The Meaning of Free Speech; and Kairys, "Freedom of Speech," pp. 153–67.

13. Coleman v. MacLennon, 78 Kan. 711, at 734–35, 98 P. 281, at 289 (1908).
And see In re Banks, 56 Kan. 242, 42 P. 693 (1895).

14. Coleman v. MacLennon, 78 Kan. at 720–21, 98 P. at 284.

15. Ibid., p. 720, 98 P. at 284.

16. "Regulating the Press," *Nation* 100 (1 April 1915): 348–49; John W. Perry, "16
States Are Considering Press Bills," *E&P*, 21 Feb. 1931, pp. 7, 51; and ibid., 7
March 1931, p. 32 (editorial critical of injunctions).

17. Edward Paul quoted in Nelson Antrim Crawford, *The Ethics of Journalism*
(New York, 1924), pp. 134–36.

18. Walter Lippmann, *Public Opinion* (New York, 1922; reprint, New York, 1975),
p. 209; on the relationship between Lippmann's work and the free-speech ideas of
Holmes and Brandeis, see Cover, "The Left, Right, and First Amendment," pp. 363–
71. On the Florida law, see Thomas W. Hoffer and Gerald A. Butterfield, "The Right
to Reply: A Florida First Amendment Aberration," *JQ* 53 (1976): 111–16, and Miami
Herald Pub. Co. v. Tornillo, 418 U.S. 241 (1974) (declaring Florida's reply law unconstitutional). On the Ohio reply law, see *E&P*, 1 Feb. 1930, p. 20; ibid., 22 Feb.
1930, p. 36.

19. Roscoe Pound, "Equitable Relief against Defamation and Injuries to Personality," *HLR* 29 (1916): 640–70, at 651. See also the elaborate brief and supporting evidence compiled for the proposition "that the Minnesota Nuisance Law should be
adopted by every state in the Union." Lamar T. Beman, comp., *Selected Articles on
Censorship of Speech and of the Press* (New York, 1930), pp. 145–68, 195ff. Finally,
see the later legal analysis in Estella Gold, "Does Equity Still Lack Jurisdiction to Enjoin a Libel or Slander?" *BrkLR* 48 (1982): 231–63.

20. Act of 20 Apr. 1925, Ch. 285 1925 Minn. Laws 358 (held unconstitutional,
Near v. Minnesota, 283 U.S. 697 [1931]). In the absence of other citations, discussion
of the background of the *Near* case is based upon Fred W. Friendly's *Minnesota Rag*
(New York, 1981) and Reed L. Carpenter, "John L. Morrison and the Origins of the
Minnesota Gag Law," *JH* 9 (1982): 16–17, 25–28. See also Paul L. Murphy, "*Near v.
Minnesota* in the Context of Historical Developments," *MinnLR* 66 (1981): 95–160.

21. State ex re. Olson v. Guilford, 174 Minn. 457, at 462, 219 N.W. 770, at 772
(1928); see also State ex rel. Olson v. Guilford, 179 Minn. 40, 228 N.W. 326 (1929).

22. Near v. Minnesota, 283 U.S. 697, 723–38 (J. Butler dissenting).

23. Ibid., at 713, 715.

24. Brandeis quoted in Friendly, *Minnesota Rag*, pp. 130–31. For a discussion of

Brandeis's changing views on constitutional guarantees of free speech, see Cover "The Left, Right, and First Amendment," pp. 371–87.

25. Near v. Minnesota, 283 U.S. at 719–20.

26. Chaplinsky v. New Hampshire, 315 U.S. 568, 571–72 (1942). The views of Murphy, a staunch libertarian on most free-speech issues, closely paralleled those of the ACLU on the law of libel. During the 1920s, for example, endorsement of mainstream libel doctrines seemed compatible with the ACLU's social activist stance. In 1926 the ACLU refused a direct request to become involved in a defamation suit brought by Norman Thomas, one of its own board members, against Joseph T. Cashman, a lecturer for the National Security League. In rejecting Cashman's request for assistance, the ACLU's Forest Baily argued that the group's interest in free speech did not "extend to the field of utterances which are at issue because of their supposed libelous character." Because the law regarded truth "as an adequate defense," the ACLU assumed that Cashman could place his trust upon the accuracy of his statements about Thomas with "utmost security." "Press Release," 21 April 1925, *American Civil Liberties Union Records and Publications, 1917–1975* (Microfilm Edition, 1976), Reel 1. Indeed, the ACLU's leadership, including Arthur Garfield Hays, used libel suits as weapons in their fights against various right-wing and ultra-patriotic groups. See, e.g. Schwimmer v. Commercial Newspaper Co., 228 N.Y.S. 220 (1928). See generally, Murphy, *The Meaning of Free Speech*, pp. 221–22, 356–57.

On Justice Frank Murphy's fear of "anti-democratic libels," see David M. Bixby, "The Roosevelt Court, Democratic Ideology, and Minority Rights: Another Look at United States v. Classic," *YLJ* 90 (1981): 741–815, at 770–74. For an example of a full-scale justification for the use of libel law as a weapon against antidemocratic forces, see my discussion of David Riesman's views, Chapter 9, pp. 229–31. The United States Supreme Court, in 1942, did have the opportunity to rule directly on libel law; but, when the Justices divided 4–4, the Court could render no decision. Sweeney v. Schenectady Publishing Co., 122 F.2d 288 (2d Cir., 1941), aff'd by an equally divided Court, 316 U.S. 642 (1942). This case, one of a series of chain libel suits by U.S. Congressman Martin Sweeney, was notable for several reasons, other than its appearance before the U.S. Supreme Court. First, the case reflected deeper tensions about how the law should respond to racial and ethnic defamation. A majority of the Court of Appeals for the Second Circuit held that it was libelous per se, under New York's defamation laws, to allege, as Drew Pearson had done of Congressman Sweeney, that a person was prejudiced against Jews. (Pearson had charged that Sweeney opposed an appointee to the federal judiciary on the basis of the nominee's religious faith.) Ibid., at 290–91. Second, Justice Charles Clark issued a vigorous dissent, one that insisted that the majority's holding threatened serious damage to the ability of the press to comment upon the actions and opinions of public officials. In practice, he argued, the traditional defense of truth could provide insufficient protection in libel suits by public officials. Ibid., at 291–92 (J. Clark dissenting). For an analysis of the general lines of division within the Court of Appeals for the Second Circuit, see Marvin Schick, *Learned Hand's Court* (Baltimore, 1970). On Drew Pearson's libel problems with Martin Sweeney, see Douglas A. Anderson, A *"Washington Merry-Go-Round" of Libel Actions* (Chicago, 1980), pp. 102–27, 263–65.

Although defamation involving alleged ethnic and religious defamation by people such as Sweeney divided members of both liberal and Jewish groups, this time they lined up solidly behind Pearson and the *Schenectady Union*; several Jewish organizations joined the ACLU in filing briefs urging the U.S. Supreme Court to overturn the Circuit Court holding. But the Court, with Justice Robert Jackson withdrawing, split down the middle, a result that delayed a Supreme Court ruling on political libel for another twenty-two years and that sent Pearson and the *Union* back to the District Court for another hearing. (On a motion for reconsideration, Justice Jackson again withdrew, and the Court again reached no decision.) 316 U.S. 710 (1942).

27. Allan Nevins and Frank Ernest Hill, *Ford: Expansion and Challenges, 1915–1933* (New York, 1957), p. 132; Louis Nizer, *My Life in Court* (New York, 1961), pp. 17–152, 287–346.

28. On the continuing flow of publications by law professors and teachers of journalism on libel law, especially on its relationship to political questions and guarantees of free speech, see, e.g., William G. Hale, *The Law of the Press* (St. Paul, Minn., 1923) (collection of lectures, given by a law professor at two schools of journalism), esp. pp. 130–38; Frederick S. Siebert, *The Rights and Privileges of the Press* (New York, 1934) (text by professor of journalism), esp. 330–37; Francis H. Bohlen, *Cases on the Law of Torts*, 2d ed. (New York, 1934), pp. 771–839 (chapter on defamation), pp. 840–93 (separate chapter on privileged statements and publications); John Hallen, "Fair Comment," *TLR* 8 (1929): 41–100; Clarence Morris, "Inadvertent Newspaper Libel and Retraction," *IlLR* 32 (1937): 36–49; Fowler Harper, "Privileged Defamation," *VaLR* 22 (1936): 642–64.

For the concern of the mainstream press about defamation law, see *Editor & Publisher*, the leading trade publication of the American newspaper industry. See, e.g., *E&P*, 29 Jan. 1927, pp. 269–73; ibid., 25 Jan. 1930, pp. 257–58; and ibid., 30 Jan. 1948, pp. 306–8.

29. *ALIP* 14 (1936–37): 135.

30. Ibid., pp. 136–57. See also American Law Institute, *Restatement of the Law of Torts*, 3 vols. (St. Paul, Minn., 1938), 3: Sec. 606–7, 275–85. Van Vechten Veeder had been one of the most influential spokespersons, earlier in the twentieth century, for rejection of the old Cooley position and acceptance of the neo-Hamiltonian approach. See Van Vechten Veeder, "Freedom of Public Discussion," *HLR* 23 (1910): 413–46. A judge in New York state, Veeder was considered one of the early twentieth century's foremost experts on the law of defamation.

31. Leon Green, "The Torts Restatement," *IlLR* 29 (1935): 582–607, at 582–83.

32. Francis H. Bohlen, *Cases on the Law of Torts*, 2nd ed. (Indianapolis, Ind., 1925); Leon Green, *The Judicial Process in Tort Cases* (St. Paul, Minn., 1931), pp. 1427–85 ("Social Relations"), pp. 1486–1525 ("Professional Relations"), pp. 1531–1607 ("Political Relations"). On the general impact of legal realism, see, e.g., Mensch, "Mainstream Legal Thought," pp. 26–29; on the impact of realism on tort law, see White, *Tort Law*, pp. 63–113.

33. Morris Ernst and Alexander Lindey, *Hold Your Tongue!* (New York, 1932; reprint, New York, 1950), pp. 61, 81. Any definition of freedom of press, the two authors argued, was "merely the temporary and changing attitude of our judges and our

jurors." Ibid., pp. 177–78. To Ernst and Lindey, then, there was just one case after another. Similarly, they insisted that libel doctrines, like rules in other areas of the law, bore "only [a] slight relation to actual life." Ibid., p. 83.

34. Sweeney v. Schenectady Publishing Co., 122 F.2d. 288, 291 (2nd Cir.), aff'd by an equally divided Court, 316 U.S. 642 (1942). See also, n. 26 for this chapter.

35. In the absence of other citations, discussion of Pearson's suits are based upon Douglas Anderson's thorough study, *"Washington Merry-Go-Round."*

36. Laurence H. Eldredge, *The Law of Defamation* (Indianapolis, Ind., 1978), pp. 590–91. Existence of a specialized corps of libel defense lawyers, by itself, provided an insufficient guarantee against defamation problems, of course. In the mid-1980s, although media representatives were complaining loudly about defamation suits, most experienced libel lawyers still represented defendants. See Marc A. Franklin, "Good Names and Bad Law: A Critique of Libel Law and a Proposal," *USFLR* 18 (1983): 1–49, 12–13. There were indications, though, that attorneys for libel plaintiffs were more experienced and had more organizational support in the 1980s than ever before. See, e.g., Jonathan W. Lubell, Audry J. Isaacs, and Arlene R. Smoler, "A Plaintiff's Approach to the Law of Defamation," in *Communications Law*, 2 vols. (New York, 1982), 1:647–720.

37. Nevins and Hill, *Ford*, pp. 133–40; Eldredge, *Defamation*, pp. 591–92.

38. Oliver Pilat, *Drew Pearson: An Unauthorized Biography* (New York, 1973), pp. 140–47.

39. Anderson, *"Washington Merry-Go-Round,"* p. 52. Ernst and Lindey specifically noted how the slow-moving American legal system worked against plaintiffs determined to take defamation actions to trial. *Hold Your Tongue!*, pp. 18–20.

40. Marc Galanter, "Why the 'Haves' Come Out Ahead: Speculations on the Limits of Legal Change," *LSR* 9 (1974): 95–160, at 97–119.

41. David Riesman, "Democracy and Defamation: Fair Game and Fair Comment II," *ColLR* 42 (1942): 1282–1318, at 1285; David Dudley Field, "The Newspaper Press and the Law of Libel," *IR* 5 (1876): 479–91; Zechariah Chafee, Jr., *Government and Mass Communications*, 2 vols. (Chicago, 1947), 1:101, quoting from a book review by Arthur Garfield Hays.

42. Anderson, "Washington Merry-Go-Round," pp. 142–43.

43. Marvin Berger, "Detecting Libel Before It Appears," *E&P*, 29 May 1937, p. 7; Riesman, "Democracy and Defamation II," p. 1309, n. 114. Drew Pearson refused to use libel insurance because companies generally reserved the right to take advantage of retraction provisions in state defamation laws. See Morris, "Inadvertent Newspaper Libel and Retraction," pp. 36–49. Pearson considered such provisions a form of censorship. Drew Pearson, *Drew Pearson Diaries*, ed. Tyler Abell (New York, 1974), p. 360 n.

44. Chafee, *Government and Mass Communication*, I: 103. Similarly, in *The First Freedom* (New York, 1946), the prominent liberal attorney Morris Ernst reiterated the conclusion of his earlier work on libel law: the law, in practice, gave the American press almost no trouble. Thus, Ernst proposed laws relieving electronic media of any threat of defamation suits—the applicability of laws developed for the print media to broadcasting was unclear in 1946—so that the holder of a broadcasting license could stand on the same ground as "the owner of a printing press who, as a practical matter,

is free of libel suits." Ibid., p. 262. The ACLU, an organization in which Ernst played an important role, also saw no pressing problems, in the 1940s, with libel law. Board of Directors Minutes, 21 Apr. 1947, *ACLU Records*, Reel 10.

45. Quoted in Michael Schudson, *Discovering the News: A Social History of American Newspapers* (New York, 1978), p. 152.

46. Casper Yost, *The Principles of Journalism* (New York, 1924), pp. 46–47, 118.

47. Nancy Barr Mavity, *The Modern Newspaper* (New York, 1930), pp. 14–16, 20–21.

48. Schudson, *Discovering the News*, pp. 121–59, at 151; Mavity, *Modern Newspaper*, p. 48; Leon Nelson Flint, *The Conscience of the Newspaper* (New York, 1925), p. 108; Silas Bent, *Ballyhoo: The Voice of the Press* (New York, 1927); for an example of one of Bernarr McFadden's libel suits, see *E&P*, 8 Feb. 1930, p. 52; Crawford, *Ethics of Journalism*, p. 227; Albert F. Henning, *Ethics and Practices in Journalism* (New York, 1932), pp. 31–33. See also the more penetrating critique of the limitations of journalism in Lippmann, *Public Opinion*, pp. 201–30. See also Catherine L. Covert and John D. Stevens, eds., *Mass Media between the Wars: Perceptions of Cultural Tension, 1918–1941* (Syracuse, N.Y., 1984).

49. Robert H. Phelps and E. Douglas Hamilton, *Libel: Rights, Risks, Responsibilities*, rev. ed. (New York, 1978), p. 1; Paul Ashley, *Say It Safely: Legal Limits in Journalism and Broadcasting* (1948; reprint, 1956), pp. 6, 18–26; Philip Wittenberg, *Dangerous Words: A Guide to the Law of Libel* (New York, 1947). See also the cautionary tone of Ella Cooper Thomas, *The Law of Libel and Slander* (New York, 1949).

50. See Jerold S. Auerbach, "The Patrician as Libertarian," *NEQ* 42 (1969): 511–31; Jonathan Prude, "Portrait of a Civil Libertarian," *JAH* 60 (1973): 633–56; and Peter H. Irons, " 'Fighting Fair': Zechariah Chafee, Jr., the Department of Justice, and the 'Trial' at the Harvard Club," *HLR* 94 (1981): 1205–36.

51. Chafee, *Government and Mass Communication*, 1:97.

52. David Riesman, "Democracy and Defamation: Fair Game and Fair Comment I," *ColLR* 42 (1942): 1085–1123, at 1092–1111.

53. Ibid., pp. 1117–23; Riesman, "Democracy and Defamation: Control of Group Libel," *ColLR* 42 (1942): 727–80, at 779.

54. Riesman, "Democracy and Defamation II," pp. 1311–12.

55. Riesman, "Democracy and Defamation II," pp. 1300–1308, 1314–18; Riesman, "Group Libel." Riesman's approach to political communication grew out of the so-called bullet theory of propaganda, which was the conventional wisdom from about World War I to the 1940s. According to this view, antidemocratic propaganda mowed down the inert masses, much like bullets from a gun. See Mark Yudoff, *When Government Speaks* (Berkeley, Cal., 1983), pp. 74–75.

56. Karl Loewenstein, "Legislative Control of Political Extremism in Europe," *ColLR* 38 (1938): 591–622, 725–74; on Roosevelt's attitude toward the far right and Pelley, see Leo P. Ribuffo, "United States v. McWilliams: The Roosevelt Administration and the Far Right," in *American Political Trials*, ed. Michael Belknap (Westport, Conn., 1981), pp. 201–32, at 204–5; see also U.S. v. Pelley, 132 F.2d 170, 176 (7 Cir., 1942), cert. denied 318 U.S. 764 (1942), reh. denied, ibid., p. 801. For Lasswell's faith in his approach and its application to court trials, see Harold D. Lasswell et al., eds., *Language of Politics* (New York, 1949), pp. 173–232.

57. See generally, Donner, *Age of Surveillance*.

58. See Beauharnais v. Illinois, 343 U.S. 250 (1952); Joseph Tannenhaus, "Group Libel," *CLQ* 35 (1950): 261–302; Loren Beth, "Group Libel and Free Speech," *MinnLR* 39 (1955): 167–84; and Harry Kalven, Jr., *The Negro and the First Amendment* (Chicago, 1965), pp. 7–53. Linking *Beauharnais* and *Times* v. *Sullivan*, Professor Kalven noted Justice William O. Douglas's dissenting comment in 1952: "in the next [libel] case a Negro would be haled before the Court for protesting in heated terms, lynch law in the South." Quoted in ibid., pp. 52–53.

59. See Chafee, *Government and Mass Communications*, 1: 101ff., and Richard C. Donnelly, "The Right of Reply: An Alternative to An Action for Libel," *VaLR* 34 (1948): 867–900.

60. See Owen Lattimore, *Ordeal by Slander* (Boston, 1950); Stanley I. Kutler, *The American Inquisition* (New York, 1982), pp. 183–214; Fred W. Friendly, *Due to Circumstances Beyond Our Control* (New York, 1967), pp. 62–65. See also Arnold M. Rose, *Libel and Academic Freedom: A Lawsuit against Political Extremists* (Minneapolis, Minn., 1968); William L. Dwyer, *The Goldmark Case* (Seattle, 1984); and Harold L. Nelson, *Libel in News of Congressional Investigating Committees* (Minneapolis, Minn., 1961).

61. See Allen Weinstein, *Perjury: The Hiss-Chambers Case* (New York, 1978), pp. 161–95, and William L. Marbury, "The Hiss-Chambers Libel Suit," *MdLR* 41 (1981): 75–102 (reminiscences by Hiss's attorney).

62. On the *Faulk* suit, see Louis Nizer, *The Jury Returns* (New York, 1966), pp. 225–438, at 436, 438, and John Henry Faulk, *Fear on Trial* (New York, 1964).

63. Dix Noel, "Defamation of Public Officers and Candidates," *ColLR* 49 (1949): 875–903, at 875; Vernon X. Miller, *Selected Essays on Torts* (Buffalo, N.Y., 1960), p. 194.

64. See Murphy, *The Meaning of Freedom of Speech*; Kairys, "Freedom of Speech," pp. 149–63; and Harry Kalven, Jr., "The Concept of the Public Forum: Cox v. Louisiana," *SCR* (1965): 1–32.

65. See Alan Trachtenberg, *The Incorporation of America* (New York, 1982); Emily Rosenberg, *Spreading the American Dream* (New York, 1982); R. Jeffrey Lustig, *Corporate Liberalism* (Berkeley, Cal., 1982); and Robert W. Gordon, "Legal Thought and Legal Practice in the Age of American Enterprise, 1870–1920," in *Professions and Professional Ideologies in America*, ed. Gerald L. Geison (Chapel Hill, N.C., 1983), pp. 70–110.

66. Lustig, *Corporate Liberalism*, pp. 109–49, is very suggestive in his discussions of the ways in which group-based analysis came to dominate social and legal thought. On law in particular, see ibid., pp. 91–95, 116–20, 140–42. David Bixby's account of liberal concern for the protection of minority rights adds another dimension consistent with the argument advanced here. See Bixby, "The Roosevelt Court," pp. 743–86.

67. See Note, "Developments in the Law—Defamation," *HLR* 69 (1956): 875–960.

68. See Robert W. Gordon, "Critical Legal Histories," *StanLR* 36 (1980): 57–125, esp. pp. 114–25, and Mark V. Tushnet, "Deviant Science in Constitutional Law," *TLR* 59 (1981): 815–27.

69. Chafee, *Government and Mass Communication*, 1:109–14.

CHAPTER TEN

1. New York Times v. Sullivan, 376 U.S. 254, at 256 (1964).
2. Ibid., at 278.
3. On the proslavery offensive of the 1830s, see William W. Freehling, *Prelude to Civil War* (New York, 1966), pp. 301–60; on the prosegregationist campaigns of the 1950s and early 1960s, see Numan V. Bartley, *The Rise of Massive Resistance* (Baton Rouge, La., 1969).
4. My view of the civil rights movement is especially indebted to the analysis in Francis Fox Piven and Richard Cloward, *Poor People's Movements* (New York, 1977), pp. 181–263. In this chapter I argue that the law of defamation must be understood against the complex tensions within both liberal politics and a liberal legal-constitutional order. My view of the larger legal-political issues draws upon a vast literature, but it has been especially enriched by Garry Wills, *Nixon Agonistes* (New York, 1969); Charles Lindbloom, *Politics and Markets* (New York, 1977); Theodore Lowi, *The End of Liberalism*, 2d ed., (New York, 1979); Ira Katznelson, *City Trenches* (New York, 1981); Christopher Lasch, *The Culture of Narcissism* (New York, 1979); Frank J. Donner, *The Age of Surveillance* (New York, 1980); Alan Wolfe, *The Limits of Legitimacy* (New York, 1977), and *America's Impasse* (New York, 1982); Alan Matusow, *The Unraveling of America* (New York, 1984); Roberto Unger, *Knowledge and Politics* (New York, 1975), and *Law and Modern Society* (New York, 1976); Jerold Auerbach, *Unequal Justice* (New York, 1976); David Kairys, ed., *The Politics of Law* (New York, 1982); Marc A. Galanter, "Why the 'Haves' Come Out Ahead: Speculations on the Limits of Legal Change," *LSR* 9 (1974): 95–160; C. Edwin Baker, "Scope of the First Amendment Freedom of Speech," *UCLALR* 25 (1978): 964–1040; "Symposium—Freedom of Expression: Theoretical Perspectives," *NWULR* 78 (1983): 937–1357; Steven Shiffrin, "Liberalism, Radicalism, and Legal Scholarship," *UCLALR* 30 (1983): 1103–1217; Gerald Frug, "The Ideology of Bureaucracy in American Law," *HLR* 97 (1984): 1276–1388; and "Symposium: A Critique of Rights," *TLR* 62 (1984): 1363–1617. Although Stanley Ingber, "The Marketplace of Ideas: A Legitimizing Myth," *DLJ* (1984): 1–91, appeared too late to be integrated more fully into my footnotes, the analysis there appears to bolster my own.
5. *Brief of Ralph David Abernathy, et al.*, at pp. 18, 29, 39. New York Times v. Sullivan, 376 U.S. 254 (1964). Samuel R. Pierce, "The Anatomy of an Historic Decision, New York Times v. Sullivan," *NCLR* 43 (1965): 315–63, emphasizes the origins of *Sullivan* in the civil rights movement.
6. See Corliss Lamont, ed., *The Trial of Elizabeth Gurley Flynn by the American Civil Liberties Union* (New York, 1968); Jerold S. Auerbach, "The Depression Decade," in *The Pulse of Freedom*, ed. Alan Reitman (New York, 1975), pp. 64–76. Michal Belknap, *Cold War Political Justice* (Westport, Conn, 1977); and Stanley I. Kutler, *The American Inquisition* (New York, 1982).
7. Meiklejohn's classic works were *Free Speech and Its Relation to Self-Government* (New York, 1948) and *Political Freedom: The Constitutional Powers of the People* (New York, 1960; reprint, New York, 1965). "Part I" of the latter volume reprints the entire text of *Free Speech*. The quoted passages are from his final restatement, "The First Amendment Is an Absolute," *SCR* (1961): 245–66, at 248–49, 255, 257.
8. Carlson v. Landon, 342 U.S. 524, 555 (1952) (Justice Black dissenting). For a

friendly critique of Justice's Black's approach to First-Amendment issues, by a fellow cold-war libertarian, see Harry Kalven, Jr., "Upon Rereading Mr. Justice Black on the First Amendment," *UCLALR* 14 (1967): 428–53. Later critics have been less kind, viewing Black's general approach as "little more than a disguised form of balancing." Martin H. Redish, "The Warren Court, the Burger Court and the First Amendment Overbreadth Doctrine," *NWULR* 78 (1983): 1031–70, at 1043. Redish's essay is part of a broader movement in First-Amendment theory that criticizes the cold-war libertarians' efforts to frame general free-speech theories and to develop strict categories of protected speech. See, e.g., Steven Shiffrin, "The First Amendment and Economic Regulation: Away from a General Theory of the First Amendment," *NLR* 78 (1983): 1212–83. Evident in much of the revisionist view of cold-war libertarianism is a view of politics that is much more skeptical of the positive potential of citizen participation. See Vincent Blasi, "The Checking Value in First Amendment Theory," *ABFRJ* (1977): 521–649, esp. 561–62.

9. Edmund Cahn, "Freedom of the Press: The Libertarian Standard," in *Confronting Injustice: The Edmund Cahn Reader*, ed. Lenore L. Cahn (Boston, 1966), pp. 134–47. See also, "The Firstness of the First Amendment," ibid., pp. 86–104.

10. Meiklejohn, "The First Amendment Is an Absolute," p. 259.

11. Edmund Cahn and Hugo Black, "Justice Black and the First Amendment 'Absolutes': A Public Interview," *NYULR* 37 (1962): 549–63, 557–58. See also David L. Grey, "Black on Libel: So Firm . . . in his Foundation," in *Justice Hugo Black and the First Amendment*, ed. Everette E. Dennis, Donald M. Gillmor, and David L. Grey (Ames, Ia., 1978), pp. 66–80. As Professor Grey emphasizes, Justice Black simply believed that the whole idea of suing for libel made no sense; a veteran of political wars in his native Alabama and a firm advocate of the maxim "sticks and stones may break my bones but words can never hurt me," Justice Black considered libel suits unnecessary on principle. Ibid., pp. 69–73. Although he joined Justice Black's libel opinions, William O. Douglas was somewhat less opposed on principle. He even considered suing one Washington columnist for concocting what Douglas viewed as "fabricated lies" originating in the Nixon administration, but was persuaded that a suit would only give the defamation more publicity. William O. Douglas, *The Court Years, 1939–1975: The Autobiography of William O. Douglas* (New York, 1980), pp. 200–201.

12. Edmund Cahn, "Freedom of the Press: Responsibility for Defamation," in *Confronting Injustice*, ed. Cahn, pp. 147–60, at 154, 159.

13. Harry Kalven, Jr., "The Law of Defamation and the First Amendment," in *Conference on the Arts, Publishing, and the Law* (Chicago, 1952), pp. 3–18, at 3.

14. Ibid., pp. 7–8, 9, 15.

15. Harry Wellington, "On Freedom of Expression," *YLJ* 88 (1979): 1105–42, at 1111. Thomas Emerson, *The System of Freedom of Expression* (New York, 1970), p. 5, and *Toward a General Theory of the First Amendment* (New York, 1963), p. 28. *Toward a General Theory* originally appeared as an article in *YLJ* 72 (1963): 853–956. Emerson specifically rejected realism as an appropriate mode for free-speech analysis. See *Toward a General Theory*, pp. 29–30, n. 3. And in contrast to other cold-war libertarians, Emerson initially took a rather casual view of the libel question in First-Amendment theory. See *Toward a General Theory*, pp. 68–71. Later, in response to

developments after about 1964, he adopted a position similar to that of his fellow cold-war libertarians. See *System of Freedom of Expression*, pp. 517–43.

16. On broad trends in legal consciousness, see G. Edward White, *Patterns of American Legal Thought* (Indianapolis, Ind., 1978), pp. 99–135, 136–62; Elizabeth Mensch, "The History of Mainstream Legal Thought," in *The Politics of Law: A Progressive Critique*, ed. David Kairys (New York, 1982), pp. 18–39, at 26–37; and Robert Gordon, "New Developments in Legal Theory," in ibid., pp. 281–93. The characterization of "rights justifications" is from Duncan Kennedy, "Legal Education as Training for Hierarchy," in ibid., pp. 40–61, at 48. The broad question of the value of legal rights has been debated extensively by members of the critical legal studies movement. See, e.g., Staughton Lynd, "Communal Rights," unpublished paper prepared for Eighth National Conference on Critical Legal Studies, March 1984. An entire issue of *Stanford Law Review*, StanLR 36 (1983), focuses on the critical legal studies movement, including various approaches to the rights problem.

17. Frank J. Donner, *The Age of Surveillance* (New York, 1980), pp. xvii–xxii, 3–29, 149–50 (Emerson's image to the FBI).

18. Beauharnais v. Illinois, 343 U.S. 250 (1952). This 5–4 decision in favor of a state group-libel law represented the high point for interest in using criminal prosecutions to combat antidemocratic defamation. See David Riesman, "Democracy and Defamation: Control of Group Libel," *ColLR* 42 (1942): 727–80; Joseph Tannenhaus, "Group Libel," *CLQ* 35 (1950): 261–302; and Harry Kalven, Jr., *The Negro and the First Amendment* (Chicago, 1966), pp. 7–64. In the 1970s and 1980s people connected with the feminist movement began to worry about the impact of antifemale (and antihuman) stereotypes in hardcore pornography, and this concern prompted both a search for new approaches to group-based defamations (as well as other injuries) and renewed praise for the view of the complex relationships—between political speech, the media, and groups without significant power over the ways in which they are portrayed—that supported the whole concept of group libel. See, e.g., Ruth Colker, "Pornography and Privacy: Towards the Development of a Group Based Theory for Sex Based Intrusions of Privacy," *LAI* 1 (1983): 191–238, at 233–34. See also Richard Delgado, "Words that Wound: A Tort Action for Racial Insults, Epithets, and Name-Calling," *HCRCLLR* 17 (1982): 133–81; Majorie Heins, "Banning Words: A Comment on Words That Wound," ibid. 18 (1983): 585–92; and Richard Delgado, "Professor Delgado Replies," ibid. 18 (1983): 593–97.

19. New York Times v. Sullivan, 376 U.S. 254, at 284–92 (1964). Bernard Schwartz, *Superchief: Earl Warren and the Supreme Court* (New York, 1983), pp. 531–41.

20. See pp. 167–77, and Dix Noel, "Defamation of Public Officials and Candidates," *ColLR* 49 (1949): 875–903.

21. New York Times v. Sullivan, 376 U.S., at 293–97 (Justice Black concurring), ibid., pp. 297–305 (Justice Goldberg concurring). See also, Emerson, *System of Freedom of Expression*, pp. 528–43.

22. New York Times v. Sullivan, 376 U.S., at 279–80.

23. Ibid., at pp. 273, 276. Charles A. Miller, *The Supreme Court and the Uses of History* (Cambridge, Mass., 1969; reprint, New York, 1972), discusses the concept of ongoing history.

24. New York Times v. Sullivan, 376 U.S. at 270, 279. For an analysis of the chilling effect idea and of its use by the Warren Court in other circumstances, see Frederick Schauer, "Fear, Risk and the First Amendment: Unraveling the 'Chilling' Effect," *BULR* 58 (1978): 685–732.

25. Even the Warren Court never really accepted this, and other, invitations from Professor Kalven to adopt a full-blown Meiklejohnian approach. Harry Kalven, Jr., "The New York Times Case: A Note on 'the Central Meaning' of the First Amendment," *SCR* (1964): 191–221, at 221, 221 n. 125. A summary of Professor Kalven's legacy, including his numerous articles on free expression and the Warren Court, may be found in a tribute entitled "In Memoriam: Harry Kalven, Jr.," *UChiLR* 43 (1975): 1–19.

26. Godfrey Hodgson, *America in Our Time* (New York, 1978), pp. 142–45, 152. For other analyses that suggest how forces within the media interact with social phenomena to help shape the framework of news coverage see Edward J. Epstein, *News from Nowhere* (New York, 1973); Alvin Gouldner, *The Dialectic of Ideology and Technology* (New York, 1976), pp. 119–24; and Todd Gitlin, *The Whole World Is Watching* (Berkeley, Cal., 1980).

27. Francis Murnaghan, "From Figment to Fiction to Philosophy—The Requirement of Proof of Damages in Libel Actions," *CatULR* 22 (1972): 1–38, 4; Arthur B. Hanson, *Libel and Related Torts*, 2 vols. (New York, 1969), 1:vii. See also Vernon X. Miller, *Selected Essays on Torts* (Buffalo, N.Y., 1960), p. 191 n. 2. When Miller first looked at the subject in 1947, he played down the problem of libel suits; in 1960, when he revised the piece for publication in *Selected Essays*, he then noted that libel suits "have been more numerous during the last ten years," ibid.

28. Murnaghan, "From Figment," p. 4.

29. Amicus Curie Brief of Washington Post Co., at pp. 20–22, New York Times v. Sullivan, 376 U.S. 254 (1964); Brief of the Petitioner, New York Times Co., pp. 38–58, ibid. See also Amicus Curie Brief of ACLU, pp. 18–31, ibid. This brief used the key phrase of "actual malice" and traced its application through a series of state-level, political libel cases. Ibid., p. 27 n., 28.

Once the Alabama Supreme Court rejected the appeal from the trial court level, a "Lawyers Committee on the Alabama Libel Suits," composed of twenty-three prominent attorneys from New York and Washington, issued a public letter—sent to all state bar associations and law school deans—condemning the decision. If the *Sullivan* verdict were allowed to stand, the committee argued, no paper "will be free to print the truth, where the facts about social justice would inflame, without risk of bankruptcy." The general public, the committee concluded, remained ignorant of the gravity of the segregationist threat to free expression. *E&P*, 13 Oct. 1962, pp. 12, 76, quote at 76. As the *New York Times* journalist Harrison Salisbury later wrote, leaders of the first-line northern media viewed the *Sullivan* lawsuit and similar cases on file or under consideration as grave threats to free expression and to the larger political process. See Harrison Salisbury, *Without Fear or Favor: The New York Times and Its Times* (New York, 1980), pp. 392–402.

The evidence seems persuasive, then, that various interested groups were pushing for a landmark ruling, something more than a mere technical reversal, and that the final result was not the product of last-minute maneuvering at the oral argument stage by the *New York Times*'s attorney, Herbert Wechsler and members of the Court, a scenario suggested in Arthur S. Miller and Jerome A. Barron, "The Supreme Court, The Adversary System, and the Flow of Information to the Justices: A Preliminary Inquiry," *VaLR* 61 (1975): 1187–1245, at 1204–10, 1218–22, 1230–34.

30. On the removal of blockages, see Mark Tushnet, "The Dilemmas of Liberal Constitutionalism," *OSLJ* 42 (1981): 411–26, at 412; on the larger implications of the relationship between the constitutional standard laid down in *Sullivan* and common law concepts of defamation, see Patrick O. Gudridge, "The Persistence of Classical Style," *UPaLR* 131 (1983): 663–792, esp. p. 690 n. 106.

31. One can be sensitive to the critique of *Sullivan* suggested by Arthur S. Miller and Jerome Barron without accepting their thesis that the problems could have been remedied by a better flow of superior information to the justices. Miller and Barron, "Flow of Information," pp. 1218–22. First, many of the basic ideas in *Sullivan* were contained in the briefs, especially that of the ACLU, see n. 24, and not suddenly sprung at the oral argument stage. Second, the problems with the *Sullivan* decision reflected very fundamental strains within the broader process of public communication, strains that Professors Miller and Barron have dissected in their other publications. See, e.g., Jerome Barron, *Freedom of Press for Whom?* (Bloomington, Ind., 1973), and Arthur S. Miller, "On Politics, Democracy, and the First Amendment: A Commentary on First National Bank v. Bellotti," *W&LLR* 28 (1981): 21–41.

32. Ginzburg v. Goldwater, 261 F. Supp. 784 (1966), cert. denied 396 U.S. 1949, 1051–52 (1970) (Justice Black dissenting).

33. Franklin Haiman, *Speech and Law in a Free Society* (Chicago, 1981), p. 52.

34. See Norman L. Rosenberg, "Thomas M. Cooley, Liberal Jurisprudence, and the Law of Libel, 1868–1884," *UPSLR* 4 (1980): 49–98, at 93–97, and David Anderson, "Libel and Press Self-Censorship," *TLR* 53 (1975): 422–81.

35. Curtis Publishing Co. v. Butts, 388 U.S. 130, 133–62 (1967) (emphasis added). In the same opinion, the Court also disposed of Associated Press v. Walker, another libel case with important implications for the civil rights movement. In *Walker*, a former U.S. Army General, Edwin A. Walker, who had been at the center of anti-integrationist violence at the University of Mississippi in 1962, the Court reversed a judgment for $800,000 against the AP wire service. Ibid., pp. 156–62.

Clearly, the *Butts* case indicated important fissures within the Supreme Court; and, in retrospect, it presaged the eventual retreat from a general application of the *Sullivan* principles that occurred in Gertz v. Robert Welch, Inc., 418 U.S. 323 (1974). Although three other justices joined Justice Harlan in urging that the *Sullivan* standard not be applied in *Butts*, the crucial fifth vote came from Chief Justice Earl Warren; the chief justice believed that the *Sullivan* test should apply to cases such as *Butts* and that the evidence did show actual malice. Curtis Publishing Co. v. Butts, 388 U.S., at 163. Thus, Justice Harlan, in a footnote, had to indicate that *Butts* rested on grounds other than those he had outlined in the text of his opinion. Ibid., at 133 n.

Although some of the chief justice's clerks joked that his course in *Butts* reflected his reverence for sports and respect for football coaches, very fundamental differences were tearing apart libertarian hopes that *Sullivan* might provide a unifying standard for public defamation cases. The *Sullivan* coalition did re-form when the Court extended the actual-malice test to criminal libel—Garrison v. State of Louisiana, 379 U.S. 64

(1964)—but by 1967, Court watchers, according to Harry Kalven, needed a scorecard to identify the nine players and the various defamation routes they were running. Harry Kalven, Jr., "The Reasonable Man and the First Amendment: Hill, Butts, and Walker," *SCR* (1967): 267–309, at 275. There are innumerable analyses of doctrinal deviations from *Sullivan*; see, e.g., Joel Eaton, "The American Law of Defamation through Gertz v. Robert Welch, Inc. and Beyond: An Analytical Primer," *VaLR* 61 (1975): 1349–1451. And see also the "behind the scenes" maneuvering revealed in Schwartz, *Superchief*, pp. 566–68, 612–17, 642–52. Schwartz's account, among other things, underscores the extent to which defamation law became entangled with privacy issues; it also reveals Justice Abe Fortas's considerable disenchantment with the performance of the American media.

36. Sprouse v. Clay Communications, Inc., 211 S.E. 2d 674, 682–83 (W. Va. 1975), cert. denied, 423 U.S. 882 (1975). See the excellent critical analyses of this case in David Anderson, "A Response to Professor Robertson: The Issue is Control of Press Power," *TLR* 54 (1976): 271–84, at 277–82, and Frederick F. Schauer, "Language, Truth and the First Amendment: An Essay in Memory of Harry Cantor," *VaLR* 64 (1978): 263–302, at 285–89.

37. See Mark L. Rosen, "Media Lament—The Rise and Fall of Involuntary Public Figures," *StJLR* 54 (1980): 487–517, at 512–14.

38. Rosenbloom v. Metromedia, Inc., 403 U.S. 29 (1971) (erroneous radio report that plaintiff was arrested for possession of pornographic materials). After *Rosenbloom*, according to the leading casebook on media law, "the press enjoyed a respite from libel laws." Donald M. Gillmor and Jerome A. Barron, *Mass Communication Law: Cases and Comment*, 4th ed. (St. Paul, Minn., 1984), p. 224. The proliferation of opinions in *Rosenbloom* exacerbated the doctrinal confusion that had long characterized defamation law. See, e.g., Robert Keeton, "Some Implications of the Constitutional Privilege to Defame," *VLR* 25 (1972): 59–77, esp. 75–77, and Donald M. Gillmor, "Justice William Brennan and the Failed 'Theory' of Actual Malice," *JQ* 59 (1982): 249–53.

39. Gouldner, *Dialectic of Ideology and Technology*, p. 124.

40. *E&P*, 16 March 1974, p. 9. Two years later, a number of U.S. senators introduced a bill intended to make it easier for public officials to sue for libel. See Haiman, *Speech and Law* p. 436 n. 32. It is misleading, as Haiman implies, that only Nixonian politicians had doubts about *Sullivan* and its implications. The liberal law professor Jerome Barron, for example, almost immediately argued that the Court had given the press a broad immunity from libel laws without providing any assurance that profit-oriented media corporations would really open their products to any meaningful spectrum of ideas and opinions. Jerome A. Barron, "Access to the Press—A New First Amendment Right," *HLR* 80 (1967): 1641–78, at 1656–61. And Harvard Law School's Paul Freund, though approving of Justice Brennan's *Sullivan* opinion, worried that extension of the actual-malice test might provide a "hunting license for the ruination of character and career with the safe knowledge that there is no redress." Paul Freund, "Political Libel and Obscenity," *FRD* 42 (1968): 491–503, at 494. See also Chapter 10, n. 59.

41. For a comprehensive analysis of the privatization of the means of mass communications, see Herbert I. Schiller, *Who Knows: Information in the Age of the Fortune*

500 (Norwood, N.J., 1982); for the reference to organized crime and libel suits, see Gillmor and Barron, *Mass Communication Law*, p. 224 (citing specific cases).

42. On the problems Theodore Roosevelt faced in bringing a defamation suit, see Melvin G. Holli and C. David Tompkins, "Roosevelt v. Newett: The Politics of Libel," *MichH* 47 (1963): 373–94. For two diverse views on recent cultural-psychological trends, see Christopher Lasch, *The Culture of Narcissism* (New York, 1979); Lasch, *The Minimal Self: Psychic Survival in Troubled Times* (New York, 1984); and Peter Clecak, *America's Quest for the Ideal Self* (New York, 1983). We badly need more work on the social-psychological aspects of defamation in modern American society. Until the work of Jerome Skolnick is published, Walter Probert's "Defamation, A Camouflage of Psychic Interests: The Beginnings of a Behavioral Analysis," *VLR* 15 (1962): 1175–1201, though rooted in the behavioral approaches of the 1950s, remains extremely suggestive. For an account of how a small town handles the politics of reputation, see Arthur J. Vidich and Joseph Bensman, *Small Town in Mass Society*, rev. ed. (Princeton, N.J., 1968). See also Erving Goffman, *Presentation of Self in Everyday Life* (New York, 1959); Goffman, *Strategic Interaction* (Philadelphia, 1969), pp. 124–36; and, for comparative dimensions, see F. G. Bailey, *Gifts and Poison: The Politics of Reputation* (New York, 1971), and Pnina Lahv, *Press Law in Modern Democracies* (New York, 1985).

43. On [*MORE*] and its short history, see Richard Pollak, *Stop the Presses, I Want to Get Off* (New York, 1975); On I. F. Stone's career, see the samples in I. F. Stone, *The I. F. Stone's Weekly Reader*, ed. Neil Middleton (New York, 1974), and Stone, *Polemics and Prophecies, 1967–1970* (New York, 1972); on *Ramparts*, see Warren Hinckle, III., *If You Have a Lemon, Make Lemonade* (New York, 1974); and for an overview of the press's role in the 1960s and 1960s, see Hodgson, *America in Our Time*, pp. 134–52.

44. See Edward Jay Epstein, *Between Fact and Fiction: The Problem of Journalism* (New York, 1975), pp. 3–18, esp. 9–10.

45. New York Times v. U.S., 403 U.S. 713 (1971). See the account of the confrontation in Sanford Unger, *The Papers & the Papers* (New York, 1973), and the analysis of Harry Kalven, "Foreword: Even When a Nation Is at War," *HLR* 85 (1971): 3–36.

46. In addition to the works cited in notes 43 and 44 of this chapter, my view of the relationship between the media and society has benefited from insights gathered from the following: Edward J. Epstein, *News from Nowhere* (New York, 1973); Gitlin, *The Whole World is Watching*; Gouldner, *The Dialectic of Ideology and Technology*; Jacques Ellul, *Propaganda* (New York, 1965); Ellul, *The Political Illusion* (New York, 1967), pp. 49–67; A. J. Leibling, *The Press*, 2nd rev. ed. (New York, 1975); Charles Lindbloom, *Politics and Markets* (New York, 1977), pp. 201–21; Herbert Gans, *Deciding What's News* (New York, 1980); and Stanley Cohen and Jock Young, ed., *The Manufacture of News*, rev. ed. (Beverly Hills, Cal., 1981). On the impact of libel law on smaller publications, see David A. Anderson, "The Selective Impact of Libel Law," *ColJR* (May/June, 1975): 38–42. The problems of the *Texas Observer* are discussed in a sidebar, ibid., p. 41. The case of the *Alton Telegraph* is noted in Rodney A. Smolla, "Let the Author Beware: The Rejuvenation of the American Law of Libel," *UPaLR* 132 (1983): 1–94, at 12–13.

47. Edwin Diamond, *Good News, Bad News* (Cambridge, Mass., 1978), pp. 167–

81, at 168. See also Lasch, *Culture of Narcissism*, pp. 155–58, 390–92. Perhaps the most famous case to come out of this journalistic trend involved Carol Burnett, one of a number of celebrities who sued the *National Enquirer*. See Burnett v. National Enquirer, Inc., 144 Cal. App. 3d 991, 193 Cal. Rptr. 206 (1983), and *E&P* (26 Jan. 1985), p. 33. Readers can update for themselves post-*Burnett* libel suits against the *Enquirer*.

48. Gertz v. Robert Welch, Inc., 418 U.S. 323 (1974).

49. Ibid., at 351–52. Justice Powell justified the different treatment of public and private plaintiffs, in part, on the argument that public people, especially those in political life, enjoyed greater access to the mass media than private persons and could employ the remedy of self-help more easily.

50. Ibid., at 339, 347, 349–50. Ultimately, eight years after the Supreme Court heard his appeal, Elmer Gertz prevailed, obtaining a jury award of $400,000. See Gertz v. Robert Welch, Inc., 680 F.2d 527 (7th Cir. 1982), cert. denied, 103 S. Ct. 1233 (1983).

51. The legal literature is enormous. See, e.g., Gerald Ashdown, "Gertz and Firestone: A Study in Constitutional Policy-Making," *MinnLR* 61 (1977): 645–90 (emphasizing policy considerations); and Eaton, "American Law of Defamation," pp. 1349–1451 (stressing doctrinal considerations). Three articles by Marc A. Franklin are essential: "Winners and Losers and Why: A Study of Defamation Litigation," *ABFRJ* (1980): 455–500; "Suing the Media for Libel: A Litigation Study," *ABFRJ* (1981): 795–831; and "Good Names and Bad Laws: A Critique of Libel Law and a Proposal," *USFLR* 18 (1983): 1–49. A summary of post-Gertz trends, based upon figures collected by the Libel Defense Resource Center (LDRC) is presented in Smolla, "Author Beware," at pp. 1–14. The best popular account is Anthony Lewis, "Annals of Law: The Sullivan Case," *New Yorker* (5 Nov. 1984), pp. 32–95, esp. 73–95.

52. Time, Inc. v. Firestone, 424 U.S. 448 (1976). *Firestone* seemed an especially difficult case to fit into any coherent theory of libel or into any doctrinal framework. The venerable Leon Green, for example, declared that *Firestone* was not even a legitimate libel case. He insisted that it was not "a case of libel in which the injury was to Mrs. Firestone's 'relations with other people,' but was a personal injury." Leon Green, "Political Freedom of the Press and the Libel Problem," *TLR* 56 (1978): 341–79, at 363. Green, who had long urged that legal rules be judged in a historical-functional context—see Chapter 9—concluded his analysis of post-*Sullivan* cases with this suggestion. "Libel, slander, and defamation are not required in courts of law. They deserve to be embalmed as the Pharaohs of the common law. There are more adequate tort actions to care for the wrongs of today's publications." Ibid., at 378. Another example of a defamation suit in which the plaintiff recovered nothing for alleged injuries to reputation but did obtain damages for emotional harm involved Reverend Jerry Falwell and Larry Flynt, publisher of *Hustler* magazine. See *New York Times*, 9 Dec. 1984, p. 1, and ibid., 10 Dec. 1984, p. 16.

53. See, e.g., Francis J. Flaherty, "The Law's Literary Life: Publishers Under Attack," *National Law Journal* (2 April 1984), pp. 1, 26, and Robert I. Friedman and Dan Moldea, "Networks Knuckle Under to Laxalt," *VV* (5 March 1984), pp. 10–14.

54. On the *Penthouse* case, see Pring v. Penthouse Int'l, Ltd., 695 F.2d 438 (10th Cir. 1982); on escalating legal costs, see, e.g., Smolla, "Let the Author Beware,"

pp. 13–14. See also the discussion of cases collected in Gillmor and Barron, *Mass Communication Law*, pp. 243–78.

55. On Herbert v. Lando, 441 U.S. 153 (1979), see Jerome A. Barron, "The Rise and Fall of a Doctrine of Editorial Privilege: Reflections on *Herbert v. Lando*," *GeoWLR* 47 (1979): 1002–29. On post-*Lando* decisions, see Smolla, "Author Beware." On the *Westmoreland* case and its reverberations through the media and on the continuing debate over U.S. intervention in Indochina, see, e.g., Don Kowett, *A Matter of Honor: General William Westmoreland v. CBS* (New York, 1984), and Charles Mohr, "Studies Show Vietnam Raids Failed," *New York Times*, 28 May 1984 (results of documents released as part of pretrial discovery process in Westmoreland lawsuit). The *Westmoreland* suit, especially since it was held simultaneously with a libel suit by Ariel Sharon (a former defense minister of Israel) against *Time* magazine, attracted considerable popular attention. As in the 1919 libel suit involving Henry Ford and the *Chicago Tribune*, both CBS and General Westmoreland conducted vigorous public-relations efforts. Both the *Sharon* and *Westmoreland* cases, the first of which ended with a jury verdict for *Time* and the second of which was settled without any retraction after months of trial, promised to provide the material for numerous scholarly and popular commentaries—and, perhaps, libel laws willing, even a TV docudrama. (Reportedly, the threat of legal action caused ABC to drop plans for a docudrama about Elizabeth Taylor. Smolla, "Author Beware," p. 3, n. 19.) For an early, and critical, appraisal of the results of the *Westmoreland* trial, see Alexander Cockburn, "CBS Surrenders," *Nation*, 2 March 1985, pp. 228–29. On the *Sharon* case, see Steven Brill, "Say It Ain't So, Henry," *AL* (Jan/Feb. 1985), pp. 8–13.

56. Bindrim v. Mitchell and Doubleday, 92 Cal App. 3d. 61, 155 Cal. Rptr. 29, cert denied, 444 U.S. 984 (1979), reh'g denied 444 U.S. (1980), and "Defamation by Fiction," *MdLR* 42 (1983): 387–427.

57. See, e.g., *50-State Survey 1982: Current Developments in Media Libel and Invasion of Privacy*, ed. Henry R. Kaufman (New York, 1982). The LRDC also issues regular Bulletins and even "Special Alerts."

58. Supporters of the broadest possible view of the *Sullivan* case, for example, could find reason to worry when libel suits by large groups of public officials, such as members of police departments, seemed to raise the problem of creating legal liability for general criticism of governmental bodies. See Cushman v. Day, 43 Or. App. 123, 129–30, 602 P.2d. 327, 3330–32 (1979), and Brady v. Ottway Newspapers, Inc., 84 A.D. 2d. 226, 236–37, 445 NYS 2d. 786, 793–94 (1981). On the other hand, even some prominent journalists expressed concern that the Sullivan principle had been extended too far and had contributed to unfair, although legal, coverage of public affairs. See, for example, the views of two prominent columnists, generally considered First-Amendment libertarians, Anthony Lewis, "New York Times v. Sullivan Reconsidered: Time to Return to 'The Central Meaning of the First Amendment,'" *CLR* 83 (1983): 603ff (Sullivan protection should not be applicable in cases where media is discussing issues such as the personal life of celebrities); and Nat Hentoff, "Deprecating the Legacy of Edward R. Murrow," *VV* (12 March 1985), p. 5 (press should not consider the legality but the fairness of libelous stories). Although soaring legal costs remained a real problem, some evidence suggested that media defendants continued to win the vast majority of the defamation suits that went to trial. See, e.g., Flaherty,

"The Law's Literary Life," p. 26 (most trial defeats reversed on appeal, so that about nine of every ten libel suits ultimately ended in media's favor), and Bob Brewin, "The Charge That Led to Westy's Defeat," *VV* (12 March 1985), pp. 24–25 (draft of never-delivered charge in Westmoreland v. CBS showed difficulty of showing "actual malice" under Sullivan test). Finally, the large media corporations, at least, were not without legal weapons of their own. See, e.g., "Fighting Back," *E&P* (12 Jan. 1985) (meeting libel suits with countersuits for abuse of process).

59. In 1982, for example, the ACLU, which had always tried to avoid any broad stand on the issue of libel (see Chapter 9, n. 26), adopted a formal statement that, in essence, adapted the cold-war libertarian position. Rather than viewing the issue, as it had in the past, as between two conflicting civil liberties, reputation and free speech, the ACLU apparently accepted the argument that reputation essentially constituted "a property interest," which meant that the position of libel defendants represented a preferred one for civil libertarians. In addition, the ACLU's executive director, Ira Glasser, placed great weight on the fact, evident for a long time, that the realities of the politics of libel meant only the best people—in Glasser's words, "the powerful"—could realistically invoke this tort remedy. See Gilbert Cranberg, "ACLU: Second Thoughts on Libel," *ColJR* (Jan/Feb., 1983): 42–43. Franklyn Haiman, another prominent member of the ACLU, took a similarly critical view of defamation suits, proposing to reduce their use to the most outrageous cases of "deliberate, knowing, calculated falsehood[s]" where more speech could not possibly redress the immediate injury to reputation. In addition, Haiman would draw no distinction between public and private plaintiffs; all would have to clear the steep hurdles he wished to put in their legal lanes. Finally, Haiman joined others, such as Jerome Barron, in emphasizing the need to join libel laws with some version of a right-of-reply remedy. In essence, Haiman would limit libel law "to emergency situations where the democratic process does not have time to function or where those accused of defamation would rather take their chances in a lawsuit than assume responsibility for providing the channel for a reply." Haiman, *Speech and Law in a Free Society*, pp. 43–60, esp. 57–60.

Such a position, as we have already seen, did not represent a consensus viewpoint, even among those sensitive to free-speech issues. Steven Shiffrin, for example, was only one of a number of First-Amendment scholars who disliked the categorical approaches to free-speech issues urged by people such as Haiman; he called for an eclectic balancing approach. Steven Shiffrin, "The First Amendment and Economic Regulation: Away from a General Theory of the First Amendment," *NLR* 78 (1983): 1212–83, at 1251–83. And Frederick Schauer, who tried to blend a philosophical with a policy perspective, thought that views such as Haiman's gave too little value to reputation. Schauer hoped to preserve more of traditional defamation law than Haiman, while he labored to reconcile his handiwork with a general "Free Speech Principle." Frederick Schauer, *Free Speech: A Philosophical Enquiry* (New York, 1982), pp. 32, 89, 167–77.

By the mid-1980s, proposals for changing defamation law and reconciling it with First-Amendment principles were expanding almost as fast as the number of lawsuits in the courts. For example, Smolla, "Author Beware," pp. 64–94, placed a great deal of faith in changes that would rely upon the flexibility of the common law of defamation, and Franklin, "Good Names and Bad Laws," pp. 35–49, believed that so many problems had accumulated in existing case law that legislative changes were required.

CONCLUSION

1. Christopher Hill, *The World Turned Upside Down: Radical Ideas During the English Revolution* (London, 1972), p. 12.

2. See, again, Chapter 9.

3. Elizabeth Mensch, "The History of Mainstream Legal Thought," in *The Politics of Law: A Progressive Critique*, ed. David Kairys (New York, 1982), pp. 18–39, at 27. This line of criticism, most powerfully presented by legal scholars associated with the Conference on Critical Legal Studies (CLS), has helped to prompt a rethinking of post–World War II legal thought, but it has not gone unchallenged. See, e.g., the double issue of the *Stanford Law Review* devoted to explaining and criticizing the work of people associated with the CLS, *StanLR* 36 (1984): 1ff. And see the vigorous defense of a modified version of liberal jurisprudence in Steven Shiffrin, "Liberalism, Radicalism, and Legal Scholarship," *UCLALR* 30 (1983): 1103–1217. Shiffrin applies his general theory of eclectic balancing to free-speech issues in "The First Amendment and Economic Regulation: Away from a General Theory of the First Amendment," *NLR* 78 (1983): 1212–83.

4. See Donald Gillmor, "Justice William Brennan and the Failed 'Theory' of Actual Malice," *JQ* 59 (1982): 249–55, and Martin H. Redish, "The Warren Court, the Burger Court and the First Amendment Overbreadth Doctrine," *NLR* 78 (1983): 1031–70, at 1055.

5. See, e.g., Gerald G. Ashdown, "Gertz and Firestone: A Study in Constitutional Policy-Making," *MinnLR* 61 (1977): 645–90.

6. See Frank J. Donner, *The Age of Surveillance* (New York, 1980), and J. H. Plumb, *Sir Robert Walpole*, 2 vols. (Boston, 1956, 1961). See also the critique of traditional libertarian thought's failure to confront the power of "governmental falsification of majorities through leadership, education, persuasion, secrecy, and information dissemination," in Mark Yudoff, *When Government Speaks* (Berkeley, Cal., 1983), esp. pp. 90–110.

7. Alvin Gouldner, *The Dialectic of Ideology and Technology* (New York, 1976).

8. Jerome Barron, *Freedom of Press for Whom?* (Bloomington, Ind., 1973). See also, Benjamin S. Duval, Jr., "Free Communication of Ideas and the Quest for Truth: Toward a Teleological Approach to First Amendment Adjudication," *GeoWLR* 41 (1978): 161–259, at 188–94; C. Edwin Baker, "Scope of the First Amendment Freedom of Speech," *UCLALR* 25 (1978): 964–1040, at 967–81; Laurence Tribe, "Toward a Metatheory of Free Speech," *SWULR* 10 (1978): 237–45; Paul G. Chevigny, "Philosophy of Language and Free Expression," *NYULR* 55 (1980): 157–94, at 160–61; and Mark Tushnet, "Corporations and Free Speech," in *Politics of Law*, ed. Kairys, pp. 253–61. Although some commentators have distinguished between the marketplace theory brought into First-Amendment discourse by Oliver Wendell Holmes, Jr., and the self-government theory of Alexander Meiklejohn, the two ultimately collapse into a single, liberal pluralistic model, one essentially based on marketplace imagery.

See Laurence Tribe, *American Constitutional Law* (Mineola, N.Y., 1978), p. 577; Stanley Ingebar, "The Marketplace of Ideas: A Legitimizing Myth," *DLJ* (1984), pp. 1–91; and more generally, Garry Wills, *Nixon Agonistes* (New York, 1969).

9. Norman L. Rosenberg, "Thomas M. Cooley, Liberal Jurisprudence, and the Law of Libel, 1868–1884," *UPSLR* 4 (1980): 49–98.

10. Gouldner, *Dialectic of Ideology and Technology*, pp. 121–30; Godfrey Hodgson, *America in Our Time* (New York, 1978), pp. 134–52; Todd Gitlin, *The Whole World is Watching* (Berkeley, Cal., 1980), pp. 1–18, 249–82; Edward J. Epstein, *News From Nowhere* (New York, 1973).

11. Robert W. Gordon, "Historicism in Legal Scholarship," *YLJ* 90 (1981): 9–55.

12. Robert W. Gordon, "Introduction: J. Willard Hurst and the Common Law Tradition in American Legal Historiography," *LSR* 10 (1975): 9–55, and "Critical Legal Histories," *StanLR* 36 (1984): 57–125, at 124–25.

13. Duncan Kennedy, "The Structure of Blackstone's Commentaries," *BufLR* 28 (1979): 205–382, at 213. Although Kennedy may have disowned his concept/insight—see Peter Gabel and Duncan Kennedy, "Roll Over Beethoven," *StanLR* 36 (1984): 1–55, 33–40—I trust that it can still be snatched up by others.

14. See generally, Walter Probert, "Defamation, A Camouflage of Psychic Interests: The Beginnings of a Behavioral Analysis," *VLR* 15 (1962): 1173–1201.

15. See, e.g., Mark Tushnet, "Following the Rules Laid Down: A Critique of Interpretivism and Neutral Principles," *HLR* 96 (1983): 781–827. See also, "Symposium: A Critique of Rights," *TLR* 62 (1984), 1363–1617, especially the contribution of Mark Tushnet, entitled "An Essay on Rights," *TLR* 62 (1984): 1363–1403, esp. 1386–92.

16. In the battle with legal realism, rhetoric often substituted for a genuine effort to meet the essence of the criticism. See, e.g., the discussions in Mensch, "Mainstream Legal Thought," pp. 26–37, and Edward Purcell, *The Crisis of Democratic Theory* (Lexington, Ky., 1973), pp. 159–78. For thoughtful attempts to come to terms with the post-1970 critique of liberal legalism and the rule of law, see Stanley I. Kutler, *The American Inquisition* (New York, 1980), esp. pp. 243–46, and Shiffrin, "Legal Scholarship," pp. 1174–1216.

17. See Paul Brest, "The Misconceived Quest for the Original Understanding," *BULR* 60 (1980): 204–38, and Tushnet, "Following the Rules," pp. 786–804.

18. For summaries of this view of the law, see Robert Gordon, "New Developments in Legal Theory," in *The Politics of Law*, ed. Kairys, pp. 281–93, and "Critical Legal Histories," pp. 114–25; for an account that emphasizes the fragility of legal protection for critical expression, see David Kairys, ed., "Freedom of Speech," in *Politics of Law*, ed. Kairys, pp. 140–71; debates over the public-private controversy are collected in "Papers from the University of Pennsylvania Symposium on the Public/Private Distinction Held at the University of Pennsylvania on January 23, 1982," *UPaLR* 130 (1982): 1289–1609; the public-private boundary drawing in post-*Gertz* libel cases is briefly discussed in Rosenberg, "Thomas Cooley," pp. 93–96. For a related issue, see Mark Tushnet's critique of Justice William Rehnquist's attempt at boundary drawing in Paul v. Davis, 424 U.S. 693 (1976), a case that, ironically, saw the Burger Court hold that reputation was not a form of liberty or a property right protected by the Fourteenth Amendment. Tushnet, "The Constitutional Right to One's Good Name: An Examination of the Scholarship of Mr. Justice Rehnquist," *KyLJ* 64 (1976): 753–66.

Paul v. Davis provoked a lengthy, impassioned dissent from Justice William Brennan who argued that the majority opinion, by Justice Rehnquist, ignored the value of reputation. 424 U.S., at 714–36. See also Sidney Zion, "A Tale of Two Libel Themes," *Nation* (29 Sept. 1984), pp. 288–90 for a comparison of Paul v. Davis with cases protecting the reputations of the best men.

19. See, e.g., Tushnet, "Corporations and Free Speech," pp. 253–61, and Donner, *Age of Surveillance*.

20. See, e.g., the strange career of Wesley Sturges in Grant Gilmore's *The Ages of American Law* (New Haven, Conn., 1977), pp. 80–81.

21. Arthur Selwyn Miller, *Democratic Dictatorship* (Westport, Conn., 1981), pp. 4–5, 164–66.

22. See, e.g., Karl Klare, "Law-Making as Praxis," *Telos* 40 (Summer 1979): 123–45; Andrew Fraser, "The Legal Theory We Need Now," *SR* 40–41 (1978): 147–87; C. Edwin Baker, "The Process of Change and the Liberty Theory of the First Amendment," *SCLR* 55 (1981): 293–344; Paul Chevigny, "Philosophy of Language," pp. 176–94, and "Dialogic Right of Free Expression: A Reply to Michael Martin," *NYULR* 57 (1982): 920–31; and Peter Gabel and Paul Harris, "Building Power and Breaking Images: Critical Legal Theory and the Practice of Law," *NYURLSC* 11 (1982–83): 369–411, esp. 386–88. See also Ed Sparer's "friendly critique," which generally focuses upon free-speech issues. Ed Sparer, "Fundamental Human Rights, Legal Entitlements, and the Social Struggle: A Friendly Critique of the Critical Legal Studies Movement," *StanLR* 36 (1984): 509–74, at 512–35, 539–47. And, finally, Staughton Lynd has proposed refocusing First-Amendment liberties in terms of communal rights. Lynd, "Communal Rights," *TLR* 62 (1984): 1417–41, esp. 1430–35.

Bibliography

BOOKS

Abzug, Robert. *Passionate Liberator: Theodore Dwight Weld and the Dilemma of Reform*. New York, 1980.

Allen, David. *In English Ways*. Chapel Hill, N.C., 1981.

Anastaplo, George. *The Constitutionalist: Notes on the First Amendment*. Dallas, Tex., 1971.

Anderson, Douglas. *A "Washington Merry-Go-Round" of Libel Actions*. Chicago, 1980.

Auerbach, Jerold. *Unequal Justice: Lawyers and Social Change in Modern America*. New York, 1976.

Bailey, F. G., ed. *Gifts and Poison: The Politics of Reputation*. New York, 1971.

Bailyn, Bernard. *The Ordeal of Thomas Hutchinson*. Cambridge, Mass., 1974.

————. *The Origins of American Politics*. New York, 1968.

———— and Hench, John B., eds. *The Press & the American Revolution*. Worcester, Mass., 1980.

Baker, Jean. *The Political Culture of the Northern Democrats in the Mid-Nineteenth Century*. Ithaca, N.Y., 1983.

Banning, Lance. *The Jeffersonian Persuasion*. Ithaca, N.Y., 1980.

Barron, Jerome. *Freedom of the Press for Whom?* Bloomington, Ind., 1973.

Belknap, Michal. *Cold War Political Justice*. Westport, Conn., 1971.

Benton, William Allen. *Whig-Loyalism*. Rutherford, N.J., 1969.

Beth, Loren P. *The Development of the American Constitution, 1877–1917*. New York, 1971.

Billias, George Athan. *Elbridge Gerry: Founding Father and Republican Statesman*. New York, 1976.

————, ed. *Law and Authority in Colonial America*. Barre, Mass., 1965.

Bledstein, Burton. *The Culture of Professionalism*. New York, 1976.

Bloomfield, Maxwell. *American Lawyers in a Changing Society, 1776–1876*. Cambridge, Mass., 1976.

Boorstin, Daniel. *The Image: A Guide to Pseudo-Events*. New York, 1962.

Boyer, Paul. *Urban Masses and Moral Order in America, 1820–1920*. Cambridge, Mass., 1978.

Breen, Timothy. *The Character of a Good Ruler*. New Haven, 1970.

Brewer, John. *Party Ideology and Popular Politics at the Accession of George III*. London, 1976.

Brown, Wallace. *The King's Friends*. Providence, R.I., 1965.

Buel, Richard. *Dear Liberty: Connecticut's Mobilization for the Revolutionary War*. Middletown, Conn., 1980.

————. *Securing the Revolution*. Ithaca, N.Y., 1972.

Burnham, Walter Dean. *Critical Elections and Mainsprings of American Politics*. New York, 1970.

Bushman, Richard L. *From Puritan to Yankee: Character and the Social Order in Connecticut, 1690–1765*. Cambridge, Mass., 1967.

Cahn, Edmund. *Confronting Injustice: The Edmund Cahn Reader*. Edited by Lenore L. Cahn. Boston, 1966.

Calhoon, Robert M. *The Loyalists in Revolutionary America, 1760–1781*. New York, 1973.

Chafee, Zechariah, Jr. *Free Speech in the United States*. Cambridge, Mass., 1941.

Chamberlin, Bill, and Brown, Charlene J., eds. *The First Amendment Reconsidered*. New York, 1982.

Chambers, William Nisbet. *Political Parties in a New Nation*. New York, 1963.

————, and Burnham, Walter Dean, eds. *The American Party Systems*. New York, 1975.

Champagne, Roger J. *Alexander McDougall and the American Revolution in New York*. Schenectady, N.Y., 1975.

Chapin, Bradley. *Criminal Justice in Colonial America, 1606–1660*. Athens, Ga., 1983.

Clark, Charles E., and Shulman, Harry. *A Study of Law Administration in Connecticut*. New Haven, 1937.

Clecak, Peter. *America's Quest for the Ideal Self*. New York, 1983.

Cloward, Richard, and Piven, Francis Fox. *Poor People's Movements*. New York, 1978.

Cohen, Stanley, and Young, Jock, eds. *The Manufacture of News*. Revised Edition. Beverly Hills, Cal., 1981.

Countryman, Edward. *A People in Revolution*. Baltimore, 1981.

Covert, Catherine L., and Stevens, John D., eds. *Mass Media Between the Wars*. Syracuse, N.Y., 1984.

Crosskey, William Winslow. *Politics and the Constitution*. 3 vols. Chicago, 1953–80.

Crouthamel, James. *James Watson Webb*. Middletown, Conn., 1969.

Czitrom, Daniel. *Media and the American Mind*. Chapel Hill, N.C., 1982.

Dargo, George. *Law in the New Republic*. New York, 1983.

————. *Roots of the Republic*. New York, 1974.

DeArmond, Anna J. *Andrew Bradford: Colonial Journalist*. Newark, Del., 1949; reprint, New York, 1969.

Demos, John. *Entertaining Satan: Witchcraft and the Culture of Early New England*. New York, 1982.

Diamond, Edwin. *Good News, Bad News*. Cambridge, Mass., 1978.

Diggins, John Patrick. *The Lost Soul of American Politics: Virtue, Self-Interest, and the Foundations of Liberalism*. New York, 1984.

Dinkin, Robert J. *Voting in Provincial America*. Westport, Conn., 1979.

Donner, Frank J. *The Age of Surveillance*. New York, 1980.

Douglass, Ann. *The Feminization of American Culture*. New York, 1978.

Drinnon, Richard. *Rebel in Paradise: A Biography of Emma Goldman*. New York, 1961; reprint, 1976.

Dubofsky, Melvin. *We Shall Be All: A History of the IWW*. New York, 1969.
Duniway, Clyde. *The Development of Freedom of the Press in Massachusetts*. Boston, 1906.
Dwyer, William L. *The Goldmark Case*. Seattle, Wash., 1984.
Eaton, Clement. *The Freedom of Thought Struggle in the Old South*. 2d ed. New York, 1964.
Eisenstein, Elizabeth. *The Printing Press as an Agent of Change*. 2 vols. London, 1979.
Eldredge, Laurence H. *The Law of Defamation*. Indianapolis, Ind., 1978.
Ellis, Richard. *The Jeffersonian Crisis: Court and Politics in the Young Republic*. New York, 1971.
Ellul, Jacques. *The Political Illusion*. New York, 1967.
_____. *Propaganda*. New York, 1965.
Emerson, Thomas I. *The System of Freedom of Expression*. New York, 1970.
Emery, Edwin. *History of the American Newspaper Publishers Association*. Minneapolis, Minn., 1950.
_____, and Emery, Michael. *The Press in America*. 4th ed. Englewood Cliffs, N.J., 1978.
Erikson, Kai. *Wayward Puritans: A Study of the Sociology of Deviance*. New York, 1966.
Ernst, Morris, and Lindey, Alexander. *Hold Your Tongue!* New York, 1932; reprint, New York, 1950.
Fischer, David Hackett. *The Revolution of American Conservatism*. New York, 1965.
Flaherty, David. *Privacy in Colonial New England*. Charlottesville, Va., 1972.
Formisano, Ronald P. *The Transformation of Political Culture: Massachusetts Parties, 1790s–1840s*. New York, 1983.
Franklin, Marc A. *The Biography of a Legal Dispute*. Mineola, N.Y., 1969.
Friedman, Lawrence M. *A History of American Law*. New York, 1973.
_____, and Percival, Robert V. *The Roots of Justice*. Chapel Hill, N.C., 1981.
Friendly, Fred W. *Due to Circumstances Beyond Our Control*. New York, 1967.
_____. *Minnesota Rag*. New York, 1981.
Gans, Herbert. *Deciding What's News*. New York, 1980.
Gerlach, Larry R. *Prologue to Independence: New Jersey in the Coming of the American Revolution*. New Brunswick, N.J., 1976.
Gillmor, Donald M., and Barron, Jerome. *Mass Communication Law: Cases and Comment*. 4th ed. St. Paul, Minn., 1984.
Gilmore, Grant. *The Ages of American Law*. New Haven, 1977.
Gitlin, Todd. *The Whole World Is Watching*. Berkeley, Cal., 1980.
Goebel, Julius, Jr. *History of the Supreme Court of the United States: Antecedents and Beginnings to 1801*. New York, 1971.
Goffman, Erving. *Presentation of Self in Everyday Life*. New York, 1959.
Goodwyn, Lawrence. *The Populist Moment*. New York, 1978.
Gouldner, Alvin. *The Dialectic of Ideology and Technology*. New York, 1976.
Greenberg, Douglas. *Crime and Law Enforcement in the Colony of New York, 1691–1776*. Ithaca, N.Y., 1976.
Haiman, Franklyn S. *Speech and Law in a Free Society*. Chicago, 1981.

Hall, Van Beck. *Politics Without Parties: Massachusetts, 1780–1792.* Pittsburgh, 1972.

Hanson, Arthur B. *Libel and Related Torts.* 2 vols. New York, 1969.

Hartog, Hendrik, ed. *Law in the American Revolution and the American Revolution in Law.* New York, 1981.

Haskins, George L. *Law and Authority in Early Massachusetts.* New York, 1960.

———, and Johnson, Herbert A. *Foundations of Power: John Marshall, 1801–1815.* History of the Supreme Court of the United States, vol. II. New York, 1981.

Hentoff, Nat. *The First Freedom.* New York, 1980.

Higgenbotham, Sanford W. *The Keystone in the Democratic Arch: Pennsylvania Politics, 1800–1816.* Harrisburg, Pa., 1952.

Hill, Christopher. *Milton and the English Revolution.* New York, 1975.

———. *The World Turned Upside Down: Radical Ideas During the English Revolution.* London, 1972.

Hinckle, Warren, III. *If You Have a Lemon, Make Lemonade.* New York, 1974.

Hodgson, Godfrey. *America in Our Time.* New York, 1978.

Hoerder, Dirk. *Crowd Action in Revolutionary Massachusetts, 1765–1780.* New York, 1977.

Hoffer, Peter Charles, and Hull, N. E. H. *Impeachment in America, 1635–1805.* New Haven, 1984.

Hofstadter, Richard. *The Idea of a Party System.* Berkeley, Cal., 1969.

Horwitz, Morton J. *The Transformation of American Law, 1780–1860.* Cambridge, Mass., 1977.

Howe, Daniel Walker. *The Political Culture of the American Whigs.* Chicago, 1979.

Hurst, James Willard. *Law and the Conditions of Freedom in the Nineteenth-Century United States.* Madison, Wis., 1956.

Hyman, Harold, and Wiecek, William. *Equal Justice Under Law: Constitutional Development, 1835–1875.* New York, 1982.

Jensen, Richard. *The Winning of Midwest.* Chicago, 1971.

Johnson, John W. *American Legal Culture, 1908–1940.* Westport, Conn., 1981.

Johnson, Paul. *A Shopkeeper's Millennium.* New York, 1978.

Johnston, Robert M., Jr. *Jefferson and the Presidency.* Ithaca, N.Y., 1978.

Juergons, George. *Joseph Pulitzer and the New York World.* Princeton, N.J., 1966.

———. *News from the White House: The President-Press Relationship in the Progressive Age.* Chicago, 1981.

Kalven, Harry, Jr. *The Negro and the First Amendment.* Chicago, 1965.

Katznelson, Ira. *City Trenches.* New York, 1981.

Keller, Morton. *Affairs of State.* Cambridge, Mass., 1977.

Kennedy, David. *Over Here: The First World War and American Society.* New York, 1980.

Kerber, Linda. *Federalists in Dissent.* Ithaca, N.Y., 1970.

Kohn, Richard. *Eagle and Sword.* New York, 1975.

Konig, David. *Law and Society in Puritan Massachusetts: Essex County, 1629–1692.* Chapel Hill, N.C., 1979.

Kross, Jessica. *The Evolution of an American Town: Newton, New York, 1642–1775.* Philadelphia, 1983.

Kutler, Stanley I. *The American Inquisition*. New York, 1982.

Lahv, Pnina. *Press Law in Modern Democracies*. New York, 1985.

Lasch, Christopher. *The Culture of Narcissism*. New York, 1979.

_____. *The Minimal Self*. New York, 1984.

Laurent, Francis W. *The Business of a Trial Court: 100 Years of Cases*. Madison, Wis., 1959.

Lawhorne, Clifton O. *Defamation and Public Officials*. Carbondale and Edwardsville, Ill., 1971.

_____. *The Supreme Court and Libel*. Carbondale and Edwardsville, Ill., 1981.

Leder, Lawrence. *Liberty and Authority: Early American Political Ideology*. Chicago, 1968.

Levy, Leonard W. *Emergence of a Free Press*. New York, 1985.

_____. *Freedom of Speech and Press in Early American History: Legacy of Suppression*. Cambridge, Mass., 1960; reprint, New York, 1963.

_____. *Jefferson and Civil Liberties: The Darker Side*. Cambridge, Mass., 1963; reprint, New York, 1973.

_____. *The Law of the Commonwealth and Chief Justice Shaw*. Cambridge, Mass., 1957.

_____. *Treason Against God: A History of the Offense of Blasphemy*. New York, 1981.

_____, ed. *Freedom of the Press from Zenger to Jefferson*. Indianapolis, Ind., 1966.

Lindbloom, Charles. *Politics and Markets*. New York, 1977.

Lockridge, Kenneth. *A New England Town: The First Hundred Years*. New York, 1970.

Lofton, John. *The Press as Guardian of the First Amendment*. Columbia, S.C., 1980.

Lowi, Theodore. *The End of Liberalism*. 2d ed. New York, 1979.

Lustig, R. Jeffrey. *Corporate Liberalism*. Berkeley, Cal., 1982.

Lutz, William. *The News of Detroit*. Boston, 1973.

McCormick, Richard P. *The Second American Party System*. Chapel Hill, N.C., 1966.

McDonald, Forrest. *Alexander Hamilton*. New York, 1979.

_____. *The Presidency of George Washington*. Lawrence, Kans., 1974.

_____. *The Presidency of Thomas Jefferson*. Lawrence, Kans., 1976.

McWilliams, John P. *Political Justice in a Republic: James Fenimore Cooper's America*. Berkeley, Cal., 1972.

Main, Jackson Turner. *Political Parties Before the Constitution*. Chapel Hill, N.C., 1973.

Malone, Dumas. *Jefferson the President: Second Term, 1805–1809*. Boston, 1974.

Marcus, Robert. *Grand Old Party*. New York, 1971.

Matusow, Alan. *The Unraveling of America*. New York, 1984.

May, Lary. *Screening Out the Past: The Birth of Mass Culture and the Motion Picture Industry*. New York, 1980.

Meiklejohn, Alexander. *Free Speech and Its Relation to Self-Government*. New York, 1948.

Miller, Arthur Selwyn. *Democratic Dictatorship*. Westport, Conn., 1981.

Miller, Charles A. *The Supreme Court and the Uses of History*. Cambridge, Mass., 1969; reprint, New York, 1972.

Miller, Perry. *The Life of the Mind in America*. New York, 1965.

Morgan, Edmund. *American Slavery, American Freedom: The Ordeal of Colonial Virginia*. New York, 1975.

Morison, Samuel Eliot. *Harrison Gray Otis, 1765–1848*. Rev. ed. Boston, 1969.

Moss, Sidney P. *Poe's Literary Battles: The Critic in the Context of His Literary Milieu*. Durham, N.C., 1963.

_____. *Poe's Major Crisis: His Libel Suit and New York's Literary World*. Durham, N.C., 1970.

Mott, Frank Luther. *American Journalism: A History, 1690–1960*. 3d ed. New York, 1962.

Mueller, Claus. *The Politics of Communication*. New York, 1973.

Murphy, Paul. *The Meaning of Free Speech: First Amendment Freedoms from Wilson to Roosevelt*. Westport, Conn., 1972.

_____. *World War I and the Origin of Civil Liberties in the United States*. New York, 1979.

Nader, Laura, ed. *Law and Culture in Society*. Chicago, 1969.

Nash, Gary. *Quakers and Politics: Pennsylvania, 1681–1726*. Princeton, N.J., 1968.

_____. *The Urban Crucible*. Cambridge, Mass., 1979.

Nelson, Harold L., ed. *Freedom of the Press from Hamilton to the Warren Court*. Indianapolis, Ind., 1966.

_____. *Libel in News of Congressional Investigating Committees*. Minneapolis, Minn., 1961.

Nelson, William E. *Americanization of the Common Law: The Impact of Legal Change on Massachusetts Society, 1760–1830*. Cambridge, Mass., 1975.

_____. *Dispute and Conflict Resolution in Plymouth County, Massachusetts, 1725–1825*. Chapel Hill, N.C., 1981.

Nevins, Allan, and Hill, Frank Ernest. *Ford: Expansion and Challenges, 1915–1933*. New York, 1957.

Nizer, Louis. *The Jury Returns*. New York, 1966.

_____. *My Life in Court*. New York, 1961.

Noonan, John T., Jr. *Persons and Masks of the Law*. New York, 1976.

Nord, David Paul. *Newspapers and New Politics: Midwestern Municipal Reform, 1890–1900*. Ann Arbor, Mich., 1981.

Nye, Russel B. *Fettered Freedom: Civil Liberties and the Slavery Controversy, 1830–1860*. East Lansing, Mich., 1963; reprint, Urbana, Ill., 1972.

Oberholzer, Emil, Jr. *Delinquent Saints: Disciplinary Action in the Early Congregational Church of Massachusetts*. New York, 1956.

Outland, Ethel R. *The "Effingham" Libels on Cooper*. Madison, Wis., 1929.

Owen, Bruce. *Economics and Freedom of Expression*. Cambridge, Mass., 1975.

Paul, Arnold. *Conservative Crisis and the Rule of Law*. Ithaca, N.Y., 1960.

Perry, Michael. *The Constitution, the Courts, and Human Rights*. New Haven, 1982.

Phelps, Robert H., and Hamilton, E. Douglas. *Libel: Rights, Risks, Responsibilities*. Rev. ed. New York, 1978.

Pierce, Clyde. *The Roosevelt Panama Libel Cases*. New York, 1959.

Pivar, David. *Purity Crusade*. Westport, Conn., 1973.

Plucknett, Theodore F. T. *A Concise History of the Common Law*. 4th ed. Boston, 1956.

Pocock, J. G. A. *The Machiavellian Moment*. Princeton, N.J., 1975.

Pollack, Richard. *Stop the Presses, I Want to Get Off*. New York, 1975.

Potter, David. *Freedom and Its Limitations in American Life*. Stanford, Cal., 1976.

Pred, Allen. *Urban Growth and the Circulation of Information*. Cambridge, Mass., 1973.

Preston, William. *Aliens and Dissenters: Federal Suppression of Radicals, 1903–1933*. Cambridge, Mass., 1963.

Prosser, William L. *Handbook of the Law of Torts*. 4th ed. St. Paul, Minn., 1971.

Purcell, Edward. *The Crisis of Democratic Theory*. Lexington, Ky., 1973.

Reid, John Philip. *In a Defiant Stance: The Conditions of Law in Massachusetts Bay, the Irish Comparison, and the Coming of the American Revolution*. University Park, Pa., 1977.

Roebar, A. G. *Faithful Magistrates and Republican Lawyers: Creators of Virginia Legal Culture, 1680–1810*. Chapel Hill, N.C., 1981.

Rose, Arnold M. *Libel and Academic Freedom: A Lawsuit Against Political Extremists*. Minneapolis, Minn., 1968.

Rosenberg, Emily S. *Spreading the American Dream*. New York, 1982.

Rowe, G. S. *Thomas McKean: The Shaping of an American Republicanism*. Boulder, Colo., 1978.

Rutland, Robert Allen. *The Ordeal of the Constitution*. Norman, Okla., 1966.

Salisbury, Harrison. *Without Fear or Favor: The New York Times and Its Times*. New York, 1980.

Schauer, Frederick. *Free Speech: A Philosophical Enquiry*. New York, 1982.

Schiller, Dan. *Objectivity and the News: The Public and the Rise of Commercial Journalism*. Philadelphia, 1981.

Schiller, Herbert. *Communication and Cultural Domination*. New York, 1976.

———. *Mass Communications and American Empire*. Boston, 1971.

———. *Who Knows: Information in the Age of the Fortune 500*. Norwood, N.J., 1982.

Schlesinger, Arthur M., Sr. *Prelude to Revolution: The Newspaper War on Great Britain, 1764–1776*. New York, 1958.

Schudson, Michael. *Discovering the News: A Social History of American Newspapers*. New York, 1978.

Schwartz, Bernard. *Superchief: Earl Warren and the Supreme Court*. New York, 1983.

Scott, Arthur P. *Criminal Law in Colonial Virginia*. Chicago, 1930.

Shaw, Peter. *The Character of John Adams*. Chapel Hill, N.C., 1976.

Shick, Marvin. *Learned Hand's Court*. Baltimore, 1970.

Siebert, Frederick S. *Freedom of the Press in England, 1476–1776*. Urbana, Ill., 1952.

Silverman, Robert A. *Law and Urban Growth*. Princeton, N.J., 1981.

Smith, Culver G. *The Press, Politics, and Patronage: The Government's Use of Newspapers, 1789–1875*. Athens, Ga., 1977.

Smith, James Morton. *Freedom's Fetters: The Alien and Sedition Laws and American Civil Liberties*. Ithaca, N.Y., 1956; reprint, 1966.

Spater, George. *William Cobbett: The Poor Man's Friend*. 2 vols. New York, 1982.

Spinrad, William. *Civil Liberties*. Chicago, 1970.

Sproat, John G. *The Best Men: Liberal Reformers in the Gilded Age*. New York, 1968.

Stewart, Donald. *The Opposition Press of the Federalist Period*. Albany, N.Y., 1969.

Stourzh, Gerald. *Alexander Hamilton and the Idea of Republican Government*. Stanford, Cal., 1970.

Tachau, Mary Bonsteel. *Federal Courts in the Early Republic: Kentucky, 1789–1816*. Princeton, N.J., 1978.

Trachtenberg, Alan. *The Incorporation of America*. New York, 1982.

Tribe, Laurence. *American Constitutional Law*. Mineola, N.Y., 1978.

Unger, Roberto. *Knowledge and Politics*. New York, 1975.

———. *Law and Modern Society*. New York, 1976.

Vaughn, Stephen. *Holding Fast the Inner Lines: Democracy, Nationalism and the Committee on Public Information*. Chapel Hill, N.C., 1980.

Vidich, Arthur J., and Bensman, Joseph. *Small Town in Mass Society*. Rev. ed. Princeton, N.J., 1968.

Wall, Robert Emmet, Jr. *Massachusetts Bay: The Crucial Decade, 1640–1650*. New Haven, 1972.

Wallace, Anthony F. C. *Rockdale: The Growth of an American Village in the Early Industrial Revolution*. New York, 1978.

Walsh, Justin. *To Print the News and Raise Hell!* Chapel Hill, N.C., 1968.

Weinstein, Allen. *Perjury: The Hiss-Chambers Case*. New York, 1978.

Wells, Evelyn. *Fremont Older*. New York, 1936.

White, G. Edward. *The American Judicial Tradition: Profiles of Leading American Judges*. New York, 1975.

———. *Patterns in American Legal Thought*. Indianapolis, Ind., 1978.

———. *Tort Law in America: An Intellectual History*. New York, 1980.

Wiebe, Robert. *The Search for Order*. New York, 1967.

Wills, Garry. *Cincinnatus: George Washington and the American Enlightenment*. Garden City, N.Y., 1984.

———. *Explaining America*. Garden City, N.Y., 1981.

———. *Nixon Agonistes*. New York, 1969.

Wilson, Harold C. *McClure's Magazine and the Muckrakers*. Princeton, N.J., 1970.

Wilson, Major L. *Space, Time, and Freedom*. Westport, Conn., 1974.

Wolfe, Alan. *America's Impasse*. New York, 1982.

———. *The Limits of Legitimacy*. New York, 1977.

Wood, Gordon S. *Creation of the American Republic*. Chapel Hill, N.C., 1969.

Yudoff, Mark. *When Government Speaks*. Berkeley, Cal., 1983.

Zuckerman, Michael. *Peaceable Kingdoms: New England Towns in the Eighteenth Century*. New York, 1970.

Zvesper, John. *Political Philosophy and Rhetoric: A Case Study of the Origins of American Party Politics*. New York, 1977.

ARTICLES

Abel, Richard L. "The Rise of Capitalism and the Transformation of Disputing: From Confrontation over Honor to Competition for Property." *UCLA Law Review* 27 (1979):223–55.

Adair, Douglass T. "Fame and the Founding Fathers." In *Fame & the Founding Fathers: Essays by Douglass Adair*, ed. Trevour Colbourne, pp. 3–26. New York, 1974.

Anderson, Alexis J. "The Formative Period of First Amendment Theory, 1870–1915." *American Journal of Legal History* 24 (1980):56–75.

Anderson, David. "Libel and Press Self-Censorship." *Texas Law Review* 53 (1975): 422–81.

———. "The Origins of the Press Clause." *UCLA Law Review* 30 (1983):455–541.

———. "A Response to Professor Robertson: The Issue is Control of Press Power." *Texas Law Review* 54 (1976):271–84.

———. "The Selective Impact of Libel Law." *Columbia Journalism Review* (May/June, 1975):38–42.

Ashdown, Gerald G. "Gertz and Firestone: A Study in Constitutional Policy-Making." *Minnesota Law Review* 61 (1977):645–90.

Auerbach, Jerold S. "The Depression Decade." In *The Pulse of Freedom*, ed. Alan Reitman, pp. 64–76. New York, 1975.

———. "The Patrician as Libertarian." *New England Quarterly* 42 (1969):511–31.

Baker, C. Edwin. "The Process of Change and the Liberty Theory of the First Amendment." *Southern California Law Review* 55 (1981):293–344.

———. "Scope of the First Amendment Freedom of Speech." *UCLA Law Review* 25 (1978):964–1040.

Baldasty, Gerald. "The Boston Press and Politics in Jacksonian America." *Journalism History* 7 (1980):104–8.

Barron, Jerome A. "Access to the Press—A New First Amendment Right." *Harvard Law Review* 80 (1967):1641–78.

Becker, Laura. "The People and the System: Legal Activities in a Colonial Pennsylvania Town." *Pennsylvania Magazine of History and Biography* 105 (1981):135–49.

Beth, Loren. "Group Libel and Free Speech." *Minnesota Law Review* 39 (1955):167–84.

Bixby, David M. "The Roosevelt Court, Democratic Ideology, and Minority Rights: Another Look at *United States v. Classic*." *Yale Law Journal* 90 (1981):741–815.

Blanchard, Margaret A. "Filling in the Void: Speech and Press in State Courts Prior to Gitlow." In *The First Amendment Reconsidered*, ed. Bill Chamberlin and Charlene J. Brown, pp. 14–59. New York, 1982.

Blasi, Vincent. "The Checking Value in First Amendment Theory." *American Bar Foundation Research Journal* (1977):521–649.

Bogen, David. "The Free Speech Metamorphosis of Mr. Justice Holmes." *Hofstra Law Review* 11 (1982):97–189.

Botein, Stephen. "'Meer Mechanics': Strategies of Colonial Printers." In *Perspectives in American History* 9, ed. Donald Fleming and Bernard Bailyn (1975):131–225.

_____. "Printers and the American Revolution." In *The Press & the American Revolution*, ed. Bernard Bailyn and John B. Hench, pp. 11–57. Worcester, Mass., 1980.

Bowler, Clara Ann. "Carted Whores and White Shrouded Apologies." *Virginia Magazine of History and Biography* 85 (1977):411–26.

Breslau, Elaine G. "Wit, Whimsy, and Politics: The Uses of the Tuesday Club of Annapolis, 1744 to 1756." *William and Mary Quarterly* 32 (1975):295–306.

Brest, Paul. "The Misconceived Quest for Original Understanding." *Boston University Law Review* 60 (1980):204–38.

Buel, Richard, Jr. "Freedom of the Press in Revolutionary America: The Evolution of Libertarianism, 1760–1820." In *The Press & the American Revolution*, ed. Bernard Bailyn and John B. Hench, pp. 59–97. Worcester, Mass., 1980.

Cahn, Edmund, and Black, Hugo. "Justice Black and the First Amendment 'Absolutes': A Public Interview." *New York University Law Review* 37 (1962):549–63.

Carpenter, Reed L. "John L. Morrison and the Origins of the Minnesota Gag Law." *Journalism History* 9 (1982):16–17, 25–28.

Carroll, Thomas F. "The Evolution of the Theory of Freedom of Speech and of the Press." *Georgetown Law Journal* 11 (1922):27–45.

Chevigny, Paul G. "Dialogic Right of Free Expression: A Reply to Michael Martin." *New York University Law Review* 57 (1982):920–31.

_____. "Philosophy of Language and Free Expression." *New York University Law Review* 55 (1980):157–94.

Colker, Ruth. "Pornography and Privacy: Towards the Development of a Group Based Theory for Sex Based Intrusions of Privacy." *Law and Inequality* 1 (1983):191–238.

Cover, Robert M. "The Left, the Right, and the First Amendment: 1918–1928." *Maryland Law Review* 40 (1981):349–88.

Cranberg, Gilbert. "ACLU: Second Thoughts on Libel." *Columbia Journalism Review* (Jan/Feb., 1983):42–43.

Crouthamel, James. "The Newspaper Revolution in New York, 1830–1860." *New York History* 45 (1964):91–113.

"Defamation by Fiction." *Maryland Law Review* 42 (1983):387–427.

Delgado, Richard. "Professor Delgado Replies." *Harvard Civil Rights–Civil Liberties Law Review* 18 (1983):593–97.

_____. "Words That Wound: A Tort Action for Racial Insults, Epithets, and Name-Calling." *Harvard Civil Rights–Civil Liberties Law Review* 17 (1982):133–81.

Dennis, Everette. "The Press and the Public Interest: A Definitional Dilemma." *DePaul Law Review* 23 (1974):937–58.

Duval, Benjamin S., Jr. "Free Communication of Ideas and the Quest for Truth: Toward a Teleological Approach to First Amendment Adjudication." *George Washington Law Review* 41 (1972):161–259.

Eaton, Joel. "The American Law of Defamation through Gertz v. Robert Welch, Inc. and Beyond: An Analytical Primer." *Virginia Law Review* 61 (1975):1349–1451.

Ellis, Richard. "The Impact of the Revolution on Politics in the 1790s." *Reviews in American History* 1 (1973):504–7.

_____. "The Impeachment of Samuel Chase." In *American Political Trials*, ed. Michal Belknap, pp. 57–78. Westport, Conn., 1981.

Emerson, Thomas I. "First Amendment Doctrine and the Burger Court." *California*

Law Review 68 (1980):422–81.

Engel, David H. "Cases, Conflict, and Accommodation: Patterns of Legal Interaction in an American Community." *American Bar Foundation Research Journal* (1983): 803–74.

Fine, Sidney. "Anarchism and the Assassination of McKinley." *American Historical Review* 56 (1955):777–99.

Finkleman, Paul. "The Zenger Case: Prototype of a Political Trial." In *American Political Trials*, ed. Michal Belknap, pp. 21–42. Westport, Conn., 1981.

Fitzroy, Herbert. "Punishment of Crime in Provincial Pennsylvania." *Pennsylvania Magazine of History and Biography* 60 (1936):242–69.

Flaherty, Francis J. "The Law's Literary Life: Publishers Under Attack." *National Law Journal* (2 Apr. 1984):1, 26–28.

Formisano, Ronald P. "Deferential-Participant Politics: The Early Republic's Political Culture, 1789–1840." *American Political Science Review* 68 (1974):473–87.

Franklin, Marc A. "Good Names and Bad Law: A Critique of Libel Law and a Proposal." *University of San Francisco Law Review* 18 (1983):1–49.

———. "The Origins and Constitutionality of Limitations on Truth as a Defense in Tort Law." *Stanford Law Review* 16 (1964):789–848.

———. "Suing Media for Libel: A Litigation Study." *American Bar Foundation Research Journal* (1981):795–831.

———. "Winners and Losers and Why: A Study of Defamation Litigation." *American Bar Foundation Research Journal* (1980):455–500.

Fraser, Andrew. "The Corporation as Body Politic." *Telos* 57 (1981):5–40.

———. "Legal Amnesia: Modernism Versus the Republican Tradition in American Legal Thought." *Telos* 60 (1983):15–52.

———. "The Legal Theory We Need Now." *Socialist Review* 40–41 (1978):147–87.

Friedman, Lawrence M. "Legal Culture and Social Development." *Law and Society Review* 4 (1969):29–44.

Friedman, Robert I., and Moldea, Dan. "Networks Knuckle Under to Laxalt." *Village Voice* (5 March 1985):10–14.

Frug, Gerald. "The Ideology of Bureaucracy in American Law." *Harvard Law Review* 97 (1984):1276–1388.

Gabel, Peter, and Kennedy, Duncan. "Roll Over Beethoven." *Stanford Law Review* 36 (1984):1–55.

———, and Harris, Paul. "Building Power and Breaking Images: Critical Legal Theory and the Practice of Law." *New York University Review of Law and Social Change* (1982–83):369–411.

Galanter, Marc A. "Why the 'Haves' Come Out Ahead: Speculation on the Limits of Legal Change." *Law and Society Review* 9 (1974):95–160.

Gilje, Paul. "The Baltimore Riots of 1812 and the Breakdown of the Anglo-American Mob Tradition." *Journal of Social History* 13 (1980):547–64.

Gillmor, Donald M. "Justice William Brennan and the Failed 'Theory' of Actual Malice." *Journalism Quarterly* 59 (1982):249–53.

Glancy, Dorothy. "The Invention of the Right to Privacy." *Arizona Law Review* 21 (1979):1–39.

Gold, Estella. "Does Equity Still Lack Jurisdiction to Enjoin a Libel or Slander?"

Brooklyn Law Review 48 (1982):231–63.

Gordon, Robert W. "Critical Legal Histories." *Stanford Law Review* 36 (1984):57–125.

———. "Historicism in Legal Scholarship." *Yale Law Journal* 90 (1981):1017–56.

———. "Introduction: J. Willard Hurst and the Common Law Tradition in American Legal Historiography." *Law & Society Review* 10 (1975):9–55.

———. "Legal Thought and Legal Practice in the Age of American Enterprise, 1870–1920." In *Professions and Professional Ideologies in America*, ed. Gerald Geison, pp. 70–110. Chapel Hill, N.C., 1983.

———. "New Developments in Legal Theory." In *The Politics of Law*, ed. David Kairys, pp. 281–93. New York, 1982.

———. "Review of Tort Law in America." *Harvard Law Review* 94 (1982):903–18.

Green, Leon. "Political Freedom of the Press and the Libel Problem." *Texas Law Review* 56 (1978):341–77.

———. "The Right to Communicate." *New York University Law Review* 35 (1960):903–24.

Greenawalt, Kent. "Speech and Crime." *American Bar Foundation Research Journal* (1980):645–785.

Greenberg, Douglas. "Our Town." *Reviews in American History* 9 (1981):454–58.

Gudridge, Patrick O. "The Persistence of Classical Style." *University of Pennsylvania Law Review* 131 (1983):663–792.

Gunther, Gerald. "Learned Hand and the Origins of Modern First Amendment Doctrine: Some Fragments of History." *Stanford Law Review* 27 (1975):718–73.

Handford, P. R. "Tort Liability for Threatening or Insulting Words." *Canadian Bar Review* 54 (1976):563–89.

Hartog, Hendrik. "The Public Law of a County Court: Judicial Government in Eighteenth Century Massachusetts." *American Journal of Legal History* 20 (1976):282–329.

Heins, Margorie. "Banning Words: A Comment on Words That Wound." *Harvard Civil Rights–Civil Liberties Law Review* 18 (1983):585–92.

Hemphill, C. Dallet. "Women in Court: Sex Role Differentiation in Salem, Massachusetts, 1636–1683." *William and Mary Quarterly* 39 (1982):164–75.

Hindus, Michael Stephen. "The Contours of Crime and Justice in Massachusetts and South Carolina, 1767–1878." *American Journal of Legal History* 21 (1977):212–37.

Hoffer, Thomas W., and Butterfield, Gerald A. "The Right to Reply: A Florida First Amendment Aberration." *Journalism Quarterly* 53 (1976):111–16.

Hoffman, Daniel. "Contempt of the United States: the Political Crime That Wasn't." *American Journal of Legal History* 25 (1981):343–60.

Holli, Melvin G., and Tompkins, C. David. "Roosevelt v. Newett: The Politics of Libel." *Michigan History* 47 (1963):338–56.

Horwitz, Morton J. "The Conservative Tradition and the Writing of American Legal History." *American Journal of Legal History* 17 (1973):275–94.

Hutchinson, Allan C., and Monahan, Patrick J. "The 'Rights' Stuff: Roberto Unger and Beyond." *Texas Law Review* 62 (1984):1477–1539.

Ingebar, Stanley. "The Marketplace of Ideas: A Legitimizing Myth." *Duke Law Jour-*

nal (1984):1–91.

Irons, Peter H. " 'Fighting Fair': Zechariah Chafee, Jr., the Department of Justice, and the 'Trial' at the Harvard Club." *Harvard Law Review* 94 (1981):1205–36.

Kairys, David. "Freedom of Speech." In *The Politics of Law*, ed. David Kairys, pp. 140–71. New York, 1982.

Kalven, Harry, Jr. "The Law of Defamation and the First Amendment." In *Conference on the Arts, Publishing, and the Law* (Chicago, 1952):3–18.

———. "The New York Times Case: A Note on the Central Meaning of the First Amendment." *Supreme Court Review* (1964):199–222.

———. "The Reasonable Man and the First Amendment: Hill, Butts, and Walker." *Supreme Court Review* (1967):267–309.

———. "Upon Rereading Mr. Justice Black and the First Amendment." *UCLA Law Review* 14 (1967):428–53.

Keeton, Page W. "Defamation and Freedom of the Press." *Texas Law Review* 54 (1976):1221–59.

Keeton, Robert. "Some Implications of the Constitutional Privilege to Defame." *Vanderbilt Law Review* 25 (1972):59–77.

Kelly, Alfred. "Constitutional Liberty and the Law of Libel." *American Historical Review* 74 (1968):429–52.

Kennedy, Duncan. "Legal Education as Training for Hierarchy." In *The Politics of Law*, ed. David Kairys, pp. 40–61. New York, 1982.

———. "The Structure of Blackstone's Commentaries." *Buffalo Law Review* 28 (1979):205–382.

———. "Toward an Historical Understanding of Legal Consciousness: The Case of Classical Legal Thought in America." *Research in Law and Sociology* 3 (1980):3–24.

Lasch, Christopher. "Democracy and the 'Crisis of Confidence.' " *democracy* 1 (1981):25–40.

Leonard, Thomas C. "News for a Revolution: The Exposé in America, 1768–1773." *Journal of American History* 67 (1980):26–40.

Levy, Leonard W. "Did the Zenger Case Really Matter?" *William and Mary Quarterly* 17 (1960):35–50.

———. "Liberty and the First Amendment: 1790–1800." *American Historical Review* 68 (1962):22–37.

Lewis, Anthony. "The Annals of Law: The *Sullivan* Case." *New Yorker* (5 Nov. 1984):52–95.

———. "*New York Times v. Sullivan* Reconsidered: Time to Return to 'The Central Meaning of the First Amendment.' " *Columbia Law Review* 83 (1983):603–25.

Lyman, Peter. "The Politics of Anger: On Silence, Ressentiment, and Political Speech." *Socialist Review* 57 (1981):55–74.

Lynd, Staughton. "Communal Rights." *Texas Law Review* 62 (1984):1417–41.

Mann, Bruce H. "Rationality, Legal Change, and Community in Connecticut, 1690–1760." *Law and Society Review* 14 (1980):187–221.

Marbury, William L. "The Hiss-Chambers Libel Suit." *Maryland Law Review* 41 (1981):75–102.

Mayton, William T. "Seditious Libel and the Lost Guarantee of a Freedom of Expression." *Columbia Law Review* 84 (1984):91–142.

McDonnell, Richard H. "The Chambersburg Valley Spirit." *Pennsylvania Magazine of History and Biography* 104 (1980):200–220.

Mensch, Betty. "Freedom of Contract as Ideology." *Stanford Law Review* 33 (1981): 753–72.

Mensch, Elizabeth. "The History of Mainstream Legal Thought." In *The Politics of Law*, ed. David Kairys, pp. 18–34. New York, 1982.

Merry, Sally Engle. "Going to Court: Strategies of Dispute Management in an Urban Neighborhood." *Law and Society Review* 13 (1979):891–925.

Miller, Arthur Selwyn. "On Politics, Democracy, and the First Amendment: A Commentary on *First National Bank v. Belloti.*" *Washington and Lee Law Review* 28 (1981):21–41.

———, and Barron, Jerome A. "The Supreme Court, The Adversary System, and the Flow of Information to the Justices: A Preliminary Inquiry." *Virginia Law Review* 61 (1975):1187–1245.

Murnaghan, Francis. "From Figment to Fiction to Philosophy—The Requirement of Proof of Damages in Libel Actions." *Catholic University Law Review* 22 (1972):1–38.

Murphy, Paul L. "*Near v. Minnesota* in the Context of Historical Developments." *Minnesota Law Review* 66 (1981):95–160.

Noel, Dix. "Defamation of Public Officers and Candidates." *Columbia Law Review* 49 (1949):875–903.

Pessen, Edward. "Who has the Power in the Democratic Capitalistic Community: Reflections on Antebellum New York City." *New York History* 52 (1977):129–53.

Pierce, Samuel R. "The Anatomy of an Historic Decision, *New York Times v. Sullivan.*" *North Carolina Law Review* 43 (1965):315–63.

Pomerantz, Sidney. "The Patriot Newspaper and the American Revolution." In *The Era of the American Revolution*, ed. Richard B. Morris, pp. 301–31. New York, 1939.

Potter, Janice, and Calhoon, Robert M. "The Character and Coherence of the Loyalist Press." In *The Press & the American Revolution*, ed. Bernard Bailyn and John B. Hench, pp. 229–72. Worcester, Mass., 1980.

Presser, Stephen B. "A Tale of Two Judges: Richard Peters, Samuel Chase and the Broken Promise of Federalist Jurisprudence." *Northwestern University Law Review* 73 (1978):26–111.

Probert, Walter. "Defamation, A Camouflage of Psychic Interests: The Beginnings of a Behavioral Analysis." *Vanderbilt Law Review* 15 (1962):1173–1201.

Prude, Jonathan. "Portrait of a Civil Libertarian." *Journal of American History* 60 (1973):633–56.

Rabban, David. "The Emergence of Modern First Amendment Doctrine." *University of Chicago Law Review* 50 (1983):1205–1355.

———. "The First Amendment in Its Forgotten Years." *Yale Law Journal* 90 (1981): 516–95.

Ragan, Fred. "Justice Oliver Wendell Holmes, Jr., Zechariah Chafee, Jr., and the Clear and Present Danger Test for Free Speech: The First Year, 1919." *Journal of American History* 58 (1971):24–45.

Redish, Martin H. "The Warren Court, the Burger Court, and the First Amendment Overbreadth Doctrine." *Northwestern University Law Review* 78 (1983):1031–70.

Riesman, David. "Democracy and Defamation: Control of Group Libel." *Columbia Law Review* 42 (1942):727–80.

———. "Democracy and Defamation: Fair Game and Fair Comment I." *Columbia Law Review* 42 (1942):1085–1123.

———. "Democracy and Defamation: Fair Game and Fair Comment II." *Columbia Law Review* 42 (1942):1282–1318.

Roper, Donald. "James Kent and the Emergence of New York's Libel Law." *American Journal of Legal History* 17 (1973):223–31.

———. "Justice Smith Thompson: Politics and the New York Supreme Court in the Early Nineteenth Century." *New York Historical Society Quarterly* 51 (1967):128–39.

Rosen, Mark L. "Media Lament—The Rise and Fall of the Involuntary Public Figure." *St. Johns Law Review* 54 (1980):487–517.

Rosenberg, Norman L. "Alexander Addison and the Pennsylvania Origins of Federalist First-Amendment Thought." *Pennsylvania Magazine of History and Biography* 108 (1984):399–417.

———. "The Law of Political Libel and Freedom of Press in Nineteenth-Century America: An Interpretation." *American Journal of Legal History* 17 (1973):336–52.

———. "The New Law of Political Libel: A Historical Perspective." *Rutgers Law Review* 28 (1975):1141–83.

———. "Thomas M. Cooley, Liberal Jurisprudence, and the Law of Libel, 1868–1884." *University of Puget Sound Law Review* 4 (1980):49–98.

Saxton, Alexander. "Problems of Class and Race in the Origins of the Mass Circulation Press." *American Quarterly* 36 (1984):211–34.

Schauer, Frederick. "Fear, Risk, and the First Amendment: Unraveling the 'Chilling' Effect." *Boston University Law Review* 58 (1978):685–732.

———. "Language, Truth, and the First Amendment: An Essay in Memory of Harry Cantor." *Virginia Law Review* 64 (1978):263–302.

Shiffrin, Steven. "The First Amendment and Economic Regulation: Away from a General Theory of the First Amendment." *Northwestern University Law Review* 78 (1983):1212–83.

———. "Liberalism, Radicalism, and Legal Scholarship." *UCLA Law Review* 30 (1983):1103–1217.

Silver, Isidore. "Libel, the 'Higher Truths' of Art, and the First Amendment." *University of Pennsylvania Law Review* 126 (1978):1065–98.

Smith, James Morton. "The Grass Roots Origins of the Kentucky Resolutions." *William and Mary Quarterly* 27 (1970):221–45.

Smolla, Rodney A. "Let the Author Beware: The Rejuvenation of the American Law of Libel." *University of Pennsylvania Law Review* 132 (1983):1–94.

Sparer, Ed. "Fundamental Human Rights, Legal Entitlements, and the Social Struggle: A Friendly Critique of the Critical Legal Studies Movement." *Stanford Law Review* 36 (1984):509–74.

Steirer, William F., Jr. "A Study in Prudence: Philadelphia's 'Revolutionary' Journalists." *Journalism History* 3 (1976):16–19.

Stevens, John, et al. "Criminal Libel as Seditious Libel, 1916–65." *Journalism Quarterly* 43 (1966):110–13.

Stewart, Potter. "Or of the Press." *Hastings Law Journal* 26 (1975):631–37.

Stout, Harry S. "Religion, Communications, and the Ideological Origins of the American Revolution." *William and Mary Quarterly* 34 (1977):519–41.

"Symposium: A Critique of Rights." *Texas Law Review* 62 (1984):1363–1617.

"Symposium—Freedom of Expression: Theoretical Perspectives." *Northwestern University Law Review* 78 (1983):937–1357.

"Symposium: National Security and Civil Liberties." *Cornell Law Review* 69 (1984): 685–894.

Tannenhaus, Joseph. "Group Libel." *Cornell Law Quarterly* 35 (1950):261–302.

Teeter, Dwight L. "Decent Animadversions: Notes Toward A History of Free Press Theory." In *Newsletters to Newspapers*, ed. Donovan H. Bond and W. R. McLeod, pp. 237–45. Morgantown, W. Va., 1977.

———. "The Printer and the Chief Justice: Seditious Libel in 1782–83." *Journalism Quarterly* 45 (1968):235–42, 260.

Thomas, Brook. "The Pioneers, or The Sources of American Legal History: A Critical Tale." *American Quarterly* 36 (1984):86–111.

Titus, John. "Statement of Fact Versus Statement of Opinion—A Spurious Dispute in Fair Comment." *Vanderbilt Law Review* 15 (1952):1203–46.

Tribe, Laurence. "Toward a Metatheory of Free Speech." *Southwestern University Law Review* 10 (1978):237–45.

Tushnet, Mark V. "The Constitutional Right to One's Good Name: An Examination of the Scholarship of Mr. Justice Rehnquist." *Kentucky Law Journal* 64 (1976):753–66.

———. "Corporations and Free Speech." In *The Politics of Law*, ed. David Kairys, pp. 253–61. New York, 1982.

———. "An Essay on Rights." *Texas Law Review* 62 (1984):1363–1403.

———. "Following the Rules Laid Down: A Critique of Interpretivism and Neutral Principles." *Harvard Law Review* 96 (1983):781–823.

———. "Talking to Each Other: Reflections on Yudoff's *When Government Speaks.*" *Wisconsin Law Review* (1984):129–45.

Vaughn, Stephen. "First Amendment Liberties and the Committee on Public Information." *American Journal of Legal History* 23 (1979):95–119.

Veeder, Van Vechten. "Freedom of Public Discussion." *Harvard Law Review* 23 (1910):413–46.

———. "History of the Law of Defamation, I." *Columbia Law Review* 3 (1903):546–73.

———. "History of the Law of Defamation, II." *Columbia Law Review* 4 (1904):33–56.

Wade, John W. "The Communicative Torts of the First Amendment." *Mississippi Law Journal* 48 (1977):671–711.

Wellington, Harry. "On Freedom of Expression." *Yale Law Journal* 88 (1979):1105–42.

Westbrook, Robert B. "Politics as Consumption." In *The Culture of Consumption*, ed. Richard Wightman and T. J. Jackson Lears, pp. 345–73. New York, 1983.

Wilentz, Sean. "On Class and Politics in Jacksonian America." *Reviews in American History* 10 (1982):45–63.

Wills, Garry. "What's Wrong with this Magazine?" [*MORE*] (June, 1975):6–8.

Wood, Gordon S. "Conspiracy and Paranoid Style: Causality and Deceit in the Eighteenth Century." *William and Mary Quarterly* 39 (1982):401–41.

Zimmerman, Dianne L. "Requiem for a Heavyweight: A Farewell to Warren and Brandeis' Privacy Tort." *Cornell Law Review* 68 (1983):291–368.

Zion, Sidney. "A Tale of Two Libel Themes." *Nation* (29 Sept. 1984):288–90.

Index